FROM MAN TO MAN
(or *PERHAPS ONLY . . .*)

FROM MAN TO MAN

OR

Perhaps Only

by

OLIVE SCHREINER

with an introduction by

S. C. CRONWRIGHT-SCHREINER

*"Perhaps only God knew what
the lights and shadows were."*
THE CHILD'S DAY

GROSSET & DUNLAP : *Publishers*

by arrangement with Harper & Brothers

Dedicated

to

My Little Sister Ellie

Who died, aged eighteen months, when I was nine years old.

———————

Also

to

My Only Daughter.

Born on the 30th April, and died the 1st May.

———————

She never lived to know she was a woman.

CONTENTS

PAGE

INTRODUCTION BY S. C. CRONWRIGHT-
SCHREINER ix

A NOTE ON THE GENESIS OF THE BOOK . xix

I. THE PRELUDE—THE CHILD'S DAY 3

II. THE BOOK—THE WOMAN'S DAY

CHAPTER

I. SHOWING WHAT BABY-BERTIE THOUGHT OF
HER NEW TUTOR; AND HOW REBEKAH
GOT MARRIED 47

II. A WILD-FLOWER GARDEN IN THE BUSH . 64

III. THE DAM WALL 75

IV. SHOWING HOW BABY-BERTIE HEARD THE
CICADAS CRY 97

V. JOHN-FERDINAND SHOWS VERONICA HIS
NEW HOUSE 115

VI. HOW BABY-BERTIE WENT A-DANCING . . 120

VII. RAINDROPS IN THE AVENUE 140

VIII. YOU CANNOT CAPTURE THE IDEAL BY A
COUP D'ÉTAT 217

IX. CART TRACKS IN THE SAND 292

X. HOW GRIET SAT ON THE STONE WALL AND
WATCHED THE GNATS 320

XI. HOW THE RAIN RAINS IN LONDON . . . 327

XII. FIREFLIES IN THE DARK 390

XIII. THE VERANDA 434

NOTE BY S. C. C. S. AS TO THE ENDING OF
THE NOVEL 461

INTRODUCTION

O N the first day of May, 1873, Olive Schreiner, then
just eighteen, was living in tents at New Rush, the
two-year-old Diamond Diggings now known as Kimberley. On that day she entered in her journal that she had
written out the first chapter of *Other Men's Sins,* a name
that does not appear again; but, when she was governess
at the farm Ratel Hoek, she entered in her journal on the
3rd of August, 1876, that she had made up her mind "to
write *A Small Bit of Mimosa* and *Wrecked* in one"; on
the 21st of the same month that she had "Got some idea of
Saints and Sinners"; and on the 10th of September
"Saints and Sinners is growing clearer." I am inclined
to think that, when she decided to blend *A Small Bit of
Mimosa* and *Wrecked* (both then mentioned for the first
time), she incorporated *Other Men's Sins* into the same
plan. At any rate, we now have this novel fairly started;
for *Saints and Sinners* was "the original germ," as she
styled it, of *From Man to Man.* Not only did she tell
Havelock Ellis this in 1884, but it is abundantly clear
otherwise. For instance, in September, 1883, she enters
in her London journal that she is "At the Jew and 'Rain
in London,'" which is now Chapter XI of this novel;
and she adds: "Thought of a name, *From Man to Man."*
This title is taken from a sentence of John (later Lord)
Morley's, which runs as follows, except that I have forgotten the adjective: *"From man to man nothing matters
but . . . charity."* The missing word connotes "boundless," "all-embracing," or some such large and generous
attitude of mind.

Olive sailed to England for the first time early in
March, 1881, taking with her *Saints and Sinners* (as far

as it was completed), in addition to *The Story of an African Farm*. While governessing at Ratel Hoek and Lelie Kloof she had apparently made considerable progress with *Saints and Sinners*. For instance, at Lelie Kloof, in October, 1880, this entry occurs in her journal: "Had an idea about Bertie this afternoon—suicide, quite *strong*"; Bertie being one of the two chief characters of the novel. Such a reference seems to indicate that she had already made considerable progress in the plan of the work, for Bertie's death is bound to come late in the book.

From May, 1876, to November, 1883, this novel is always referred to as *Saints and Sinners;* thereafter it is styled *From Man to Man*. I have no recollection that, after November, 1883, she ever referred to it, in speech or in writing, by any other name than *From Man to Man;* though, while we were "detained" by the British military at Hanover during the greater part of the Boer War, I typed "The Prelude," the first six chapters and part of the seventh, as she revised them in 1901 and 1902.

When we lived at De Aar, from 1907 onwards, it was her custom (necessitated by ill-health) to leave home every year to escape the great summer heat of the upper Karoo. She often spent a large part of such absences in Cape Town; she was there in 1911, and then had "The Prelude" and the first six chapters retyped in triplicate and sent to me by the typist from Woodstock (a suburb of Cape Town). Knowing what the package contained, I do not think I opened it then; I have no recollection of having done so; nor do I remember having then seen the alterations she had made in the Dedication and the Title. I put the package carefully away, and, when I left De Aar in December, 1919, stored it there with my other things. Olive, who had sailed to England early in December, 1913, was unable to return to South Africa; and so, being free on retiring from De Aar, I went to England in 1920. She returned to South Africa in August of that year, leaving me to follow after the winter, but she died in her sleep at Wynberg in December.

I returned to South Africa in February, 1921, but was too much occupied to get my De Aar things down to Cape Town and go through the papers until the end of that year; then I opened the Woodstock package that had been posted to me in March, 1911. At that time I knew the book as *From Man to Man,* and by no other title; and I was familiar with the dedication, which, before the death of our baby in 1895, ran, *"To My Little Sister, Ellie, who died, aged eighteen months,"* with the relative couplet that now appears in the present dedication. In the Hanover typing of 1901-02, the title and dedication remain the same except for the following addition: *"Also to My daughter and only child, Born the 30th April 1895, and Died the 1st May, aged one day. She never lived to shed a woman's tears."* In the Woodstock typing of 1911 the title appears as *The Camel Thorn,* but the pen has been run through it and a new title, *Perhaps Only,* substituted therefor. (The Camel-thorn, Afrikaans *Kameeldoring,* is *Acacia giraffæ.*) The new title is taken from a sentence uttered by the little child in "The Prelude": *"Perhaps only God knew what the lights and shadows were."* She wrote this sentence (which appears on p. 67 of "The Prelude") beneath the typing of the Woodstock title-page. I give a facsimile of the sentence as she wrote it with the pen, and in the same relative position.

The Woodstock dedication, as then typed, reads thus:—

Dedicated
to
My Little Sister Ellie
Who died, aged eighteen months, when I was nine years old.

———

Also
to
My Only Daughter.
Born on the 30th April, and died the 1st May.

———

She never lived to know she was a woman.

The last line, so typed, stands wholly excised by Olive with pen and ink. The couplet under the dedication to little Ellie, as it now appears in this book, indicates the astounding effect Olive claims the infant's brief life and early death had upon her own life.

Except that the title (*The Camel Thorn*) is crossed out and *Perhaps Only* is written above it in largish letters, the "prelim." page of the Woodstock typing is as follows :—

THE CAMEL THORN
Prelude
The Child's Day

The Book
The Woman's Day

Part 1
(List of six chapters as they now appear.)

The original plan, or one of the early plans, of the novel was, as I understand it, that *The Child's Day* should be Part 1, *The Woman's Day* Part 2, and *Rebekah* Part 3. I give a copy of an old page, just as I found it in Olive's handwriting :—

Chapter 8. Bertie wants Dorcas to hold her hand.
Chapter 9. Showing how Veronica took hens to the old farm.
Chapter 10. Bertie ties ribbons round the kittens' necks.
Chapter 11. Bertie seeks for the country and cannot find [it].
Chapter 12. "Sally is my Sweetheart
                  Sally is my darling."

End of Part 2.

Rebekah.

Chapter 1. Great White Angels.
Chapter 2. Rebekah's Books are Dead.
Chapter 3. The Waterfall.
Chapter 4. Muizenberg.
Chapter 5. Sartje.
Chapter 6. Koonap Heights.
Chapter 7. The Old Farm.
Chapter 8. Baby-Bertie.

Chapter 9. A Bit of Mimosa.
Chapter 10. How the Wax Flowers Smell.

I now give a list of the chapters of what the whole novel was at one time meant to be, just as I found it :—

Perhaps Only.

Prelude: The Child's Day.
The Book: The Woman's Day.

Part one of the Woman's Day

Chapter 1. Showing what Baby-Bertie thought of her new tutor and how Rebekah got married.
Chapter 2. A Wild-Flower Garden in the Bush.
Chapter 3. The Dam Wall.
Chapter 4. Showing how Baby-Bertie heard the Cicadas cry.
Chapter 5. John-Ferdinand shows Veronica his new House.
Chapter 6. How Baby-Bertie went a-dancing.
Chapter 7. You cannot capture the Ideal by a Coup d'Etat.

Part 2 of the Woman's Day.

Chapter 1. Fireflies in the Dark.
Chapter 2. The Little Black Curl.
Chapter 3. The Rocks again.
Chapter 4. Koonap Heights.
Chapter 5. The Glittering of the Sand.
Chapter 6. Veronica.
Chapter 7. The Lure Light.
Chapter 8. A Bit of Mimosa.
Chapter 9. The Kopje.

The End.

The thirteen chapters, as presented in this book, are all in the order in which Olive meant them to be. Chapter XIV, "The Pine Woods," was begun; but as there are less than a thousand words, as they are of no importance to the narrative, are unrevised, and lead nowhere, I do not think it necessary to give them. After the opening lines, Rebekah and Drummond begin a conversation which, as far as it goes, has no significance, except possibly for its last few lines :

" 'Have you ever hated anyone?' he asked.

"She sat upright: 'No, not if hatred means the wish

to injure. I have loathed people; I have tried to forget some people.'"

There the manuscript ends. There is not another word of the novel or of anything in connection with it. It is as though nothing more had ever been written. It was a custom with her to retain not only her first rapid drafts, but also any manuscript she had gone over and revised. For instance, there were three drafts of *The Buddhist Priest's Wife*, each progressively shorter than the previous one and none of them quite complete; to get the final draft I had to sort out the last two drafts in several ways—by handwriting, by age of the paper, and so one—then get the (often wrongly numbered) sheets into consecutive order respectively, then compare and adjust them. It was much the same with *On the Banks of a Full River*, and with several other of her writings. And so it was with this uncompleted novel; there were a considerable number of drafts of parts; there were fragments, revisions, etc.; but none of these had any relation to the book after the thirteenth chapter, except the few words, already referred to, of the fourteenth. I feel certain that she had "finished" the novel in her mind; I think she had not only thus "finished" the plan of it, but had done so in considerable detail in parts; nothing, however, short of clear proof, will convince me that she wrote down any more after the few words I possess of the fourteenth chapter. I am unable to think she destroyed any of the manuscript of the fourteenth chapter or of any later chapters. After all her assertions, verbal and written, it may seem difficult to believe that her actual writing ceased with the beginning of Chapter 14; and yet that seems to me by far the most likely explanation. (Readers are referred, for comparison, to the strange story, related in the *Life*, of the "Big Sex Book.") Considering that she kept so much of the rejected, revised and incomplete manuscripts of other books while still working on them, that she actually did the same with this specially loved and valued novel, knowing well also the unreliability of her statements about her work, I am simply unable to believe she destroyed the balance of the manuscript of *From Man to Man.* I do not believe a balance existed. Well, there is the fact, which, extraordinary as it is, yet cannot seem so extraordinary to me as it may to other people. I have been carefully through all her papers; the manuscript of the novel, in whatever confusion, was in one bundle (as was, I think, each of her other sets of manuscripts); and there is not a single scrap of paper after the few opening lines of the fourteenth chapter. It is my considered opinion that she wrote no further than where the manuscript now ends, but that later, at various times and irregular intervals (sometimes intervals of years), she went back to the beginning and to other early parts and set to work on revision. If she had quite abandoned all hope of further work on this beloved book, if she had decided on its destruction and had had sufficient strength to carry out such decision (which I doubt), she would, in my opinion, have destroyed the whole novel except "The Prelude"; she would not have destroyed merely a portion of the unrevised manuscript and left the revised and unrevised remainder. But I do not believe she ever abandoned all hope of still doing some work on the novel, and I do not believe she had it in her heart to destroy this greatly loved offspring of her mature mind any more than it could be in her heart to destroy a child of her physical body.

At the end of Chapter XIII, I give a brief account of what she told me as to the ending of the book. It is remarkable and fortunate that the novel does not stop until the tale is told almost to completion, and that the short account I am able to add will largely satisfy a legitimate desire of those whose interest will lie mainly in the incidents of the narrative; though, to all who love her work and recognize her power, there must ever remain the deep regret that she was unable to wind up the tale herself.

As to the name of the book, I have decided after much thought not to use the title I prefer (and which indeed I wish the book could be known by), but to adopt the one already familiar from its frequent use in the *Life* and *Letters*—the only title I ever heard Olive use. It seems to me that some confusion would result from the exclusive use of *Perhaps Only;* I do not feel at all sure that she would have used it; I am inclined to think she would have retained the title *From Man to Man.* As far as I know, the titles *Camel Thorn* and *Perhaps Only* were never mentioned to any person. Yet, though I believe I have decided rightly, I deeply regret that *Perhaps Only* —— (so she wrote it) cannot be used except as an alternative title. As apparently her last choice, one might well expect it to be the most suitable, expressing with rare art, by the use of those words taken from the wondering and deep-piercing mind of the child, a kind of stunned reluctance to judge the meaning (if there be a meaning) and the incomprehensibility of the "ethic" if there be an ethic) in the awful and mysterious living cosmos.

For purposes of this *Introduction* I went carefully through both the *Life* and the *Letters* and copied out practically every reference to the novel contained therein. When all the extracts were before me in chronological order, I decided to leave them to tell their own tale. And so there follow, as a kind of supplement to this *Introduction* and without comment, nearly all of such references, made by herself and in her own words.

In dealing with the unrevised original text of the novel all I could do legitimately was, as far as possible, to give it to the world in the form in which Olive left it. I have striven to present it exactly as she might have presented it, if she herself, without further rewriting, had reduced to its final word-form the unrevised manuscript that came into my hands.

Olive loved this book more than anything else she ever wrote, and, of the book, she loved "The Prelude" best. I have therefore printed "The Prelude" (*The Child's Day*) just as it stands in the Woodstock typing of 1911, **and as revised by herself at the time.**

It may interest readers to know that many references to "the old farm" are applicable to Klein Ganna Hoek, the farm where she was governess in 1875 and 1876, and where she wrote nearly all of *Undine* and much of *The Story of an African Farm*. But some other farm or farms, which I cannot identify, though I suspect Ratel Hoek for one and possibly Lelie Kloof, must also have been in her mind. "The Child's Day" is certainly almost wholly autobiographical: to take one small incident—she herself built the little mouse-house on the bare rock at Witteberg and waited for the mouse and then fashioned her hand to imitate the mouse entering into it.

S. C. CRONWRIGHT-SCHREINER.

CAPE TOWN, SOUTH AFRICA,
March, 1926.

A NOTE ON THE GENESIS OF THE BOOK

LIFE. *April* 7, 1873. (Diary, Kimberley.) "Thought out and began to write *Other Men's Sins*."

LIFE, *p.* 92. *May* 1, 1873. (Diary, Kimberley.) "I have, since I last wrote, written out the first half of the first chapter of *Other Men's Sins*."

LIFE, *p.* 126. *August* 3, 1876. (Diary, Ratel Hoek.) Made up her mind "to write *A Small Bit of Mimosa* and *Wrecked* in one. I think it will be good."

LIFE, *p.* 127. *August* 21, 1876. (Diary, Ratel Hoek.) "I have got some idea of *Saints and Sinners*, and this morning came the thought of—A strong quiet married love; the characters strongly drawn. It will be my next work."

LIFE, *p.* 127. *September* 10, 1876. (Diary, Ratel Hoek.) "*Saints and Sinners* is growing clearer."

LIFE, *p.* 128. *October* 1, 1876. (Diary, Ratel Hoek.) "Finished writing but not writing out [that is, copying out] the first chapter of *Saints and Sinners*."

LIFE, *p.* 130. *May* 5, 1877. (Diary, Ratel Hoek.) "I am writing to-day the scene on the beach."

LIFE, *p.* 131. *September* 30, 1877. (Diary, Ratel Hoek.) "We have got a week's holiday. I am going to try and read through, fill in, all the MS. of *Saints and Sinners*. I am just correcting the scene between Mr. and Mrs. Drummond."

LIFE, *p.* 139. *October* 23, 1880. (Diary, Lelie Kloof.) "Had an idea about Bertie this afternoon—suicide, quite *strong*."

LIFE, *p.* 151. *October* 18, 1881. (Diary, London.) "I am going to try and write at my *Saints and Sinners* to-morrow, but I am so sick and weak. Where am I blowing to? Where am I going to?"

LIFE, *p.* 153. *March* 26, 1882. (Diary, London.) "I am going to revise my *Saints and Sinners*."

LIFE, *p.* 157. *October* 14, 1882. (Diary, London.) "I want to get it [*New Rush*] off my hands, then my delightful *Saints and Sinners*."

LIFE, *p.* 157. *January* 22, 1883. (Diary, London.) "I am going to begin at my *Saints and Sinners* in earnest to-morrow; have put the MS. open and ready."

LIFE, *p.* 158. *September* 1883. (Diary, London.) "I am at the Jew and 'Rain in London.' Thought of a name, *From Man to Man.*"

LIFE, *p.* 159. *November* 20, 1883. (Diary, London.) "I am going to work at *Saints and Sinners.* When will it be revised?"

LETTERS, *p.* 12. *February* 25, 1884. (England: To Havelock Ellis.) "I intend bringing out another book [this novel] towards the end of the year."

LIFE, *p.* 167. *March* 9, 1884. (Diary, London.) "I am where Bertie is at Lodging house."

LETTERS, *p.* 24. *July* 2, 1884. (England: To Miss Louie Ellis.) "I must get my book [this novel] copied out and ready by November."

LETTERS, *p.* 28. *July* 12, 1884. (England: To Ellis.) "I am so depressed thinking of my work. You see, dear one, I have so cut up and changed the thing [this novel] that there is hardly anything left, and I don't know how to put it together. This afternoon I nearly got up and burnt the whole MS. I would give hundreds of pounds if I had never touched it and [had] published it just as it was. I think it was the Devil made me unpick it. Ach, I will set my teeth and work at it and make it something better than it was. I can't have Bertie and Rebekah die. They are as much to me as ever Waldo and Lyndall were. You know, all these months when I have been in such suffering, and have had that yearning to do something for others that I feel when I am in pain, I have always built upon the fact that *From Man to Man* will help other people, for it will help to make men more tender to women, because they will understand them better; it will make some women more tender to others; it will comfort some women by showing them that others have felt as they do. Now if I were to let it fall to the ground I should feel that so much of my life had been wasted, gone for nothing."

LETTERS, *p.* 32. *July* 16, 1884. (England: To Ellis.) "Last night it suddenly flashed into me, the solution of all my difficulties with *From Man to Man.* It has been brooding in the background of my mind these many days, and now it has suddenly come. I shall have no more difficulty with it, it is as clear as daylight. I have got what I wanted. It is so splendid. I mean the feeling is. I get so excited I don't know what to do."

LETTERS, *pp.* 33 *and* 34. *July* 21, 1884. (England: To Ellis.) "I have done a little good work to-day and yesterday; worked with such intense enjoyment, and then I know my work is good. A feeling of pleasure thrills all through me. This book is going to be awfully outspoken; *An African Farm* was nothing to it. . . . You will think perhaps that I'm writing sheets and sheets, but I'm not. It's wonderful what a lot of thought and feeling goes just to make a few lines."

LETTERS, *p.* 34. *July* 24, 1884. (England: To Ellis.) "I want . . . to show what a wonderful power love has over the physical and through it over the mental nature, over what we call the soul, the inner self. In this book I have tried to show it. But you see, when I wrote it I did not know what the last three years have taught. I can only try to show it here and there."

LETTERS, *p.* 38. *August* 7, 1884. (England: To Ellis.) "I never know *why* I write things in a certain way when I write them, but I can generally find out if I think afterwards. What you mean is what I call 'writing ribbed!' I don't know when I invented that term for a certain style of writing. I am changing a whole chapter of *From Man to Man* from what I call the plain into the 'ribbed' style. Sometimes the plain is right, sometimes the ribbed. I *think* I generally write descriptions in the plain and philosophise or paint thought in the ribbed. (You know in knitting there are two stitches, one makes a plain surface and the other makes ribs. Ribbed knitting goes up and down, up and down.)"

LETTERS, *p.* 43. *August* 29, 1884. (England: To Ellis.) "Of course the subject of my book is prostitution and marriage. It is the story of a prostitute and of a married woman who loves another man, and whose husband is sensual and unfaithful. When I've got this work off my soul I shall look round at other sides of life."

LETTERS, *p.* 46. *November* 21, 1884. (England: To Ellis.) "I am not adding to my book. It grows smaller and smaller. I am sure that all I am doing is improvement. Condense, condense, condense. But it's the most mentally wearing work."

LETTERS *p.* 49. *December* 5, 1884. (England: To Ellis.) "I am writing such a funny, that is to say singular, scene. I don't know how it came into my head, where Veronica goes to look at a man's clothes. It is in the place of a whole condensed chapter."

LETTERS, *p.* 49. *December* 9, 1884. (England: To Ellis.) "I am working. But my story gets smaller and smaller and smaller. I can't help myself. I am driven on to make it smaller. The last part of the book doesn't need any condensing or much touching. It is good, I know. The question is whether anybody ever gets through the first. It's that abominable Veronica and John-Ferdinand gave me all this work."

LETTERS, *p.* 50. *December* 15, 1884. (England: To Ellis.) "Just now I do not exist; my book exists; that is all, as far as my daily life goes: Bertie sitting there that hot day in the bush, with John-Ferdinand. That is why writing makes me happy because then my own little miserable life *is not*."

LIFE, *p.* 170. ? *January* 1885. (England, Diary.) "Am going to

work this morning. 'Baby-Bertie goes a-dancing.' Love my
work so."

LETTERS, *p.* 60. *February* 26, 1885. (England: To Ellis.) "I have
not read at all to-day, or thought about anything, but Bertie
and Rebekah. I have such a nasty bit to revise to-morrow. I
don't think it's interesting because I didn't enjoy writing it.
It's about two mean scandal-talking women, and I can't bear
writing about mean people. I don't dislike writing about
wicked ones; it doesn't pain me if they're large. I've done
with Rebekah's diary."

LETTERS, *p.* 61. *March* 2, 1885. (England: To Ellis.) "If I had
ever read Schopenhauer, or even knew before I came to England
that such a man existed, one would say I had copied whole ideas
in the *African Farm* and *From Man to Man* from him. There
is one passage of his on the search for philosophic truth that
reads like a paraphrase of my allegory in the *African Farm*.
There's something so beautiful in coming on one's very own
inmost thoughts in another. In one way it's one of the greatest
pleasures one has."

LETTERS, *p.* 62. *March* 4, 1885. (England: To Ellis.) "I *am* going
to finish off my scandal-talking women to-day. Somehow I
can't bear them. I wish there were only noble people in the
world, *intense* if wicked. But there are so many of these
others."

LETTERS, *p.* 64. *March* 17, 1885. (England: To Ellis.) "I send
you a little present. It's some gorse I got this morning at the
top of the hill at Ecclesbourne. It's the walk Bertie went with
the Jew servant. They went past there. Only it was misty,
not beautiful and sunny like to-day."

LETTERS, *p.* 66. *March* 29, 1885. (England: To Ellis.) "Only
about 130 pages revised, and four or five hundred more! When
will it be done? Yet I can't quicken myself. My mind must
work at its own pace."

LETTERS, *p.* 68. *April* 2, 1885. (England: To Ellis.) "I have got
a horrid bit of my work to revise now; then I have only one
more horrid bit; all the rest is delightful to the end." [*On the
4th April*]: "I am going nearly mad with my work. I have
written this chapter out *nine* times. Now I'm going back to
the first, only I've torn it up."

LETTERS, *p.* 98. *May* 13, 1886. (England: To Ellis.) "I won't
see anyone any more for the next three months till my book's
done." [*On May* 14*th*]: "Will my book ever, ever, ever be
done? Every word of it is truth to me, and more and more
so as the book goes on."

LETTERS, *p.* 100. *May* 29, 1886. (England: To Ellis.) "All day
yesterday I was writing and thinking about the unity of the

Universe and our love of truth arising from that conception. I sat up till one, writing. I couldn't sleep when I went to bed."

LIFE, *p.* 172. *September* 12, 1886. (England, Diary.) "Writing out little story, too much smashed to do big work."

LETTERS, *p.* 108. *January* 1, 1887. (Clarens: To Ellis.) "Am thinking of having *From Man to Man* copied by typist when I have money."

LETTERS, *p.* 112. *March* 30, 1887. (Clarens: To Ellis.) "There came to me yesterday such a beautiful new scene for my book. It helped me so; but I have no strength to write it. It's where Rebekah says: 'Forgive us our sins as we forgive those that trespass against us.' Oh, Harry, just for *one* year's health to work in!"

LETTERS, *p.* 120. *June* 20, 1887. (England: To Ellis.) "Do you know, I'm going to finish my book. I'm getting jolly hard, like I used to be at the Cape. I can work now."

LIFE, *p.* 179. *December* 7, 1887. (Alassio: Diary.) "I worked all day, up and down, planning. Didn't know before that Rebekah went to sea in a sailing ship and heard 'From too much love of living.' Some woman whose heart is lonely will be comforted by what I write, as I have been by what others write."

LETTERS, *p.* 124. *December* 12, 1887. (Alassio: To Ellis.) "I love my new book so, a hundred times better than I ever loved *An African Farm.*" [*On December* 13*th*]: "Such an odd kind of peace and rest is with me ever since I made a scene to-day in which Rebekah talks to her little son [? sons]."

LETTERS, *p.* 125. *December* 18, 1887. (Alassio: To Ellis.) "Am working hard. Never come back to myself sometimes for a couple of days and that is the only way in which work can be done. *From Man to Man* will be quite different from any other book that ever was written, whether good or bad I can't say. I never *think:* the story leads me, not I it, and I guess it's more likely to make an end of me than I am ever to make an end of it."

LETTERS, *p.* 129. *January* 24, 1888. (Alassio: To Ellis.) "Yes, it's part of Rebekah's Diary I sent you. Rebekah is me; I don't know which is which any more. But Bertie is me, and Drummond is me, and all is me, only not Veronica and Mrs. Drummond (except a little!). Sometimes I really don't know whether I am I or one of the others." [*On the* 27*th January, p.* 130]: "I am writing about those two terrible women, Veronica and Mrs. Drummond. It is so terrible to have to realise them and grapple with them. I bear all kinds of wickedness, but not meanness and smallness. I shall be glad to get back to Bertie and Rebekah, my beloveds. If they are ever so real to anyone as to me, how real they will be."

LIFE, *p*. 180. *January 27*, 1888. (Alassio, Diary.) "I am doing chapter with Veronica and Mrs. Drummond. I am doing the outburst; that relieves me so."

LETTERS, *p*. 138. *July 22*, 1888. (England: To Ellis.) "Please send back 'Prelude.' Some little bits are not in yet, one where she apologises to the baby for not having milk for it. Poor little thing! I do love her so."

LIFE, *p*. 182. *February 2*, 1889. (Mentone, Diary.) "I am copy. ing my 'Prelude.' I see my way clear to the end now. I'm so well."

LETTERS, *p*. 153. *February 2*, 1889. (Mentone: To Havelock Ellis.) "My 'Prelude' is too lovely for words. . . . The worst of this book of mine is that it's so womanly. I think it's the most womanly book that ever was written, and God knows that I've willed it otherwise!"

LETTERS, *p*. 157. *March 17*, 1889. (Mentone: To Mrs. J. H. Philpot.) "Oh, I love the two women in my book so. I'm getting to love women more and more. I love men too, so very much —only they don't *need* me."

LETTERS, *p*. 160. *April 5*, 1889. (Paris: To Ellis.) "Do you think I could write Bertie's death scene, do you think I could show all the inmost workings of Rebekah's heart, if I *realised* anyone would ever read it?" [*On April 11th, p*. 161]: "I'll be glad to get back to my novel. I love it more than I love anything in the world, more than any place or person. I've never loved any work so, and I haven't cared for it all these years."

LETTERS, *p*. 175. *January 7*, 1890. (Cape Town: To Ellis.) "Newlands is the next station to Rondebosch, where Rebekah lived. I always think when I go near Rondebosch I fancy I shall meet Rebekah coming down one of the avenues. Not Lyndall, not even Waldo, have been so absolutely real to me as she and Bertie. I cannot believe they never lived. I *say* I believe it, but I don't. You see they have lived with me fifteen years."

LETTERS, *p*. 199. *November 6*, 1890. (Matjesfontein: To Ellis.) "This life is so peaceful. I'm happy, like when I was living on those farms, writing *An African Farm*. *I feel just the same*. Life is so precious to me. You know I think in this book [*From Man to Man*] I *will* say what I want to say. I mean I've sometimes felt as if I couldn't make this book say everything I want to say as *An African Farm* said what I wanted to say then. But it will! All that is in that 'Sunlight Lay' is in it, only simply in an objective form—the first, second and third Heaven."

LIFE, *p*. 251. *April*, 1893. (Matjesfontein: To S.C.C.S.) "You know I have so many books *written*, all the real work done, needing only patient revising, and that I can only give when my nature is alive and intense; I dare not touch my work at a lower mood than the mood I wrote it in, or I shall spoil it."

LIFE, *p.* 254. *April,* 1893. (Matjesfontein: To S.C.C.S.) [*She was to sail from Cape Town on the 3rd May. Her plan was*]: "To leave England in August for some little German or Italian town and settle down there quietly and steadily to copying and revising eight or nine hours a day, then, in about a year and eight months from now, either the *Buddhist Priest's Wife* or *From Man to Man* or one of my big books will be ready. I shall then be independent." [She was back again in Cape Town late in October.]

LIFE, *p.* 271. *July* 1894. [Extract from the *Life.*] "She said that, if she had two years at the Homestead, Kimberley, she would finish her two 'big' novels, *From Man to Man* and *The Buddhist Priest's Wife.*"

LETTERS, *p.* 217. *February* 28, 1895. (Kimberley: To S.C.C.S.) "While you are at Rondebosch go for a walk in my dear wood and see that old Summer House. That part is the scene where *From Man to Man* is laid. Rebekah lives there when she is married, and always walks in those woods."

LIFE, *p.* 286. *September* 1895. (Kimberley: To Mrs. John Brown.) [Extract from *Life*]: "In September 1895 she had written to Mrs. Brown that she was working very hard, and that, if she kept well, her book on South Africa [*Stray Thoughts*] would be out early in 1896 and her big novel [*From Man to Man*] before the end of the same year."

LIFE, *p.* 339. (Hanover, Cape Colony, 1901–1902.) [During these two years she revised 'The Prelude,' the first six chapters of *From Man to Man* and part of the seventh.]

LIFE, *p.* 347. *June* 4, 1902. (Diary, Hanover.) "I am revising the sixth chapter of *From Man to Man.*" [*A few days later, p.* 348]: "Have been copying out all the evening chapter 7 of *From Man to Man.*"

LIFE, *p.* 349. *June* 24, 1906. (Diary, Hanover.) "I am revising Rebekah's letter to her husband."

LIFE, *p.* 349. *October* 10, 1906. (Diary, Matjesfontein.) "I went for a lovely walk in the afternoon to *my* koppie, Rebekah's. I'm so happy."

LIFE, *p.* 350. *February* 20, 1907. (Diary, Hanover.) "I am just finishing 'You Can't Capture the Ideal.'"

LETTERS. *February* 25, 1907. (Hanover: To S.C.C.S.) ". . . and that makes the use of a writer: not that he expresses what no one else thinks and feels, but he is the voice of what others feel and can't say. If only the powers that shape existence give me the strength to finish this book [*From Man to Man*], I shall not have that agonised feeling over my life that I have over the last ten years, that I have done nothing of good for any human creature. I am not sure of the book's artistic worth: to judge of that from the purely intellectual standpoint one must stand at a distance from one's own or anyone else's work. But I know it gives a voice to that which exists in the hearts of many women and some men, I know I have only tried to give expression to what was absolutely forced on me, that I have not made up one line for the sake of making it up."

LETTERS. *March* 5, 1907. (Hanover: To S.C.C.S.) "I am so absorbed and interested in my book I don't like to think of anything else."

LETTERS. *March* 20, 1907. (Hanover: To S.C.C.S.) [*A woman friend had sent her some papers on the Contagious Diseases Acts*]: "To me there is nothing else in the world that touches me the same way. You will see, if you read my novel, that all other matters seem to me small compared to matters of sex, and prostitution is its most agonising central point. Prostitution, especially the prostitution of men of themselves to their most brutal level, can't really be touched till man not only says but feels woman is his equal, his brother human to whom he must give as much as he takes, and the franchise is one step towards bringing that about."

LIFE. *April* 28, 1907. (Diary, Hanover.) "I like Rebekah's letter; it's too long, all to have been written in one night, but that doesn't matter."

LETTERS. *May* 23, 1907. (Hanover: To S.C.C.S.) "Oh, I wish I could get my book done before I die. It may not be any good; but I feel I have to do it. I used to feel I couldn't die till it was done, that fate wouldn't let it be. Now I know that anything may be; you trust and hope for years, but things never come. If one has done one's best, that is all. . . ." [*On the 27th.* "Oh, if I could be under conditions to finish it. I've set my heart so on finishing it before the end comes. I could do so much work now if I was strong and could get fresh air. My brain has never been so clear and strong before in one way. I tried to go for a walk yesterday but came back staggering and am only now recovering from it."

LETTERS. *October* 22, 1907. (De Aar: To Mrs. Francis Smith.) "The novel I am revising now is dedicated to her ['my little sister, Ellie.'] She lived only eighteen months, but for that 18 my life was entirely in and through her, and I watched her die. The novel I am revising is dedicated to her, and the opening chapter ['The Prelude'] is about a little girl's feelings when her new little sister is born. I sometimes think my great love for women and girls, *not* because they are myself, but because they are *not* myself, comes from my love to her."

LETTERS. *October* 1909. (De Aar: To Mrs. Francis Smith.) "I've got a bit about him [the old Greek sculptor of the Winged Victory of Samothrace] in my big novel. Oh, I do hope I shall live to finish it. All the things and people in it are my little children, and you see they'll die, if I die first. I only want to live for that, nothing else."

LETTERS. *October* 1909. (Cape Town: To Mrs. Francis Smith.) "I am sending you 'The Prelude.' Send it back when you've read it. I've got to revise it yet. It's just as it came to me many years ago one day on the Riviera. I *know* you'll understand it. I love it specially because it came to me in such a curious way. I wrote the rough draft of this novel years and years ago when I was quite a young girl, before I went to England [that is, before 1881]. In England I was too much absorbed in social problems ever to read it over even One day, I think it was in the winter of 1888, I was on the Riviera at Alassio; I was sitting at my dear old desk writing an article on the Bushmen and giving a description of their skulls; when suddenly, in an instant, the whole of this little Prelude *flashed* on me. You know those folded-up views of places one buys; you take hold of one end and all the pictures unfold one after the other as quick as light. That was how it *flashed* on me. I started up and paced about the room. I felt absolutely astonished. I hadn't thought of my novel for months, I hadn't looked at it for years. I'd never dreamed of writing a prelude to it,—I just sat down and wrote it out. And do you know what I found out—after I'd written it?—that it's a picture in small, a kind of allegory, of the life of the woman in the book! ! It's one of the strangest things I know of. My mind must have been working at it *unconsciously*, though I knew nothing of it—otherwise how did it come?"

LETTERS. *December* 14, 1909. (Muizenberg: To Mrs. Francis Smith.) "Did you get my little 'Prelude'? Please return it, darling. In the novel, when the little girl grows up, she spends some of the most important moments of her life at Muizenberg close to this spot. It's curious that I feel as though some great tragic events of my own life had taken place here. I walk again and again to the spot where years ago 'Farmer Peck's' little thatched house [now the Grand Hotel] used to stand, and think, 'Yes, here Rebekah walked.' I don't think anyone else can have an idea how real and how 'out of oneself,' something not made up by oneself but which one *simply knows*, all these people are."

LETTERS. *July* 29, 1912. (De Aar: To Miss Emily Hobhouse.) "I have never been able to add a line to any of my books since I saw you. You see, as soon as one writes and feels, one gets excited, and as soon as one gets excited one gets faint."

LETTERS. *March* 1913. (Muizenberg: To Miss Emily Hobhouse.) "It isn't the pain and weakness one minds, it's the not being able to work. My one novel especially I would have liked so to finish. I feel that if only one lonely and struggling woman read it and found strength and comfort from it one would not feel one had lived quite in vain. I seem to have done so little with my life."

LETTERS. 1918. (London: To Mrs. Francis Smith.) "Would you, sometime, tell me something: when you read that little 'Prelude' to my book I showed you the other day, did you think it was a *made-up thing*, like an allegory, or did you think it was real *about myself?* Please tell me, because, if I haven't made it clear, I must. I thought it was quite clear [that it was about herself], but the only other person to whom I've shown it didn't understand."

S. C. C. S.

CAPE TOWN.
March, 1926.

THE PRELUDE
THE CHILD'S DAY

THE CHILD'S DAY

THE little mother lay in the agony of childbirth. Outside all was still but the buzzing of the bees, some of which now and then found their way in to the half-darkened room. The scent of the orange trees and of the flowers from the garden beyond, came in through the partly opened window, with the rich dry odor of a warm, African, summer morning. The little mother groaned in her anguish.

Old Ayah, the Hottentot woman, stood at the bedside with her hands folded and her long fingers crooked, the veins on the back standing out like cords. She said, *"O ja, God! Wat zal ons nou zeg?"* [1] and readjusted the little black shawl upon her shoulders. The window was open three inches, and the blind was drawn below it to keep out the heat. The mother groaned.

At the end of the passage in the dining room the father sat with his elbows on the deal table and his head in his hands, reading Swedenborg; but the words had no clear meaning for him. Every now and then he looked up at the clock over the fireplace. It was a quarter before ten, and the house was very quiet.

At the back of the house, on the kitchen doorstep, stood Rebekah, the little five-year-old daughter. She looked up into the intensely blue sky, and then down to the ducks who were waddling before the lowest step, picking up the crusts she had thrown to them. She wore a short pink-cotton dress with little white knickerbockers buttoned below the knees and a white kappie with a large curtain that came almost to her waist. She took the kappie off and looked up again into the sky. There was something

[1] "Oh yes, God! What shall we now say?"

3

almost oppressive in the quiet. The Kaffir maids had been sent home to their huts, except one who was heating water in the kitchen, and the little Kaffirs were playing away beyond the kraals on the old kraal heap. It was like Sunday. She drew a slight sigh, and looked up again into the sapphire-blue sky: it was going to be very hot. The farmhouse stood on the spur of a mountain, and the thorn trees in the flat below were already shimmering in the sunlight. After a while she put on her kappie and walked slowly down the steps and across the bare space which served for a farmyard. Beyond it she passed into the low bushes. She soon came to a spot just behind the kraal where the ground was flat and bare; the surface soil had been washed off, and a circular floor of smooth and unbroken stone was exposed, like the smooth floor of a great round room. The bushes about were just high enough to hide her from the farmhouse, though it was only fifty yards off. She stepped on to the stone slowly, on tiptoe. She was building a house here. It stood in the center of the stone floor; it was a foot and a half high and about a foot across, and was built of little flat stones placed very carefully on one another, and it was round like a tower. The lower story opened on to the ground by a little doorway two inches high; in the upper story there was a small door in the wall; and a ladder made of sticks, with smaller sticks fastened across, led up to it. She stepped up to the house very softly. She was building it for mice. Once a Kaffir boy told her he had built a house of stones, and as he passed the next day a mouse ran out at the front door. She had thought a great deal of it; always she seemed to see the mouse living in the house and going in and out at the front door; and at last she built this one. She had built it in two stories, so that the family could live on the lower floor and keep their grain on the top. She had put a great flat stone to roof the lower story, and another flat stone for the roof on the very top, and she had put a moss carpet in the lower floor for them to sleep on, and corn, ready for them to use, above. She stepped very softly up to the house and peeped in at the little door; there was nothing there but the brown moss. She sat down flat on the stone before it and peered in. Half, she expected the mice to come; and half, she knew they never would!

Presently she took a few little polished flat stones out of her pocket and began to place them carefully round the top to form a turret; then she straightened the ladder a little. Then she sat, watching the house. It was too hot to go and look for more stones. After a while she stretched out her right hand and drew its sides together and made the fingers look as if it were a little mouse and moved it softly along the stone, creeping, creeping up to the door; she let it go in. Then after a minute she drew it slowly back and sat up. It was becoming intensely hot now; the sun beating down on the stone drew little beads of perspiration on her forehead.

How still it was! She listened to hear whether anyone from the house would call her. It was long past ten o'clock and she was never allowed to be out in the sun so late. She sat listening: then she got a curious feeling that something was happening at the house and stood up quickly and walked away towards it.

As she passed the dining-room window, whose lower edge was on a level with her chin, she looked in. Her father was gone; but his glasses and his open book still lay on the table. Rebekah walked round to the kitchen door. Even the ducks were gone; no one was in the kitchen; only the flames were leaping up and crackling in the open fireplace, and the water was spluttering out of the mouth of the big black kettle. She stood for a moment to watch it. Then a sound struck her ear. She walked with quick, sharp steps into the dining room and threw her kappie on the table and stood listening. Again the sound came, faint and strange. She walked out into the long passage into which all the bedrooms opened. Suddenly the sound became loud and clear from her mother's bedroom. Rebekah walked quickly up the cocoanut-matted passage and knocked at her mother's door, three short, sharp knocks with her knuckle. There was a noise of moving and talking inside; then the door opened a little.

"I want to come in! Please, what is the matter?"

Some one said, "Shall she come in?" and then a faint voice answered, "Yes, let her come."

Rebekah walked in; there was but a little light coming in under the blind through the slightly opened window. Her mother was lying in the large bed and her father standing at the bedside. A strange woman from the next farm, whom she had never seen before, sat in the elbow chair in the corner beyond the bed, with something on her lap; old Ayah stood near the drawers, folding some linen cloths.

Rebekah stood for a moment motionless and hesitating on the ox skin in the middle of the floor; then she walked straight up to the strange woman in the corner.

"Ask her to show you what she has got, Rebekah," said her father.

The woman unfolded a large brown shawl, inside of which there was a white one. Even in the dim light in the corner you could see a little red face, with two hands doubled up on the chest, peeping out from it.

Rebekah looked.

"Was it *this* that made that noise?" she asked.

The woman smiled and nodded.

Her father came up.

"Kiss it, Rebekah; it is your little sister."

Rebekah looked quietly at it.

"No—I won't. I don't like it," she said slowly.

But her father had already moved across the room to speak to old Ayah.

Rebekah turned sharply on her heel and walked to the large bed. Her mother lay on it with her eyes shut. Rebekah stood at the foot, her eyes on a level with the white coverlet, looking at her mother.

As she stood there she heard old Ayah whisper to the father, and they both went out, to the spare bedroom opposite. The strange woman came and bent over the mother and said something to her; she nodded her head without opening her eyes. The woman made a space at her side and laid the white bundle down in it; she put the baby's head on the mother's arm. The mother opened her eyes then and looked down at it with a half smile, and drew the quilt up a little higher to shield it. Rebekah watched them; then she walked softly to the door.

"Please open it for me," she said. The handle was too high for her.

The woman let her out.

For a moment she stood outside the closed door, looking at it, her tiny features curiously set almost with the firmness of a woman's; then she turned and walked down the passage. She saw her father and old Ayah come out of the spare room. Old Ayah locked the door and put the key into her pocket, and they went back to her mother's bedroom.

Rebekah picked up her kappie from the dining-room table, put it on, and went out again on to the steps at the kitchen door. The sun was blazing in the yard now; the very stones seemed to throw up a red reflection. Standing on the top step in the shade, Rebekah shivered with heat.

Then she wandered slowly down the steps and across the yard. She could feel the ground burn under her feet, through the soles of her little shoes. She walked to her flat stone. The mouse house stood baking in the sun with all the little crystals in the rock glittering. She sat down before the house, drawing her skirts carefully under her, the rock burnt so. She drew her knees up to her chin, and folded her arms about them, and sat looking at the mouse house. She knew she ought not to be there in the hot sun; she knew it was wicked; but she liked the heat to burn her that morning.

After a while the little drops of perspiration began to gather under her eyes and on her upper lip; she would not wipe them off. Her face began to get very red, and her temples to throb; the heat was fierce. She looked out at the mouse house from under her white kappie with blinking red eyes. She could feel the heat scorching her arms through her little cotton dress, and she liked it.

By half past eleven the heat was so intense she could not bear it, and there began to be a sound like a little cicada singing in her ears, so she got up, and walked slowly towards the house, but did not go in at the kitchen door.

She went to the back, where the wall of the house made a deep shadow, and went to the window of the spare room. It was her favorite place, to which she went whenever she wanted to be quite safe and alone. No one ever went there. The beds were generally left unmade till visitors came, with only the mattresses and pillows on them, and under one bed she kept her box of specially prized playthings. She unclosed the outer shutters. The window was so low that she could easily raise the sash and climb in from the ground. She pushed it up and stepped into the room. It was beautifully cool there and almost dark : she drew up the blind a very little to let in some light. She was walking towards the bed under which her box was, when something struck her eye. On the large table in the middle of the room there was a something with a white sheet spread over it. Rebekah walked up to it; this was something quite new.

She drew a chair to the side of the table and climbed up. She lifted the top of the sheet. Under it there was another sheet and a pillow, and, with its head on the pillow, dressed in pure white, was a little baby. Rebekah stood upright on the chair, holding the sheet in her hand.

After a while she let it down carefully, but so turning it back that the baby's face and hand were exposed. How fast it was sleeping !

She bent down and peered into its face. There was a curious resemblance between her own small, sharply marked features and those of the baby. She put out her forefinger gently and touched one of its hands. They were very cool. She watched it for some time; then she

climbed down and went to the wardrobe where the best going-to-town clothes were kept hanging. With some difficulty she unhooked a little fur-trimmed red cape of her own; with this she climbed back on to the chair and laid it across the baby's feet. It was evidently not warm enough, though the day was hot.

She bent down over it again. On the top of its head was a little mass of soft, downlike curly black hair; she put her face down softly and touched the hair with her cheek and kissed it. She dared not kiss its face for fear of waking it. She sat down beside it, motionless, for a long time, on the edge of the table. Seeing it did not stir, after a time she climbed down, and taking off her shoes and leaving them at the foot of the table, went on tip-toe to the bed and drew from under it her box.

It was a large soap box with an odd collection of things in it. On the top was a dried monkey's skin and a large alphabet book with colored pictures; below were different little boxes and bags; some held stones; one was full of brightly colored beetles and grasshoppers she had picked up dead; in one, all by itself, was a very large bright crystal, carefully wrapped in cotton-wool and tied with a string. Below, was an oblong-shaped, common brown stone about eighteen inches in length; it was dressed in doll's clothes and it had a shawl wrapped round it. Beside it was a small shop-doll with pink cheeks and flaxen hair, which she had got on her last birthday; but it had no shawl and its face was turned to the wood. The stone she had had two years, and she loved it; the shop doll was only interesting. Besides these there was a round Bush-man stone with a hole in the middle, which she had picked up behind the kraal, and a flat slate-colored stone with the impression of a fossilized leaf, which she found on the path going up to the mountain; and, at the very bottom in the corner was a workbox, with a silver thimble and needles and cottons inside, which she thought very grand; and two little brightly colored boxes with chocolates and peppermints with holes through them like whistles, which

she had got on Christmas Day, but thought too pretty to eat; and there was also a head of Queen Victoria, cut out of the tinsel label of a sardine tin, and which she kept wrapped up in white paper.

She took all the things out of the box and handled them carefully, deliberating for a while. At last she selected the alphabet book, the Bushman stone, the silver thimble and a paper of needles, Queen Victoria's head, and a stick of chocolate. When she had packed the other things back, she went with them to the table. She climbed up on the chair. She laid the thimble and paper of needles on the cushion on the left of the baby's head, and the Bushman stone and the tinsel Queen Victoria head on the right. Very gently and slowly she slipped the alphabet book under the baby's doubled-up arm; and then, turning back the silver paper at one end of the chocolate stick, she forced the other end very gently into its closed fist, leaving the uncovered end near to its mouth. Then she stood upright on the chair with her hands folded before her, looking down at them all, with a curious contentment about her mouth.

After a little time she got down and went to her box at the foot of the bed, and sat down upon it; to wait till the baby woke.

Her face was seamed under the eyes with lines hot perspiration and dust had left, and she was very tired. She leaned her arm on the bed and rested her head on it.

At half-past one it was dinner-time, and old Ayah could not find her. She often crept in the heat of the day behind the piano or into the wagon-loft, and fell asleep there where no one could discover her. So old Ayah put some dinner for her in a tin plate in the oven to keep warm.

Then everyone went to lie down; the shutters of all the doors and windows were closed, and there was not a sound in all the house but the buzzing of the flies in the darkened rooms.

Only old Ayah did not sleep to-day and was sewing a piece of white calico into a long, narrow, white robe with a stiff frill down the front for a tiny baby. She sat working in the dining room with the shutters very slightly apart to let in enough light.

When she had done it she went down the passage to the door of the spare room and unlocked it.

The first thing she noticed was that the outer shutters she had left carefully closed were partly open, that the window had been raised, and the blind was an inch or two drawn up. She walked to the table. The baby lay with the sheet removed from its face, and the Bushman stone, and thimble, and needles, and a picture, on its pillow, and the alphabet book under its arm, and the chocolate stick in its hand. She glanced round. Rebekah was still sitting on her box at the foot of the bed with her stockinged feet crossed and her head resting on her arm on the mattress, fast asleep, her shoes standing side by side at the foot of the table.

Old Ayah walked up to her and shook her by the shoulder. Rebekah opened her eyes slowly and looked at her dreamily, without raising her head.

"What are you doing in here? Couldn't you see, if the door was locked, that you weren't meant to get in here?" she said in the Cape Dutch she always spoke. Rebekah sat up, still looking round vacantly; then in an instant all came back to her and she stood up.

"Aren't you a wicked, naughty child, letting all the flies and the sun come in! What have you been doing?"

"Oh, please don't talk so loud," whispered Rebekah quickly, bending forward and stretching out her hand; "please, you'll wake it!"

"O Lord!" said old Ayah, looking at her, "what would your mother say if she knew you'd been in here playing with that blessed baby? You naughty child, how dared you touch it!"

"It's mine: I found it!" said Rebekah, walking softly up to the foot of the table.

Old Ayah came up, too.

"Oh, please," said Rebekah, putting out her hand again, "*don't* touch it! Don't touch it! I *don't* want it waked!"

She looked up at old Ayah with full lustrous eyes, as a bitch when you handle her pups.

"O my God!" said old Ayah, "the child is mad! How can it be yours? It's your mother's."

"It is mine," said Rebekah slowly: "I found it. Mietje found hers in the hut, and Katje found hers behind the kraal. My mother found hers that cries so, in the bed-room. *This one* is mine!"

"O Lord, Lord!" cried old Ayah. "I tell you this is your mother's baby; she had two, and this one is dead. I put it here myself."

Rebekah looked at her.

"This one is dead: it'll never open its eyes again; it can't breathe."

The old Hottentot woman began taking the alphabet book from under its arm and the stick from its hand, and took the things from the pillow.

Rebekah did not look at her; her gaze was fixed on the baby's face.

"Here, take these things!"

But Rebekah raised out her hand, and touched the baby's feet; a coldness went up her arm, even through the sheet. She dropped her hand.

"Child, what is it? Here!—take your shoes!"

She thrust the shoes into her hand. Rebekah held them, but let them slide between her fingers on to the floor; she was still staring at the table.

Old Ayah gathered up the child's apron and put into it the things she had taken from the baby, and forced the shoes back into her other hand.

"Here, take them, I say, and go away! And get your face washed and your hair done, and tell Mietje to put you on a clean dress and white pinafore. What would your mother say to see you looking such an ugly, dirty little fright?"

Rebekah turned away slowly, with the gathered apron in one hand and the shoes in the other, and walked to the door. When she got there she turned and looked dreamily back; then she went out into the passage.

After she had had her face washed and her hair brushed, and had got on a clean starched pink dress and a white over-all pinafore, she went to the dining room. Old Ayah had put her plate of warmed dinner on the table ready for her, and she sat down on the bench to eat it. She felt better now she was washed and had a clean starched dress on.

The heat outside was still very oppressive, and only a little light came in through the cracks in the shutter; and the blue flies were buzzing round everywhere in the dark. She did not feel very hungry, and played with her dinner, but she drank all the water in her mug. Then she pushed her plate from her, found her kappie, and went out into the great front room. All was quiet there also, and almost quite dark. She took a large worn picture-book from the side table, and opened the double door and went out on to the front stoep.[1] The vine leaves on the front wall hung dry and stiff, and even the orange leaves on the great orange trees before the door hung curled and flaccid.

It was nearly three o'clock, and the heat was hardly less intense than at midday, though there was already shade on that side of the house. The hollyhocks and dahlias in the flower garden beyond the orange trees were hanging their heads, and the four-o'clocks were curled up tight, though the trees sheltered them.

She walked down through the flower garden, on into the orchard beyond.

All was very still and brown there. The little peach trees that stood in rows were shedding their half-ripe fruit, which fell into the long yellow grass beneath them, and the fig trees along the wall had curled up the edges of their leaves. Rebekah followed a little winding foot-

[1] Stoep: stone-flagged veranda.

path among the grass to the middle of the orchard, where a large pear tree stood, with a gnarled and knotted stem. There was a bench under the tree, and the grass grew very long all about it. She looked around to find a spot where the tree cast a deeper shade than elsewhere. Here she walked round and round on the grass, like a dog, and then lay down on her back in the place she had made. It was like a nest, with the grass standing several inches high all round.

She drew up her legs, cocking one knee over the other, so that one foot waved in the air.

It was very nice. She lay for a while with her hands clasped across the top of her head, from which she had thrown her white kappie. The pear-tree leaves were so thick overhead you could hardly see any sky through them. She yawned luxuriously. Beyond the edges of the pear branches, here and there as you looked through half-closed eyes, were strips of blue sky, and some great, white masses of thunder cloud were showing in them, like ships sailing in the blue. She watched them for a while with her eyes half shut; then she took up the book that lay on the grass at her side, stood it open on her chest against her knee, and gently waved the foot that was cocked up in the air.

The book opened of itself about the middle of a certain page. On it was a picture: Peter, a great boy with a red face, looking out through the top of the letter P, and at his feet was a little pig with a curled tail. Besides this there were in the picture, in the distance, fields and a stile, and a winding path leading far away over the hills; and in the foreground was a milestone with weeds growing around it; below was written, "**P** stands for Peter and Pig."

She had had the book ever since she could remember, she had kept it very clean; there was no torn place or mark in it; but the page of *Peter and his Pig* was brown and worn round the edges. It was her favorite picture. Whenever she looked at it she wanted to make up stories. She had made one long story about it: how people were not kind to Peter and he had no one to love him but his pig, and how they both ran away together by that far-off road that went over the hill, and saw all the beautiful things on the other side. She liked this book better than her new books. She stood it up on her chest and looked into the picture. But to-day it had no meaning; it suggested nothing. Then she looked away again beyond the edges of the pear branches, where two great masses of white cloud were floating in the blue; they dazzled her eyes so she closed them.

Presently she made a story that one of those clouds was a ship and she was sailing in it (she had never seen the sea or a ship, but she was always making stories about them), and, as she sailed, she came at last to an island. The ship stopped there. And on the edge of the shore was a lady standing, dressed in beautiful clothes, all gold and silver. When she stepped on to the shore the lady came up to her and bowed to her, and said, "I am Queen Victoria. Who are you?"

And Rebekah answered her, "I am the little Queen Victoria of South Africa."

And they bowed to each other.

(The child under the tree moved her head very slightly, without opening her eyes.)

The Queen asked her where she came from. She said, "From a country far away from here: not such a *very* nice country! Things are not always nice there—only sometimes they are."

The Queen said, "I have many islands that belong to me, but this island belongs to no one. Why don't you come and live here? No one will ever scold you here, and you can do just what you like."

Rebekah said, "I should like it very much; but I must first go and fetch my books out of the ship." And when she had brought her books, she said to the Queen, "Here is a little box of presents I have got for all the people who live on the farm where I used to live: for my father and my mother and the servants and the little Kaffirs—and even old Ayah. Would you please give it to them as you go past?" And the Queen said she would; and she said, "Good-by, little Queen Victoria!" And Rebekah said, "Good-by, big Queen Victoria!" and they bowed to each other, and the old Queen went away in the ship in which she had come.

Then she was all alone on her island. (She had never seen an island except a lump of ground in the furrow, with some thyme and forget-me-nots growing on it; but when she grew up she found she had pictured that island just as a real island might have been!) The island had many large trees and bushes, and the grass and thyme and forget-me-nots grew down to the water's edge. She walked a little way and she came to a river with trees on each side, and on it were two swans swimming, with their long white necks bent. She had had a book with the picture of a swan swimming in a lake, and she had always thought she must die of joy if she should see a real swan swimming up and down. And here were two!

A little farther, on the bank of the river, there was a little house standing. It was as high in proportion to her as grown-up people's houses are in proportion to them. The doors were just high enough for her to go in and out at, and all things fitted her. One room was covered with books from the floor to the ceiling, with a little empty shelf for her own books, and there was a microscope on the table like her father's which she was never allowed to touch; but this one was hers!

Outside, in the garden, there were little rakes and spades that came as high as her shoulder. (Rebekah had always had to dig with a man's spade that made her arms ache.) At the side of the house there were all the things lying one uses for building houses; and a pile of bricks; and a bit of bare ground where you could make as much mud as you liked and make more bricks. But she hadn't time to stay and make bricks then. She went on farther.

Presently she came to a place where the trees hung very low down over the water and the grass was very thick;

and there, from a large white bush, hanging right over and nearly touching the water, she saw a snow-white pod nearly as long as her arm. It was like a pea pod, but it was covered all over with a white, frosted silver. She reached down over the edge and tried to pick it. It was very heavy; at last she broke it off and carried it away in her pinafore, and she sat on a bank with it on her lap. She pressed with her finger all up and down the joint, and slowly the pod cracked and cracked, and opened from one end to the other, like a mimosa pod does.

And there, lying inside it, like the seeds lie inside the pod of a mimosa tree—was a little baby. It was quite pink and naked. It was as long in proportion to her, as a Kaffir woman's new baby is in proportion to a Kaffir woman, when she first finds it. She tried to lift it out but it was tied to the pod like the mimosa seeds are, with a little curled-up string. She broke the string and lifted it out; then she wrapped it up in her pinafore and skirt and put its head on her arm and carried it home.

(The book, which was still standing up against her knee, here fell over softly into the breast of the child under the pear tree.)

When she got it home she fed it with milk from a tiny bottle as one feeds a hand-lamb, and she wrapped it up in a soft white shawl, and put it on her bed and lay down beside it. She held it close against her with one arm, and stroked its hair softly with the other hand.

"Go to sleep, my baby," she said; "you must be very tired this first day. The world is so large. To-morrow you can see all the things, and I'll tell you about them.

"If you should wake in the night, my baby," she said presently, "and hear anything, don't be afraid: just call to me. I'll be close by. And if you hear the clock ticking, *don't* think it means any of those dreadful things— it doesn't! I'll stop it if it makes you sad. And if you want to see the angels, then just shut your eyes and press on them *hard* with your two fingers, like this——" (The child under the tree moved her hand as though to raise it

to her eyes, but did not). "Those black things with th
light all round which you see going round and round when
you press your eyes, are the angels' heads; just like it says
in the hymn:

> 'And through the hours of darkness keep
> Their watch around my bed.'

They are good angels, though they are black in the middle.
I always used to see them when I was a little girl and I
pressed my eyes. I'll put a chocolate stick under your
pillow, that you can find it and suck it if you feel lonely.
Don't be sorry you are come into the world, my baby. *I*
will take care of you!"

She was going to rise from the bed; then she remembered other things that had to be said, and lay down again.

"When you are grown older, I'll teach you the multiplication table and spelling, because you can't grow up if
you don't know these things. I know how bad it is to
learn them; I had to when I was little, and so at last I
grew up.

"Kaffirs grow up without learning tables or spelling;
that's why it would be nice to be a Kaffir. If you've
something hard to learn, pray God to help you; sometimes
he does and sometimes he doesn't. If he doesn't, it's
because you've prayed wrong; but it's no use praying
again on that same day, especially if it's hot;—wait till
the next."

Again there was a long pause.

"My baby, I shall *never* call *you* 'a strange child'! You
can climb trees and tear your clothes; but if you find any
birds' nests, you mustn't take the eggs; you can just put
your hand in and feel; and, if it's a very little nest, you
must only put one finger in. Especially cock-o-veet's eggs
you must *not* take! Kaffir boys take birds' eggs."

Again there was a pause.

"My baby, shall I tell you a little story? It's one I
made myself, and a rather nice little story:

"Once there was a little girl, and she went for a walk in

the bush. And when she had gone a little way, a cock-o-veet [1] came flying up to her and took hold of her pinafore by the corner with its beak. And the little girl said, 'Cock--o-veet dear, what is it?'

"And the cock-o-veet said, 'Make your hand like a little round nest.'

"So she made it so—so!" (The child as she lay under the tree with her closed eyes drew the fingers of her right hand together and made a hollow.)

"And the cock-o-veet sat down in her hand; and when it got up, there—was—a little—real—blue—egg—lying there!

"And the little girl said, 'Oh, cock-o-veet!'

"And the cock-o-veet said: 'Put the egg in my nest, and I will sit on it and make a little bird come out, for you!' And the cock-o-veet showed the little girl where her nest was; and she put the egg in; and the cock-o-veet sat down on it, and said, 'Good-by; I'll call you when it comes out.'

"And when she had gone farther she saw some monkeys sitting up in the high trees, little, long-tailed monkeys; and they put their hands out to her. And she looked up and said, 'Oh, little monkeys, what do you want?'

"And they said, 'Come up in the trees and have tea with us.'

"And she said, 'What kind of tea do you have, oh, monkeys?'

"And they said, 'Nam-nams and Kaffir plums.'

"So she climbed up and sat with them on a branch, and they gave her of their nam-nams and Kaffir plums with their little black hands, and she gave them some cakes out of a little bag she had with her.

"And when they had finished the monkeys kissed her, and she kissed them, and she climbed down and went on.

"And presently she came to a place where some very large rocks were lying deep in the bush, and the trees were

[1 Kokkewiet: The bush-shrike, a very handsome bird with resonant call notes of great beauty—a prime favorite of Olive's.]

hanging over them, and it was dark under the rock. And the little girl thought it looked rather like a tiger's sleeping place!

"And when she looked under the rock, there *was* a great tiger lying! And she said, 'Oh, tiger!'

"And the tiger winked with its eyes—so!

"And she said, 'I'm rather frightened of you, Mr. Tiger!'

"But the tiger said, 'Come here!'

"So she came.

"And the tiger said, 'You can just play being my cub if you like!'

"So she lay down by the tiger, and the tiger rolled her over and made believe to bite her.

"And the tiger said, 'Cubbie, would you like to sleep a little? You look rather tired.' And it made a place for her between its front legs, where she could lie down with her head on its side, and it was nice and soft.

"And the tiger said, 'If the flies trouble you, I'll just switch them away with my tail!'

"And the little girl said, 'I'll just leave my little bag of cakes open so that if you like you can help yourself while I'm asleep.'

"And she went to sleep on the tiger. And when she woke the tiger licked all over her face and said, 'Good-by'; and she went on.

"And by and by, as she was going up a very steep road right up on the mountain, there was a lion standing right before her.

"And the little girl said, 'Oh, Mr. Lion!'

"And he said, 'Come up to me!'

"So she came up; and he rubbed his head against her pinafore and she rubbed her head in his stiff curls.

"And the lion said, 'Aren't you afraid to come walking in the bush alone?'

"And she said, 'Oh, no!'

"And he yawned.

"And she said, 'Don't you open your mouth so *very* wide, please! It's so *very* big!'

"And he said, 'I'm only yawning a little; it's nothing.'

"And the little girl gave him some of her cakes. She said, 'I've made them myself.'

"He licked his mouth and said they were nice cakes; and he said he would walk home with her. She said there was no need, because perhaps the people at the farm house mightn't quite like it; but that if ever he had a thorn in his foot he must let her know and she'd take it out. He said he hadn't a thorn just then, but he'd let her know when he had. So they rubbed their heads against each other, and she went away."

(The mouth of the child under the tree was drawn in at the corners as if half smiling, a quiet smile.)

"Then the little girl went down the mountain and into her father's garden. And, just as she was going in at the gate under the dam wall, she heard something go puff— puff—puff! And she looked round, and, there, just by her, was a great puff-adder sitting up! And she said, 'Oh, Puff-puffie!'

"And the puff-adder said, 'Come with me, my dear!'

"And the little girl said, 'But Puff-puffie, I'm rather afraid!'

"And the puff-adder said, 'Don't be, my dear; *I* never bite little girls!' And she took the little girl to a hole in the wall, where all her little puff-adders were. And she said, 'You can put your hand in and take a few out. They've all got little poison bags, but they don't use them. They only eat grass and sand; and they like a little drop of milk now and then when they can get it.'

"And the little girl put her hand in and took out the little puff-adders, till her pinafore was full.

"And she said, 'I shall not forget to bring them a little drop of milk when I have any!' And she put them back in the hole, and she wished good afternoon to the puff-adder, and the puff-adder wished her good afternoon and went to sleep under a stone.

"And then the little girl went down farther in the garden; and she hadn't gone very far when she saw a great cobra lying on the grass, with his bright eyes looking at her.

"And she said, 'Oh, Mr. Cobra!'

"And he said, 'Good afternoon, my dear. Won't you take me on your lap and warm me a little? I'm so cold to-day!'

"So she held out her pinafore and the cobra climbed in: he made her pinafore quite full. And she walked to the sod wall with him and sat down on the top, where the sun could shine on him, and she sang to the cobra; and he went to sleep in her lap.—And that's the end of the story."

(The child under the tree seemed to be dropping asleep also; her lips had ceased to move, and her breath came evenly, but her mind went on.)

"You know that's only a story, my baby. You can't really go into the bush and do so with all the animals. They don't understand—yet. Perhaps, if you could talk to them—from a long way off—so that they knew what you meant— My father brought a tiger down from the bush once, that they had caught with a trap. I was sorry for him because he was shut up in a cage and looked so sad. So I saved my meat for him at dinner, and I took it out to him when the others were asleep; his eyes were quite nearly shut and his head was on his feet. But just when I put my hand in with the meat he jumped up; he tried to bite me. I didn't tell anyone.

"Only dogs understand. If a great dog comes at you, my baby, don't you run away. Just say 'Sibby! Sibby! Sibby!' and make—so—with your fingers; say 'P-o-o-r dog, *p-o-o-r*, P-O-O-R little Sibby!' Even if he's big, you can say 'little'; dogs always like to be called 'little.' Even if he's got his mouth on a side—so—and you can see his one tooth, don't be afraid; just stand and talk to him. He'll understand. But other things don't. The best thing is to feed them.

"My baby, was it a nice little story I've told you? If

I tell you a secret, you mustn't tell anyone else! I'm a person that makes stories! I write *books!* When I was little I used to scribble them in a copybook with a stick, when I didn't know how to write. But when I grew up I learned to write;—I wrote real books, a whole roomful! I've written a book about birds, and about animals, and about the world; and one day I'm going to write a book something like the Bible. If you like to make up stories, I shall never let anyone laugh at *you,* when you walk up and down and talk to yourself. I know you *must.*

"There are some stories I didn't make that I like too. There's one I like best of all. Shall I tell it you?"

(The child under the tree moved her arms a little as if drawing something closer to her.)

"It's rather a hard story because it's a grown-up people's story; I heard it one Sunday afternoon; my father read it to my mother. They thought I couldn't understand, but I did. I don't know if I tell it right, because I only heard it once, but I often looked at the picture. I'll make it as easy as I can.

"You see, it's called *What Hester Durham Lived For.* Hester Durham was a woman, and she sat by the table talking; and the minister came and talked with her. And she said: 'Oh, I wish I was dead! My husband isn't very kind to me, and my boy, whom I loved so much, is dead; and now I wish I was dead, too.'

"And the clergyman (that is a minister) said to her, 'Oh, you mustn't say that; perhaps one day you'll have something to do for some one.'

"And so the lady went away to India—that's a land far away where black people live—and the black soldiers (they call them sepoys) wanted to kill them. They came all round the house, calling and yelling, with swords and sticks. They were only women and children there; and all of them were very frightened; even the old black ayah. But Hester Durham was not afraid. In the picture they are all standing round her and some of them have caught hold of her dress, and some are lying on the ground close to her; and you can see the men's faces outside, with their eyes very big, wanting to come in and kill them all, and their mouths open, screaming! Then it says in the Book:—'*Alone, like a rock in a raging sea, Hester Durham stood there.*' They hadn't been *so* afraid, because she was there to comfort them. And at last the sepoys did come in, and killed them all; but—'*to comfort those frail women and children in their last hour of despair, that was what Hester Durham lived for*'—those are the words I heard my father read. It's rather a difficult story; but you'll know what it means when you're grown up, when you are five years old—I did—though it is difficult.

"I can teach you many things, my baby; poems; there's a nice one:

'The Assyrian came down——'

And another:

'Like mist on the mountains,
Like ships on the sea——'

"But the nicest of all is about a woman. The Romans came and they took away her country and they beat her till the blood ran off her back on to the ground, and they were cruel to her daughters. The Romans were people who took other people's countries; and she got into a chariot and her two daughters and her long hair flying in the wind; and under the tree sat an old man with a long white beard;—and he said—

'Rome shall perish; write that word
In the blood that she hath spilt——' "

(The child under the pear tree with her eyes still fast closed raised her right hand, and her lips moved making a low sound.)

" 'Rome, for Empire far renown
Tramps on a thousand States;
Soon her pride shall kiss the ground:
Hark!—The Gaul is at her gates!' "

(The child under the tree lifted her hand higher and waved it dramatically with her eyes still closed.)

"And the Gauls did come; and they knocked at the gates, and they burned it down. 'Hark!—The Gaul is at her gates!'—I'm glad they burned it. Aren't you?"

(The child's hand dropped.)

"It's a long poem. I'll teach it you. I could understand it all except 'For-Empire' and 'far-renown.'—I don't know what 'far-renown' is—or 'for-empire—'"

(The child under the tree knit her forehead a little.)

"Grown-up people's things are nicer than children's. I didn't like *Jane Taylor's Hymns for Infant Minds.* You'll never have to learn them. The Bible is nice, especially about Elijah, and some texts; one beautiful one—'And instead of the thorn tree shall come up the fir tree; and instead of the briar shall come up the myrtle tree.' It's just like water going—so—!! But Miss Plumtree's Bible stories are horrid! My mother used to read them to me."

(The child under the tree turned her head a little to one side and bent it, as though bringing it nearer to something that lay on her arm.)

"My baby, do you know who Charles is? He's the boy who always plays with me. You won't mind if I love him more than you, because I've known him so very long. He always tells me stories, and I tell him stories, and we walk up and down together. He's a little older than me. He's not a *real* boy, you know! I made him up. He is the Prince Consort of South Africa, and I am the Queen.

"I don't like *real* boys. We had two came to visit us once: they were my cousins. Frank was the biggest. Before they came I meant to play with them and show them all my things; but afterwards I didn't: I wouldn't even show them my flat stone. Frank laughed at me and called me Goody-no-shoes. Well, I didn't mind that so much, it's not so bad as to be called a 'tomboy,' or 'a strange child'!—but he was so unkind to the cat! He held her up by her tail. I don't like cats; they eat birds; but you can't do *that* to them! He used to come after me when I wanted to be alone, and say, 'Ha, ha, miss! I've found you!' and he said I'd have to marry him when I grew up, but I said I never would."

She paused for a long while.

"I liked him better than John-Ferdinand—that was his brother. One day John-Ferdinand saw the little Kaffir maid break the churn stick, and he went and told old Ayah; and old Ayah beat her. Frank and I saw it, too, but we didn't say anything. Frank said I ought to say to him—

> 'You tell tale tit,
> Your tongue shall be slit,
> And every dog in the town
> Shall have a little bit!'

"It wasn't such a very nice little poem; my mother said I mustn't say it up. I just tell you what Frank said. He knew many other little poems—

> 'Four and twenty tailors
> Went to catch a snail——'

and

> 'Boobee—Boobee! Black-face!'

"They are not such very nice poems; but rather funny; and you can say them up if you like. I won't mind. He could make wagons—but I was glad when they went away. I don't like live boys: they are something like Kaffirs. Jan married Mietje, our Kaffir maid, and he used to beat her. I'm glad I'm not a Kaffir man's wife.

"My baby, I'm so glad you are a little girl. I'll make you a pair of thick trousers to climb trees in; these white ones tear so when you slide down, and then the people call you 'tomboy'!

"Now put your arms tight round mother's neck, and hold mother tight."

(The child under the tree turned yet slightly more on

to her side, and moved her left arm as though she were drawing something nearer to her.)

"Mother will tell you just one little story before you go to sleep, a very easy one.

"Once there was a little blue egg in a nest, and the mother bird sat on it. And one day out came a bird; it had no feathers and its eyes were shut, and the mother bird sat on it. By and by the feathers began to come and the eyes opened. And one night, when the mother bird was fast asleep in the nest and the little bird was under her, it put out its head from under the mother's wing and looked. And what do you think it saw? It saw all the stars shining! And it sat up and looked at them!

"That's the end of the story." She paused for a while.

(The child under the tree knit her brows a little, and her hand moved softly up and down on her bosom.)

"My baby, I'm so sorry I have to give you food out of a bottle—Kaffir women have milk for their babies—and cows and sheep, too—but I am like the birds."

(She moved her hand over her little flat breast.)

"I'm so sorry. Now go to sleep, my baby. Put your arms round mother's neck. You must always try to be a good little girl: I always did when I was little—at least —I didn't always—but you must, please. Now go to sleep. Mother will sing you a little song."

(The child under the tree made a queer piping little sound in her throat, and half-formed words came from her lips.)

> " 'London's burning!
> London's burning!
> Fire! Fire!
> Bring some water! Bring some water!
> London's burning!
> London's burning!' "

(The song died away, and the child under the tree lay quite motionless; but her dream still went on.)

She thought when the baby had gone to sleep that she got softly off the bed and went out. The evening air was blowing over the island, and it was near sunset. She went to the side of the house where the building materials lay. She was going to build a play room for the baby. She rolled up her sleeves and dug a foundation and filled it with stones. (She had seen the workmen build the wagon house.) Then she mixed mud, and took off her shoes and socks, and danced in it. (She had seen the Kaffirs treading the mud to build the wagon house, but she had never been allowed to help.) Then she began to build. She took the bricks in one hand and the trowel in the other; she threw the bricks round in one hand and cut off the rough points with the trowel, as the workmen did. Then she placed each brick carefully on the layer of mortar, and tap-tapped them with the end of the handle of the trowel to see if they were quite straight.

When the little wall was two layers high, she looked round. The sun was setting on the island, and over the trees a strange soft evening light shone. There was a pink glow in the sky, and it reflected itself on everything. She stood perfectly still, holding the trowel in her hand, and looked at it. The swans were swimming up and down in the quiet water, far away, with their necks bent. They left a long snow-white mark in the water, like the swans in the picture.

> "The swan swam in a silvery lake.
> Well swam the swan!"

A spasm of delight thrilled up the spine of the child under the pear tree. When a full-grown woman, long years afterwards she could always recall that island, the little house, the bricks, the wonderful light over earth and sky, and the swans swimming on the still water.

After a time she half opened her eyes and looked up. Above her was the pear tree, with its stiff branches of dull green leaves. Slowly she raised herself into a sitting posture and looked round.

All about lay the parched yellow grass, and the little dried peach trees, with their shriveled leaves and drooping yellow peaches.   Everything was brown and dry; she stretched herself and yawned.

Then she stood up.   Suddenly she saw a herd of little pigs a short way off, feeding under the peach trees.   They had got in through a hole in the wall and were eating the fallen fruit among the grass.   They would soon make their way up to the flower garden.

With a shout and whoop she rushed off after them, waving her kappie at them by one string.   The little pigs squeaked and grunted and scattered in all directions.   She chased them till she had got them in a herd all together, and drove out through one of the gaps in the sod wall. Then she stood on the wall and shouted frantically after them, still waving her kappie, though they were all running as fast as they could, with their little curled-up tails. She stood on the wall and waved till they disappeared behind the kraals.

The severest heat of the afternoon was now past, and there was a certain mellow haziness beginning to creep into the afternoon air.   She shaded her eyes with her hand and looked away over the flat below the homestead, where the thorn trees grew.   There seemed a kind of soft, yellow, transparent veil over it all; and there were little gnats in the air.   Presently, as she stood dreamily gazing, she saw some figures moving far away in the flat below the house, near the great dam with the willow trees. The foremost figure carried something on its shoulders; it looked like Long Jan the Kaffir.   Then came her father, and then two Kaffir boys with something over their shoulders that looked like spades.   She could not see well; they were so far away and the soft yellow haze made things dreamy.   They passed through the new lands and then they went out of sight, behind the great willow trees which grew round the dam.

She stood still, looking out at them very drowsily, thinking of nothing in particular and hardly noting them.

Suddenly a small shrill voice called from the back steps of the house, "Get down from that wall, child, will you!

Standing there with nothing on your head! You'll be burnt as black as a Kaffir before your mother gets up. Put your kappie on!"

It was old Ayah, who had come to the back door to throw water into the pigs' wash.

Rebekah climbed from the wall on the garden side, and walked away; but she did not put her kappie on; she tied it round her waist by its long strings and walked back to the pear tree. Everything seemed a little bald and empty; she had no wish to make more stories, and there was nothing to do. It seemed to her, all at once, that it was a very long afternoon. Then there came back to her the picture of her mother lying in the bed with the baby's head on her arm, which she had been trying to put from her all day. She saw the embroidered wrist of her mother's nightdress, and she saw her mother drawing up the cover to shield the baby's head. She tried to think of something else.

There was a strange little blind footpath among the grass under the pear tree on the left side. It was a few feet long, trodden hard and flat and led to nothing. She had made it by walking up and down there when she and Charles made stories and talked.

She began to walk up and down in it now, rather dragging her feet. By and by she and Charles began to talk; she talked in a quite audible voice, now for Charles and then for herself. They told each other no stories, but they began to discuss a little about the house of stramonium stalks they were going to build; he said what he thought was the best way of making the roof would be with stramonia branches; she said she thought peach branches would be stronger and better. But neither had much of interest to say that afternoon.

It began to get cooler now. The large white butterflies that had sat with folded wings during the great heat were beginning to hover over the brown grass; and there was a faint movement in the air, which showed that the evening cool was going to begin.

Then, as she walked, her eye caught sight of a white ball sticking on the bark of the pear tree. She walked round to the stem to look at it, and broke a bit of dry bark off to get it out. It was a soft fluffy ball. She put it on the ground and opened it carefully with two sticks, bending over it, her knees drawn up almost to her chest, and all her little white knickerbockers showing. Inside of it were little gray things that looked like tiny spiders' eggs. She examined it carefully and long, sticking her under lip out over the upper. It was very curious. She was going to examine it more closely, when she caught sight of a row of black ants walking across her own footpath, like a file of little soldiers, one after the other; each one had a pink egg in its mandibles. A few inches farther was another line of little black ants returning across the footpath, probably to fetch more of the eggs which were in some nest hidden in the grass. She wheeled round, still on her heels, with a hand on each knee to balance herself, and watched them closely. Presently a huge ant, like those running up and down the stem of the pear tree, dashed into the path from the grass and seized one of the tiny ants that were carrying the eggs. The ant dropped the egg. The large ant held it exactly in the middle with its large nippers. In an instant she started up, drew her lips tighter, and seized a stick of straw, and tried to divide them; but the large one held so tightly she found she would crush both. She took two withered leaves and softly tried to separate them. The large one caught the leaf with its nippers and the small one got free; it ran away to look for its dropped egg. The large one was clinging angrily to the leaf and trying to bite it. She bent intently over it, watching it.

Suddenly she looked up. She had a curious feeling that some one was looking at her! She looked round and up into the pear tree, still balancing herself carefully in her half-sitting position; there was nothing there but the green dried leaves, and all about nothing but the long brown grass, in some places partly trodden down, in others still standing upright.

She looked back at the ants. Then she glanced round again inquiringly. Two feet from the round spot in the grass which she had trodden down to lie in was the head of a large yellow cobra. Most of its body was hidden in the grass; but its head was out and it was watching her. It was the color of the grass, pale yellow with brown marks. Had it been there all the afternoon? She stood softly upright and stared at it. It looked at her with its glittering unblinking eyes. Then it began to move. Krinkle! krinkle! krinkle! It drew its long body out over the grass, with a sound like a lady walking in a stiff starched print dress. She gazed at it in fixed horror, motionless.

She was not afraid of snakes. When she was three years old she had carried one home in her pinafore, as a great treasure, and been punished for doing so. Since she understood what they were, she was not afraid of them, but they had become a nightmare to her. They spoiled her world. Krinkle, krinkle, krinkle!—it moved away over the grass toward a hole in the sod wall, winding its long six feet of body after it.

She seized her book and ran up the path through the orchard. According to rule, she should have gone to the house and called people to look for it and kill it. But she ran quickly through the flower garden and up the steps on to the front stoep; then she stood still. Her heart was beating so she could hear it; she had a sense of an abandoned wickedness somewhere: it was almost as if *she herself* were a snake, and had gone krinkle! krinkle! krinkle! over the grass. She had a sense of all the world being abandonedly wicked; and a pain in her left side. When her heart had stopped throbbing quite so loud, she opened the door slowly and went into the large front room.

No one had remembered to open the shutters that afternoon, though it was almost sunset; it was dusky in the room even with the door open. On the wall hung two

great framed pictures of Queen Victoria and the Prince
Consort, in regal dress. She always played the Queen
was herself, and the Prince, Charles; and once, when no
one was about, she had put a chair on the side table and
climbed up on it, and kissed her own hand, and put it
high up where she could touch Charles' face with it.

But to-night she did not look at them. The chair in
which her mother always sat stood empty beside the little
work table, and the footstool before it was covered with
dust. She opened the drawer of the table and took out a
calico duster and carefully dusted the chair and stool.
When she had put the duster back, she opened another
drawer and took out a spelling book. She drew her own
little square wooden footstool between her mother's chair
and the open door and sat down on it, with her spelling
book in her hand. She began to learn a short column of
spelling which she should have learned in the morning.
She held up the book before her so that the light from the
door might fall on the page, and spelled out—

"T-h-e-i-r—their."

She repeated it a few score of times; then she went on
to—

"T-h-o-s-e—those."

And then turned to her multiplication table. It was
printed on the cover of the book. She was learning six-
times. She repeated slowly over and over to herself—

"Six times six is—thirty-six,
And six times six is—thirty-six."

The soft, fading evening light was creeping over the
orange trees outside the door.

She drawled slower—

"And, six times six is—thirty-six,
And, six times six is—thirty-six,
And, six times six is—thirty-six,
And, six times six—is—thirty-seven,
And, six times six—is—thirty-seven."

She repeated it slowly about a hundred times, sometimes
right, and sometimes wrong, looking out dreamily all the

while over the book, through the open door, her mind almost a complete blank; then she paused. In a moment, something had flashed on her! She knew now what those figures had meant which she had seen walking down in the flat in the afternoon when she stood on the sod wall. She knew now what it was Long Jan was carrying; she knew why her father walked behind him, and the two Kaffir boys had spades over their shoulders. In an instant she knew well, and with an absolute certainty, that if she went down to the great dam behind the willow trees beyond the new lands, she would find there a little mound of earth, and that the baby from the spare room would be under it. All day she had not let herself think of that baby since old Ayah had driven her out of the room. She knew, also, something else; she knew at that moment —vaguely, but quite certainly—something of what birth and death mean, which she had not known before. She would never again look for a new little baby, or expect to find it anywhere; vaguely but quite certainly something of its genesis had flashed on her.

She stood up in the quickly darkening room, put her multiplication book back into the drawer, and walked straight to the door that opened into the dining room, and closed it behind her.

In the dining room also it was getting dark now, though it looked towards the west and the window was open, and here also it was very quiet. This was generally the noisy time of the day, when there was a stir and a bustle everywhere; her mother was generally giving out rations, and the herds and maids who had come from the huts to fetch their food stood about the storehouse door outside, laughing and talking. The Kaffir maids who worked in the house were generally chatting loudly in the kitchen; and the little Kaffirs, who might not approach at any other time, often stood about the kitchen steps, waiting for their mothers; and from the milking kraal you could hear the men shouting to the cows and calves, and calling to one another; and the dogs felt the excitement and barked;

and above everything could always be heard old Ayah's voice, in a shrill, small key, giving orders everywhere, which no one ever obeyed. But to-night it was all quiet: you could only hear the lowing of the cows and the bleating of the sheep. The men hardly shouted. The rations had been given out early in the morning, and the little Kaffirs had been told not to come about the back door.

Through the great square window the twilight was beginning to come in. She would not go to her mother's room, and she had nowhere else to go. She sat down on a deal bench without a back that stood against the wall. No one came to light the candles; and you could see the dim outlines of the tall clock in the corner, and the wooden chairs and tables standing out as shadows from the whitewashed walls. Presently, as it grew quite darker, a bat came in at the window and flapped about from side to side and went out again. Then the room grew pitch dark. Rebekah drew her legs up under her on the form, and leaned her head back against the whitewashed wall.

By and by the two Kaffir maids came in from the milk house, each carrying a bucket of milk. They had a lighted candle. They went through the dining room into the pantry; they were laughing and talking softly; the light from the open pantry door came back into the dining room.

Presently old Ayah came in from the mother's bedroom.

"What are you sitting here all alone in the dark for, child?" she said.

She went into the pantry, and came out with a large basin of bread and milk sop, and a little pannikin of pure milk. She set them down on the side of the table next to the bench with a tallow candle beside them in a low candlestick.

"Why didn't you eat your dinner, little white face?"

Rebekah sat upright; old Ayah pushed the table a little nearer to her, and she began to eat. She had not known before that she was hungry. Now she ate ravenously and drank at the milk out of her pannikin.

Old Ayah went back into the pantry and scolded the maids in Dutch because the wooden milk-pail was leaking. Very soon the maids and old Ayah came back to the dining room, and rested the pail on the end of the dining table to examine what was gone wrong. One of the maids held the lighted candle, while the other was chewing tallow to put in the cracks.

"What's the baby like, old Ayah?" asked the maid holding the light, as old Ayah examined the leak.

"A fine child," said old Ayah, without looking up. "She'd make four of *that* child when she was born. Its hands are nearly as large as hers now."

The maid who was chewing the tallow pressed some down on the open seam.

"Where has *she* been all day?" she asked, nicking her head at Rebekah.

"Oh, God knows!" said old Ayah. "I've hardly seen her. You might as well try to keep your eye on a *mierkat* among its holes as on *that* child."

They talked of her to her face as if she were a stone wall.

Rebekah kept on eating her supper, gazing straight into her basin, and taking large mouthfuls.

"Look at her now!" said the first Kaffir maid. "How she eats! She's trying to swallow the spoon!"

"Sy's 'n snaaks se kind!" said old Ayah. ("She's a strange child!")

Rebekah kept on eating steadily and looking into the basin. It hurt her so that they talked of her.

When they had done stopping the hand-pail, the two maids went to the kitchen and old Ayah went back to the mother's room. Immediately they were gone Rebekah pushed her basin with what was left in it from her and leaned back on the bench. She drew up one leg, leaned her elbow on the bench, and rested her head against the whitewashed wall. She was very tired. She watched the tallow candle fixedly; it was burning up red, and flickering a little, as the moths and night flies that came in through the open window fluttered round it. It seemed so long since she had got up in the morning. It was her bedtime, but no one came to tell her to go to bed.

Then she began to watch the wick of the tallow candle more fixedly as it burned larger and redder. She pressed two of her fingers on her eyes, half closing them; then she saw two candles; she took them away, and there was only one. She wondered how that was, and tried it again. When she moved one finger a little the one light went up slowly and stood over the other; she moved the other finger, and they came so close they were almost one. She took her hand away and looked at the candle, half closing her eyes; she did not see two candles now, but only four long rays of red light, the two higher ones darker and the two lower lighter. She was slowly getting very interested in it.

She held up her hand and let the light shine through her fingers; the hand made a long dark shadow on the wall to the left of the room. Why was the shadow so much longer than the hand, she wondered, and why did it fall just where it did? She moved her hand and watched the shadow move. If only one were grown up, one would know all about these things! She dropped her hand on her side. Perhaps, even grown-up people didn't know all. Perhaps only God knew what lights and shadows were!

She lay still watching the candle. The wick had burned so long it was beginning to droop and turn over a little on one side. The next morning she would get up early before anyone was up and begin learning her multiplication table and spelling; perhaps she would know it before evening. She would not play once the whole day nor make up stories. She would learn the whole day. It would all help to make you grow up quickly and know everything!

It was half past eight now. Her eyelids began to droop; she only kept them open with a strong effort; she could not bear to go to sleep; but her head bowed, nodding even though she leaned it against the wall.

Suddenly she sat bolt upright; her eyes opened widely. They seemed to grow larger and larger at each instant. She listened intently. From her mother's bedroom there came a sound, a loud, wailing cry. Rebekah got off the bench and stood rigid and upright. Her small sharp-cut face, pale before, became now a deadly white. There was silence for a moment; then another cry, then another, and another, each louder and longer than before. Her hands doubled into fists; she turned a bright pink. The crying went on. She raised her chin; her throat swelled till it looked like the full throat of a tiny woman; the veins stood out like little whipcords. She drew in the corners of her mouth. Again there was a cry, but this time fainter. A dark purple flush came up over her forehead; her eyelids drooped. She rushed out at the door, striking herself against it. She flew up the dark passage to the door of her mother's room. She tried to reach the handle, but it was too high. With hands and feet she struck the panels of the door till they rebounded.

"Let me in! Let me in! I say, let me in! I will—I—will—I say—I will come in!"

The baby inside had left off crying.

Rebekah heard nothing but the surging of the blood in her own ears. Old Ayah opened the door.

"Let me in! Let me in! I will come in!"

Old Ayah tried to put her back with her hand.

"Leave me alone! Leave me alone!" she cried; "You are killing it like the other one! Leave me alone, I say! Leave me alone!"

Old Ayah tried to hold her fast, but she caught the Hottentot woman's skirts and twisted them round with her arms and legs.

The little mother from the bed asked in a sleepy voice what was the matter.

"Don't ask me what is the matter!" cried old Ayah indignantly, in Cape Dutch. "Ask the Father of all Evil! This child is mad!"

She wrenched her skirts free from Rebekah's grasp and thrust her into the room. Rebekah stood on the ox skin in the center of the floor, vibrating from the soles of her feet to her head.

The candle was on a stand beside her mother's bed, and threw its light full on her as she lay with the baby's head on her arm and her hand with the white frill thrown across it. On the right side of the great four-poster bed they had pinned up a red cotton quilt, with great lions and palm trees printed on it, to keep off the draught from the open window; and the quilt reflected a soft red light over the mother and child. In the far right-hand corner of the room was Rebekah's own little cot, where she had slept ever since she was born.

"God only does know what possesses this child!" said old Ayah, fixing her twinkling black eyes on Rebekah and talking at her. "If she were my child, I wouldn't let her come into the house at all, where respectable people live who like to be indoors. I'd just tie her fast with a chain to a monkey post outside, and let her go round and round there. Then she could eat Kaffir beans like a baboon, and climb, and scream as much as she liked!"

"What did you make such a noise for, Rebekah?" the little mother said gently. "Did you think they were hurting the baby?"

Rebekah said nothing; the blood was leaving her head and running into her heart, and she felt faint.

"Twisting a person's clothes almost off their backs! Can't one even wash and dress a child without this little wild thing coming howling and dancing round one!" Old Ayah smoothed out her crumpled skirt.

"Do you want to see the baby, Rebekah?" asked her mother.

Rebekah walked unsteadily to the foot of the bed and stood beside the great wooden bedpost.

Old Ayah took up the baby's bath and walked out of

the room with it, muttering that some children ought to live with the baboons.

"If you would like to come and see the baby, you can climb up," said her mother drowsily, with half-closed eyes.

Rebekah waited a moment, then she clambered softly up on to the bed, and sat down at the foot, half kneeling, with her back against the post. Her mother, who was very tired, had reclosed her eyes. The baby's red face pressed against the mother's white breast. The light shone on them both.

Rebekah drew up her knees and clasped her arms round them, and sat watching.

"It's drinking, isn't it, eh, mother?" she said at last very softly.

"Yes," said her mother, without opening her eyes.

"It's *your* little baby? Eh, mother?" she whispered again softly, after a long pause.

Her mother nodded dreamily.

Rebekah stroked her little skirts down over her knees. "It *must* drink!" she said after a time. "It *must* have milk, eh, mother? It's your little baby, eh, mother?" she added after a long pause.

But the little mother made no answer; she had dropped away into sleep.

Rebekah sat watching them.

By and by the baby moved its hand which struck out from the white flannel wrapper about it; it opened its fingers slowly; it stretched them out one after the other and closed them up again into a fist. Rebekah watched it intently.

Presently she leaned forward, resting one elbow on the bed, and slowly stretched out her other hand, and with one forefinger touched the hand of the baby. Her mouth quivered; she sat up quickly and watched them again. She leaned her head back against the post at the foot of the bed and sat gazing at them, her eyes never moving.

At half-past nine old Ayah came in again, bringing in

a hot-water bottle and an etna to warm the gruel during the night.

"My fatherland's force!¹ You not in bed yet! Are you going to sit up till morning?"

The mother woke up. "Have you been sitting here all this while, Rebekah?" she asked gently.

Old Ayah put the warm water bottle at the mother's feet.

"She'd never go to bed if she could help it!" old Ayah muttered. "It's my belief, if you came in at three o'clock in the morning, you'd find her sitting up in her bed, talking to the spiders in the dark. She'd talk to the stars if she hadn't anything else to talk to, just not to go to sleep like other children!"

"Mother," said Rebekah in a very slow, clear voice, stroking down her knees—"mother, will you let me have *your* baby to sleep by me for a little while?"

She spoke each word slowly and distinctly, as one who repeats what he has carefully prepared.

"No, dear," said the mother; "it's too small; you can't have it to sleep with you yet."

"Have it to sleep with you!" said old Ayah. "I should think not! Why, you'd kill it!"

"I should take great care of it," said Rebekah, very slowly, still stroking her knees, her eyes very wide open and fixed steadily on her mother; "I wouldn't lie on it nor let it fall. I only want to take care of it and teach it."

"Teach it! Teach it, indeed!" said old Ayah, tucking in the mother's feet. "You just want to teach her to be a naughty tomboy like you. We'll take care she doesn't play with you and learn all your wild ways."

Rebekah stroked her knees more heavily. "I didn't

[¹ "My fatherland's force!"—So Olive wrote it. But the expression is Africaans ("Dutch") and should be *My Vaderland se vos* (pronounced almost "May vahderlahnd ser fos"), probably a corruption of an old Nederlands expression, meaning My fatherland's God.]

mean to teach her anything wrong," she said slowly; "I wasn't even going to teach her to hate *you*."

"Hate me! Rather! I should think not! What next? Why should you teach her to hate me?"

Rebekah turned her eyes on to old Ayah and gazed at her. "Because *I* hate you so!" she said.

"Don't quarrel with her any more, Ayah," said the mother; "the child really doesn't know what she is talking about; she's half asleep already. Come, get off the bed, Rebekah, and go and undress. You can't have the baby."

But Rebekah sat motionless. Slowly the tears gathered under her eyelids. She closed them, and the tears lay in large heavy drops under the lashes without falling.

She raised her face with its closed eyes to the canopy of the bed.

"Oh, I can't bear it! I can't bear it!" she said slowly. "What shall I do? What shall I do? Oh, what shall I do?" She moved her upturned face with its closed eyes slowly from side to side. "I meant to love it so! Oh, I meant— All my things—my Peter book—all my stones. Oh, if you will let me love it!" The bed shook, but no tears fell from the closed eyes. She stroked her knees with both hands. "It's not any use!—you see—it's not any use!—I have tried!—I have tried!—Oh, I wish I was dead—I wish I was dead—I wish I was dead!"

Even Old Ayah looked at her in silence.

"The child is really three parts asleep," said the mother.

"It's been a long trying day for her, running about with no one to look after her. She is but a baby, though she is so old-fashioned. Get off the bed, Rebekah, and old Ayah will undress you."

But Rebekah felt her way to the foot of the bed and slid down.

"I can undress myself," she heaved.

She stood on the floor in the middle of the room with her eyes still closed, the lids swollen and fastened together, and unbuttoned her things one by one, letting them drop on the floor, until she stood there in her little white shift,

her small naked shoulders still vibrating. Old Ayah
brought her her nightdress.

"Diss 'n snaaks se kind!" she muttered. ("'Tis a
strange child!")

Rekebah slipped it over her own head, and then, with
her hand stretched out, she felt her way to the bed in
the corner. She climbed up over the side of the cot and
lay down. The long vibrating movement still went on;
it was almost as if a man were crying.

"I can't have that," said the little mother. "She'll go
on with it half the night in her sleep. I know the child.
I think she dreams of things. Take the baby and lay it
by her just for a little while. It's been a long day and
she's very tired."

Old Ayah shook her head forebodingly; but she took up
the baby, wrapped it in its shawl, and carried it across the
room. She turned back the cover and made a place for it
beside Rebekah. The child stretched out her arm for its
head; the Hottentot woman laid it down on it and drew
the cover up over both. Then she turned and went out,
to fetch the gruel and the night light.

The elder sister slipped her hand under the shawl till
she found the baby's hand; she clasped her fingers softly
into its tiny fingers, and held them. With the other hand
she tried to draw its body up close against her.

Presently there was a queer quavering little sound, as
though some one were trying to sing; but nothing came of
it; then all was quiet.

When old Ayah came back in fifteen minutes everyone
in the room was quiet and asleep.

She put the gruel and night light down on the drawers,
and came to the bedside to remove the baby. But when
she turned down the cover she found the hands of the
sisters so interlocked, and the arm of the elder sister so
closely round the younger, that she could not remove it
without awakening both.

Old Ayah shook her head and drew the cover up softly.
She blew out the candle and put the night light down on

the floor beyond the bed, and walked softly towards the door of the room with her naked yellow feet, her figure casting a long dark shadow on the wall. When she got to the door as she passed out she turned and looked back. Along the floor the night light shone, casting deep shadows into far corners, especially that in which the two children lay!

But they were all sleeping well.

THE BOOK

THE WOMAN'S DAY

CHAPTER I

Showing What Baby-Bertie
Thought of Her New Tutor;
and How Rebekah Got Married

TUCKED away among the ribs of a mountain in the
Eastern Province of the Cape of Good Hope is a
quiet, tree-covered farm. The owner of this farm twenty-five years ago was an Englishman, a gentleman in the
rough and unveneered fashion; a man fond of his books,
of his trees, of his land; little given to speaking, much
given to thinking, and seldom going farther than his own
beacons. In truth, there was little to tempt anyone
farther; the neighbors were unlettered, velskoen-wearing
Dutchmen, or equally unlettered English settlers, and
they did not often trouble their neighbors with a visit—
a fact which no one regretted except the little mother,
who was of a lively and sociable turn and who rejoiced
greatly over even the arrival of an old Boer *tante*. It
was a quiet, monotonous life; the farmer himself, the
little mother, their children, with a score of Hottentot
and Kaffir servants, completed the catalogue of the farm's
inhabitants; the human inhabitants, for of wild animal
life there was no want. In the bush that covered the
mountain sides were leopards, who came down at night
and carried off lambs from the kraals; in the tall trees
in the bush were little gray, long-tailed monkeys, and
wood-doves, and cock-o-veets, who cried and called all
day; in the rocks that crowned the mountain troops of
baboons climbed and fought; and down in the valley

among the thorn trees [1] were mier-kats and great tortoises, and hares who paid visits to the lands. Almost all day from the open windows of the house you might see at intervals the sheep among the long grass on the mountain side or down in the flat; or catch sight of, far off, moving specks, which were the goats moving in and out among the thorn trees. All day long the great glass doors and windows stood open; through them came the scent of orange blossoms from the orangery before the door, and from the garden beyond where the hollyhocks and dahlias and marigolds and four-o'clocks made a bed of color. In springtime there was the sweet scent of the blossoms from the long orchard beyond the flower garden; and in the summer, at Christmas time, the flat was a sea of gold with the yellow flowers of the thorn trees, and the honey scent came up to the house; and in autumn there was a faint, acid smell from the falling figs and peaches which lay on the ground in the brown trampled grass, and which the little Kaffirs and pigs came over the gaps in the wall to revel among.

Over the nek came the road from the town. It wound in and out, in and out, a line of white among the thorn trees. It disappeared altogether on the flat, till it came out near the mielie lands, and by the great dam with the willow trees. In that dam on hot summer nights the frogs loved to croak. Baby-Bertie, the farmer's younger daughter, said she loved to hear them as she lay in her bed at night; but Rebekah, her elder sister, said it was a sad sound and made one think of when one was a child, long ago. But Bertie, Baby-Bertie, as they called her, was only fifteen and two months, and she had not a very long, long ago to think of. Rebekah, her sister, was twenty, and had once been on a visit to Cape Town, and knew a great deal, and had read a great deal, and that

---

[1] The mimosa, generally called thorn tree in South Africa; a tree with a delicate acacia leaf and long white thorns from an inch to three inches in length, and with a sweet-scented yellow honey blossom.

might make it seem a long time since she was a child; but to Bertie it was only yesterday, though she could already touch the oranges no other woman on the farm could reach, and her chin was higher than her father's shoulder. So, to her, the croaking of the frogs at night was as pleasant as the lowing of the cows when they came down the mountain side in the evening.

On one afternoon Baby-Bertie stood at the window of the spare room, putting dahlias and lilies into a slender green glass; Rebekah, her sister, knelt in the room behind her, pinning a white valance round the bed. Outside, all the flat was full of yellow blossoms, for the thorn trees were in flower. Once or twice Bertie put her head far out of the window, and looked across the flat, and drew it back again.

She was a velvety creature, with long eyelashes turned back till they almost touched her straight eyebrows. Her forehead was low and very broad, the hair hanging over it in brown curls, up each one of which you might have slipped a finger, but what one looked at most were the large round brown eyes and the velvety cheeks. Rebekah, her sister, was a small woman, with dark, fine hair, wavy, and parted down the middle; she had a very white face, except when she flushed, and then it seemed as if the blood might burn through the skin. You could always see the veins in her temples. When she was a child she used to run behind the bed and kneel down and repeat Bonar's hymn:

> "Calm me, my God, and keep me calm!
> Let Thine outstretched wind
> Be as the shade of Elim's palm——"

because her heart beat so fast sometimes she thought it was going to burst. Now she seldom needed to pray that; she was always busy with her books and her microscope and collections of insects, and stones, when she was not busy working in the kitchen or milk room, or helping her father with his farming.

And now she was to be married the next day to her cousin Frank, who had come from Cape Town to fetch her. He was tall and large, and fair, and full, with blue eyes and a light mustache; he smoked cigars and wore very spotless shirts and collars, whether they were white or striped and colored.

He had always wanted to have her for his wife since a boy of eleven he came with his parents from England to visit their relations in South Africa. He had gone back to England, but ten years later he had come out again and settled in Cape Town to manage a branch of his father's business, and he had visited the farm once a year for four years, and had always asked Rebekah to marry him when he came, but she always said she could not. Now everyone was surprised: she had suddenly written to him that she would; and she was to be married the next day and the wedding breakfast was already laid out in the back dining room, with a white cloth pinned over it to keep the dust off. She was to be married in a lilac silk in the large front room; and her father and mother and Bertie and the servants would be there, and Queen Victoria and the Prince Consort would look down from the picture frames upon the wall.

Rebekah had wished there should be no feast and to be married in her little blue gardening dress, but her mother and Bertie said a wedding was no wedding without these things; and even the bridegroom laughed at the idea.

The magistrate was coming from the town to marry them, because Rebekah wanted no Church service. Frank was willing; he said it did not matter in the country, where no one knew what you did, though he would have liked it done in the town where everyone would have noticed it.

He was the only man who had ever asked Rebekah to marry him, except his brother, John-Ferdinand, whom she had met when she went to Cape Town two years before, and who had asked her, but she had refused him.

Except for that visit to Cape Town and a visit to the seaside once with her mother when she was a child, she had never left the farm, except to drive into the next up-country village for the day's shopping. There the shop-clerks and young business men seemed people so far out of her world that she hardly knew who they were. Once the young bank clerk invited himself out to the farm and spent a day and night there, but she only spoke to him when she poured out the tea to know if he would have more, and spent the afternoon by herself in the kloof. His account of his visit did not encourage other young men to come; and only the little mother suspected what he had been there for. Rebekah had never been to a ball or a theater or paid a formal call, and her world was a very little world except in the direction of books.

Now she and Bertie were getting the spare room ready, because Bertie's tutor was coming, who was to teach her when Rebekah was gone. Bertie herself had no greater appetite for books and learning than her hand-lamb for carrots, which it ate, as it were under compulsion, if you offered them to him, for fear of paining you, but under no other conditions whatever. But Rebekah and her father both said she ought to learn more.

This tutor was a delicate young man from England, who had advertised for a situation on a farm where he might, in return for teaching three hours a day, receive his board.

No one had seen him, but he had good credentials, and Rebekah said men were generally better teachers than women; and everyone followed Rebekah's advice on the farm.

Bertie put her head out of the window again; but there was nothing to be seen except the flat, shimmering in the afternoon sunshine, and the white road over the nek.

"Perhaps Jan has got drunk and turned the cart over; or perhaps it has broken down," she said, straining her head farther.

"It is not four yet," her sister said.

Bertie drew her head in and took the glass with the dahlias and white lilies to the mantelpiece. She stood looking at them.

"Do you think he will like them, Rebekah?"

At this moment three little Kaffirs whom Bertie had set to watch on the top step of the loft ladder set up a series of frantic yells. Bertie put down the loose flowers she had just begun to collect and rushed from the room. Rebekah pinned on. She never seemed very much excited now, even when she found a new germ under her microscope, or when one of her grafts budded, or a new book came from town; and those were the things she seemed to care for most. Soon after Bertie put her face in at the door again.

"Rebekah, do come and see him! He's just come! He is so lovely and small! He's hardly a bit bigger than you! I thought I should be afraid of him, but I'm not a bit! He's smaller than I am. He keeps on smiling. He's got coal-black hair. He's got a little curl just like a drake's tail right above his ear! Do come and see him!"

Rebekah was pinning the last fold.

"Oh, come, Rebekah! He's shaking hands with father and mother and coming up the steps already!" She rushed out again.

Rebekah rose from her knees slowly, and then stooped to gather the flowers Bertie had thrown away in her haste; she looked round once to see that the room was all in readiness. Then she went into the front room. A little man was sitting at the end of the sofa, who certainly looked not more than twenty-five years old, though he had given his age as thirty-five in his credentials. He was sitting with his hands between his knees; but he smiled, and rose as she came in, with his face slightly turned down. His forehead was rounded and protruding, and had a gleam upon it as though oiled; his nose was small, and was rounded except at the point, where it seemed to have been sliced off, leaving a small square tip. Rebekah shook hands with him; but his restless, beadlike small eyes looked away at the piano. When she had gone out, he sat down again and talked to the little mother, who sat at her work table, while Bertie, too excited, or not venturing to come in, peeped through the dining-room door as she passed.

That afternoon they had their tea at four o'clock in the little front workroom, because the wedding breakfast was laid out in the dining room. The room opened with a large window on to the front stoep. All the family collected there except Frank, Rebekah's cousin, who lay out under the orange trees before the door on his back on a reed mat, smoking, and whose tea had been carried out to him by Bertie. He looked very cool in a spotless gray suit, with a white shirt and no waistcoat. He was reading a yellow-backed book, and his pointer, whom he had brought with him in case there was any shooting, lay near his feet, with her head upon her paws.

Presently he lifted his hand as he read and drew her nearer by the ears; she winced a little, but crept up and put her nose against his arm. By and by, when he had emptied his cup, he raised his large not ungraceful body and sauntered to the house with the cup.

In the small sitting room the others had finished their tea and had all left, except Rebekah, who sat dreamily in her place near the window, cutting stars out of the orange peel on her plate. She had been up since five that morning, busy with housework and preparations for the next day, and was tired.

Presently there came the scent of a whiff from a cigar through the open window, and then her cousin Frank put his handsome face and shoulders in.

"All alone?" he said.

He stretched out his hand and set the empty cup down on the table. "Come out and sit under the orange trees? It's splendidly cool there."

"I can't; I've so many little things to do yet if we are to start to-morrow at eleven."

He folded his arms on the window ledge and drew softly from his cigar.

"How nice you look in that dress," he said slowly. She was dressed in white muslin, with a little blue sleeveless jacket cut away from the waist. "I like that jacket; it shows your little waist—What a little ting-ting-kie [1] it is!" He put out his large, soft, well-shaped hand, and let it rest gently on her waist for a moment. Then he drew it back and refolded him arms on the window, and smoked. He blew a long whiff of smoke softly at her; he knew she liked it.

She began collecting the empty teacups on to the tray. There was a quiet contentment in his eye as he watched her.

"What do you think of the new arrival?" he said, taking his cigar from his mouth and holding it between his two first fingers.

"I dislike him."

Frank laughed. "He's not attractive. I'm sure he uses cocoanut oil for his hair. One can forgive a man a great many sins but, not that." He put his cigar between his lips again and drew a long whiff. "Don't you think it's a little dangerous, too?"

"What?" Rebekah looked up at him quickly.

"Oh, settling him and Bertie down every day for three hours with nothing but the table to divide them and French verbs to unite them! It's a dangerous thing for any young man, or old either, to have a head of curls like Bertie's dancing within three feet of him!"

"I think——" she said.

He blew a whiff of smoke softly towards her across the table, which did not reach her, and laughed. "Oh, I know just what you are going to say—men should teach women and women should teach men. What difference does it make? But it's not the Garden of Eden yet!

[1] The ting-ting-kie is a slight, very lively bird, not much larger than a humming-bird, often seen moving quickly about among the grass and low bushes in South Africa. [The Cape wren-warbler.]

Bertie'll be the finest-looking woman in Africa in a few years. Have you noticed how she's developed since I was here six months ago?"

Before Rebekah could answer, Bertie thrust her head in at the door to say old Ayah wanted her to come and see if the cakes were done, and dashed away again; and Rebekah took up the tray to carry it out with her.

"Then you won't come out under the trees with me? I must go and be lazy alone! What a busy little ting-ting-kie! Well, to-morrow!——" He kissed the fingers of his left hand towards her and turned away from the window, his dog following close at his heels. As he walked along the stoep he hummed in a soft sweet tenor:

> "Ten little nigger boys fuddling over wine,
> One got so jolly drunk, then there were nine!"

He went back and lay down on his mat under the orange trees, and Rebekah went to see if the cakes were burning.

At nine o'clock that evening Rebekah sat out on the stoep. It was a dark night; the beetles buzzed about, among the vine leaves on the wall about her head. She was sitting on the step opposite the front door with her back turned to it; a square of light fell from the open door across the stoep beside her and dimly lighted up the stems of the orange trees beyond. She rested her elbows on her knees and sat looking out into the dark. After a while she glanced through the open door. In the room behind her she could see the little mother sitting in the rocking chair in the far corner beside the work table, rocking herself and smiling and nodding her head, keeping time at the wrong places, and Percy Lawry, the new tutor, sitting at the piano, playing; and Bertie standing with her elbow on the top of the piano, with her eyes fixed on his face, so that, at a movement of his head, she might turn the page for him. She could see her lover lying on the sofa with his large arm thrown across his fore-head, listening to the music, which was good; and in the room beyond she could catch sight of her father sitting at the bare table reading, with his grizzled beard pressed against his breast. She looked in for a moment, and then she looked away again.

What was she leaving it for, that quiet, peaceful life? She folded her arms on her knees. What was she leaving it for? The light that streamed out from the door lay in a square about her, and the little night flies gathered thicker above her head. To-night, almost too late, she took up the old balances and began to weigh again, as she had done before. What was she leaving it for, that quiet, peaceful life?—that life in which the right was pleasantest and easiest to do, and lay right ahead; in which there was no being torn asunder living between "I would" and "I must"; a life in which there was just as much to be done for others as might yield a grateful sense of satisfaction, yet leaving space for the individual life undisturbed; a placid, peaceful life, into which the noisy, babbling, worried, worrying world crept only once a week through the post-bag of the boy who brought the letters and newspapers from the town; a life in which news from the outer world came to one with a freshness it could never bear for those living in the hurry and turmoil of the great streams of life; a studious life, in which one might grow wise exceedingly over plants, and suck whatever joy there was in insects and stones; a thoughtful life, in which one might read and creep into the hearts of books, as they can only be crept into when the wheels of the daily life are grinding soft and low; a life in which suffering was small, and pleasure, if gray-tinted, calm and constant. What was she leaving it for? She looked back again into the room, and then out into the dark. The scale looked heavy.

On the other hand, there was—well—a vague, insatiable hunger? Books, black beetles, well-performed duties—she had tried them all, and she was dying of hunger. Was it for that, that of which the far-off blue and purple mountains whisper when they say: "Come! Come! Come! We have that to give you know not of! Come!

Come! Come to us!"? Or was it a voice from that primal depth of nature which, before man was man, called beast to beast and kind to kind? Which, through all the ages, has summoned the human woman, in spite of the great Chaldean curse, "I will greatly multiply thy sorrow and thy conception," along one path? An ox at the roadside, when it is dying of hunger and thirst, does not lie down; it walks up and down—up and down, seeking it knows not what;—but it does not lie down.

She looked back into the sitting room, where her cousin Frank still lay, with his large rounded arm in its gray coat sleepily thrown across his forehead, his full, well-shaped lips almost smiling.

For four years, when he had placed the question before her, she had always decided she could not go with him. Why was it that, six months before, his face had become always present to her; and at night even she saw his hands, and heard his soft, sweet voice? She looked out again into the dark; and she knew as she sat there in the dark with her elbows on her knees, that, if she had been wholly free that night, and had to decide over again, she would yet have decided exactly as she had done.

She folded her arms closer on her knees and looked out at the dark stems of the orange trees, while the little night beetles fluttered thicker and almost rested on her dark head.

After a while the others went to the back dining room to drink coffee, and took the lamps with them; Rebekah still sat on alone in the dark, only a faint streak of light coming from the door of the dining room beyond the passage.

Then Bertie came out with a cup for her, feeling her way along the uneven stoep with her feet.

"I can hardly see you, the light has dazzled my eyes so." She sat down beside her sister on the step, close to her, holding the coffee cup for her.

"I hope the little Kaffirs will come and call me very

early in the morning, before it's light. Will you wake me if they don't? I want to go up in the bush and fetch more creepers and berries." She slid her hand through her sister's arm and let it rest in her lap; she still held the saucer of the cup. "If I tell you something, you mustn't tell anyone, Rebekah! But we've made an arch up in the bush, and just before you are married we are going to bring it down, the little niggers and I, and fasten it over the front door; and you and Frank will have to go out under it! Don't tell anyone: it'll be such a surprise! And we're going to fasten a paper bag of rice in the top, and just as you go out one of the little niggers is going to poke it with a long stick, and all the rice'll come down on you. All Frank's collar and shirt will be full, and your dress, but you won't mind, eh?"

She took the empty coffee cup from Rebekah and put it down, and then slipped her hand into hers, so that their palms lay against each other.

"Do you know that something happened this evening, Rebekah?" She bent her head closer. "Frank gave me your wedding ring to try on. I went into the kitchen to show old Ayah, and when I was taking it off it fell under the woodpile, and we had such a trouble to find it. We had to pack all the wood out. Old Ayah was angry with me; she said it was unlucky to try on other people's wedding rings. She said if you did you never married and that the most dreadful thing in the world happened to you. She wouldn't tell me what. It's only a 'geloofie,' [1] isn't it, eh, Rebekah? Rebekah, what *is* the most dreadful thing that *could* happen to anyone?"

"It would depend on who the person was," Rebekah said, still dreaming her own thoughts; but she drew her sister's head closer into hers.

"It must be so nice to get married." Bertie said. "But when I get married I shan't go so far from the farm. I should like to be married to some one with a farm near here, and then you could come and visit me every

[1] Superstition.

year and I could come and visit you. It must be so nice
to be married. But I should like to have a pure-white
dress to be married in, not a mauve one like yours."
Bertie laid her head on her sister's shoulder. "I suppose
I shall be married some day; only I don't know whom
I shall find to marry here. Perhaps some one will come
like Frank did—from far away. Rebekah, can I come
and visit you some day soon?"

"Yes, dear, as soon as you've learned a little more
you shall come to me for a long time—a year or six
months if you like." Bertie sat silent, with her cheek
resting softly on her sister's shoulder, the crown of her
head pressed against her sister's cheek.

Sometimes I think, if one should live to be ninety, and
all the sights and sounds of the world about become dim
to one, that then, as one sits alone in the firelight dreaming, or out in the sunshine, the child sister who was young
with us will come back and sit with us there. No one will
see her; and we two shall sit there alone, she with her
long, flowing hair; and we shall look out at life together
with our young eager eyes that have known no mighty
sorrow. I think it is, perhaps, that she may sit there
with us, that we treasure her memory so all life through.
We two shall be always young when we are together.

After Bertie had gone back into the house through the
dark front room, Rebekah's lover came through it, feeling
his way; he came out on to the stoep.

"Where is my little Goody-two-shoes? All alone in
the dark, as usual?" He felt for her with his hands, and
raised her up. "What an unsociable little mortal it is!
Come and walk with me."

He put her hand through his arm and drew the little
blue shawl she had across her arm about her. He lit
his cigar, and they paced up and down on the long stoep.
Her head hardly reached his shoulder. "Chilly to-night,"
he said.

By and by the little mother came into the front room and, when she had bid them both good night, left the lamp on the table; and they paced on together.

"I must go to bed now," Rebekah said, after a few minutes. "I have to be up so early to-morrow."

"Don't make yourself too tired. We have a long day's journey before us."

He drew her close up to him and before him. They were standing in front of the door where the lamplight fell full on them. He raised her hands in his and put them alternately softly to his lips. He put down his head and whispered something very softly. Her cheeks turned the color of the pale carnation she had fastened to his buttonhole before supper.

"Good night, my little one! My queen! My love."

Suddenly, with a little curious caressing movement, she raised herself and put her face against the side of his as he bent.

"What is it? Do you want to say something?"

She said nothing; but he thought he felt the soft touch of her lips against his neck; then she glided quickly from him.

He stretched out his arms towards her, for her to come back to him; but she shook her head softly and called out, "Good night," and the little figure in blue and white fluttered away through the front room.

He turned round slowly to pace up and down to finish his cigar before he took up the lamp and retired.

When Rebekah left him she went out into the long passage. She called out a second "Good night" at the door of her mother's room as she passed, and both her parents answered it; then she went to her own room at the end of the passage.

She lit a candle and set it on the table, and then sat down on the side of her small bed. The window was standing open and the pitch darkness seemed to come in through it from outside; it looked out towards the kloof on the mountain, and the bush came down close to it.

That little room had been hers for fifteen years, ever since she had given up to the new baby the cot in her mother's room.

It was bare and dismantled now. In one corner were two boxes, packed and corded, which contained her luggage ready for to-morrow's journey. Above the little table were marks on the wall where a book-shelf had been taken down. When her father first put it up for her, it was one little shelf containing a few children's books; but it had slowly mounted upward till there were shelves holding fifty or sixty volumes. A tall rough glass cabinet that had stood in the corner, in which she had kept her fossils and insects and her microscope, was packed up, too; and above her bed, at the head, was a square mark on the wall and the holes of four tacks. When she was a child of six she had found in an old copy of the *Illustrated London News* a rough print of Raphael's Madonna della Sedia, and she had cut it out and fastened it there. No one told her it was a great picture, but when she looked at the little John, and the baby with its hand inside its mother's breast glancing round, and the mother with her striped shawl looking down at it, a thrill of quiet joy ran through her, that no other picture made her feel. She called it "*My* picture." Now it was taken down and folded away with her other things to go to her new home.

She sat on the side of her bed and looked out of the window. A curious weight and heaviness seemed suddenly to rest on her. The wick of candle which stood on the table began to burn long and red and bend over a little as the soft night breezes blew it. She snuffed it and then took up the light, and walked to the door at the end of her room which led to Bertie's.

Baby-Bertie lay on her bed with her arms thrown back on the pillow above her head. The sleeve of her nightdress had fallen back and showed her round arm, so small at the wrist, so large above the elbow; and one button at the neck had become unfastened and showed her small white throat; her face was flushed, though the window stood wide open and night air came in over the bed. The pillow was covered with a tangle of her brown curls.

Almost every night when, as a very small child, she had been moved into that room, Rebekah had lain by her to sing her to sleep; and when she grew older Rebekah had still crept in to lie beside her to talk and caress her before she slept. To-night Rebekah put the light down on the floor and knelt beside the bed. She put her head down upon Bertie's breast, under Bertie's arm, and pressed it there. It was as though, to-night, it was she who wanted to be caressed. But Bertie slept on—a deep, calm sleep. Presently Rebekah rose and partly closed the window, that the air might not blow so fully upon her. On a chair near the bed Bertie had laid out the lilac silk wedding dress Rebekah was to wear the next day, and the white tulle veil lay over it; the orange blossoms Bertie would gather early in the morning. Beside it, on another chair hung the muslin gown Bertie herself was to wear.

Rebekah did not glance at them; she took up the light and went back to her room. Through the open window you could hear the baboons shouting and calling to one another high up on the mountain side.

She undressed slowly. When she stood ready at the bedside in her nightdress she took from under the pillow an envelope, and sat down again on the side of her bed and opened it. It was brown and worn, but you could still see the address. It held the first letter her cousin Frank had written to her, after his visit six months before, when she had written to him, telling him she had changed her mind and would marry him. She read it again: "My one love! My own love! My only love!"

She had slept with it under her pillow ever since. In the envelope were parts of other letters. She took them out and looked at them. She did not need to read them; she knew them by heart. She kissed them one by one and then put them back in the envelope and the envelope under her pillow. When she had got into bed she put out the light, but two hours later she still lay awake. She could hear the baboons outside in the dark, shouting and fighting among the rocks on the mountain side.

The next day Rebekah got married.

CHAPTER II

A Wild-Flower Garden in the Bush

FOR a while after Rebekah went things seemed askew and out of tune at the old farm; but they soon made grooves for themselves and ran on smoothly enough.

In the bush the wood doves cooed to one another, and the cock-o-veets called; the little gray, long-tailed monkeys climbed the trees and slid down by the monkey-ropes: the hares and porcupines visited the lands at night by the great dam; and the leopard sometimes came down on very dark nights to prowl about the kraals; and snakes made their nests and reared their young in the garden and under the dam walls. The great flat stone still lay baking in the sun on hot days; and the trapdoor spiders made lids to their nests and lined them with white silk and opened and shut them, though no little child with passionately interested eyes sat patiently waiting to see them open or shut; and at evening, the avondbloem [1] in the grass on the mountain opened their drab-tinted flowers and sent their rich sweet scent far and wide; though the small personage that had moved among them for twenty years, as a child and woman, was gone.

If the father missed his wise little daughter when he went down to the lands to see how a new variety of wheat was doing, and had no one to advise with over his grafts and flutes, or to discuss with him new remedies for cattle disease, he said nothing, but buried himself deeper than ever in the pages of his Swedenborg. And the little mother, if she missed her eldest daughter on baking days,

[1 Aandblom: evening flower (a species of hesperantha).]

and in the vegetable garden, and every day when rations were given out, yet found great consolation from the fact that she had now a new subject to lament over.

Old Ayah said that everything had gone wrong since Miss Rebekah went, and that there was no one to keep order, or who knew how things ought to be done; but she cooked the food and scolded the little Kaffirs, just as of old, and shook her head continually over the tergiversations of mankind in general.

Baby-Bertie missed her. She cried herself to sleep for several nights after she went; but even for her time brought compensations. After a while there were long weekly letters from Rebekah and great excitement when the boy came with the post-bag over the nek. She told about her little house, and its furniture, and the garden; and now and then there were little parcels with bits of muslin or silk to be made up into kappies or aprons for Bertie or the little mother, and odds and ends for old Ayah and the servant: and all these brought a new element of excitement into life, and were something to look forward to.

And there was the new tutor. Everyone liked him at the farm, except perhaps the father; and he only showed dislike, if he felt it, by speaking even less than usual if he was by.

The little mother liked him. He would sit listening to her for hours while she lamented over the hardships of her life and described her home in England, which she had left as a girl twenty-five years before. It had been a simple country parsonage, but, seen through the refracting mist of twenty-five years of African life, it had slowly assumed always increasing proportions in luxury and beauty. The schoolmaster could paint beautiful illumined mottoes, with borders copied from the flowers which Bertie brought him. He painted one to hang in the mother's bedroom, for her birthday, with a border of roses and lilies, and on it the motto, "Blessed are the pure in heart."

Bertie liked him. He did not trouble himself as to whether she remembered what he taught her; and he could play beautiful dreamy music, especially on Sunday afternoons, when Bertie, whom nothing else could keep long quiet, would crouch in the corner with her cat in her lap and cry softly, she did not know why.

When her three hours of school was over, he often helped her to work in the flower garden, which she had taken care of since Rebekah left, because Rebekah liked it so. Up in the bush he helped her to make a little garden for wild flowers, which he said would do better up there in their natural soil than down in the old soil of the farmhouse garden. She and he went often to see how the things were growing; and that was something new to Bertie, who had not been fond of the bush as Rebekah was, and had hardly ever gone there.

Then the autumn came. The gentians and everlasting-flowers had died in the grass on the mountain side; and the thorn trees in the flat were covered with long seed pods, and their thorns became a more shiny white. Nothing important had happened at the farm since Rebekah left, except that one old batch of Kaffir servants had left and another had come; and the turkeys and goslings and chickens had bred out well and the yard was full; and the little mother had made two fine boilings of soap.

Then the winter passed and the spring came. It was ten months since Rebekah had gone. And then came the news she had a baby. The little mother cried. Old Ayah cried also, and said she felt sure the Cape Town servants would mismanage all the house while Rebekah was ill. And the father said, "Rebekah? Rebekah? Can it be?" and walked out to the far lands. And Baby-Bertie first laughed and then cried, and then ran away to tell her tutor the news—and then things settled down again.

One afternoon, when everyone had risen from the afternoon nap, the little mother sat sewing at her work table in the corner of the front room. The door on to the stoep was open, and through it she could see Percy Lawrie, the tutor, sitting on a chair on the stoep, reading. By and by Bertie came round to the front of the house from the yard and sat down on the edge of the stoep, just before him.

She threw off her kappie and fanned herself with it; and then looked up towards the chair where her tutor sat.

"You aren't angry with me, are you, Mr. Lawrie?" The tutor glanced down from his book at her, and then with one restless little black eye glanced in the direction of the open door where from his position he could see the mother sitting.

"No, Miss Bertie; oh no, of course not."

"Because you said——"

He made a quick movement as if to drive away one of the bees that was coming towards him: "Miss Bertie, there it is close to your forehead!"

She shook her head. "I don't mind." Then stretching out one hand towards him with a deprecatory little gesture: "I couldn't bear you to be angry with me! I don't like anyone to be angry with me—not even the servants! You *do* love me, don't you?"

She looked up at him with the expression a puppy dog might have when looking up into the face of a master he half fears he may have offended.

"Certainly I am not angry with you, Miss Bertie. I have no reason to be. You do your lessons very well."

"Baby-Bertie!" called the little mother from the sitting room, "go to the yard and see if the hen is letting the goslings she brought out get to the little dam. Don't let her drive them back to the fowl house. Make haste."

Bertie rose slowly and went round the house again to the yard.

A little later the mother went to the kitchen door herself and found Bertie sitting on the lowest step with her white apron full of goslings which she had been feeding, and which she was going to carry down to the dam, as the hen refused to lead them. The black hen moved round her feet restlessly, anxious as to what was to become of her brood.

The mother stood on the top step.

"Baby-Bertie," she said a little uncertainly, "I want to speak to you."

Bertie lifted her head and half turned it to her.

The little mother hesitated.

"Just now, when you were round on the front stoep, I was sitting in the front room and heard you speaking to your tutor. I didn't quite like the way in which you spoke to him, dear."

Bertie turned her head more fully and looked up into her mother's face. "Well, I didn't mean to be rude to him," she said; "but after dinner, when you all went to lie down, he asked me to go up with him to see our plants in the kloof, and I didn't want to go because I wanted to sleep. He seemed cross about it, but I didn't mean to be rude to him."

"Oh, you weren't rude to him, dear," said the little mother nervously; "it's not that." The brown eyes that looked up into hers abashed her. "You were quite polite to him; but you know, Bertie, girls and women don't ask grown-up men if they love them. You are not a real baby, Bertie, although we call you so. But it's all right, my dear," she added quickly, seeing the surprise on Bertie's face, "only don't ask any man that again, dear. Take the goslings down to the dam."

The little mother turned and hurried quickly into the house; Bertie rose slowly with the goslings in her apron and walked away towards the small dam beyond the wagon house, with the black hen anxiously following her.

It was about ten days after that the little mother fell ill. She had one of her bad sick headaches which sometimes kept her in bed for several days. All the house was kept perfectly still for her, and even the cocks were driven away from the back door because their crowing disturbed her. Bertie gave up all her lessons and waited on her, bringing in little basins of soup or of gruel she had made, and driving away the little Kaffirs if they came to play too near the farmhouse, and keeping everything in order like an old, experienced housewife. Even old Ayah allowed she was turning into a wonderful housewife since Rebekah left, though she would never allow she was as good. The little mother almost liked to lie in bed and see her trip softly in and out of her room, with her gruel and soup and fresh flowers, in her white muslin dress.

On the morning of the fourth day the little mother was better and fell early into a heavy sleep. About half past eleven o'clock she woke, and lay expecting Bertie to come in: but all the house was still; Bertie had put no new flowers in the vase beside her, nor brought in her lemon and water. For more than half an hour the little mother lay there waiting and wondering. Then the quiet grew oppressive; she rose and partly dressed herself, and went out into the passage. There was not a soul stirring in the house nor a sound to be heard but the far-off voices of the men as they called to their oxen plowing in the mielie lands. She went to the kitchen and found old Ayah standing before the fire shredding "snysels" [1] into the soup-pot; she said she had not seen Bertie since just after breakfast; the father was gone to the far mielie lands and the Kaffir maids to wash the churns at the fountain. The little mother went back to her own room, but, feeling restless, she went out again to the room that used to be Rebekah's and was now Bertie's, and opened the door. Bertie was sitting there with her arms folded on the low dressing table before the window and her head resting on them. The little mother stepped gently up to her, thinking she was asleep. She laid her hand softly on her shoulder. Bertie raised her head slowly and looked into her mother's face. "Are you ill, my baby?" she asked, bending down. Bertie said nothing. There was in the large eyes the look that an animal has when it is in pain; the mute fear of a creature that cannot understand its own hurt.

[1 Snysels: dough cuttings, for soup.]

She dropped her head upon her arm again.

The little mother saw nothing in it but the look of one who has a violent sick headache.

"You are ill, my baby, you are very ill! Lie down on the bed and let me cover your feet with the rug." She took Bertie's arm and walked beside her to the bedside. Bertie moved heavily. "You have done too much these last few days—you have taken too much care of me. Do not let your feet hang down so, dear. So—that is better! You take after me with these terrible headaches. I always had them when I was young."

The little mother drew down the window blind. "Lie still; I'll go and tell old Ayah to bring you hot water for your feet. We'll get Mr. Percy Lawrie to ride over to Mrs. de Wet's and bring some blue-gum leaves; they are wonderful things for these sick headaches."

She trotted out of the room, forgetting wholly in her anxiety that she herself had been ill. At the kitchen door she met old Ayah, and told her what ailed Bertie, and discussed the blue-gum leaves. Old Ayah said they would have to send one of the Kaffir boys on foot for them, as, about half past ten that morning, Mr. Percy Lawrie had come down from the bush and had said he must ride into the town for the post at once, himself, and had gone on the only horse in the stable.

When the Kaffir boy had been found and sent off, old Ayah made up the fire to get some warm water, and the little mother went back to Bertie with a glass of lemon; but she was lying with her face close to the wall, as though she were asleep, and did not stir when spoken to; and the little mother stepped softly out again.

That evening at eight o'clock the horse came back from the town; but there was a strange boy riding it whom Mr. Lawrie had hired in the town. And there was a letter from him among the other post, in which he said that when he got to town he found a letter from his English relations awaiting him, which told him that his mother was dangerously ill and very anxious to see him before she died; it was therefore necessary for him to take the first post-cart and go on to the Bay [1] at once, if he wished to catch the next mail steamer for England; so he regretted he could not return to the farm to say good-by. They need not concern themselves about any clothes, music, or books that he had left, but might give them away; neither need they trouble about his last half-quarter's salary, as he was leaving without notice. He thanked them for all their kindness. He did not send any special message to Bertie, but wished to be kindly remembered to all.

As soon as she had read the letter, the little mother hurried away to Bertie's room to tell her the news. She had refused to take any supper; but she had undressed herself and was still lying on the bed with her face to the wall. The little mother sat in the rocking chair by the bedside and rocked herself, and cried intermittently. She said it was always so, troubles never come singly; first she had been ill, then Bertie, and now the dear, good schoolmaster had gone away in such trouble! But Bertie said nothing. The little mother asked her if she had pain; she said, no, only her head ached, and turned her face deeper into the pillow.

In the middle of the night the mother got up and came and stood at the door of Bertie's room, then opened it and went in softly. She thought she had heard some one crying bitterly; but when she got to the bedside Bertie was lying motionless and seemed to be asleep, with her face turned towards the dark, and the little mother went away, thinking it must have been the owl hooting, who came every night to see if any stray chickens were left out.

But the next morning very early, before anyone was up, Bertie got up and dressed herself, and went for a walk up into the kloof. When she came back she went straight to her own room and lay down, and took nothing all day but a little tea.

In the evening a little Kaffir herd, who had been up in the bush to look for some goats, came back with the news

[1] The Bay: Port Elizabeth.

that Bertie's little wild-flower garden was destroyed; that all the plants had been pulled up by the roots and the ground trampled flat; but when the little mother went to tell Bertie about it she took no notice, and lay with her eyes half shut.

The next day she got up at the usual time and said she was well, that her head did not ache; but she ate hardly anything, and was white-faced, with rings under her eyes; and old Ayah and the little mother agreed that she had been very seriously unwell.

As the days passed she went as usual about what household duties she had, but remained white and silent, seldom speaking to anyone and taking no interest in anything. As soon as her work was ended she went back to her own room, and closed the door and lay on the bed. The little mother thought she had been studying too hard; but old Ayah said it was a sickness which young girls often suffered from when they were about sixteen, and advised saffron root boiled in milk. Once or twice again at night the little mother thought she heard the sound of low crying, but when she went to Bertie's room all was silent, and she felt sure it must be owls on the roof.

Twice Bertie began a letter to Rebekah; but both times she tore the letter up, and it was never sent.

Of the little schoolmaster Bertie never spoke, though the little mother was always talking of him, speculating as to why he did not write again before he left Port Elizabeth, or as to whether his mother would be alive when he got to England. All the bits of music which he had left behind, with his name written on them, disappeared, one by one; and from the walls the mottoes he had painted with frames of everlasting flowers about them, which he had helped Bertie to make, vanished. Only in the little mother's bedroom her motto with the painted border of lilies and roses still hung; otherwise there was nothing to recall him in the house.

One Sunday afternoon, two months after he went away, it had been a strangely sultry day, and since dinner Bertie had been lying down in her own room. About half past four the storm burst; the lightning flashed incessantly, the thunder crashing close over the roof, while the rain fell in torrents till you could not see the wagon house; the tiny stream that came down from the kloof was a roaring, foaming river, and all the little footpaths were rushing streams.

Just before sunset, when it was all over, Bertie came out of her room and went to the back of the house which faced the sunset, and sat down on the rough stone step at the floor of the milk room.

All the earth had been washed clean and fresh. The little streams in the footpaths had ceased to run, but in all the hollows in the hard ground were pools of water, and you could hear the stream still rushing in the bed of the mountain torrent.

Baby-Bertie leaned her head back against the door; a rich, fragrant odor rose from the fresh earth; she drew the white shawl she had thrown over her head closer round her face, and sat watching the wet world. The sun was setting at the end of the great valley below the farmhouse; all the west was a bloody pall of crimson, all the east a faint reflection of its redness. On the water of the great dam by the willows, in the windows of the farmhouse, in the puddles in the roadway, on the wet leaves of the thorn trees, even there it was reflected; and the little flat and the lower hills on the other side of the valley and the tall mountains were all touched with its redness. A curious feeling came over her as she sat there watching it; it was as though a strong great hand were put out and took fast hold of her heart, that trembled and was so heavy, and held it fast. A curious quiet came over her. Was there not something that might make the past as if it had never been, and the "I have done it" as meaningless as "I have dreamed it"?

She sat gazing at that drenched world. It seemed as though the great hand stretched itself out and stroked her.

Slowly the crimson vanished and a faint glow lingered only at the far end of the valley.

Her father, as he passed her on his way back from the sheep kraals, laid his hand upon her shoulder. "It grows late and cold," he muttered; and she stood up and followed him into the house.[1]

When Bertie went to her bedroom that night and closed the door, she felt no terror of the room, as she had done lately; even thought it was better to be there alone than anywhere else. After she had got into bed it seemed as though a great hand made an arch over her and she crept in under it and was safe. She drew the cover up high about her and clasped her arms about a pillow, as if it were a person, and drew it close to her. Even then the croaking of the frogs filled her with no horror; and when she fell asleep, she slept till morning without waking.

[1 Olive once drew attention to this rhythmic paragraph thus, and commented upon it:

Her father, as he passed her
On his way back from the sheep kraals,
Laid his hand upon her shoulder:
"It grows late and cold," he muttered.]

CHAPTER III

The Dam Wall

THORN KLOOF was expecting visitors, and the life-blood stirred in its sluggish old veins. From the superannuated chairs and churns in the loft, to the china in the front room cupboard, everything was turned upside down and inside out and washed and scrubbed and reno-vated. Even the pigsty was whitewashed and had a new trough, and the kraal walls were built up higher with thorn branches.

For the visitors were many and important whom Thorn Kloof was expecting, and it behoved it to put on its best face. Even the little Kaffirs who danced about naked all day on the old kraal heaps knew that something unusual was about to happen, and came to the house to beg for cast-off clothing, paper collars, or old shoes, in which to bedeck their small naked bodies; and they danced about in the sunshine more contentedly than ever, with a collar, or a boot, or a torn waistcoat. All day the Kaffir maids were busy scrubbing and cleaning, laughing and chatter-ing; and all day the little mother trotted about giving orders, and old Ayah clucked and scolded; and Griet, the little Bushman girl, whom Bertie had got from her drunken mother a little while before for a pair of old shoes and a bottle of wine, rushed about hither and thither, doing nothing, but flaunting her little yellow petti-coats in everybody's face, and chattering at the top of her voice, and tormenting the Kaffir maids. Bertie herself got up before sunrise every morning to gather oranges and figs for preserves, and was busy all day making jams and almond cakes.

It was just four full years since Rebekah married, and now she was coming to visit them for the first time, bringing with her her three small children, the eldest of whom was three years and three months old, and the youngest a new-born baby of eight weeks. She had almost died when it was born, and was coming home to rest for a while. Of late years she had often not written long letters though she wrote every week; she seemed always to be having a baby or nursing it, or to be otherwise engaged. Her husband was not coming with her, she wrote, as his business kept him in Cape Town, and later he was going for a six weeks' hunting trip into the Western Karroo. But her husband's brother, John-Ferdinand, was coming; he had come out again from England for his health, and was going to buy a farm in South Africa and settle there. He was coming to ask his uncle's advice as to the choice of a place.

A few weeks later there was also coming another visitor, a lady from England, who was delicate and recommended to their care by their English relatives; but no one knew much of her, or could tell what she would be like.

The excitement at the old farm was intense; everything was in motion.

One Saturday afternoon the wagon they had sent to the coast to fetch Rebekah came over the nek. The little mother began to cry as soon as they told her it was coming; and then everyone gathered at the back door to wait for it. Bertie would have liked to put on her kappie and run through the thorn trees to meet it, but she thought her mother would rather they all met Rebekah together.

At last the wagon drew up at the kitchen door, and Rebekah herself got out first. She looked smaller and more like a child than ever, with her little white face and her large eight-weeks baby on her arm. While the little mother was kissing her and crying, the driver handed down to the father a stout, fair boy of two, and then lifted down a shy boy of three, who looked like Rebekah and hid his face in his mother's skirt as soon as he got to the ground. They all gathered close round Rebekah. Bertie caught up the boy of two and covered him with kisses, and ran towards the house with him; the little mother took the baby from Rebekah and began to cry afresh; old Ayah caught hold of its long white skirt and began to cry also; and Griet did all she could to coax the shy boy to take his face from his mother's gown and let her carry him; but he kept his face carefully turned away as they walked towards the house.

They were so absorbed in Rebekah and her children they did not notice John-Ferdinand, her cousin, who had been walking some way behind the wagon, and who had now come up. He was a tall, slender man, with a very small, delicate head and face, and black hair, curling close to his head, and eyes of such an exceedingly dark blue they seemed black, except in certain lights. His fingers were very long and tapered, and his hands transparently white.

Only the father saw him, and went up to shake hands with him, and said he was glad to see him. When he went away to give orders about the oxen, John-Ferdinand stood alone by the great whitewashed brick oven that jutted out from the side of the kitchen.

He was dressed in dark clothes and wore a soft, black felt hat; he leaned his elbow almost gracefully on the oven and stood watching the unpacking of the wagon. The Kaffir maids had come up from the huts now, and were dragging mattresses, pillows, boxes, canisters, and bundles, out of the wagon, and throwing them down in heaps or carrying them into the house, all laughing, running, and talking. Over all Griet, with her small, yellow-brown, Bushman face, with its touch of Hottentot, was giving pretended orders to the Kaffir maids, and screaming in a shrill voice; tumbling in and out of the wagon over the heads of the others, doing nothing and glorying in the confusion.

Presently Bertie came to the back door to see how they were getting on. Then she noticed John-Ferdinand standing alone by the oven. It seemed to her he must feel lonely and neglected standing leaning there, no one speaking to him, and she ran down the steps towards him. He reminded her of the picture of Charles the First the night before his execution in her old school history, with his deep-blue eyes looking out so gravely. When she came near him she suddenly felt shy, and almost turned away; but he came slowly forward to meet her.

"You are my cousin Baby-Bertie, are you not? I think you were not born when I was here twenty-one years ago."

He spoke gravely and held out his white hand. Bertie took it shyly.

"I have heard much of you from my brother and his wife; I think I should have known you anywhere had I met you."

Bertie said nothing, and hesitated; then, seeing a large canister standing on the front box of the wagon ready to be carried into the house, she turned towards it and seized it. Her cousin came forward.

"That is too heavy for you." He took it from her very gently and gravely. When their hands were near each other on the canister, she noticed how brown, and even rough, her hands were compared with his. She wrapped her right hand up quickly in her little silk apron as she walked behind him to the house. He put the canister down solemnly on the kitchen table; she thanked him quickly, and he went slowly out again.

That night, when Rebekah lay on the bed in the spare room, hushing her babies to sleep, Baby-Bertie came in. She had changed since the old days when Rebekah married and Percy Lawrie was her tutor. The exuberant brown curls were gathered into a knot at the back of her head, which showed better the beautiful outline of her small round neck and broad shoulders and the small round head. She had grown, as Frank prophesied, into a magnificent woman; but she had become quiet, the noisy gaiety of her early girlhood had passed, and she spoke and moved almost heavily. She would have been almost majestic if it had not been for the infant-like expression of the face, and something uncertain and almost wavering in her walk, rising from the fact that her feet were almost too small for her body. Her rich coloring was more perfect than ever; but in her round brown eyes there was a slight wistfulness, almost as though asking a perpetual question; and the corners of her small full-lipped mouth were more drawn in than they had been, as though always wearing a placid, half-smile.

She stood at the foot of Rebekah's bed, dressed in a white muslin gown with blue bows down the front. Rebekah's eldest son lay at her back, with his arms twisted round her neck, and her baby lay at her breast; but the little fat blue-eyed boy had already gone to sleep in his cot in the corner.

She crept on to the bed and laid her head softly on her sister's knee.

"It is so nice to have you here, eh, Rebekah," she said slowly. "It seems like long ago." She uncovered the baby's feet and looked at them: "Aren't they beautiful?" She held them in her hands. "So soft and warm!" She held her cheek against them for a moment, and then laid her head back again on Rebekah's knee.

Rebekah smoothed her hair with her free hand. "Aren't you very lonely here sometimes, Baby-Bertie?" she asked after a time.

Bertie smiled, the soft dreamy smile that was seldom wholly absent from her face. "No," she said. "Sometimes I feel as if I should like to go to Cape Town and be with you and the children; and sometimes I feel as if I would like to go somewhere and see people and things and be where other people are." She rubbed her cheek softly against Rebekah's knee. "And then again I feel, no, it's better to be here shut in safely by the old mountains." A slightly troubled look crept into her face; then she said: "You know it isn't because I don't want to be with you, Rebekah; I am always wanting you; like when I was little." They were silent for a time, as the little

boy with his arms round his mother's neck was just drop‧
ping asleep. "Rebekah," Bertie whispered, as he seemed
to have gone off, "does cousin John-Ferdinand always
look so grave?"

"Yes; he does not often smile; I never heard him
laugh."

Bertie lay still. "Keep on stroking my hair, Rebekah;
I like it so. Don't you like people to touch you—I mean,
if you like them?" After a while she added, "He's very
clever, isn't he?"

"He took his degree well at the university."

Bertie caressed the baby's feet softly with her hand.
"Don't you think he's very beautiful, Rebekah?"

At first Rebekah thought she meant the baby, then she
understood.

"Yes, in a way. Most people think so. His beauty
doesn't touch me."

"I feel so afraid of him, Rebekah. He's not merry
like Frank, who used always to be laughing and joking.
Do you feel afraid of him, Rebekah?"

"No."

"Oh!" said Bertie, and lay still.

Presently Griet came in to tell Bertie the milk was come
and it was time to get supper ready. Soon after the
little mother came in and sat in the rocking chair at the
bedside and told Rebekah how much greater her troubles
were than they used to be: the maids did less work than
ever, and her father was more silent and said, "Um!
Um!" in answer, when you tried to talk with him. She
said Bertie was a dear, good, beautiful child, but she spoiled
Griet and was like her father in not caring to talk much.
She said how happy Rebekah must be with a husband
always ready to chat and laugh, and how nice it must be
to live in a town where you could get your bread ready
baked, and all kinds of things you couldn't get on a farm;
and she lamented on till Bertie came to call them to
supper.

A few nights after, when the father and little mother lay in bed, the father reading with his book open on his breast and the candle on the stand near his head, the little mother said, "Rebekah *is* changed, you know."

The father made a sound, which might mean attention or not, from under his thick iron-gray mustache.

"It's always, when you talk to her, as if she were thinking of something else; as if she didn't quite see you. She's different, she's quite different from what she used to be!"

"The cares of life," muttered the father, still looking at his book, and growing sleepy.

"What cares has she?" said the little mother. "She hasn't quite such an easy life as she would have had if she'd married John-Ferdinand. I've sometimes wondered why she didn't marry him, with the twelve thousand pounds of his own his aunt left him, when Frank had only his business. But, after all, I should have chosen Frank! He's so big and strong, and he's doing well, she says. Of course, she has a great many children and only one servant and an outside boy, and no nurse—but she *will* look after the children herself—Rebekah always did work harder than anyone else! She never complains, but it's as if she was thinking of something else. Even when she——"

But the father's book had dropped over on to his chest and he was breathing heavily; and the little mother put the light out.

During the days that followed Rebekah's arrival the womenfolk at the house did not see much of John-Ferdinand. Sometimes he was out riding with the father, to look at the farms in the country round, to see if any suited him; and when he was at home he took his book after breakfast and roamed away with his rug into the bush and did not come back till dinner. After the afternoon sleep and tea he generally went for a walk again. At meal times he sometimes talked a little to the father and Rebekah about books. He was annotating a copy of Tennyson's *Idylls of the King,* and generally had it with his pencil in his pocket. The little mother feared he must feel lonely, and offered him the gun to go out shooting; but he said he never hunted; and she felt ashamed, as if she had offered him something wrong.

Yet, after the first ten or twelve days had gone, he began to stay more in and about the farmhouse. Sometimes, when in the morning Rebekah lay under the orange tree with her boys creeping about her, catching at the orange blossoms as they fell and stuffing them down her neck or making little heaps of them on the reed mat, and the baby lay on her arm, and Bertie was sitting at her feet shelling peas or peeling fruit, and chatting away softly about the wild cat that had stolen all her last brood of turkeys, or the man on the next farm who would quarrel about the beacons, or the sheep that had strayed in her father's veld, it would happen that Bertie would look up suddenly and see John-Ferdinand standing close behind them with his hands resting on the head of his cane, looking down at them; and she would at once become still and shell her peas or peel her fruit in silence, while John-Ferdinand said a few words to Rebekah, or walked on into the garden. He began also to sit a good deal, too, in the back dining room, reading at table, where Bertie passed and repassed as she went about her work between the pantry and kitchen.

One morning, when Rebekah had been there more than three weeks, Baby-Bertie was kneeling in the pantry, making Boer biscuits. She had the dough in a large wooden trough on a low bench, and the black pans she had to fill placed across and across on the end. She was kneeling on a footstool because she was too tall when she stood. She had finished kneading and was just going to begin making up, when she looked round and saw John-Ferdinand standing in the pantry door, watching her with his grave eyes, and his delicate head a little on one side.

"Rebekah isn't here," she said quickly and shyly; "she's gone down to the garden; and mother is in the ration room."

"I am not looking for either of them, thank you."

He stood still, and then came a step nearer.

"May I come in and watch you?"

He seated himself on the wooden churn that was turned upside down in the corner between the bench and the dresser. He leaned forward slightly and watched her. A lock of her brown hair had escaped and hung in one little ringed curl over her low, broad forehead; her sleeves were turned up far above her elbows and she had on a great snow-white coarse apron covering her dress.

She put the making-up board across the trough and broke off a lump of dough and began to make it up. She turned it this way and that, her downy cheeks growing pinker and pinker. First she tried to make snake curls, but they often broke in two as she was twisting them; then she made up double balls, and the one would hardly stick on to the other; she tried quickly three or four different patterns. She knew John-Ferdinand must think her so stupid, not even to be able to make up biscuits well. She would not have minded so much if the curl had not been hanging over her forehead, and she could not lift it off because her hands were doughy.

At last the six pans were full, and she stood up with a flushed face.

John-Ferdinand had not spoken once all the time.

He rose also.

"I am going for a walk in the bush up in the kloof," he said. "Will you come with me?"

"I—oh—I don't know. My hands are full of dough."

"But you can wash them," he said gravely, almost smiling.

Baby-Bertie called to the girl to take the pans away and went to her own room. She put on her best white dress and a large white kappie with embroidery round it. Then she came out without saying a word to anyone; and John-Ferdinand and she walked round the back of the house and up towards the kloof.

First they went through the belt of small thorn trees,

with seed pods just forming and the soft green this year's thorns turning white and hard, and with little honey-creepers hanging from here and there; and on, past the great round kunee trees, in whose depths you could hear the little birds hopping, though you could not see them; and on, into the real bush, where the tall forest trees grew straight and high over the bed of the mountain torrent and made a great stillness in which the woodpeckers worked and there was always shade. Here the monkey-ropes hung from the trees, and the Kaffir bean trees shed their great seeds till the ground was brown with them; and here and there out of the banks hung the great roots that the Kaffirs used to make medicine of. They crossed the bed of the mountain torrent, where the little stream of water, not thicker now in the dry weather than two fingers, was running among the great rocks, making clear pools here and there. On the other side of the torrent the path grew quickly steeper and the mountain side rose abruptly. She took the narrow upward footpath made by the Kaffir maids when they went to fetch wood; the nam-nams [1] and jasmine shrubs made a thick wall on either side, and the wild asparagus hung out long waving arms. By and by they came to a patch where olive-wood trees grew thick among fragments of fallen rocks covered with long dry moss. Just here, suddenly, they came to a small open space; two mighty rocks that must have fallen from their home in the crags on the mountain tops centuries before lay there, covered with long dry moss and red lichens. In the crack in one a tall slender young tree was growing, and the space between them was bare, covered only by a smooth carpet of moss and sorrel, with little fern leaves intermingled here and there; and the small, sweet-scented mountain geranium with its tiny pale blossom was growing close to the foot of the rocks. A bush of the tall scarlet geranium, with its brilliant blossoms, grew up against one rock. On the other side the bush rose like a solid wall, nam-nams and sweet-henries mingling with the larger

[1 A shrub with a small edible berry (also "num-num").]

trees. The bare space between the rocks and the bush was just like a little almost square room, with a rich soft carpet.

John-Ferdinand broke away a branch of scarlet geranium, which left clear a little mound covered with fern and moss, close to the foot of one rock.

"Sit there," he said. "This is my little parlor. I come here often."

She sat down upon the mound, and he stretched himself at her feet on the carpet of moss and sorrel.

"It is very nice here," she said.

"Yes," he answered.

She took her great muslin kappie off and laid it across her knee. "It's quite cool," she said.

"Yes," he said.

Then they were quiet for a long time. At last he stretched out his hand, and from the branch of scarlet geranium he had broken he began plucking the brightest blossoms and mixing them with the small fern leaves in the carpet. When he had gathered a tiny bunch he laid it upon her knee.

"They are very beautiful," he said.

"Yes," she answered. Then he stretched out his hand and scattered them again over the moss and sorrel.

"Oh—I liked them!"

"They do not belong to you. I should not have given them to you," he said slowly. "This is yours."

He rose and from the wall of bush he plucked a small spray of the plumbago [1] that hung out everywhere.

"This is the sweetest flower of South Africa," he said. He placed it on her knee close to her hand, and lay down again on the carpet at her feet.

"Those others are not for you," he said, looking up at her. "They are for women in crowded ballrooms and

[1] Plumbago, or sweet-henry, as the frontier children call it, is a delicate, pale-blue flower, growing on a large partly creeping shrub. Its skylike flowers are sensitive and curl up if roughly touched or plucked.

theaters. They can live there in the hot, stifling air. These are yours—they would fade there in a moment."

Bertie touched softly with her finger the delicate blue leaves and the spirally curled buds.

He turned round on to his face again; the crushed leaves of the tiny mountain geraniums sent up a sweet aromatic odor as he moved.

"Would you mind my reading?" he asked.

"Oh no."

He took out his book and laid it open before him on the turf, and leaned on his folded arms, reading at her feet.

Baby-Bertie fastened the sweet-henry spray he had given her with a pin to the front of her white dress; then she sat still. She could hear the wood doves cooing and the cock-o-veets calling in the cool morning air.

There was much wondering at the farmhouse and no little searching when dinner time came near and Baby-Bertie was not to be found. It was an unheard-of thing that she should wander farther than the kraals, or the milk house, or at most the end of the orchard. Griet, Bertie's little Bushman maid, who had been sent to look for her and who had searched for her even in the oven at last, now sat down on the step of the loft ladder and howled, covering her face with her pinafore and knocking her heels against the lower rung, but partly peering out from the side of her pinafore now and then to see what effect her grief had on the group of little Kaffirs gathered below to watch her. She declared that the great spook with red eyes, whom she had seen at the fountain the evening before when she went to fetch water, had certainly carried off Miss Bertie and eaten her. The little Kaffirs looked up at her with wonder and awe. They regarded her as a person highly favored and much gifted.

Presently she saw Bertie coming down the kloof road in the hot sun, for the day had now grown warm, with John-Ferdinand following her; and the sweet-henry on her breast curled up, but still fastened there.

Then Griet got down quickly and stood with her face buried in the wall of the gable, sobbing bitterly. (She had seen Bertie go up the kloof road, and knew where she was all the time.) She thought Bertie would stop as she passed her to find out the cause of her grief, and when she did would pat her on the head and perhaps promise to give her the point of the sheep's tail, to console her.

But Bertie walked by her without seeing her.

"Daddy-long-legs! Why didn't he stay in his own country!" Griet whirled round from the gable wall, making her little skirts stand out all stiffly. "Daddy-long-legs! Why did he ever come here! Taking our Miss Bertie away from us, to walk with him! Let him stay in his own country!" She whirled till there was only a cloud of yellow petticoats, and the little naked Kaffirs looked on.

After that day everyone knew where Bertie was when she was not to be found in the milk room or the kitchen or the garden.

She and John-Ferdinand often went for walks. Sometimes they went in the early morning, when the dew was on the grass and you were afraid to set your foot down because you broke the spangles, and when the calves were putting their faces through the wet bars of their kraals and the cows were lowing for them, and the sheep had their backs dark with the dew, as they streamed out of their kraals, with the herd boy with his two sticks in his hand behind them; and when, as you walked through the mimosa trees and touched a branch, the dew rained down on you, and the long beams of the early sun made them sparkle like a shower of diamonds.

Sometimes they went in the evening up the steep bare spur of the mountain side that lay to the left of the farmhouse where the long waving grass grew; and they passed the herd boy coming down with his flock of curly Angora goats, a great Boer-goat leading them with a bell round his neck, and the Angoras running hither and thither on every side to have a last nibble at the few thorn trees among the long grass. Then they sat high up on the ridge and saw the sun set at the end of the valley, and the farmhouse on the other spur of the mountain below them looked like a white speck among the dark orange trees; and they watched the long curls of blue smoke rising in the still air from the Kaffir huts, where the maids were lighting the evening fires with mielie cobs; and they saw the line of dust which hung over the road by which the sheep were going to the kraal; and in the dry grass about them the avondbloem (evening flowers) were coming out, and the air was full of the sweet night scent. Then they would walk down the steep stony footpath together, and say nothing; except John-Ferdinand asked her which was the best footpath to take, or she told him the name of one of some little night insects which began to buzz by them. They were very silent.

But especially in the middle of the day, when it was too hot to walk anywhere else, they went up to the little parlor in the bush. John-Ferdinand lay on the ground and read, and Baby-Bertie took out sewing she had brought with her and sat at the foot of the rock; and they stayed there long hours, often without speaking.

The little mother was glad she went out with him; it was a change for Bertie and it was bad to have a visitor one did not know how to entertain. No one thought it strange she should like to walk out with her cousin. Only Griet resented it. She turned up the little flattened ball in the center of her face which was her nose whenever she mentioned him.

When Bertie was at home she was unusually silent, and went about her work more quietly than ever; only the placid half-smile that was always upon her face was deepened into something softer.

Rebekah was quiet, too. When she was not actively attending to her babies she was always reading. She read when she woke in the morning, in the gray dawn she drew back the curtain and lay on the side of the bed with her book stretched out that the early light might fall on it, while the baby lay drinking at her breast. She read at night, when supper was over and she could go to her own room and shut her door and lie reading without interruption, sometimes till the old cock at the wagon house began to crow; and often when she blew the light out she found the square of the window was already becoming dimly visible. She read in the afternoon, for a large part of the time when everyone else slept. Even when she was taking care of her children under the orange trees or in the orchard, she had always a book in her hand; and if one came near to interrupt her, she looked up with an eager, sharp look—the look of a hungry dog eating a bone, when some one comes near him.

She seemed like a creature returning to its old habitat and resuming its old instincts and habits; but never, even when she was a child and first learned to read, had she read with such a concentration of almost fierce avidity. It was as though she hardly saw the world about her; even Bertie and her parents and the old farm she saw as through a mist, and only the world of her thought was real to her.

But one evening, when Baby-Bertie was in the milk room skimming the pans, Rebekah came with a mug to fetch fresh cream for her children. It was quite dark in the milk room already, and Bertie bent over the table, holding a lighted tallow candle in one hand, and the saucer in the other, with which she went over the pans, putting the cream into the little wooden cream vat at her side.

Rebekah stood still for a moment just inside the doorway. The light of the candle her sister held shed its yellow light full upon her, on her plain white dress and lovely down-turned face, and made her stand out from the dark shadows which filled the rest of the low room, almost illuminated. Rebekah stood looking at her for some seconds; then she came in and put her mug on the end of the long table. Bertie filled it. Still Rebekah waited, watching her work.

Suddenly Bertie said: "Rebekah, I wish I was different and not like I am! I wish I was clever. I am so big and heavy! I am so stupid!—I wish I were like you!" She looked up, and under her curled lashes the candle-light showed a tear had gathered.

"I can understand about work and such things," she said slowly, looking back at her work, "but I can't talk about books and all the clever things other people talk of. Sometimes, when father and you and Cousin John-Ferdinand are talking together at meal times—sometimes I wish I was dead. I want so to be different!" She bent down over her work. "Rebekah, do you think anyone could ever love me who was very clever and not stupid like I am?"

Rebekah, looking at the lovely face half turned from her as it bent over its work. She almost laughed softly: "You need not fear people will not love you, darling; you will be loved wherever you go; I am only afraid you will be loved too much."

"Rebekah, I like so to be loved!"

Rebekah made a little caressing movement as though she would have put out her hand and touched the hand nearest her in which Bertie held the candle; then she heard the baby crying through the spare-room window and hurried away with her mug. Before Bertie had finished the milk the quiet dreamy smile had settled down on her face again.

The next morning, as Rebekah lay under the orange trees, with her book in her hand and her baby asleep on her arm, her boys playing beside her, John-Ferdinand came out of the house and appeared to be looking for some one and then turned to pass on to the orchard. Rebekah put down her book and told him she wished to go for a walk with him.

"I am sorry I cannot," he said. "I have asked Bertie to go with me as soon as her work is done."

"That does not matter. I shall not keep you long."

She rose and, calling Griet to watch the children, led the way round the corner of the house and past the kraals. She took the short cut through the mimosa trees towards the great dam in the flat. John-Ferdinand followed her with the copy of Milton he had been reading showing from his breast pocket. The path among the trees was so narrow that the thorns in the mimosa trees pecked at them as they passed.

When they got to the dam, Rebekah led the way along the narrow footpath that ran on to the broad top of the earthen wall that formed the dam. The path was almost overgrown with love-grass and chickweed and widows; and the great willow trees which grew at intervals hung over the path and dipped their branches into the water beyond. Rebekah and John-Ferdinand stood knee-deep among the weeds under the willows. They had not spoken all the way down, and they still stood silent for a few minutes.

On the other side of the dam, where the water was shallower, the lilies and water plants floated; and the goslings swam in and out among them and disappeared and reappeared among the chickweed and wild mustard that grew rank to the water's edge. Beyond them was a little mound where Bertie's twin sister, who had died when she was born, had been buried. Bertie often came down to weed about it and keep it clear; but during the last weeks she had forgotten it, and the weeds had almost overgrown it.

Rebekah took off her kappie and held it in her hand.

"John-Ferdinand," she said, "I wish to speak to you about Bertie."

John-Ferdinand bowed his head gravely, to show he was attending, and looked down at her.

"She has led a lonely life here. A woman who grows up alone on a solitary farm in South Africa is not quite in the position of most other women. A child of ten, who has lived in a village or town and has gone to a school and grown up among other children, has more knowledge

of the world in a thousand ways than she can have even
at fifteen or twenty. She may know much of books, and
be skilled in domestic labor or—she may even be excep-
tionally advanced intellectually in many ways; she is still
a child in the knowledge of men and life. Bertie does not
know even the world of books."

John-Ferdinand bowed again, and looked down at her
with his dark head delicately poised a little on one side.

"You have seen a great deal of her since you came
here. I do not blame you; it was natural you should. She
is the only interesting thing here, and she is very beautiful. But I am afraid she may possibly grow to care a
little for you, John-Ferdinand, seeing no one else."

John-Ferdinand moved as if he were about to speak,
but she raised her hand and stopped him.

"She has said nothing of her feeling towards you to
me; I am acting entirely on my own judgment. But she
has seen no men in her life but a few shop clerks and
farmers' sons who may have come here on business or
have served her in a shop when she was in town; you are
the first man of mental and physical attractions with whom
she has been thrown into close contact. It has been almost
inevitable that she should be attracted by you, and it has
been almost as inevitable that you should feel attracted
towards her. And yet, when you marry, you will probably
require in your wife certain qualities which Baby-Bertie
has not: more intellect and more calm strength of character. Now, if this is the case, John-Ferdinand"—she
looked up at him—"and you feel that, in spite of her
great beauty, she is not the type of woman you can make
your wife, then I think you ought to go away from the
farm and not seek to meet her again. It is an absorbing
love she would love you with, John-Ferdinand—a love
you probably cannot understand. You might become all
the world to her. Some women with complex, many-
sided natures, if love fails them and one half of their nature dies, can still draw a kind of broken life through the
other. The world of the impersonal is left them: they can

still turn fiercely to it, and through the intellect draw in a kind of life—a poor, broken, half-asphyxiated life, not what it might have been, like the life of a man with one lung eaten out by disease, who has to live through the other alone—but still life. But Bertie and such as Bertie have only one life possible, the life of the personal relations; if that fails them, all fails. If you chop down the stem of a mimosa tree, years after you may come and find from the bottom of the old dead stem sprouts have sprung, which will even bear flowers, though there will never be the glory of the central stem; but an aloe has one flower, once; if you cut that down, nothing more comes. If the life of personal relations fails Bertie, all will have failed her; I want to save her from this. You are a man of principle, John-Ferdinand; I know you are a man who always does what he believes to be his duty. I think you will feel it your duty to go, if you know you cannot care for her."

"Rebekah," he said softly, still looking at her, "I love your little sister. She is the one absolutely pure and beautiful thing life has ever yet shown me. From all the world of men and women I turn to her to find in her the one absolutely spotless, Christ-like thing I have known. I am a nobler and better man when I am in her presence. No other woman ever could be, or ever will be, to me what she is. When as a youth I asked you to marry me I was drawn to you by your intellect, your strange intensity and delicate physical refinement and beauty, and your devotion to your duties. My feeling for her is wholly different. For the first time I understand now how men have made a god of woman—the eternal virgin mother!— If I am all the world to her, Rebekah, she is more than all the world to me."

Rebekah looked up at him and then away across the water. There was no mistaking the ring of sincerity in the man's voice; his dark-blue eyes were moist with unshed tears. They stood quiet for a moment. The willow

trees sifted down the last of the spring's little dried
catkins on Rebekah's brown hair and on John-Ferdinand's
black felt hat.

"If I have not yet spoken to her of my love, Rebekah,
it has been because she has seemed to me almost too pure
and sacred a thing for me to approach. Can you understand? Have you never felt, on a solitary mountain side,
that some delicate flower you have found growing there
was too beautiful to be plucked?—that it was too pure
for your finger to touch it? When your father has helped
me to secure a farm in this neighborhood, so that I shall
not need to take her far from her parents and her old
home, I shall lay my love before her. I hope it will not
be long before I take her to myself forever."

Rebekah looked away from him to where the little goslings swam in and out among the water lilies.

"If that is so," she said slowly, "I have no right to say
more, and perhaps I should (? not) have said what I
have." She gathered together her little skirts and turned
to lead the way along the little footpath. Then suddenly
she turned. "If I knew," she said, "that you would
ever fail her, I, I, with my own hand would rather take
her life and see her lying buried there, beside her little
sister." The crimson flush had risen suddenly over her
face, darkening even her forehead; it died away in an
instant and left the face paler than before. She walked
on before him, the black widows shaken from bushes as
they passed sticking fast to her skirts and to his black
trousers. When they got off the dam wall she took the
path among the thorn trees and walked so fast John-
Ferdinand could hardly keep up with her. When they
had climbed almost to the top of the long rise on which
the house stood, she stood still for an instant and took out
her penknife and cut a large many-horned gall growth
from one of the mimosa branches. "I am collecting
these," she said, half turning to him, "to see whether the
galls on the different species of mimosa are all quite alike,

or whether they are different on different species of the tree." Then she walked on quickly.

When they came out of the thorn trees at the kraals they saw the white tent of a cart which stood outspanned near the back door.

"The woman from England must have come," she said. "They were expecting her to-day."

As they came nearer the house they saw Bertie standing on the top kitchen doorstep, and beside her a tall woman with square shoulders, dressed in a starched mauve cotton dress, with white collar and cuffs. Bertie, in her white muslin and blue ribbons, was motioning with her right hand, evidently pointing out to the stranger the interesting points in the landscape, from the wagon house and pigsty to the great dam and the road over the nek, which could all be seen to advantage from the top of the steps. As they approached the steps, Bertie and the newcomer came down to meet them. She had light hair of an almost drab shade touched with yellow and parted down the center. It was brushed smoothly down on each side, showing strikingly the large, flat-topped, broad shape of the head. Her forehead was high and arched in the middle, and her large eyebrows were even more arched, so that between them and the pale-blue eyes below, over which the eyelids habitually drooped, almost the whole bulb of the eyeball showed under its eyelid. Her eyelashes were thick and almost white, and drooped over her cheeks readily as she looked down. She walked towards them with a long, even stride that contrasted with Bertie's wavering uneven little footsteps.

She held out a large, flat, cool hand to Rebekah and John-Ferdinand when Bertie introduced her.

It was not easy to say what her age was; it might have been anything between twenty-eight and thirty-eight; the perfect placidity of her face might make her appear older than she was, or, being old, might make her appear younger.

"You must have had a warm drive from the town," John-Ferdinand said.

"No, it was very pleasant," she said slowly; "the view was very interesting."

Then they all turned and went into the house.

CHAPTER IV

Showing How Baby-Bertie
Heard the Cicadas Cry

"WHEREIN lies this woman's charm?"

This question Rebekah had asked herself more than once before Veronica Grey had been at the farm three weeks.

She looked at the angular high shoulders, at the rather large mouth, somewhat drawn down at the corners as in a fixed half smile; at the thickening finger tips on the large, flat, snow white hands; and at the white eyelashes— and found no immediate answer.

Everyone at the farm seemed to like her except Griet.

The father liked her. He seldom went to his mielie lands to examine the new varieties of grain he was experimenting with, or to the orchard to look at his grafts, but he took her with him. Her past life in a villa in the south of London could hardly have yielded her an extensive knowledge of African field growths, and she did not know a mielie land from a wheat field, or a bed of sweet-potatoes from one of pumpkins; but she always said, "Ah, yes," when the father discussed the varying growth in his beds and their manures; and when she looked at the grafts she said, "How *very* interesting!" or, "How *wonderfully* they are growing!" and the father liked her company.

The little mother liked her. On days when she had a headache and went to lie down, Veronica came and sat in the rocking chair beside her bed, knitting, and saying nothing; and when the little mother was better and able to talk, she sat rocking and listening to all her complaints, and never tried to put a good complexion on to her troubles; she only said, "How strange!" or, "That is just what my mother often said!" and the little mother liked her.

Bertie liked her; she was something new to take care of. When the hand-lambs and all the poultry had been fed, and there were no sick Kaffirs to attend to, and Rebekah's children needed nothing, there was always still Veronica. She used to bring a glass of milk to her bed at six in the morning, when the cows were first milked, and little cups of broth or beaten-up egg and wine between breakfast and dinner; and she insisted on her sleeping in the next room to her own, which used to be Rebekah's, so that if she woke in the night and needed anything she might knock on the wall and not feel lonely—as Bertie herself still often felt, when she woke in the night and had to clasp a pillow to her and hold it tight in her arms to make herself feel as if there were some one sleeping by her and caring for her. She ironed Veronica's white dresses herself, because the maids could not make them smooth and stiff enough.

John-Ferdinand liked her. When Bertie was busy with her housework, he used to read aloud to Veronica from the *Idylls of the King* or *Paradise Lost,* and she would sit knitting and listening. Often she would drop the work into her lap and sit with her hands across upon it and her blue eyes fixed on the cover of the book he was reading from; for half an hour she would sit motionless, listening; and sometimes she asked him to read a long passage over again; and that he liked most of all.

Old Ayah liked her; she said she gave no trouble and kept her room beautifully neat: there was never a thread or a scrap of paper on her carpet; and her large flat-soled thick English boots stood exactly side by side under the dressing table, toe to toe; and her gloves lay ready on the dressing table, in case she should be going out, finger to finger and thumb to thumb; and she gave old Ayah who did her room a shawl she had knitted.

As for Rebekah, she was so busy attending to her children and reading that she seldom spoke to anyone; and no one noticed that she never addressed a remark to Veronica, and generally left the room or the stoep when Veronica came there.

But Griet showed her dislike actively. One evening, when she went to the fountain to fetch water for the baths, she found a fine large toad under a stone, with great warts on his back. Carefully catching it with two sticks, she put it into the pail, which she carried home on her head and emptied into Veronica's bath. She hoped that when Veronica got up the next morning and stepped into the bath she might not notice it till she was in. About the time Veronica usually got up, Griet stood outside her bedroom door, first on one leg and then on the other, rolling her eyes and holding her breath, momentarily expecting to hear a step into the bath and then a wild cry and a flight across the floor. But instead a calm voice called to her from the bedroom, "Griet, I think there is something moving in my bath; come in and see what it is and take it out!" And Griet, bursting with rage, had to come in and recapture her toad. "How did that 'thin-eyes' know that I was there!" she cried indignantly when rehearsing the story to herself as she emptied the bath; and her defeat increased her antipathy; but she contented herself with setting Veronica the cracked plate at teatime, and the bluntest knife at dinner; and occasionally putting a small drop of aloes into the coffee she took to her room in the morning; in which case Veronica always left it undrunk.

One Saturday night, when Veronica Grey had been just eight weeks at the farm, the father and John-Ferdinand came home to supper. They said they had signed an agreement with the owner of the next farm, the tops of the tall blue-gum trees about whose homestead were just visible over the nek when you climbed the mountain side, to sell his farm to John-Ferdinand for five thousand pounds, and to give him possession at once.

There was much talking about it at the supper that evening. Veronica Grey said she had often wondered what that farm was like, and John-Ferdinand said they should all go and see it the next week. Only Rebekah could not go, as her visit had come to its close, and she was leaving at daybreak on Monday morning in the ox-wagon to begin her journey to Algoa Bay, [1] from which she would go by sea to Cape Town.

After supper, the mother, who had a headache, went early to bed, and Rebekah went to her own room; the father sat with his books in the dining room; Bertie, who was finishing a dress for Griet to wear the next day, sat by the lamp at the center table in the front room sewing, and John-Ferdinand sat beside her reading, but now and again he looked away from his book and watched her fingers as they sewed. Veronica sat in an armchair in the far corner of the room knitting; as she knitted, from time to time her eyes, from under their long white lashes, rested on the two who sat together at the table. At last she rose and gathered her work into its bag, and went to the little mother's bedroom.

"Would not you like me to come and sit by you a little?" she asked; and she seated herself on the rocking-chair beside the bed. For a long time there was nothing to be heard but the tick, tick of her needles. By and by, however, her hands dropped into her lap and she sat looking at the painted motto that hung on the wall opposite the bed with its border of lilies and roses.

Then the little mother, who had been half dozing, woke up, feeling much better, and showed an inclination to talk.

Veronica said that was a very pretty motto on the wall. The mother lay on her side and told her all the story of Percy Lawrie, how he had stayed on the farm and taught Bertie, and how nicely he could paint; how he had had bad news from England and had gone away

[1] Port Elizabeth.

suddenly and they had never heard any news of him
again. Veronica listened, and knitted, and rocked herself.
Then the little mother gradually got drowsy again and
went off to sleep.

When she was sleeping soundly, Veronica rose and
rolled up her work and put it into the little bag upon her
arm, and went out of the room, closing the door behind
her. In the passage all was quiet, but you could hear
Bertie at the piano singing sacred music, and John-Ferdinand's voice singing the bass, through the closed door of
the front room. The long passage itself was dark; but
through the half open door of John-Ferdinand's bedroom
at the far end shone a light. He had evidently not put
his candle out when he went to supper. As she went
towards her own room she passed John-Ferdinand's door.
She looked round quickly; every other door into the passage was closed, and John-Ferdinand's and Bertie's voices
could still be heard singing.

With a long, light, smooth step she passed into John-
Ferdinand's room. The candle stood on the dressing
table. She looked round the room. It was the first time
she had ever stood alone in a man's bedroom. Her father
had died in her early childhood and her brother was
grown up and had gone to China before she could well
remember, and in the quiet home in the south of London,
where her widowed mother and four unmarried sisters
lived, no men visitors had ever come. She stood just
inside the door and looked round. On a rack against the
wall behind the door hung a row of articles of man's
clothing—coats, and jackets, and waistcoats, and trousers;
under the dressing table was a row of boots, and a pair
of man's slippers stood beside the bed. She walked up
to the clothes behind the door and passed her hand softly
over them; she took down a greatcoat and felt the velvet
collar and the buttons; she rubbed her cheek gently
against the shoulder of the coat. So a man's shoulder
felt when you put your face against it. She took down
a pair of trousers, stroked them, and hung them up again;

she felt the buckles at the back of a waistcoat; then she walked to the washing-stand. There was nothing there but the ordinary soap, and sponge, and toothbrush, that any woman might have used, as John-Ferdinand did not shave but clipped his soft beard; but she touched the soap and toothbrush with her finger. She went to the bedside; there was a large braided bag before the pillows; she turned back the flap; there was a man's thick linen garment inside; she did not take it out, but stood listening to hear if anyone were coming. But Bertie and John-Ferdinand were still singing in the front room, and there was no other sound. She turned to the dressing table; there were his brushes and combs and a large bottle of lavender water. On each side of the glass was a small pile of books. She ran her fingers quickly over them. From under the looking-glass protruded the end of a closed, old-fashioned, portrait case. She drew it out and tried to open it; she moved the little hook that fastened it. Inside the case was an old daguerreotype portrait. It was the portrait of a little child of four with a mass of brown curls about its head; the face was smiling; there were dimples in the cheek and in the chin; the child seemed bursting with life and joy, and in its hand it held a bunch of flowers. The old tinted daguerreotype had the color of life, the cheeks and lips were red. She held it sloping towards the candle, at such an angle that she could see it truly through the glass. There was no mistaking whom it represented. It was Bertie as a child, and the only photograph of her in existence. John-Ferdinand had begged the loan of it from the mother, that he might send it to Cape Town with Rebekah to have a life-size enlargement taken from it.

Veronica looked down closely into the face, and her eyes contracted slowly at the inner corners. Quickly she put the case down open on the table, and, placing her large flat thumb on the face, she pressed; in a moment the photograph had cracked into a hundred fine little splinters of glass radiating from the face, which was indistinguishable. With smooth quickness she closed the case and slipped it under the looking-glass, without one bit of glass falling from its place. She stood listening to hear whether anyone was coming. There was no one; and with one or two long, even steps she glided out of the room; with three or four more she had reached her own and closed the door.

The next day the morning broke peaceful and windless, but it promised to be unusually hot later. A deep Sunday stillness reigned about the farmhouse after breakfast. The Kaffir servants were gone to their huts to have their Sunday rest; old Ayah sat at the kitchen door slicing salad and keeping an eye on the pots inside with the Sunday dinner. Griet had gone off to the far lands to pick some green mielies, swearing vengeance upon all the world because she had been accused by old Ayah of breaking Bertie's photograph when she dusted John-Ferdinand's room, and had narrowly escaped the force of old Ayah's hand by Bertie's intervention. The father, in his Sunday best, was reading Swedenborg in the front room, with his hair very much brushed. The little mother was busy in her bedroom, and Rebekah with her boys was, as always, out under the orange trees upon the mats.

John-Ferdinand came out at the front door, looking for Bertie to go for a walk with him. Rebekah did not glance up from her book as he passed, and he walked on through the flower garden and down into the orchard beyond.

Of late, without actually shunning him, Bertie had seemed to elude him; it seemed almost as though she feared to be alone with him; yet when he spoke to her there was a wavering in her color, and a soft brightening about her face she could not hide.

He wandered into the orchard. The long dry grass was brown under the trees, the young unripe peaches had fallen by hundreds into it, and the leaves of the peach trees were beginning to grow yellow for want of rain. At the great pear tree in the middle of the orchard, on the bench, which Rebekah had had put up around the stem when she was sixteen, he saw some one sitting. At first he thought it might be Bertie, but when he came closer he saw it was Veronica Grey.

She was dressed in one of her spotless, stiff cotton dresses with broad, stiff, white linen collar and cuffs; a great straw hat with only a simple band of ribbon tied about the crown lay on the bench beside her, and a book of Sunday sermons lay open beside it. The little sunbeams came through the pear tree branches and played on her smoothly brushed yellow and drab hair; but her eyes were fixed on the row of peach trees before her, and her long white fingers were clasped together upon her knee.

John-Ferdinand stood still at a little distance and watched her. It was a curious picture of placid calm, not a line in figure or dress moving as she sat under the soft playing shadows and lights. He stepped closer to her and asked her if she had seen Bertie. Without unclasping her hands she turned her face towards him and said slowly, "No," and then looked back again at the trees.

John-Ferdinand turned away; yet as he wandered up through the orchard the placid picture under the tree was with him. He walked through the flower garden and out at the gate at the north gable of the house, and took the little footpath among the mimosa trees that led up into the kloof.

Now he was thinking only of Bertie. He pictured the farmhouse among the blue-gum trees as it would be when he and Bertie lived there; Bertie, with her beautiful face and queenly figure lighting up the world about her, till lambs and servants and everyday work reflected that beauty that had made the old farm so lovely to him. He saw her as she had looked that morning at breakfast, when some one had told her that her old Kaffir man she was nursing was worse, and she had left her breakfast and gone out with a jug of hot milk in one hand, and the bottle of medicine in the other, to go to the huts and see if she could do anything for him; as deeply concerned as if it mattered to anyone but herself whether there was one old woolly head in the world more or less. A creature so full of loveliness and love for every living thing, was she not satisfying to the whole soul and body of a man? As he followed the little footpath among the trees, his mind ran on to the long years that were to come; he saw children with their mother's fawnlike eyes looking up at him and calling him father, and the thing he loved lying always in his bosom to comfort and complete his life: it was as though he looked up a long valley where ridge succeeds ridge in new colors, till the far end was reddened with sunset glory.

So far had his thought led him, that he had crossed the almost dry bed of the mountain torrent and had reached their little room and almost trodden on a little ungloved hand, before he saw that Baby-Bertie was before him, sitting at the foot of their rocks, with one hand resting on the moss beside her.

"Why did you come without me?" he said, as he lay down on the turf beside her, so close that his folded arms rested on the edge of her white dress. He had never before done so. "I thought I should find you here."

She was dressed in her best white Sunday dress, with bows all down the front, and a blue ribbon round her neck.

"Do you know what I was thinking of as I came up?" he said, after a while. "I seemed to be looking into the future; and it seemed to me," he added softly, "that I was looking down a long sun-lit path that passed over ridge after ridge, each one more beautiful than the last, till the end, far beyond human sight, lay hidden in glory."

Bertie sat quiet; she was thinking of no beauty in the future, only of a hand very near to her, that she would have liked to bow down to and kiss humbly.

John-Ferdinand spoke in a yet lower voice: "Nothing can ever alter, nothing can ever change, our happiness, that springs from such deep love. Death itself will be but going home to the Father's house to be made perfect there in that which made us loved and loving here." He looked up at her. "For those who love as we love, there is no parting, and no death, only eternal union."

She listened, and the sound of his voice was music to her; but of the meaning she took in little.

"I do not like to think of what will come," she said, bending her head. "I like all things to be just as they are, now; never, never to change! I wish they would always be just so!"

He too at that moment seemed content with an unchanged present. He lay still watching the little hand that rested on the sorrel close to his; and once he looked up at the opening overhead, across which at intervals small thunder clouds were already beginning to move quickly against the hot blue sky. Why did it seem so hard to take that woman to his arms and tell her how he loved her? Why did she seem, without repulsing him, to move away from his hands when he meant to put them out and hold her?

It was already nearly midday, and a sultry stillness was beginning to settle down over the bush. Nothing broke it but the shrill cry of some cicadas hidden in the thickets and in the stems of the trees.

Then he rose from the ground, leaned his elbow against the rock, and bent down over her.

"Bertie, my darling," he said softly, "you must not miss me too much if I go away next week. I shall only be gone for a few days, that I may get all that will be necessary for our new home. And then I will come back to you, and you will come to me, and we will be together for ever; never to part while life is left us. You are my wife now, already my darling; are you not?"

He bent down and wound his left arm round her, half drawing her up to him. For a moment it seemed as though she would have leaped up and nestled close to him; then she loosened herself from his arms and sat down again on the bank. "You must not touch me, you must not kiss me—you must stand still, just where you are—against the rock—I want to say something to you—I want to tell you something."

For a moment he tried to draw her to him again; then silently, wondering, he obeyed her. She sat on the mound at his feet. There was that in her voice that compelled him to listen, and the dimpled hand that had rested on the turf was on her knee now and quivering. Her face he could not see; he looked down at her waving hair that hung in little curls about her forehead.

For a moment she was quiet. He waited; but still she said nothing.

"My little Baby, what is it you want to say to me? I have not long ago told you how I love you, only because I thought you knew, as I knew, how you loved me."

He bent over her again, with his face above her head.

"I do not know what to say—stand back as you were before—with your arm against the rock."

He obeyed her, and waited.

"Long ago I had a schoolmaster; his name was Percy Lawrie. I—I liked him—I liked him very much. He was very kind to me. I liked him at first, then afterwards I hated him———" The hands she had now folded together in her lap were covered in the palms with a cold perspiration. "I did not know—he said he would be angry with me—I did not want him to be angry with me—I didn't want to—I didn't know, you see! Oh, what shall I do! —What shall I do!" She half started up, and then sank down on the mound again.

John-Ferdinand looked down at her, white, motionless.

"He went away that day—I never saw him any more!"

John-Ferdinand leaned heavily on his arm on the rock above her, his face an ashen white. The scent of the crushed geraniums on which he stood seemed to rise up overpoweringly strong; and the only sound was the crying out of the cicadas: they seemed glorying in the hot stillness of the bush.

John-Ferdinand took his elbow from the rock.

For a moment Bertie made a movement as though she would have moved up close to him; then she sat down motionless.

"Bertie, do you mean that you gave yourself to him?"

She nodded.

He waited in silence.

"My poor cousin!" he said slowly.

There was a cicada in the bush, just to the left, that cried louder and louder; its cry seemed to ring through her brain; she wondered when it would leave off.

"Let us go home, Bertie," he said slowly.

She stood up from the mound. The bush had become very hot and deadly still; only the cicada's cry seemed ringing everywhere. She began to walk down the little path; John-Ferdinand followed her. The leaves of the plumbago bushes on either side hung flaccid and curled, and even the asparagus branches drooped, waiting for the storm that must come later. They crossed the bed of the mountain stream and climbed the bank on the other side where the great roots hung out, and the ground was covered with the fallen Kaffir beans; the leaves and dried sticks cracked under their feet as they walked. Just here, where the trees were tallest and met overhead and the monkey ropes hung down, and where there was deep shade and stillness, they met Veronica Grey coming up from the farmhouse into the bush, holding her stiff white skirt about her with one hand and in the other, which drooped in front of her, her half-open book, with her fingers between the leaves. She smiled tranquilly as she passed them.

"What a peaceful Sabbath stillness reigns up here!" she said; and she walked on higher into the bush, as John-Ferdinand and Bertie went down.

When they had got beyond the belt of tall trees where the small mimosa trees and scattered kunee trees grew, she turned suddenly and looked up at him.

"I hurt you so. I hurt you so!" she said.

He looked down at her.

"It is not pain that matters, Bertie; it is sin," he said slowly.

She looked up into his white drawn face, with its compressed nostrils. Then she gathered her skirts tight about her and fled down the winding footpath. An outstretched branch of mimosa caught in her skirt and tore it from top to bottom; but she did not pause. In an instant she was out of sight. There was nothing, when John-Ferdinand passed the next winding, but the tiny rag of white muslin with its blue bow hanging from a thorn to show she had been there.

That night, at ten o'clock, all the boxes and bedding had already been packed into the ox wagon, which was drawn out before the back door prepared for Rebekah's start the next morning before dawn. The yokes were laid out in order before the wagon, and the riems [1] hung over the side ready to inspan in the dark; and the oxen were sleeping in the kraal. The household had retired early, as they had to rise so soon; only Rebekah was still busy in her room arranging the clothes which the children would require to put on in the morning and tying up the last parcels.

When she had finished, she went to Bertie's room. Bertie had been there since before dinner, complaining of feeling unwell; and even the great thunderstorm which had burst in the afternoon had not revived her.

Rebekah opened the door very gently, fearing to awake her if she had dropped asleep. But Bertie was kneeling on the floor in the middle of the room, a large box open before her and a candle balanced on one corner; while Griet, with much alacrity, was adding the contents of the lowest drawer in the chest to the pile of clothes that lay on the floor at Bertie's side. Bertie was putting the articles one by one into the box.

Rebekah set down her candle on the dressing-table and walked up to her, looking down with astonishment. Ber-

[1 Riems: rawhide thongs.]

tie did not look up, but went on mechanically fitting the articles in.

"Bertie, what is this?" Rebekah asked.

She did not look up. "I am going with you," she said shortly, in a voice almost low and gruff; and went on packing. Her face was turned downwards; her lips looked heavy and protruding; but there was no sign of her having wept.

Rebekah put her hand on Bertie's arm: "How is this, Bertie? What is it?"

"I am going with you." There was a dull, dogged persistency in the tone.

"But does mother know of this?"

"I am going with you."

Griet, who had just added the very last article of the drawer to the heap on the floor, stood with her eyes rolling and glittering, delighted with the general confusion and the excitement of something unusual happening, though she did not understand what. Rebekah sent her out to go to her bed. When the door was closed, she knelt down beside Bertie.

"What is the matter, my dear one? You have always said you would not leave the farm or go with me, when I have asked you. Has anything happened?"

Bertie said nothing; her heavy face was still turned down. There flashed on Rebekah the remembrance of John-Ferdinand's white stiff face all that day.

"My darling, is there anything I can do to help you? Anything I can say?"

"Go and tell mother I am going with you," she said slowly. "Make her understand I am going. I *will* go."

Rebekah stood up, but bent down again, putting one hand on her shoulder. "There is nothing I might say to John-Ferdinand, which could be of any use to you, is there?"

In an instant Bertie had leaped to her feet and caught both Rebekah's hands in hers.

"Oh, no, no! Rebekah, promise me—you will never—

never speak to him of me—never ask him about me—
never ask him anything! Promise me, Rebekah! Promise me!"

For the only time in her life Rebekah saw Bertie transfixed with passion.

"I will do whatever you ask of me, dear one."

Bertie sank back again on her knees before the box,
and Rebekah went out to see the father and the little
mother in their bedroom, and tell them of Bertie's resolve.
The little mother, who had been half-asleep, woke up and
began to whine that it was all so sudden; that she could
not bear sudden things; that Bertie had no clothes; that
she ought to have told them before; that it was unlike
Bertie to take people so by surprise. But when Rebekah
had explained that the new clothes could be better got
in Cape Town; that the little mother had always wished
her to go with her for a visit; that Bertie needed change
and ought to see something of life after twenty years on
the farm; and, when the father had expressed his full
approval of her going, the little mother, still whimpering,
insisted on getting up and going to see Bertie; but gave
her consent. Bertie gave her as little explanation as she
had given Rebekah. She only said stolidly she was going.
And the little mother was at last persuaded by Rebekah to
go back to her bedroom, still whimpering that she couldn't
bear surprises; that she wouldn't have wondered if it had
been Rebekah, but that Bertie took after her and never
took anyone by surprise; that perhaps after all Bertie
took after her father also; and she had no child who really
resembled her! But she had no valid objection to make;
when Rebekah had bid her good night and she found the
father was asleep and she had no one to hear her, she got
quietly into bed and was soon asleep.

When Rebekah had helped Bertie to pack all her things
and they had strapped the last box, it was nearly twelve
o'clock. They had spoken only of the work they were
busied with. When all was done, Rebekah put her arm
softly about Bertie and drew her head on to her breast.

"There is nothing you would like to tell me, Bertie?"

"No, nothing." She almost drew herself from her sister; who, when she had helped her to undress, went to her own room for a few hours' rest, before the early start.

At half-past three the next morning the driver came and knocked at all doors and bedroom windows to rouse them, and everyone lit candles and got up.

It was still absolutely dark outside. The men were at the kraal, sorting out the oxen, and old Ayah stood before the kitchen fire, drawing her little yellow handkerchief tighter about her shoulders, and watching the flame and smoke go up about the kettle, and saying, "Oh, ja, Heere!" partly because she wanted to persuade herself she was quite wide awake, and partly because it was so chilly. Under the dining-room table Griet, who had just awakened, was sitting upright on the skin on which she slept and rubbing her eyes and blubbering, partly with cold and sleepiness, and partly because old Ayah had told her that Bertie was going away for six months.

When old Ayah had made the coffee and put it on the dining-room table, they began to file in one by one, and stood round the table drinking it and making believe to eat dried biscuit;—the father in his great overcoat with the collar turned up; the little mother in her dressing gown with a shawl over her head; Rebekah in her traveling dress with a large white kappie; while Griet, on the bench in the corner, sat holding Rebekah's baby, the two boys having been already carried out fast asleep to their bed in the wagon. Then Veronica came in, fully dressed in her starched gown, with collar and cuffs, her hair smooth and the braids coiled carefully at the back, and a pale blue scarf over her shoulders pinned up neatly at one side. They stood round the table drinking the coffee and eating the biscuit, almost in silence. Only Baby-Bertie and John-Ferdinand were not yet there.

As Bertie came out of her bedroom into the long passage she saw John-Ferdinand come out of his room. It was almost dark at her end of the passage, and she stood still, thinking he would pass on to the dining room without noticing her. But he saw her and came up the passage towards her. She drew herself close to the wall as if to let him pass, but he stopped when he reached her.

"Bertie," he said, standing near her, and speaking in a slow even voice, "I fear you may think I dealt very hardly with you yesterday. If you feel that, by my expressing my love for you and showing it as I have done, I have at all committed myself to you, I am still willing to marry you, if you feel that I should do so! My poor cousin!"

"Oh no!" she said in a quick, thick voice. "No! no! no!" Holding her skirt that it might not touch him, she ran down the passage to the dining room, and John-Ferdinand passed slowly out through the dark front room and round to the back of the house where the wagon was standing.

A little later they were all gathered about the kitchen doorsteps to say good-by. The light streamed in a great square from the door. Rebekah said good-by and climbed into the wagon to take her baby. The father folded Bertie in his great arms and kissed her eyes and her mouth. The little mother cried and reminded her of some of the clothing she ought to buy for herself as soon as she got to Cape Town. Old Ayah and Griet caught hold of her at the same time, both crying; then Veronica, standing in the middle of the doorway, held both Bertie's hands fast in hers and looked full into her face. "I hope," she said, "you will have a happy, a very happy, time in Cape Town. I shall do all I can to fill your place to your dear father and mother. Come back soon!"

Bertie drew her hands from her and went down the steps.

John-Ferdinand stood in the dark beside the oven. Bertie would have walked quickly by him and got into the wagon, but he stepped forward and put into her hand a hand as cold as hers. Then the father helped her to climb in, and the driver clapped his whip and called aloud to the oxen, and slowly the great wagon began to roll away in the dark. Bertie flung herself down on the bed beside the children and buried her face in a pillow; but Rebekah moved to the back of the wagon and sat leaning against the back plank. As the wagon rounded the kraal she could still see in the bright square of light at the kitchen doorway her father and mother, and Griet and old Ayah standing at the foot of the steps and Veronica standing full in the door, and John-Ferdinand slowly mounting the steps to go in. Then the house passed out of sight. Half an hour later, as the wagon was climbing the nek, Rebekah, who still sat looking out at the back, could see in the first gray breaks of dawn the farmhouse glimmering as a white speck among the peaceful orange trees. But Bertie still lay with her face buried in the pillow, as though she were sleeping heavily. [1]

[1] In those days there was no railway in the Eastern Province, and persons going to Cape Town were obliged to make the whole journey overland by wagon or cart, taking several weeks; or they might travel by wagon or cart as far as the Bay (Port Elizabeth) and take the steamer round the coast to Cape Town. Even by this route a journey such as Rebekah's would take twelve days or fourteen.

CHAPTER V

John-Ferdinand Shows
Veronica His New House

THE old farm was curiously quiet after Bertie and Rebekah went.

Veronica tried to fill Bertie's place: she poured out the tea and coffee at table, and got the mother to show her how to make bread, and even went to the milk room at night to skim the milk; but she was so curiously still in all her movements that the house seemed quiet and empty.

Griet resented bitterly her attempts to fill Bertie's place. Why should she sit in Miss Bertie's chair, attend to Miss Bertie's flowers, and even move into Miss Bertie's bedroom? And Griet, as far as she was able, took care it did not go well with the bread making; and the flower gardening did not prosper as in Baby-Bertie's time.

In the afternoon, when she was sent out by Veronica to water the flowers, after working for a little while she would carefully peer through the stems of the orange trees and look up and down the orchard; and if she saw no one coming, she would kneel down quickly and, producing from her little yellow print sleeve a sharp table knife, would slip it under the sod at the root of some balsam or larkspur or brilliantly colored four-o'clock and cut the stem off two inches below the surface. The next day when Veronica came to inspect the garden she found it drooping, and a day or two after Griet was ordered to pull it up and throw it away. When Veronica asked her what she thought was the cause of the flowers withering, she always fixed her twinkling black eyes on

Veronica's face and said, "Worms, worms!"—a reply which satisfied Veronica, who in her ignorance of gardening did not note it as remarkable that only the annuals died, while the perennials, which would still be there when Bertie returned in six months, were left untouched. Also, why Veronica's bread never rose, and why it sometimes had a strong taste of garlic, and she had at last to leave it for old Ayah to make, was a mystery Veronica never fathomed.

John-Ferdinand had left the farm the day after Bertie and Rebekah went, to go to the next little up-country town to get workmen and material for enlarging and repairing the house on his farm, and also to buy some furniture for it. If he regretted purchasing it, there was now no way left of getting rid of his bargain.

At the end of ten days he returned to his farm; but to everyone's surprise, though it was only a half hour's ride on horseback from the old farm, he never came over. It was as though he had no wish to see the place. When he wanted the father's advice on any matter, he sent over a boy with a letter; or he asked him to come over and see him.

At last one afternoon, when he had been on his new farm over five weeks, John-Ferdinand drove over to ask the father's advice about using the dredger to enlarge his dam.

His aunt insisted on his staying to supper, and when it was over, as it was already late and there was no moon, he slept the night there.

The little mother, who was much concerned at his loneliness at his new farm and the fact that he had only a Kaffir cook, begged him to come over often; and after that night his visits were not infrequent. He generally drove over in the evening, when his day's work of superintendence was ended, and had supper with them. After supper the father went to his books, and then to bed; and as the little mother often could not sit out on the stoep on account of her neuralgic-headaches, and as the evenings were now too hot to sit indoors, John-Ferdinand and Veronica often sat on the stoep alone.

Sometimes they talked of England and the places they had both been to; oftener, as they sat in the half-darkness, he recited passages from Young's *Night Thoughts* or Keble's Hymns, which Veronica said she admired much; and sometimes they sat quiet and rested.

After a time it became almost a rule that he should drive over in the evenings, and sleep at the old farm, returning to his own early in the mornings; and on Sunday he always came and spent the whole day. In that way, as the little mother said, he got at least one good meal a day, and it was a break in the solitary monotony of his life. She told him to bring over all his darning and mending; and, as she was generally busy, Veronica did it for him.

One night, about three months after Bertie had gone, he asked the mother if she would drive over with him to his farm the next morning and help him hang his curtains, and give him advice about arranging the china and linen, which had just arrived from England, and which he had ordered before he bought the farm, in view of his marriage with Bertie.

The little mother said she could not go, as it was baking day, but that, if Veronica would go, she would send over two of the best of the Kaffir maids to help her in arranging the things; and the next morning Veronica drove over with John-Ferdinand.

They came back in the evening just as it was getting dark, and for three days running Veronica went to help him.

The next time the little mother wrote the weekly letter to Rebekah, she said:

"There is generally no news to give you from this dull place, but to-night there is great news, that will very much surprise you.

"Veronica Grey went over with John-Ferdinand to help him to arrange his house for several days, and,

when they came back last night, after supper he told me
and your father he wished to speak with us, and he told
us he had asked Veronica to marry him, and that they
were engaged and would be married in a few weeks. I
was surprised, though your father did not seem to be;
I think nothing surprises him. I am very glad about it.
It was lonely for him there; and it will be very nice to
have relations there. Veronica has been very good trying to help me since Bertie left, and I feel almost as if
she were my daughter! Tell Bertie; I know she will be
glad.

"John-Ferdinand had seemed ill and depressed during
the last months. It's living alone there, and not getting
proper food. It will be so good for him to have her to
take care of him. Her health is much better now; her
cough is almost gone; you would hardly know her, she
looks so bright. She is not much of a housekeeper; her
bread always turns out bad, and the flower garden hasn't
done well since she looked after it; but she is well off
and they will always be able to have good servants and
need not trouble much about the farming. They seem
made for each other.

"It will be very nice for Bertie, when she comes home,
to have them so near for company. Tell her her hand-
lamb of last year, which has been running with the
sheep, has got two lambs. I hope the air is suiting her
better than you said it did at first. I will write to her
next week. I will make you the biltong as soon as it gets
cooler. I feel so excited still about the engagement I can
hardly write."

Six weeks afterwards Veronica Grey and John-Ferdinand were married. Veronica said there was no need to
wait for letters from England, as she knew her mother
would be delighted to hear of her marriage; and if she
were married at once she could help John-Ferdinand to
get the house and farm quite straight. The clergyman
came from the town and they were quietly married at
the old farm, and Veronica promised the little mother

when she said good-by that they would come over every Sunday and spend the day with her. As the cart drove away with them to their farm, the little mother cried, she hardly knew why; but Griet shouted hurrah and tossed up her little skirts, and then turned round and round like a dervish, till you could see nothing but a whirl of yellow skirts and two little spindle legs; and the little mother left off crying and told her not to make such a spectacle of herself.

CHAPTER VI

How Baby-Bertie Went A-Dancing

TUCKED away among the great oak avenues in the suburbs of Cape Town was Rebekah's home. You might ride mile after mile on a hot summer's day and never feel the sunshine on you, for the great oak trees met over your head; and here and there to the right and left were houses buried behind hedges, with trees touching the roofs, and verandas, and flower gardens.

Everywhere was the scent of fir trees; and pine plantations stretched away up the mountain sides; and now and then there were vineyards stretching acre on acre, with the sunlight shimmering through their leaves, and with white and purple grapes kissing the ground. Behind all rose the mountain's side, sloping away towards the Devil's Peak. On sunny days, as you looked up at it, it seemed as though that side of the mountain were a giant, tranquilly leaning backwards and watching with great godlike, placid eyes the pine woods and the dwellings of men curled about his feet.

It was very peaceful in the great avenues. Sometimes carts drove along and foot-passengers walked there; in summer the acorns fell, and in winter the leaves strewed the sidewalks, and the beautiful tracery of the bare oak branches showed against the clear blue sky, and the lovely green of the pines and of the flower gardens seemed the brighter because the oak trees were bare.

In the houses at night you always heard the trees everywhere rustling with a sound like the distant moaning of a sea. Yet, if you entered a train at one of the little stations, in half an hour or a little more you might be on the other side of the mountain and in the old seaport town itself, with its long streets, principally of single-storied houses, but also here and there of double, with small-paned windows, much as the old Dutch loved to build a hundred years ago. In the streets were Malays; and fish carts blowing their horns; and Dutchmen, and Englishmen, and men of all nations and colors and mixtures; and in the side streets were little Malay and colored children playing happily in the gutters before their doors, or sitting on the stoep steps with a bunch of grapes in the one hand and a lump of bread in the other; and everywhere the peaceful, sleepy life of the old South African town crept on slowly; with its open drains, and its old families, and its old quiet methods of business, still prevailing. And above it all towered the stupendous front of Table Mountain, its beetling crags seeming to look down always with a stern calm contempt on the little seething world of men below.

Round the Peninsula swept the Southern Sea, pale blue and deep green in fair weather, and black in storms; but always, whether in storm or in fair weather, restless and passionate as no other sea on earth is—the Cape of Storms.

Rebekah's house was divided from the avenue by a tall hedge of blue plumbago, so high you saw no one that was passing in the avenue beyond, except it might be their heads, if they were very tall. It was a small house, two great oak trees that grew in the back yard overhanging its roof; and before it was a little flower garden always brilliant with flowers in both summer and winter; and there was a small veranda between two jutting-out wing rooms. Under the windows ran a little rockery; and on the left side of the garden was a little rose hedge of monthly roses almost always in bloom, which Rebekah had planted when she first came to live there.

Across the rose hedge was a large house with a rough grass lawn and some oak trees growing around it; and in the rose hedge was a small gate which Frank had had put there a year after they were married, as people they knew lived next door, and he wanted a passage between the houses.

It was to this little house among the trees that Rebekah brought Baby-Bertie; and gave her as a bedroom the left-wing room, with a green wall-paper, which looked out into the flower garden.

But for a long time after she came Bertie seemed to take no interest in anything. She had no wish to see the people and the sights of the town; and for most part of the day she sat in the iron rocking chair on the veranda, watching the flower garden indifferently; she did not even notice the parrot swinging himself above her and calling to her from the cage over her head; and the needlework she had brought out lay often untouched in her lap all the morning.

When Frank came home at evening with his laughter and talk, it did not rouse her. Sometimes he brought men in for a game of billiards in the billiard room at the back of the house. Sometimes they had supper at eleven, and came out afterwards to sit on the veranda and smoke; but Bertie generally slipped away to bed, and seemed to feel no interest in them. She, who had always been fastidious about her clothes, and as a little child had loved bright ribbons and shoes, now often wore one white dress till it was frowsy and tumbled. Rebekah had never asked her for an explanation of her sudden desire to leave the farm and come with her, nor had she ever offered one; and the name of John-Ferdinand was never mentioned between them. In her heart Rebekah did not grieve if any misunderstanding had separated her cousin from her sister.

Rebekah, who had only one little colored maid to help her, was generally too busy with her household work and children to have much time to spend with her; but she brought her cups of soup and plates of fruit; and she bought her material to make new dresses, but Bertie put them away in a drawer without troubling to make them. Now and then a neighbor who had rooms in the large house across the little rose hedge came over through the little gate and brought her fancy work, and sat on the veranda with Bertie and talked to her. She was a Mrs. Drummond, a little slight woman, with so long a neck and waist that when she sat, or until she stood beside another woman, she looked almost tall. She was always beautifully dressed; whatever she wore was graceful and was perfectly thought out. If she changed her scarf or waistcoat, she changed also her breast pin and earrings to match them; she was as thoughtfully dressed in the morning, in a cotton wrap with little moonstones set in dull silver in her ears, as in the afternoon when she wore Indian muslin and lace, or in the evening, when she wore delicate Chinese silks and little diamond stars for earrings. Even her little drawing room was softly draped in Indian silks or Oriental tapestries in a way other people's were not; there was not a hard outline or bare corner. The curtains at the window were tied back with gold filigree work that matched the brown and gold wall paper; and her little real China tea cups matched her own slippers, and both harmonized with the Indian footstool on which she rested her feet. If you picked up in the avenue a bow she had dropped from her dress, you might have guessed it must be hers from its graceful limp fall. Other women tried to imitate her dresses and the draperies of her little drawing room, but they never made their things look quite as hers did.

She was not pretty, but she was too graceful to be plain. Her hair was neither dark nor light; and she had large white teeth which some people said were false, and some real, and which she always showed when she smiled, as she did continually, with a sudden short movement of her upper lip, which moved alone, while the rest of the face was at rest, as though it was mechanically drawn up and then suddenly let down again. Her face was oblong, and was long, like her neck and her body; and

she generally preferred to sit instead of standing and
walking, when it was possible, because her long neck and
waist made her look more tall and graceful, when the
shortness of her legs was hidden. She often sat leaning
a little forward, with her hands drooping over the edge
of her lap, and with her head very slightly on one side,
as that showed the outline of her chin, which she knew
was the best point about her.

She had come to the Cape from England with her
husband two years before Rebekah was married; but he
had gone to travel in the interior of Africa, while she
had remained in Cape Town; he had gone on from Central
Africa to India and Burmah and the Far East, and had
never come back during the seven years.

When Mrs. Drummond first came, men had been very
attentive to her, and women had imitated her dress and
manners much. Now, the men who knew her began
often to discuss her at their Club and in their smoking
rooms; she had said she was twenty-eight years old when
she came, and she was twenty-eight still; and they sometimes speculated as to when she would have another
birthday, and as to whether the huge coil of hair at the
back of her head were real or artificial; and they mimicked
her little mannerisms; but the women still copied her
dresses, though not quite so much as at first; and both
men and women came to the croquet parties she gave on
the lawn of the large house, part of which she had hired.
She went to dances and receptions, and at dances still
got partners, though not so many as at first; and young
girls and older women still thought that if Mrs. Drummond wore or did anything, it must be "the right style."
Sometimes the men made jokes about her husband's long
absence ribaldly, and the women now and then discussed
it seriously; but, on the whole it attracted little attention;
it had come about so gradually. She had always said he
was coming back in six months, or in eight, or next year
(she said so still), and she showed handsome silks and
embroideries she said he sent her from the East, and she

told the women he wrote to her every week and was always longing to come back to her; so people never found the matter of great interest.

She had known Rebekah's husband before he married; she and her husband had come out in the same steamer, when he was returning from a visit to Europe; and it was she who had chosen the little house next door for him, when he had determined to marry, and helped him to furnish it. They were both musical, and sang in the same glee club, and had belonged to the same church choir; but at the time Bertie came they did not see much of each other. He had left the choir, and he laughed as other men did about the twenty-eight years and the large unchanging coil of fair hair at the back of her head; and the little gate that he had had put in the rose hedge, that he might go over more easily to practice his music with her, was now almost unused, and the grass grew in the path.

But as soon as Bertie came she called and offered to come and sit with her as she so seldom went out; and almost every afternoon she tripped over with the little silk bag over her arm; the bag varied to match each costume, and in it she carried the fancy work she was always doing for church bazaars. Sometimes she chatted to Bertie about her work, and told her about the bazaars; and sometimes she told her of her friends in England, her father a retired army officer, and their little place in the country; and sometimes she talked of the presents her husband sent her from the Far East, and what a clever man he was. She said he had a whole box full of manuscripts, that he wouldn't print just because he didn't care to, or he might have made a heap of money; but generally she talked of dresses and the prices of things in the shops in Cape Town; and now and then she told some gossip about people Bertie had never seen, why some lady was never called on, or how a certain young girl was getting herself talked about. But generally she talked of more trivial matters. Rebekah never came out and sat with them while she was there, but sent them out tea and cake. And Bertie would sit still listening to her. Often Mrs. Drummond stayed so late that when Frank came home in the evening she was still sitting there.

One afternoon, when she had just left, and Bertie sat with her hands crossed on her work and one little foot with its slipper half off dragging under the rocking chair, her brother-in-law opened the garden gate and came up towards the steps. Rebekah had heard him and had come to the front door to meet him. She had always met him there in the first days of their marriage, when he had called out from the gate, "Where is Goody-two-shoes?" and whistled for her; and now, when he did not call or whistle, she still met him there every day when she heard the click of the gate and the step on the gravel. As he gave her his bag in the doorway he said: "Great news! What do you think! The immaculate John-Ferdinand writes he is to be married to a Miss Veronica Grey, a lady who was staying at the farm for her health. He says you know her. John married!" he laughed.

As Rebekah took his bag from him she glanced round at Bertie; she was sitting bolt upright and looking out over the flower garden. Rebekah drew him in; but Bertie heard him laughing from the dining room, "I wonder whether he proposed to her, or she to him!—the saintly John!"

When Rebekah went on to the veranda again she found Bertie gone, and only her slipper lying under the rocking chair.

When supper-time came Bertie did not appear, having gone to her room feeling unwell, she said, and the next day was so unwell that Rebekah sent for a doctor, who said she was suffering from anæmia and must take rest and a tonic; and for some weeks she lay about eating little, seldom even sitting on the veranda to be talked to by Mrs. Drummond, but lying on a sofa Rebekah had placed there for her, often seeming half asleep. She even discontinued the short weekly notes she had been in the habit of writing home. Rebekah took care that John-Ferdinand's engagement was never mentioned before her, and she wished she could have prevented her receiving the little mother's letters, which were always full of news of preparations for the marriage.

Then came the news of John-Ferdinand's wedding. The little mother's letters were full of it: and Rebekah watched Bertie anxiously. But a strange change came over her. She lolled about no more. She seemed suddenly to wake up from a sleep. She was suddenly always active and restless. She laughed, and talked, and romped wildly with the children whom she had hardly noticed before. She began making the dresses, the material for which Rebekah had bought her when she first came. Sometimes she suddenly insisted on turning out a whole room and shaking the carpets and washing the windows herself; and then she would rush over to Mrs. Drummond's to get advice about trimming a new hat. When she came back she would begin weeding a flower-bed, or go into the kitchen to make a cake. She seemed able to do anything except to rest quietly or be alone. When her dresses were made, Mrs. Drummond insisted on her coming to her croquet parties and introduced her to people. Soon invitations came to her for dinner parties and dances, and, as Rebekah did not go out, she went under Mrs. Drummond's care or with Frank; and Mrs. Drummond taught her to dance. After a time the invitations became so numerous that she was always busy getting a new dress ready or repairing an old one, and seemed to live in a low fever of excitement. Frank took her to concerts and entertainments, and was proud of the attention his pretty sister-in-law awakened everywhere.

One evening, a little more than two months after the marriage, Bertie, who was going to a whist party with Mrs. Drummond, knelt partly undressed on the floor before her sister with her back turned to her, that Rebekah might arrange her hair for her. All the while she talked restlessly about the dress Mrs. Drummond was going to wear that night, and about the way she was going to change the old wedding dress which Rebekah had given her into a dancing skirt for herself. Suddenly in the midst of her talk she glanced round. "Rebekah, aren't you laughing at me? You think me so foolish!" She turned herself round and clasped her large beautifully shaped white arms round Rebekah's little body. "I talk of nothing but dressing and dancing! You must think me so foolish!—but, Rebekah, when you want to forget anything, you can read and think; you are so clever— and you have your children—I—I am so stupid—I can't help it!" She laid her head against Rebekah's breast and nestled to her like a little child. Rebekah pressed her lips on the bare white shoulder. "Rebekah, you will not let me go back to the farm? You will keep me here?" she said quickly. "I can never go back; I won't go back!—Never! Never! Promise me! Promise me!" Then, giving Rebekah no time to reply, she sprang up and ran away to her own room to finish dressing.

That was the first and last time at which, either then or afterwards, to any human being Bertie ever referred directly or indirectly to John-Ferdinand's relation with herself.

When three months more had passed, Bertie had had three proposals of marriage. One was from a very wealthy young man, whose estate adjoined a tiny fruit farm Rebekah had bought a few miles out in the country, and who had seen Bertie walking in the vineyard with Rebekah's children, and who had found out where she lived and got an introduction to her. Another was from an English officer whom she had met at Mrs. Drummond's, who was spending two months at the Cape on his way to India, and who asked her to marry him the fourth time he saw her; and one was from a young beardless, pen- niless, civil servant, whom she had danced with once or twice. Bertie refused them all. Frank and Mrs. Drum- mond both thought her very foolish to refuse the English officer, who had appealed to both to further his suit, and

who was a man with a large private income, of an aristo-
cratic English family, and a first rate fellow. But the
only suitor who seemed to concern Bertie at all was the
young civil servant. She cried when she told Rebekah
how miserable he looked when she refused him, and said
she would not go to dances any more, if dancing with
people made them miserable; but her restlessness and
dislike of being quiet or alone soon made her go again.

At this time there came a letter from John-Ferdinand
saying he and his wife were coming for a short visit to
Cape Town, as they had taken no honeymoon when they
were married, and asking Rebekah to take rooms for
them in the large house next door, in which Mrs. Drummond also had her rooms, and where John-Ferdinand
had himself stayed when in Cape Town before.

Rebekah took the rooms; but when John-Ferdinand
and his wife came, she and Bertie with the children had
gone to her little fruit and vine farm, and only the
servants were in the house, as Frank also was away up-
country on a shooting trip.

This little farm Rebekah had bought two years after
her marriage, partly with the money her father had
given her as her wedding gift, and partly she had paid
for it by placing a bond on it. Her husband had laughed
loudly at first at the idea of her buying and farming it,
but as they were married by ante-nuptial contract and
he was not responsible for her debts, and as he was
never much interested in any matter which did not immediately concern himself, he did not interfere.

Now he rather approved of it, as it saved the expense
of taking the children to the seaside when they needed
change, and supplied the household with fruit and vege-
tables free of charge. Rebekah kept an old German and
his wife there to look after it with the help of a colored
boy, and drove out herself when she had a half a day to
spare; and when her husband went away, as he often did,
for hunting or fishing expeditions, she took the children
and stayed there till he came back. She herself had

helped to mend the roof of the old cottage and to plaster and whitewash the walls, and with her own hands had planted and grafted trees and vines. She liked the labor in the open air, and she was studying books on wine-making so that if in time she were able to buy two vineyards adjoining she could make wine.

During the first days Veronica and John-Ferdinand spent much of their time sight-seeing, as she had never visited Cape Town before; but he introduced her to Mrs. Drummond, and in the mornings, which he generally spent walking in the pine woods with his book, after the first days Veronica was invited by Mrs. Drummond to sit in her private drawing-room with her and work and drink coffee at eleven. They were unlike physically and mentally, but they had tastes which harmonized. While Veronica sat upright on a high-backed chair knitting heavy squares for a bed quilt, Mrs. Drummond on a low settee, with her head a little on one side, chose carefully the shades of silk for an altar cloth which she was making. They discussed their work and the prices of things in Cape Town shops; and Mrs. Drummond chirped continually the news of the place, especially the house over the way, and Veronica listened. She said that when Rebekah was married she went at first a great deal with her husband to dances and entertainments and dinners, but after about a year and a half gave it all up and never went out visiting any more. She said she never entertained now except little men's suppers which she cooked herself for the men who came sometimes to play billiards with her husband in the evenings and to which she never asked women or sat down herself. She said it was so strange, she thought, that they should have a billiard table, when they had such a small house otherwise and kept only one servant and a stable boy. She believed Rebekah had paid for the building of the billiard room herself. She had had it done while her husband had been away on a long business trip—the contractor who had built it had repapered her bedroom and had himself told her that Rebekah had paid for the room as a surprise to her husband. Mrs. Drummond supposed it was to keep him at home she built it. She said women didn't seem to care for Rebekah—she didn't think a woman had called there for over a year; she thought many of them didn't even know she existed, as she never went to church. She said she thought men cared for her as little as women; she had never seen a man call there, except when her husband was at home. It seemed so strange to her that Rebekah should have gone away to the farm with Bertie and the children just when she knew Veronica was coming, and looked inquiringly over her silks at Veronica.

Veronica said Rebekah was always strange.

Mrs. Drummond said, Yes, she was; she used to dig in her garden with a big spade where people could see her quite well over the gate; she had heard some one say that when she was out at her farm they had seen her climb up a ladder right on to the roof, mending a smoky chimney.

Veronica said some people were born with those mannish ways. It was not Rebekah's mother's fault, as she was quite a sweet womanly woman.

Mrs. Drummond also had much to tell of Bertie; of how dull she had seemed when she first came, and how she had improved. She told of her dancing and her dresses, and about the English officer (Bertie had not told her of her two other suitors), and she said she liked Bertie better than Rebekah.

Veronica said she thought she liked Rebekah the better of the two, though she was so strange, and not always very nice and womanly in her ways. She said it seemed to her that Bertie always cared too much to attract men's attention.

Mrs. Drummond drew her upper lip up sharply and held her head a little more on a side. She said some people couldn't help attracting men's attention; and she looked very sideways with her eyes at Veronica's square shoulders and the flat foot showing below her plain skirt. She said one wondered how some women ever got married at all; but Veronica was looking down at her own square of bed quilt.

Mrs. Drummond said she thought a woman ought to take care of her appearance; that Rebekah had worn the same old brown silk dress for three years whenever she went out shopping to town, only altering it a little every year as the fashions changed, that it might not look too striking. She said a woman who could afford to build a billiard room ought to dress better. They spent all the mornings together.

Sometimes in the afternoon they went into town shopping together also; and, when they did not, they all three had tea under the oak trees on the lawn out of Mrs. Drummond's delicate little china cups, unless it was her croquet afternoon.

At last, the last day came of their visit to Cape Town. Then Veronica proposed to her husband that they should go and look at Rebekah's house and garden. She said the little mother would be so disappointed if they came back and could tell her nothing about it. John-Ferdinand felt sure his brother and sister-in-law would not object, and they walked over. They paced about Rebekah's little garden; the front door was not locked, and they went in. John-Ferdinand sat down in the drawing-room at the table to look at some books, and Veronica went to inspect the house. The stable boy was away exercising the horses and the servant girl resting in her room across the yard, and Veronica passed alone from room to room. In the dining room she noted the things on the mantle-piece and the sideboard, and Rebekah's work basket and sewing machine on the table in the corner; she examined Rebekah's bedroom and the things on the dressing table and washing stand, and Frank's little dressing room that opened from it, with its large dressing table and new carpet and comfortable easy chair; she went through to the children's bedroom opening out of Rebekah's, and

tried the handle of Rebekah's little study which led out
of the children's room, but that was the only place in the
house which was locked. She examined the kitchen and
outer pantry and the things on the shelves, and passed
down the passage to the billiard room which was built out
at the left side. She examined the cues, which she had
never seen before, and lifted the holland cover to look
at the green cloth on the table; and went to the spare
room which was now Bertie's bedroom and looked at
all her dresses hanging in the wardrobe and the whole
row of boots and shoes under the dressing table, and
unlocked and examined the large new dressing case upon
it with brushes and scent bottles heavily mounted in real
silver, which Bertie had received through the post from
some unknown admirer on her last birthday. She even
went into the yard and lifted the lids of the tanks that
held the water for the bathroom. When she had seen
everything, she went back to the little drawing-room.

John-Ferdinand was still sitting at the table with his
elbows resting on it; his head was supported by his hands;
he was looking down so intently that he did not notice
Veronica's soft entrance, till she had stepped up behind
him and put her large cool hands over both his eyes.
"Who is it?" she said with grave playfulness. He did
not speak, but taking each of her hands in one of his,
took them down from his eyes and resting them on his
shoulders held them fast there, while he looked back up
into her face.

"What are you studying so deeply?"

"Only this," he said, glancing down.

It was not a book that was open before him, but an album
of photographs. On the page before him was a picture of
Bertie which had just been taken at the request of her
father and mother. Mrs. Drummond, who had gone with
Bertie to have it taken, had insisted it should be in full
evening dress, that her beautiful arms and shoulders might
show. The photographer also had tried to make what he
believed to be an effective picture. He had turned her

head a little over her shoulder and raised her chin, so that
the lovely lines of the neck and upturned chin were not
lost. He had put in her left hand a bunch of artificial
flowers which she held against her breast, and he had required her to draw her lips in a smile. The picture resembled an imaginary type of beauty in a book of engravings
rather than Bertie. The simplicity and directness of pose
and manner, amounting almost to awkwardness, which
was the character of her beauty, was lost.

Veronica looked down at the book over his shoulder.

"It is very finely taken, is it not?" she said. "How well
they take portraits here!"

He looked down at the face too. "It's very handsome,
and just like her!"

He loosened one of her hands, and with his right drew
her to his side and made her kneel down beside him. He
turned to her and took her face softly between both his
hands and looked down into it—

> "'And learn how pure,
> How sweet can be,
> My own wife's face!'"

he said softly.

A faint flush rose into Veronica's cheeks as he looked
down into her face. He put one arm round her shoulders
and drew her nearer to him.

"My wife," he said, "I want to confess something to
you."

But then he was silent. She crossed her hands upon his
knees and looked up at him. "What is it, my husband?"

His hand rested again on the side of the album; he was
looking down at it.

"I told you once," he said, "on that day on the farm
when we became engaged, that I had once been much attracted by my young cousin, but that we had had a difference, and I felt I could not marry her. But one thing I
never told you—that, after she left the farm, she was
always with me. Wherever I went I seemed to see her.

I dared not come to the old place because it reminded me of her. At last I wrote a letter telling her I could not live without her, and asking her to come back and marry me. —That evening, when I rode over to her father's farm, for the first time after she had left, I came over partly that I might give it to the boy who was going to the town the next morning to post.—But you were so kind to me that evening—do you remember?—We sat out on the stoep, and I repeated that passage of Tennyson's to you that you liked so? It seemed to rest me to be with you, as if I got rid of her face as I saw it last look at me. And somehow, I did not post the letter that night, though it was in my pocket.—Looking back now, though I didn't realize it at the time, I am sure it was your influence upon me that kept me from sending it."

"Yes, dear!" she said.

"But, do you know, I did not destroy that letter? For weeks still I kept it in my pocket, and at any moment it might have been sent.—Then came that day when you came over to my farm to help me put things right in my house. Even then I still always had the feeling that perhaps I was getting that house ready for her.—But, darling, you know what happened that afternoon when we stood together on the back veranda? I never can quite understand it. It seemed as though some power stronger than myself were drawing me to you—and my arms were about you, and your head was on my breast, and you were to be my wife, before I knew! That night, when I went to my bedroom, I burnt the letter.—But, Veronica, my wife, do you know, that even since that time, that face has come in between you and me?" He raised the palm of his hand from Bertie's portrait. "At night I have dreamed of it; the scent of geraniums and the sight of plumbago flowers have brought it back to me, even the darkness of the night has brought it to me. It has been a white face with great innocent eyes—a child's face, that I have always seen.—It has mingled with all our life together at the farm. When I saw the sheep come out of the kraal in the morning with the dew on their backs—when I saw the thorn trees, or smelt an evening flower, a kind of sudden trembling has come over me.—Even when you first proposed we should come here for our holiday, you know how I resisted you? And still more when you proposed we should stay here in this house near to them—I felt I could not see her—could not be near her—and yet deep in my heart I knew it was best; that I must see her again, or the spell would never be broken." He looked down at the portrait, half of which his hand covered. "Even since I have been here and I have heard from you how she has devoted herself to pleasure, even when you told me of her flirtation with that English military man for whom she yet cared nothing—it made no difference to me. But now—when I look at that—all is gone!" He raised his hand and dropped it again on the face of the picture. "When I see *that,* I know it has all been an idle dream! She could never really have been mine—never been anything to me. Never have been what you are—

> 'What have I done
> That God should choose a wife for me?'"

He bent down over her. "My darling wife! Look up at me!"

Veronica raised her eyes to his, and pressed her head close to his breast.

"Do you forgive me, my darling?"

She drew his head down with her hand so that his cheek rested on her hair; and then they heard the maid servant coming into the passage, and Veronica rose to her feet to explain to her how it was they were there.

Late that night, when Veronica and John-Ferdinand lay in bed in the large room in the boarding house, the wind was blowing through the pine trees and among the oak trees in the avenue, making them crack their great branches and tap the roofs of the houses. It was just a quarter to one when John-Ferdinand woke and lay liste ing to the wind; then on the other side of the large bed he heard Veronica move.

"Are you awake?" he asked.

"I have not yet been asleep," she said.

He stretched out his arm and drew her a little nearer to him.

"You are not troubling about anything I told you this afternoon, beloved! You know it is all past?"

"Oh yes!" she said.

He drew her closer to him, her head resting on his shoulder, his arm passing under her neck.

"You trust me utterly?"

"Oh yes! my dear one." They both lay looking upwards in the dark, and heard the wind tearing at the branches of the trees.

"There is *nothing* troubling you, my dear one?" He turned his face more towards her.

"No, nothing, dear—at least," she hesitated, "there is perhaps one very little thing—such a very little thing, that you will think me foolish! You must tell me if I'm wrong. You always know so much better what is right and wise than I."

"What is it, my dear one?" He put out his right hand and took her left that lay on the white coverlet.

She spoke slowly, lisping a little as a child might, talking to its mother: "It's such a little thing—such a small thing—but, you know, ever since we were married it has sometimes made me a little sad, I've felt as if you didn't *quite* trust me!"

"What is it?—There is nothing I know, or feel, or think I would not share with you!"

"Oh, it's only a little thing!—I've wondered sometimes," she murmured softly, "why you didn't tell me what you and Bertie quarreled about! You told me you had a difference; but you never said what it was. You didn't even tell me to-day."

He was quiet for a moment; then he said, "I did not tell you because it was a matter more hers than mine.—She did not ask me to make any promise not to repeat it—she asked nothing—but I took it that she was speaking to me in confidence. I could never have told anyone but you—but you are not some one else. You are me, myself! When I speak to you I speak within my own soul."

"But you must not tell me anything, dear, that you would rather not. I always know that what you wish to do is right! You know better than I."

"But I want to tell you! There shall be nothing that divides between us." He turned on his side and drew her nearer to him, so that from shoulder to feet their long straight figures lay side by side.

"The reason why I could not marry my cousin," he said, "was this"—and then he told her the story of the parlor in the bush and what Baby-Bertie told him.

Half an hour later the wind was still blowing as wildly as ever; but they lay asleep with their hands interclasped and his breath on her face.

The next day when all their trunks were strapped for starting, John-Ferdinand went to the station to call a cab. He returned sooner than he had expected, as he had met one in the avenue. As he came back into the bedroom, Veronica was sitting with her traveling cloak on, and her hat on the table beside her, bending over the dressing table, writing. She thought it was the maid come to begin carrying things down, till he stood almost at her shoulders. She started lightly, and spread her broad hand over the page on which she was writing.

"What is it?" he asked, bending over her.

A faint tint of roses rushed into her white cheeks.

"A little surprise for you.—A secret.—Something you mustn't know about."

He stooped and pressed his cheek against her smooth head, and turned to help the maid carry down the packages.

An hour later they were driving through Cape Town on their way to the docks.

"I wish to stop at the post office," she said. "I have

st about something I forgot to order at a
I want sent on to me."

got to the post office he offered to get out
a. for her: but she said she was tired of sitting
and ild rather get out herself, and before he could
speak, had jumped out and put it in the box. The letter
was addressed to Mrs. Drummond, but in a large, round
hand, quite unlike her own angular small one. When she
had put it in the box, they drove down to the docks, and
in two hours they had sailed away to their home in the
Eastern Province.

CHAPTER VII

Raindrops in the Avenue

WHEN Bertie and Rebekah came back from the fruit farm, Rebekah was busy putting her house right, and no one noticed that, on the first morning she went to see Mrs. Drummond, Bertie did not stay so long as usual, nor was there anyone to note that, neither on that day nor the next, nor the day after, did Mrs. Drummond come to see her.

But on the day after that, as Bertie sat sewing in the veranda, Mrs. Drummond came with her workbag on her arm and sat in the low cane chair opposite her; and Bertie thought it must have been her own fancy which had made it seem that Mrs. Drummond had not been so glad to see her when she returned from the farm.

Mrs. Drummond said it was a fine afternoon, and made a remark about the new pattern she was tatting; and Bertie answered her; then they sat silent for a while, with the rich warm scent from Rebekah's flower garden coming up to them.

Then Mrs. Drummond said, without raising her head, that her cousin, John-Ferdinand's wife, seemed a very nice woman. Bertie said yes, and asked Mrs. Drummond if she thought it would not look better if she featherstitched the sleeve of the baby's dress she was making. Mrs. Drummond said she thought so: and then there was quiet again with only the sound of Bertie's needle and Mrs. Drummond's shuttle and of their sleeves rustling against their sides as they worked. The parrot, who had been to sleep, woke suddenly and began throwing down grains of mielies on Bertie's head. Then Mrs. Drummond drooped her head on the opposite side from the one on which it had been drooping before and said, "Did you never go to school when you were a girl?"

"No," said Bertie, without looking up, "my sister taught me out of her old books; and my mother taught me to sew."

Mrs. Drummond drooped her head lower than before, looking at her work. "So you never had any real teacher to teach you?" she said.

"No," Bertie said. "At least," she added, hurriedly, "once—for a few months—I had a teacher."

Mrs. Drummond drooped her head yet lower.

"I suppose," she said, half glancing up, "it was a lady whom you had to teach you?"

Bertie said quickly, "No—it was a man—he did not stay long.—Don't you think that the oranges I sent you yesterday were just right for marmalade?" she added quickly.

"Yes-s," said Mrs. Drummond slowly; then she looked up fully into Bertie's face.

For a little while Bertie heard only the click of the tatting shuttle, as it turned to let the thread out, and the tick of her own needle; the scent from the flower garden seemed to come up almost overpoweringly.

"Yes, the peels of the oranges were very fine and thick," Mrs. Drummond said slowly.

"I will go and fetch you some tea," Bertie said quickly, rising. "Rebekah will have made it by this time."

"Oh, no, thank you," Mrs. Drummond said. "I have some people coming to have tea with me, and must go at once or they will find me out.

"Oh, please do not trouble!" she said, as Bertie darted to pick up her ball of tatting cotton which had dropped from her lap as she rose. Bertie caught it and handed it to her, and she put it in her bag. "How very nice your sister's flower garden looks this afternoon—she always seems to have more flowers and sweeter smelling than anyone else! Good afternoon!"

Then the little figure in its large-figured Japanese silk dress fluttered across the garden and out through the gate in the rose hedge and across the lawn to the house beyond.

When Mrs. Drummond was gone Bertie sat in the rocking chair, sewing. There was a stain of red on each cheek deeper than the red of the damask rose in Rebekah's garden; gradually it turned to pale pink and then white.

The next afternoon Mrs. Drummond had her weekly croquet party, but she did not send over to ask if Bertie was coming, and Bertie helped Rebekah to preserve the oranges they had brought, and did not go, but in the evening she went to explain why she had not been.

She found Mrs. Drummond in her bedroom before the chest of drawers, putting them neat. Mrs. Drummond did not pause in her work and hardly looked up; and when Bertie had stood beside her chatting for a little while she went away. Mrs. Drummond seemed preoccupied. For two weeks after that she did not meet her again; then she overtook her in the avenue. Mrs. Drummond talked of some purchases she had made in Town and said good-by at the gate. Then for a week she did not see her again. Twice Bertie had gone as far as the rose hedge, meaning to ask her whether she had done anything to pain her; but both times she had turned back when her hand was on the gate.

Then came a Wednesday evening when Bertie was going to an evening party at a house two avenues off. It was to be a young-people's dance in honor of the fifteenth birthday of the daughter of the house, and, as most of the dancers would be under thirty, she needed no older woman to go with her; and Frank was going, who, as he grew older, preferred going to the dances and picnics where very young girls were rather than to those where there were women nearer his own age.

As the house was close at hand they were to walk, and Rebekah had brought Bertie to her own room to dress her, because of the large glass there.

"Don't you think it looks nice?" Rebekah asked.

Bertie was standing before the wardrobe door; she looked like a head of a large white hydrangea, in the gauze dress Rebekah had helped her to make. "Oh, I think it looks lovely!"

Rebekah, standing behind her, looked at the dress critically. Her own small, delicate face was drawn and white, as though needing rest. "Your hair is not high enough if you are to wear the flowers under it," she said.

She mounted a footstool and stood behind Bertie and unwound the coils of back hair to pin them higher.

Then Bertie said in her low, soft drawl, "Rebekah haven't *you* ever wanted to go to dances? Don't you want to dance?"

"Yes," Rebekah said, "when I was a child I liked to dance. I used to go up into the kloof under the Kaffir-bean trees and dance and sing and throw up my arms till I got drunk and had to lie down on my face."

"Oh, I don't mean that kind of dancing," Bertie drawled slowly, "alone, in the kloof, by yourself! I mean with pretty dresses and other people to ask you to dance. I don't like you to stay alone here when I go, ' she said in a yet softer drawl; "you'd look so pretty if you were dressed in pretty dresses like me—you'd look like a fairy. Don't you think it would be nice to dance with other people, eh, Rebekah?"

"Perhaps," Rebekah said, "if you had some one you liked very much, and you two were quite alone—and you could go on dancing on and on forever with no one there, it might be better than dancing alone—perhaps better than almost anything. That will do, I think.'" She got off the stool.

Bertie still stood impassively with her arms hanging on either side. "Yes," she said dreamily, "it would be nice to dance with some one you liked very much; I never have. But, Rebekah, you know, I don't care very much whom I dance with now. It's the light and the noise and the going round and round I like. All the men are so kind to me, too," she added slowly, "and all the girls also; they don't mind that I dance so much all the evening. Isn't it nice of them, Rebekah?"

"Very." Rebekah was now fastening a white, half-blown rose on her breast.

"You know, I like it so when you go into a room, and they all look at you, and something so nice runs all up your body, when they all look at you and think you look nice. I like it," she said slowly. "Have you ever been to a real ball, Rebekah?"

"When I was first married. Frank went; and I wanted to go with him."

She turned to a wardrobe behind the door and took from it a dress of black diaphanous silky material speckled all over with tiny silver spangles, each carefully cut out and sewn on separately. She held it up by the shoulders.

"How beautiful!" exclaimed Bertie, crossing her hands. "I never saw such a dress. Whose is it?"

"I made it for myself," said Rebekah. Bertie came nearer to touch it. "Mrs. Drummond had one from Paris, like this, only white. Frank said it was the most beautiful dress he had ever seen. When she did not want it any more I bought it from her as a pattern." She looked down at the dress. "I cut out each little spangle separately and sewed it on. It took me three weeks to make it." She turned the dress over. "This was the wreath to wear with it," she said, holding up a wreath of frosted leaves.

"You must have looked beautiful," Bertie said. "Your teeth, your dark hair—and the spangles—just like the night! Did Frank like it?"

"He said it was not bad."

"Do you never wear it now?"

"No, I keep it."

As she was hanging the dress up, Bertie said suddenly, "Rebekah, do you think, if Mrs. Drummond was your friend, that she—that she—would really care for you —that she—that she wouldn't—take part with anyone against you?"

"I don't know, dear. I know very little of her. We have nothing in common. I don't understand her."

At that moment Frank's voice sounded from the hall, calling out that Bertie must hurry or it would rain before they started; and Rebekah wrapped her sister up in the large, red silk opera cloak she had made for herself when she had first married and folded Bertie's white satin dancing shoes in silver paper, that she might carry them.

"Don't mend the stockings," Bertie whispered as she turned to go, half bending over her; "I'll darn them all to-morrow."

They went into the hall where Frank was waiting, and Rebekah saw they had their umbrellas and waterproofs with them. The night was of inky blackness; it seemed it might rain at any moment, and Rebekah stood in the doorway holding the candle high to light them down the veranda steps and along the path to the gate. When the two figures had gone out at it, she closed the door and turned back into the house.

In the dining room she took from the work table a large basket with the week's mending in it, and, placing the lighted candle on the top, went through the room into the one where her children slept. She paused at each bed to see that the child in it was covered; and then, still carrying the lighted candle on the basket, she opened a door at the end of the room and went into the next.

The room was a small one, made by cutting off the end of the children's bedroom with a partition. She had had it before as a study for herself where she could always hear the children call if they needed her at night. It was hardly larger than a closet, but there was a window in it and a small outer door, and both looked out on to the rockery and the plumbago hedge but on nothing else, and there was a small door close beside the window, which she had had put in that at any time she might run out and work a little in the garden. The walls were covered with a red-brown paper, and in the center stood a large oblong desk with drawers; before it stood an old armchair with a deep dent where a head had often rested. A waste-paper basket stood beside it. In the corner stood the tall wooden cabinet which she had had when she was a girl to hold her fossils and insects, and which she had brought with her when she married; on a ledge in front her microscope stood. There was no other furniture on the floor, but on the walls hung three small bookshelves. One was behind the armchair, between the window and door; and in the corner beside it, on a little wooden bracket, was a tiny statue of Hercules a few inches high in old discolored marble. This she had got from Mrs. Drummond when she first married, in exchange for a length of green silk which she had had as a wedding present. Mrs. Drummond told her her husband had bought it when he was traveling in Italy, but had left it behind with many other things he did not want when he set out on his travels in the Far East.

On another hanging bookshelf to the right of the desk were books of poetry, science, history, and travel; all of them much worn cheap editions except one handsome new copy of Darwin's *Variation of Plants and Animals under Domestication* bound in calf, which also she had got from Mrs. Drummond two years before, in exchange for some pots of roses, to stand in her drawing room. It had been sent from England addressed to her husband, but as he was now in the mountains of Japan, and had said she need send nothing on to him, she was glad to let Rebekah have it.

On the wall to the left of the desk were three very small shelves, and on them were science primers and school books from which Rebekah had taught and most of which she had bought with the money her mother gave her for herself for drying peaches when she was a child. They were all now very old. What she felt for them was what no one feels for the books out of which they have been taught by another—it was what a full grown doe might feel for a little mountain stream, which it had found for itself when it was a very young fawn wandering quite alone and parched with thirst, and from which it had drunk. It might have tasted of many finer clearer streams since then, but in none of them all would the water be to it like that in the little stream it found all for itself when it was a small thing, quite alone, and dying of thirst.

There was a *Cornwallis Grammar* with the back worn off with which she had followed her father about over the plowed lands one day, trying to get him to explain to her what a preposition really was, and, when he answered her absently in the cut dried words of the book, she had gone away behind the hedge and lain with the book open before her, and prayed that she might really understand. There was a Smith's *Latin Principia,* the gilt letters worn off its side and black back; she bought it when she was nine years old with three-and-sixpence which her father gave her when he went into the town to sell his wool and she went with him. She had bought it at a shop where they had books in the window, and had carried it home pressed against her chest all the way in the cart. She knew they would laugh at her if they knew she meant to learn Latin; but at night she sat up in her own room, writing the exercises by the light of a tallow candle she had begged from old Ayah, happy, thinking she would at last know all the Romans knew—what, she did not quite know.

On the shelf below were a number of cheap translations of Greek and Latin authors, which she had bought when she had found out she would never know Greek or Latin enough to read in the originals.

On the lowest shelf were five or six thin science primers in brown covers. She had seen them advertised in one of her father's newspapers, and she had sent money for them to a bookseller's in Cape Town who advertised them; when the parcel came by post she had opened it on her bed, and she had lain down by the books and felt nearly faint with gladness. The Botany she liked because it taught her how to examine the parts of flowers and helped to take away that almost painful longing she had felt when she looked at them to understand a little why they were as they were. The Geology she liked much; but it had distressed her because, like the botany book, it was written for people in England, and the plants and rocks and fossils mentioned she could not find in Africa. Her father had some shelves of old brown books: she had read nearly all of them; but, except the histories, none interested her much: they did not explain to her the world about her, what it was. He had one book called *Pre-Adamite Earth,* which she read and agonized and prayed over, trying to understand it; only after she had grown up she realized it was a book no human being could understand, least of all the man who wrote it. But he had a large old atlas which he gave her, which lay now on the top of her wooden cabinet. She used to lie on her back for hours, with the atlas open on her chest leaning against her drawn-up knees and with the Geography at her side for reference, and look at the different countries and seas, and picture them, and fancy she was there, especially China and Japan and Greenland and South America; till her heart got large with joy, the feeling that she was all over the world. On the shelf below were books of children's poetry, and the one or two story books she had as a child; but the books on the shelf above them were much more poetry to her. She felt so for them, that, if she had lived to be a woman of eighty and some one had suddenly come into the room where she was with one of those old worn books in his hand, her heart would have throbbed, and the memory of the hunger of the fierce young soul for knowledge, as it first looks out on life, would all have come back to her.

Over the door leading to the children's bedroom was tacked the picture of the Madonna from the *Illustrated London News* which she had had pasted over the head of her bed when she was a child. It was the only ornament the room held except the little statue of Hercules in the corner.

Often at night, as she sat alone in that room, she had

pictured to herself what great works of art must be like, or great orchestral music. She had seen or heard neither, but she dreamed of them, as she dreamed of what it must be to be one of a company of men and women in a room together, all sharing somewhat the same outlook on life and therefore thinking somewhat the same thought, and able to understand one another without explanation—a thing she knew was possible somewhere in time and space, which actually did exist though she might never know it.

On the brown carpet on the floor was a mark like a footpath where the nap had been worn off, running right round the desk. This was where she walked round and round, because the room was not large enough to allow of her walking up and down, as she used to under the trees in the kloof.

For days often, and sometimes for weeks, she did not come into this room; but she knew it was there; and there was always a quiet spot in her mind answering to it.

To-night she set the basket of darning down on the floor beside the desk and lit the reading lamp, and, when she had put the candle out, sat down in the armchair, leaning her head against its dented back.

It was a long time since she got up before sunrise that morning to warm the baby's milk, and she was tired. She was to have another child in seven months, and her legs and the lower part of her body ached; but it was never the same to her if she sat to rest in that room or any other. From her shelves, the bindings of her books looked down at her, each one a little brown face that seemed to love her. Behind each was hidden the mind of some human creature which at some time had touched her own; they were all the intellectual intercourse she had ever known. Not one was there because it was a rare or old copy, or had an expensive binding; each one was there because at some time she had lived close to it and it had penetrated her.

After a time she drew the basket nearer her and began to work. For nearly an hour she sewed on buttons and darned little worn places in little garments, till there was nothing left in the basket but a few pairs of socks and stockings; she took up one and began to darn it, but soon put it with the mended things in the basket with the unmended at the top, and then leaned back again on her chair, resting.

Outside, the rain had begun to fall; it was dropping on the thatched roof with a soft soo-o-shing sound. She lay in the chair and listened to it.

After a time she drew her chair closer to the desk, and from one of the top drawers took a book. It was an exercise book in a black cover. She laid it open on the desk.

In the drawer below were six or seven such books; some filled with the sharply pointed writing of a very small child who tries to write a flowing hand. In these were verses and short stories and little allegories told in rhyme —one very long allegory in blank verse, which was never quite finished—and one book held a story as long as a novel, and quite finished—and there were a few prose passages copied from books, which had struck the child as beautiful.

Some others were filled with the larger, more rounded handwriting of a young girl from twelve to twenty. They also held stories, but few had verses; and there were discussions on abstract questions. One book was a diary full of small daily entries, a book read, a visit found, seeds planted, but once or twice working out great plans for the life that was to be lived—countries to be visited—books to be written—scientific knowledge to be gained—all written with absolute confidence. Now and then there were passionate personal entries, almost incoherent little calls for love and friendship; but they came not often, and some had been scratched out.

There were a couple of books filled after marriage; but the entries dwindled. Months passed in which nothing was written. After a child had been born and it had been necessary to lie still for weeks, there were dissertations on some abstract matter, or an allegory; but generally there

were only short scraps: outlines of stories never to be
filled in, and short diary notes of a very practical nature:
on such a date the baby was weaned, or a new servant
was hired, or she had planted a seed in her garden and
set down the date to mark how long it took to come up.
And sometimes (generally after a long interval in which
nothing had been written) there were short notices, so
written that no one into whose hand the book should fall
could have understood them; in which dashes and letters
took the place of words; such as "Came into the billiard
room unexpectedly. J. D.—Under the table. Ran out.
Well, it doesn't matter, it doesn't matter. J. F." or
"Again—again—again—to-day!"

To-night she drew the book towards her. It was four
months since she had opened it; she had had no time since
she returned from the Eastern Province. When last she
wrote she had been sitting up for a night, to make poultices for her boy who had bad earache, and, between
whiles as he slept, she had written.

She had been carrying on a long discussion with herself
as to what was the real cause of that curious hunger for
an exact knowledge of things as they are, of naked truth
about all things small or great, material and also psychic,
which seems to haunt so many of us, and which seems so
little to have affected the thought and life of Europe
through so many ages. She had advanced the view that,
to find any true likeness to the modern feeling, we had to
go back to the life and thought of classical days, especially
to the life and thought in Greece in the fourth century
before Christ.

Here she had had to go and make a poultice, and she
had branched off on a side line when she came back, to
question if it were not just the resemblance on this point—
this common desire for an exact knowledge of reality, of
things exactly as they were, first and before all things—
which gives us that strange sense of nearness to ancient
classical thought and art. Was it not this deep reverence
for reality, even in material things, which made us feel so

curiously akin to, say, a little Greek statue, in which every muscle and organ have been carved with solemn care to follow life—sex organ and knee as devoutly as eye and forehead? Was it not this common hunger after a knowledge of reality as an end in itself which, in spite of the difference in our technical knowledge and outlook in many respects, yet makes us feel, when we read the page of a translation of some book two thousand years old, as if it might have been composed this morning by some one walking up and down in the pine woods behind the house, as well as by a peripatetic pacing the paths of a garden at Athens two thousand years ago?—Which makes us feel that if, in the sunshine on the graveled path in our own garden to-day, a certain old man with flattened nose and rough cloak were found lying, we should be able to throw ourselves down beside him with our elbows on the earth and listen to his talk and share in his outlook, almost as we might have done two thousand years ago? Is it not this which, though we know thousands of things they never knew, yet, when we read them, makes us feel—"My own! My own!"?

Is it not perhaps just the absence of this passionate desire to penetrate into the nature of all things and know them exactly as they are, which, in spite of their much nearer relation to us in order of time and by ties of blood and descent, makes us feel so infinitely more removed from the worthy Christian fathers and the sometimes gifted writers and thinkers of the Middle Ages (save a few heretics), and even from the mass of men of our own time—perhaps the very parents who bore us or begot us—persons who, living in the present, belong yet to that past which, accepting all things, found virtue in faith and not in a keen unending questioning of the facts of life; so that when we, who to-day share the new spirit, strive to come near them, we seem to be looking at them across an impassable mental chasm and through the haze of an almost infinite moral distance?

Here she had been interrupted again. When she came

back she had gone on to seek more narrowly after the cause of the new spirit.—Was it because we were more virtuous, that for us a knowledge of all reality—whether it concerned the shading of the down on a butterfly's wing, the exact nature of a handful of earth, the antennæ of a beetle, the movements of a planet, the how of sexual emotions or of social organization—was to us a matter of primary importance, all willful shutting of our eyes to it a crime, and all willful misleading of our fellows with regard to it a social wrong?—while to men of the past, or men of the present holding the attitude of the past, such knowledge was only desirable and to be sought after if direct personal advantage to individuals could be seen to flow from it, while the willful shutting of one's eyes to it, or the misleading of one's fellows with regard to it, might even be most virtuous actions if personal good seemed to flow from it?

She had held that it was not because we were more virtuous, but that the difference between the two attitudes took its rise entirely from two opposing intellectual conceptions of the nature of the Universe.

According to the old Christian conception, the Universe was a thing of shreds and patches and unconnected parts. Outside all we see and touch was the great individual Will, which had called into being wind and water, man, planet, star, stone, beast and plant, by the arbitrary action of its power, and which at any moment might return it all to nothingness, even the life that moves in animals having no permanence, and only that life in man which they called the soul having any future, though it had no past, and rose into being at an arbitrary fiat, like a stone and plant.

For the man intellectually holding this view to be true, the Universe could resemble only the heap of toys which a child gathers about it on the floor: doll, bugle, brick, book, having no subtle, living, connection with one another, being there together only because the will of the child has brought them there.

Solemnly to study each toy because, when you understand its structure, it might throw light on that of all the others, and closely to study their relation to one another—this doll lies at such an angle to that bugle—would be the work of a fool, when any moment a kick of the child might disturb all their relations.

For the man sincerely holding the old view, truth, the thing to be loved and sought after more than life, can be only a knowledge of the will of the arbitrary ruling individual, and the only thing of real importance in life must be the relation between that one indestructible element in man and the ruling individuality. Truth, as it regards the shading of a feather on a bird's wing, the movement of a planet, the order of social growth, the structure of a human body, can be of no value; it may even be a positive duty to misrepresent or repress the knowledge of facts, if they bear on, or seem to have a bearing injurious to, the relations of the individual man and the all-powerful individual.

For the man holding this view of the structure of the Universe, "truth," in the sense in which it is a thing of value, cannot be simply the knowledge of all facts and all relations, as nearly as he can attain to it; it can be only the knowledge of certain facts for a definite purpose. The suppression of Galileo's discovery that the world moved—the habitual suppressing in art of certain aspects of life—the habit of continual questioning within oneself, not "Is this thing true?" but "What will be the effect of such knowledge or such a statement?"—is not, in the man holding this old view of the Universe, a sign of low morality and anti-social feeling; it is simply the logical outcome of his view of the Universe. For him to take any other course would not be rational, would not be virtuous, would not even be sane.

For us all this has changed.

Slowly advancing knowledge has forced on us an entirely new view of the Universe. Step by step we have been brought almost to the standpoint from which many an old Greek looked out on life.

For us once again the Universe has become one, a whole, and it lives in all its parts. Step by step advancing knowledge has shown us the internetting lines of action and reaction which bind together all that we see and are conscious of.

Between the farthest star and the planet earth we live on, between the most distant planet and the ground we tread on, between man, plant, bird, beast and clod of earth, everywhere the close internetted lines of interaction stretch; nowhere are we able to draw a sharp dividing line, nowhere find an isolated existence. The prism I hold in my hand, rightly understood, may throw light on the structure of the farthest sun; the fossil I dug out on the mountain side this morning, rightly studied, may throw light on the structure and meaning of the hand that unearths it; between the life that moved in the creature that plowed in the mud of the lake shores three million years ago and the life which beats in my brain and moves in my eyes here in the sunshine to-day, I can see long unbroken lines of connection. Between spirit that beats within me and body through which it acts, between mind and matter, between man and beast, between beast and plant and plant and earth, between the life that has been and the life that is, I am able to see nowhere a sharp line of severance, but a great, pulsating, always interacting whole. So that at last it comes to be, that, when I hear my own heart beat, I actually hear in it nothing but one throb in that life which has been and is—in which we live and move and have our being and are continually sustained.

Having this view of the nature of the Universe forced on us, is it possible that our view of the nature and value of truth should not be changed?

The physiologist, when he seeks to study an organism, puts beneath his microscope an almost invisible spot of blood or shred of animal tissue, and devotes days or months to its study, not because he believes the individual shred or speck to be of any peculiar value, but because he knows that once rightly understood it may explain to him the nature of the entire organism of which it is a part. So we, who are dominated by this new conception of existence, are compelled to look upon the exact knowledge of even the smallest and most insignificant fact as sacred, never knowing when it may turn into the key which may unlock for us the meaning of part of that great universal life of which it is an integral fragment.

Holding this view of the Universe, we are compelled to walk almost awe-filled among even the small things of life; and, as the old Christian father, after much contemplation, was compelled at last to cry, "There *is* no small sin—all violation of the will of God is great," so we also are almost compelled to cry, "There is no small truth—all truth is great!"

Holding the old conception of existence, it was quite possible to believe that, between God and man, mind and matter, soul and body, there were many chinks and crannies where a lie might creep in and hide itself and be quite innoxious. For us there is no faith in such possibility; we can no more nurse a false conception without it causing injury than a foreign substance can be intruded into a highly organized body without causing disorganization and disease. Whether the truth concerns the feathers on a pigeon's wing or the constitution of a lump of earth or a psychological fact, we know that it is vital.

Here she had had to leave off the first night. When she began the next night she went on to discuss how this new intellectual conception of the nature of the Universe necessarily influenced our spiritual and moral outlook: how, for the man dominated by it, the existence of an extraneous will dealing arbitrarily with the things of existence was inconceivable, and the true revelation of the unseen and unknown beyond was to be found in the study of the seen and knowable about us; how, for us, the true act of religious worship was the search after a knowledge of all reality; how, for us, not less devout and religious than the old monk, who spent his life in copying and embroidering his missal or studying his gospel, is the man who to-day humbly devotes his life to the study of a spider's eye or the nature of a mineral, not knowing or seeking any direct benefit to flow to himself from the knowledge, but dominated by the profound conviction that the true comprehension of the smallest existence about us brings us nearer to the comprehension of the whole.

Then she went on to argue to herself that, for us, the true atheist was of necessity no longer the man who denies a knowledge of an unknown and unseen personality, but rather the man who believes that by juggling with facts he can outwit the Universe and make that which he knows is not as if it were; and that the greatest wrong a man can commit towards his fellow is the willful misleading of him as to any reality; and the sin against the Holy Ghost —the sin which hath no forgiveness—is the conscious, willful blinding of our own eyes to any form of reality.

So far she had scribbled four weeks before, when she was sitting up to make the poultices. Since then she had not thought of her discussion. But that morning, when she took the children to walk in the woods, she walked up and down under a pine tree, as they picked flowers, talking it over to herself. To-night she opened her exercise book on the desk, climbed up in the chair and drew her feet back under her, partly because it was cold and she kept them warm so, and partly because the desk was a little high. She knelt up, bending low over the book, and began to write. She wrote quickly in a large sprawling hand, because she had much to say.

She went on to illustrate how our new attitude towards truth influenced all our personal relations in practical life. She illustrated it first by the feeling of the mother who looks down at the head of her little new-born baby sleeping at her breast. The old mother, if she were religious, looked down at it and prayed for it that it might cling to the dogmas which she would teach it, and, allowing nothing to turn its faith from them, at last attain everlasting joy. The new mother, when she looks down at the little head upon her breast, whispers in her heart: "Oh, may you seek after truth. If anything I teach you be false, may you throw it from you, and pass on to higher and deeper knowledge than I ever had. If you are an artist, may no love of wealth or fame or admiration and no fear of blame or misunderstanding make you ever paint, with pen or brush, an ideal or a picture of external life otherwise than as you see it; if you become a politician, may no success for your party or yourself or the seeming good of even your nation ever lead you to tamper with reality and play a diplomatic part. In all the difficulties which will arise in life, fling yourself down on the truth and cling to that as a drowning man in a stormy sea flings himself on to a plank and clings to it, knowing that, whether he sink or swim with it, it is the best he has. If you become a man of thought and learning, oh, never with your left hand be afraid to pull down what your right has painfully built up through the years of thought and study, if you see it at last not to be founded on that which is; die poor, unloved, unknown, a failure—but shut your eyes to nothing that seems to them the reality."

Then she scribbled on to show how the new attitude influenced the emotional relations between man and woman.

All women of the past and in the present find woman's heaven when their head rests on the shoulder of the man they love and his strong arm is about them; and as dear to the women of to-day as to the women of the remotest past is the love and tenderness of the man she is bound to. But yet the cry of our hearts is not the same. Beyond the cry for passionate tenderness there is another—"Give us truth! Not jewels, not ease—nor even caresses, precious as they are to us—are the first thing we seek: give us truth. We are weary with seeking for truth and being baffled everywhere by subterfuge and seeming; in your eyes, beloved, let us never have to seek it, let it come out to meet us. The love which is not planted on a naked sincerity, which needs subterfuge and self-deception and the deception of another for its life, is a plucked flower stuck into the sand; what matter how soon it dies—it has no real life. Our love will more easily survive the most awful knowledge you can give us than the realization that you have once willingly misled us. Should you lay your head upon our knees and tell us your heart had gone forever to another, it would be easier for us to bear than that you had fed us with one subterfuge to shield us from knowledge. The highest sacrament of love we thirst for between our two souls is an almighty sincerity; if there is not this, then for us love's holy of holies is defamed."

She bent lower over her writing, scribbling quicker and quicker.

Then she painted the effect of our new feeling for reality upon the moral judgments we pass upon ourselves and others.

When we lie awake in the dark of night thinking, what causes us to start and our cheek to burn? That which makes us shift restlessly from side to side, as if we were trying to shake off something, is often not the remembrance of what men and women of the past would have regarded as our greatest crime; it may be no infringement of any decalogue that ever yet was written; it may be just some written or spoken word or some act, perhaps seeming to us, even at the moment it was written or spoken or done, to be right and even magnanimous, but which falsified our relation with another or that other's relation to some one else. We remember it with a pain which manifest wrongdoings, recognized by the world, have not left; it is, when we remember it, as if a little knife cut into our heart, and we know till death comes it will always be sticking there.

She scribbled on to show how it altered our moral judgment of others; how, for us, the great criminal was not necessarily the murderer, the ruffian, the drunkard, the prostitute, or even the frank, direct, and open liar; but, maybe, a spirit encased in a fair and gentle body, rich in many graces of character and manner, openly breaking no social law and with no need to lie directly to others, because it lies always and so successfully to itself and within itself and acts persistently in harmony with that lie: a rotten apple with dead seeds and a worm at its core, and a shining surface. The old view was that the great sin lay in not speaking truth to your fellow when thereby you caused him practical loss; for us there is one infinitely greater—the sin of the soul that refuses to see the naked truth within itself and therefore can never show it. The man who lies to his fellow poisons an external relation— but the soul which lies in itself to itself, acting always a part before itself, becomes a poison, a deadly fungus that scatters its poisonous seeds unconsciously whenever it is touched.

The rain was now falling in torrents, running off the thatched roof and streaming down the rockery and along the garden path; but she scribbled on without hearing it.

She was trying now to show the effect of the new attitude with regard to truth on our feeling for art. For the man or woman holding the old view, the story, the picture, the statue in which certain artistically necessary aspects of life are intentionally suppressed or misrepresented for certain practical ends, the human nature falsely painted because it seemed undesirable to paint it as it is, the fig-leaf tied across the loin of the noblest statue, gives no pain and is still art; while, for those of us who have long set an intellectual value on sincerity, a mental habit has been formed which makes the perception of the willful suppression of truth emotionally painful and so destroys our sense of perfection in the object in which it appears. The true reproduction of a sunrise, or a narrative that shows the working of a lofty spirit, may be more delightful art for us than the art which reproduces the texture of a lady's dress or paints the picture of a small soul; but the representation of the smallest or slightest aspect of life, if we are conscious of truth in it, in so far satisfies an emotional need in us and becomes for us, so far

at least, an object of satisfaction; while no art can be art
for us, however lofty its claims, which does not satisfy
what has slowly become a master need of our natures. A
work of art may have many other elements of beauty for
us; but it must be a revelation of truth for us, or it means
nothing. Better the true picture of a beggar in his rags
than the willfully false picture of a saint.

So she scribbled on, hearing nothing of the rain outside,
bending low over her paper with her chin pressed down
on her breast. But presently she began to write slower
and slower, and presently raised herself and sat watching
the lamp. Then she sank half back in the chair, still on
her knees and, after a time, began slowly drawing with her
outstretched hand the pictures of faces down one edge of
the page she had written on. They came out slowly, one
below the other, some with sharp features, some with dark
beards and curls, some with blunt features, some grotesque
and some beautiful; she did not seem to be looking at
them as she drew them. When she got to the bottom of
the page she dipped the pen into the ink again and sat
turning it round and round in her fingers and dipped it
again. She was questioning in how far she had been right
in her conclusions, and arguing the other side. Then she
jumped suddenly from the chair and began to pace the
room in the footpath round the desk. She clasped her
hands behind her with the pen still between her fingers,
and it made a large inkspot at the back of her little blue
print skirt.

What, after all, did she know of art, except the art in
literature? The book of photographs of great statuary,
which she had bought at great expense, had so disgusted
her with the modern fig leaves tied on with wire that she
had never brought it into her study but had thrown it into
a corner of the drawing-room. What would she really
feel if she could study plastic art in all its forms, not only
Greek, Assyrian, Egyptian, Indian, not through books at
second-hand, but actually, as though living, in climates

that produced them! [1] She shot out her hand greedily as if grasping them.

After she had walked for a time, she stopped suddenly at the door of the children's room, and, half opening it, stood listening to hear if they were still quiet and asleep; then she closed it softly and walked and walked on with her hands behind her. Her thoughts had wandered far now, though the new chain of thought was bound link by link to the old. From thinking of Greek art and literature, her thought wandered on to the old, old problem which had held so great a fascination for her, even when she was a child and read, in her father's old brown leather-covered *History of the Ancient World,* its stiff long-worded accounts of the Assyrian and Egyptian and Roman and other early empires, and had traced with a dry pen on the mildewed map in the front of the book the path over the mountains which the Goths and the Vandals and the Huns took when they came to overrun Italy and destroy Rome, till the map had worn quite thin there. It was the old, old problem that had always fascinated her: why, when a nation or a race or a dominant class has reached a certain point of culture and material advance, has it always seemed to fall back from it, and the nation or race or class to be swept away? Always the march of human progress has died out there, to be taken up again by some other race or class in some distant part of the globe or after the lapse of centuries—to die out there also after a time, never proceeding persistently in a straight line. Was there an immutable law, based on an organic and inherent quality in human nature, which caused this arrest? Was it futile for us to hope that human advance might ever proceed persistently and unbroken in one direction? Was that which governed its arrest an organic law, like that which ordains the length of a man's beard, which, however long the individual may live, when it has once

[1 What she actually wrote was: "Not through books at second hand, but to them all actually living, in climates that produced them!"]

reached a certain length will always stop growing? Is it absolutely futile to hope that humanity can ever advance as the fern palm grows, beautiful frond beyond beautiful frond opening one out of the other as it mounts up higher and higher?—or has the arrest and decay, so invariable in the past, being merely dependent on external and fortuitous conditions, having no one organic root in the human nature itself and therefore being possible to avoid?

That morning, when she had taken the children for their walk in the pine woods, she had been pacing up and down under a tree while the children picked the bluebells among the grass, and had been arguing over the matter, almost as she used to argue with Charles under the pear tree. She had taken first the standpoint that it was organic and inevitable. To-night, as she walked round the desk, she took the other view (which was really her own) and tried to defend the position that there was no sufficient evidence that this arrest and decay was really organic and therefore inevitable. One thing alone would be enough to account for it—the fact that a high advance in intellectual culture and social organization has never yet been attained by any but a minute section of the human race as a whole, and always by merely a small section of the inhabitants of any single territory. That such a minute section of humanity has never been able to maintain its advance proves nothing except that humanity, being intimately in its nature a solidarity and a whole with all its parts reacting on one another, one minute fragment can never move very far ahead of the mass without ultimately being drawn back, either by internal disintegration, brought about through that body in the society itself which has not been included in the advance, or through external and violent contact with other parts of the race which have not shared its advance.

That all so-called advanced societies have, in the past, always disintegrated and fallen back does not prove that a hard rim-line exists which humanity can never surpass, and cannot prove this while we are in possession of a fact which adequately accounts for this retrogression without any such supposition.

She paced up and down quickly and more quickly with her hands behind her, still holding the pen, and went on in her thought to illustrate her view.

What was that high point of advance, intellectual and moral, which we speak of Greece having attained in the fourth century before Christ, and from which she receded so quickly and completely—was it indeed Greece which ever reached that point? What was that much vaunted culture, that high creative energy, that passionate thirst after intellectual insight, that demand for personal freedom, that search after physical beauty, but the possession of a few males who constituted the dominant class in a few cities of Greece! What was that much vaunted culture but a delicate iridescent film overlying the seething mass of servile agricultural and domestic slaves and of women, nominally of the dominant class, but hardly less servile and perhaps ignorant, who constituted the bulk of its inhabitants? As little could it be said to have been the property of the inhabitants of the land of Greece as the phosphorescent light on the surface of the ocean is the property of the fathoms of water stretching below it whose surface it illuminates. It would be as rational to expect that such a form of culture, brought into existence for a moment by a combination of happy conditions, could hand itself down from generation to generation, expanding and strengthening as it grew, as to expect a spray of shrub, plucked and placed in a vase of water in a hothouse, though it might bloom profusely for a few days, should permanently propagate itself and persistently grow when it was without ground and had no root.

But even had things been otherwise in Greece—had its women, they who alone have the power of transmitting the culture and outlook of one generation safely to the next, been sharers in the culture and freedom and labors of its males, not merely partially in the person of a few of its *hetairai*, but in that of the bulk of its child-bearing women—had every hand that labored in the fields or the cities been that of a freeman, sharing to the full the civic rights of his State, possessing a stake in its material welfare and a culture that enabled him to rejoice in its art and share in its thought—had that happened, which never yet has happened in any land—had Greece been filled with a population homogeneous in their culture and freedom—had no untaught servile woman existed to suckle any Greek child—had no slave formed a rotten foundation stone in the social structure—had culture, freedom, and civic rights been the common property of every human who breathed on the soil of Greece—had the social superstructure been sound and homogeneous from foundation to coping stone;—even then, though the vantage gained, instead of passing away in a couple of generations, might have remained for a few hundred years and there might have been more persistent progress; yet,—could it have been even tolerably permanent?

For what was the whole of Greece itself but a mere spot on the earth's surface? What were its people but a drop in the ocean of humanity? Unless she could have walled herself in, shutting off all possibility of interaction with all the races beyond herself, sooner or later she must have been so interacted upon by the mass of humanity beyond, that change and disintegration, moral and intellectual, must have set in, and she must slowly have fallen back to the common level.

As she walked she had paused before the little statue of Hercules, and, taking it automatically from the bracket, stood holding it in one hand and softly stroking it down with the finger of the other as though she were feeling its outline: yet her eyes appeared not to see it. After a while she put it back on the stand and began pacing again.

All the civilizations of the past, in Egypt, in Assyria, in Persia, in India, what had they been but the blossoming of a minute, abnormally situated, abnormally nourished class, unsupported by any vital connection with the classes beneath them or the nations around? What had they resembled but the long, thin, tender, feathery, green shoots which our small rose trees sometimes send out in spring, rising far into the air, but which we know long before the summer is over will have broken and fallen; not because they have grown to a height which no rose tree can ever attain, for ultimately the whole rose tree may be much higher than the shoot, but because they have shot out too far before their fellow-branches to make permanence possible; having no support, wind and weather will sooner or later do their work and snap them off or wither them. Next year a dozen rich young shoots may sprout from the snapped stem and survive; it may not have shot upwards and been broken off without helping in the growth of the whole tree—but it, itself, perishes.

If the whole of our vaunted modern advance, our science, our art, our social ideals, our material refinement, were to pass away to-morrow, swept away by the barbarians we nurse within the hearts of our societies or which exist beyond: would it for a moment prove that humanity had reached its possible limit of growth, and not rather that a sectional growth is no permanent growth?—that, where the mass remain behind, the few are ultimately drawn back? (As the head of a tortoise, let it stretch it out as it will within certain limits, can never continue to advance while its hind legs are sticking in the mud; would it move, it must pull its hind legs forward. Would it prove that our loftiest ideals of human progress were futile?—man moving ever in a little ring, advancing and forever falling backward as soon as the edge is reached— and not merely that the true cry of permanent human advance must always be "Bring up your rears! Bring up your rears"? Head and heart can ultimately move no farther than the feet can carry them. Permanent human advance must be united advance!

Then she thought suddenly she heard the baby stir. She threw her pen down on the table and took up the lamp, went into the next room and bent over his cot. But he had only turned in his sleep and was resting quietly. She bent down and turned him on to his side and put the nipple of his feeding bottle into his fist and close to his lips that he might find it if he woke. She had had to wean him because of the new baby that was coming. Then she tucked the cover in at the back of his neck and went back, closed the door softly behind her and began to walk up and down.

If the advance of a nation or a race must always ultimately be stayed, partly because of the internal action of the undeveloped mass within itself which must in time disintegrate it, and partly because the interaction with humanity beyond itself must ultimately draw it down and back, how much more must it be the case that a solitary individual city can never reach its full development in a society far behind itself?

That the highest and most harmonious development of the individual which we dream of is never reached, and that the attempt to attain it seems always to lead to intense personal suffering or absolute social destruction for the individual striving, in no way proves that the ideal is ultimately beyond reach—an *ignis fatuus* which the human hand will never grasp. As the nation or the class which should first have developed so far that it turned all its energies entirely away from the creation and wielding of the arts of destruction and self-defense, and turned them entirely to the creation of the beautiful and useful arts which benefit all mankind, would, ultimately and probably very soon, be swept away, as long as anywhere on the earth's surface there were still races so retrograde that they devoted all their energies to the arts of destruction; and as the nation, which should have attained the moral standpoint at which it became no longer possible for the stronger to absorb all the good of life and in which therefore poverty and need become extinct, would inevitably be overcome by the wanting and miserable products in other societies where a lower moral standard prevailed, if any such society existed anywhere on the earth—so more surely the individual, who should arrive at a higher moral point of development and strive to realize his ideals in actual life, must inevitably suffer or be absolutely annihilated in a society which had not reached his standpoint; and this not because his ideal was inherently unattainable and might not be the ultimate goal of the race, but simply because, for its realization harmoniously and successfully, it wanted more than the solitary unit, it wanted the interaction of the whole society.

A wolf who should suddenly be smitten by the idea that, instead of tearing his fellows to pieces, it would be better if they made a league of co-operation and fellowship, and for that purpose filed down his canines, would quickly become a prey to his fellows, not because his ideal was incompatible with successful animal life, for other forms have attained to it, but because its attainment by one was impossible.

So the individual primitive man in a cannibal tribe who had become possessed with the idea that the eating of human flesh was undesirable, and who had refused to capture and feed, would have become an object of scorn and probably of hatred to his tribe and might probably have died of hunger in some time of pressure, not because his ideal was ultimately unattainable, for practically to-day the whole of humanity has reached it, but because change in the idea of his fellows and the common carrying out of agricultural and pastoral labors were necessary to its successful attainment.

The man who dreams to-day that the seeking of material good for himself alone is an evil, who persistently shares all he has with his fellows, is not necessarily a fool dreaming of that which never has been or will be; he is simply dreaming of that which will be perfectly attainable when the dream dominates his fellows and all give and share. Working it alone, it fails, because the individual is part of an organism which cannot reach its full unfolding quite alone.

The man who should have reached a point of development at which sex in all its manifestations, whether physical or mental, has become a matter for reverence, and who should find his ideal reached only by a perfectly free and even comradeship between men and women at large in human society, and the personal ideal reached only in a relationship in which the mind fully shared with the body and in which the best in each half united into the perfect human creature called forth, who would desire that all that was most self-forgetful and heroic in his nature should be brought into play in the relation, as men desire to hang only the fairest wreaths before the shrine of the chief god in their temple—could such a man ever fully realize his ideal, or even attempt to realize it, without acute suffering and many-sided failure, in a society in which the brothel reigns and the ideals which the brothel presupposes, in which sex relationships are viewed by the mass of his fellows from the two standpoints of crude and selfish physical enjoyment or of gross material benefit? Might not his very attempts to bring men and women into freer and more equal fellowship in themselves seem to produce more evil than they remedied, simply because they were not ready for it? Would he himself not be almost certainly misunderstood and his personal relations end in irrevocable failure? What would this prove but that each man is but a cell in the human organism and that what his full development might be we shall never know till others share it with him?

The man whose ideal it is that, by the non-requital of injuries and the large expansion of sympathy even towards those who inflict suffering on himself, is human good and justice finally served—does his failure to evoke any response, and his final crushing beneath the hands he refused to strike. prove anything but the solidarity of humanity and that the foremost branch which grows too far beyond its fellows must ultimately be snapped off? That no individual ever yet realized in life the highest development which the mind has dreamed of proves [? does not prove] that perfect truth and fellowship are not attainable to humanity, but that the one alone cannot compass them.

Is it not a paradox covering a mighty truth that not one slave toils under the lash on an Indian plantation but the freedom of every other man on earth is limited by it? That not one laugh of lust rings but each man's sexual life is less fair for it? That the full all-rounded human life is impossible to any individual while one man lives who does not share it? "Bring up your rears! Bring up your rears!"

She walked, whispering softly to herself. Outside, the rain had left off falling; only the drops fell from the branches of the trees over the roof as the wind moved them, and the great drops fell slowly from the thatched eaves; but she did not hear them, she was so happy talking to herself.

Now her thought shifted its standpoint. She imagined the mind she argued with to take a new view and to say, "Granting you are right and that the full developed individual and the race must be hampered and limited by that of the less developed, is it not practically our duty and for the benefit of humanity that we should forcibly suppress, cut off and destroy the less developed individuals and races, leaving only the highly developed to survive?" She imagined it to produce all the arguments for the destruction of inferior races and individuals, stating them as fairly as she could. Then she turned to the other side and stated the view which was really her own.

She walked more quickly now, but with her head still down, striking the palm of one hand now and then with the doubled-up fist of the other.

Firstly, where is any body of humans to be found impartial enough, and untouched by the warping of personal and racial prejudices, to be able to determine for the race at large just what qualities are desirable and should be preserved and which should render their possessors liable to destruction? Would not each individual composing it be warped, not merely by a weakness for his own personal qualities, mental and physical, but would not racial prejudice make impartial judgment for humanity at large impossible?—the Chinaman judging from the Chinaman's standpoint; the Hindu from the Hindu's; the Englishman from the Englishman's? Could any but a race of crowned immortal gods, untouched by human self-love with its bias, form any conclave which should dare determine, not merely what were the ideal qualities after which they individually should strive and which they should impress on the race by preaching and example, but which would justify them in physically destroying those unendowed in them?

But, granting that it were possible to find such a body of humans on the globe (which it is not and cannot be), who would draw up an infallible code of all the qualities desirable and to be sought after by expanding humanity and of all those to be crushed and undesirable to the race, two difficulties that could not be surmounted would yet remain. Firstly that, given this almost divine conclave had succeeded in drawing up a list of all the qualities which are desirable in advancing humanity—the physical qualities of muscular strength, organic soundness, physical beauty (the idea of which differs so much from race to race and even from person to person that no representative body of humans ever could agree in what it consisted)—that general vitality and harmony of parts and forces which makes physical life a joy—the mental qualities of reason, imagination and keen and quick perception—the social qualities of sympathy, kindliness, rectitude, and all other qualities desired by humans in their fellows—and should exactly define what was meant by each quality and by its reverse: would they be much nearer the solution of the question what individuals and what races should be destroyed as a weight and drawback on the development of the race, and which saved and sacrificed for as the highest development? For no extended list of desirable or undesirable human qualities could be drawn up, all of which could be found wholly incarnate in any race or individual.

You say, and rightly, physical health and strength are

among the prime necessities of the fully developed human creature. The Kaffir and the South Sea Islander have often these in their very highest perfection: are these, therefore, the races to be preserved and which others are to be sacrificed for? You say a powerful reason is essential to the advance of the race: you find your man with the powerful reason, but diseased, antisocial, using his powerful intellect only as a means of preying on his fellow, often the great criminal. You say, at least let us kill out the hopelessly unfit, the invalid and the sickly and the consumptive: under this law you may ordain to destruction the bright, the lovely and most beneficent of the race. Has my view not as much to be said for it as yours that, if any on earth should be willfully destroyed as the down-drawers of the race, it is not a Shelley or a Keats, who has enriched and beautified existence on earth beyond fifty thousand whole men; but that it is the man of perfect physical health, with far less intelligence, and organically incapable of living for anything but his own well-being, finding no joy in any kind of sacrifice for his fellows and transmitting his qualities as surely as the consumptive or the weak, who is really the disease point in humanity, the creature who prevents the noblest social institutions and personal relations from coming into existence, because his egoisms can always be calculated to make them unworkable? You say that keen perceptions and the power of dominating are characteristics of the to-be-preserved races: but what if to me the little Bushman woman, who cannot count up to five and who, sitting alone and hidden on a koppie, sees danger approaching and stands up, raising a wild cry to warn her fellows in the plain below that the enemy are coming, though she knows she will fall dead struck by poisonous arrows, shows a quality higher and of more importance to the race than those of any Bismarck? What if I see in that little untaught savage the root out of which ultimately the noblest blossom of the human tree shall draw its strength? Who shall contend I am not right?

You say, "Let it be granted that social qualities are to count as high as or higher than intellectual or physical, then at least it will be justified that all avowedly criminal individuals and classes should be destroyed."—But who are the criminals? You say the prostitute, the murderer, the robber, the gambler. But who are these? The judge who sits in his elbow chair sentencing the man who plays pitch and toss in the street and himself sits up till two o'clock over his cards—the king and the prince who, while every avenue of pleasure and good is open to them, hang round the tables of Monte Carlo—the poor man who opens his back cellar for gaming to make a wretched living— who is the gambler? Who is the prostitute—the wretched woman whom the policeman drags along the street, or the man, often of wealth and learning and power, whose selfish lust and gold alone keep alive the institution whose bitter fruit she is? When you have crushed and destroyed the woman prostitute, what have you done more than cut out the tiny rotten place on the surface of an apple, while you leave gnawing away in the dark at the core the worm that produced it? Who is the robber and murderer we have most to fear—the pirate who on the high seas grasps men and goods, the highwayman and the housebreaker, or the man who, shielding himself always carefully behind a law he sees works in his favor or knows how to evade, makes his wealth from the ill-paid labor of those in mines and factories working at the cost of life, and ornaments his wife and his daughters as much in blood-stained jewelry and garments as the robber who returning home puts on his wife's finger a ring cut from the hand of a living woman, or throws on his daughter's shoulders a garment spotted with a traveler's blood? Who is the man who robs his fellows of life and the fruit of their labor, that we may be sure he shall not slip through our fingers, leaving the wrong man there? Who is the gambler, prostitute, robber, murderer? Is he king, prince, judge, as well as beggar and tramp? How shall we make sure he gets judgment in exact proportion to his offense? And further, is there any definite action or state which, judging for the world as a whole, can be set down as marking out the criminal? Has not the buccaneer, the polygamist, the polyandrist been the hero and the virtuous man or woman of his community? Will any action more certainly bring down the judgment and social punishment of his society in some countries than refusing to bow the head to a passing wafer of flour, in others the eating of pork, or the refusal to take his dead brother's wife, or give his daughter to the chief harem? Have not robber chiefs been regarded as quite as respectable and unliable to punishment in their society as the wealthy wage robber and the prostitute king and the hangman who are with us? What definite action will you set down as marking the criminal?

You say that of course no definite concrete action can be set down as marking out the criminal, that it is one in one society and another in another, but that he is yet easily marked off: he is the man who in any society refuses to submit to the laws which its dominating power has instituted and who persists in facing the punishments and penalties it ordains; and that, if he were in all societies destroyed and prevented from perpetuating himself, his type might become absolutely extinct and the qualities he possesses die out from the human race.

Perhaps this would be so; but are you sure you know what you are doing? For on that broad road of opposition to law and authority, along which stream the millions of humanity too low to grasp even the value of laws and institutions about them, resisting them from an ignorant and blind selfishness which makes them believe they are improving their own conditions by violating them, there are found walking men of a totally different order—white robed sons of the gods with the light on their foreheads, who have left the narrow paths walled in by laws and conventions, not because they were too weak to walk in them, or because the goals towards which they led were too high, but because infinitely higher goals and straighter paths were calling to them—the new pathfinders of the race!

These men, who rise as high above the laws and conventions of their social world as the mass who violate them fall below, are yet inextricably blended with them in the stream of souls who walk in the path of resistance to law. From the monk Telemachus, who, springing into the Roman arena to stop the gladiatorial conflict, fell, violating the laws and conventions of his society—a criminal, but almost a god—up and down all the ages man has been on earth there have been found these social resisters and violators of the accepted order, the saviors and leaders of men on the path to higher forms of life.

It is true that if, persistently and with a rigor from which none escaped alive, you could in every land exterminate the resisters of social law, you might at last produce a race on earth in which even the wish or the power to resist social institutions will have died out; your prisons might be empty, your hangmen and judges without occupation. But what would you have done? Seeking to cut out humanity's corns, to remove its cataract, to amputate its diseased limbs, you would have put out its eyes, cut off its tongue, maimed its legs; unable to see or move or express, its heart would beat slower and slower and death would come.

There is no net which can be shaped to capture the self-seeking ignorant violator of law which shall not also capture in its meshes the hero, the prophet, the thinker, the leader—the life of the world!

As the oak tree cannot grow unless, with each new ring it adds, its old bark cracks and splits, so humanity cannot develop without the rupture of its old institutions and laws; and it has been exactly because the bulk of humanity have never of necessity been able to distinguish between this healthful disruptive process and unhealthful decay, and have sought to crush and annihilate the particles causing it, that the growth of humanity has been as slow as it has. To suggest the more rigorous extermination of all non-law-submitting humans is simply to suggest a slow suicide as far as human development is concerned. In all ages the multitude has looked upon Barabbas as a less violent and dangerous disrupter of social laws than the Christ—not this man but Barabbas!

But you may say the criminal is, of course, not to be marked off in all societies merely as the breaker of any of its laws, for then, of course, the man who strives after better ideals would be included with the man who strives after lower; you say the true criminal is that man who, whether within or without the law, is willing to inflict suffering and loss on others for his own gain; and undoubtedly this is the true criminal. But how is he to be found, since it is not by the committal of any definite marked-off act, or by the violation of public enactments, but by the nature of his motive, that he becomes a criminal? It is certainly not a Lucrezia Borgia, adulteress and murderer, who of necessity, judged by the standard of motive and the amount of suffering caused to others, will always come out the great criminal. The fair gentle woman, never transgressing any enacted law, always seeking for love and sympathy and determined to gain it at all cost to others and all sacrifice of direct sincerity, may inflict in the course of her life an amount of suffering and wrong before which a few direct murders count as nothing; not merely by the love she takes from others or the friends she divides, but by the much more terrible distrust of human nature she awakens; by showing that, below so much gentleness and virtue, self-seeking and rottenness may lie, she strikes at our faith in our fellows, than which no more terrible wrong can be done. Yet under what code or before which tribunal could she be condemned to death? She is the snake in the Garden of Eden; yet who can swear she has poison as she glides noiselessly by? When we all lie silent in our last sleep with our feet turned upwards, if a god of life, knowing all things, should pass us, meting out judgment according as we had caused suffering in the search after our own good, would he of necessity pause over the worn-out drunkard and the street-treading outcast? Might it not also be over the woman of virtue and philanthropy or the man, hail-fellow well-met with all men, who paid his debts of honor and owed no man anything—saying "Their lies the great criminal!"?

But, you may say, granting that we cannot determine who the criminals are who should be destroyed for the benefit of the race, or the kind or degree of ill health which should be followed by instant destruction, yet surely such an ideal body of humans should find no difficulty in desiring the annihilation of all dark and primitive races who are manifestly a down-draught on humanity.

But are they so?

Is there really any superiority at all implied in degrees of pigmentation, and are the European races, except in their egoistic distortion of imagination, more desirable or highly developed than the Asiatic? Are we not in our vanity like the parvenu who, having wrung wealth out of the labor of others and surrounded himself by the results of all human toil and knowledge, stands in his gorgeous room filled with the works of art and use of all nations and, with his hands in his pockets and his full belly, looks round with infinite satisfaction at what he has accumulated about him, and says, "All these are mine," believing really that their existence and creation have something to do with himself? Are we modern Europeans not the parvenus among the human race? From the ancient civilizations of Asia and Africa, ancient and complete, when we were merely savage, have we not got all the foundation and much of the superstructure of what we possess? Art, science, letters, all are their original creation, merely taken over by us; even our very religion, such as it is, we could not invent for ourselves, but had to take it over from a hook-nosed, swarthy, Semitic people. And, if the learning and art and industry of Asia and Africa, passing into the hands of that marvelous bloom of humanity the Greek race, in its little span improved and enlarged what it took, it yet has been no work of ours, the Northern barbarians; we were running naked and staining ourselves with woad in our woods, when the looms of India and China were producing the delicate fabrics we seek now to imitate, when Asiatics ate from golden-flowered and delicate china, when temples and statues were raised that are our wonder and admiration, when philosophers taught and thought, and books were written and great legal systems enacted, while we sat round our fires on the dung and gambled with knuckle bones or danced war dances to the shouts of our fellows. It ill becomes us, who are but the tamed children of yesterday, to talk of primitive savages. Even to-day, when we have inherited all, is it so certain that our vaunted civilization is so much statelier and on all sides wider and with nobler elements of truth lying at its foundation than the older civilizations of the yellow and brown races? Is it so sure we are the people and wisdom will die with us? Is it not possible, for instance, that there is something of deep wisdom in the Chinese ideal which gives so much of the beauty of life to the end, which gives even the woman when she is old, the mother and grandmother, so honored and tender a place in society? Is it quite wise to sacrifice all to youth, so that every man and woman fears old age and would sacrifice all to avoid it? Must not the whole of life be more beautiful when men wait for good at the end, the joy of the sunset? Is not the religion which permeates Asia, and which came to life while our fathers still dreamed of heaven as a hall where man drank wine from the skulls of their enemies, more in harmony with the teaching of modern knowledge, which is reshaping us, than even that other Asiatic religion which we have adopted? Did not the deep-seeing eye of the Buddha, hundreds of years before the Jewish teacher walked in Syria, perceive clearly beneath all the complexities of form and individuality the unity in life upon the earth? He did not get at it as the modern man of reason, slowly, by measurement and calculation; by deep perception he knew that our little brothers look out at us from the eyes of animals, that the life of no beast and bird or insect is alien and unconnected with ours, that life flows on earth as one large stream with many divided branches, and under his mystical doctrine of the transmigration of souls he covered the same radical truth which "evolution" expresses in other but perhaps more absolutely accurate terms. We Northern fair-skins have had great men; our glimpses of new truths, new masteries over matter, have added our grain to humanity's sum of riches even in the direction of creative art; but, when we look around us on what we call our civilization, how little is really ours alone and not drawn from the great stream of human labors and creation so largely non-European? We scorn the Chinaman because his women compress their feet, not perceiving how infinitely more deadly and grotesque is the compression of our bodies; we ridicule, in certain Asiatic races, the pigtail of the Chinaman or the darkened tooth of the Japanese, blinded by egoism to the infinite degradation of the Northern races in their passionate strife to imitate ever-changing costumes and modes, alike so far removed from nature and beauty that even we, when a few years are past, perceive their grotesqueness and vulgarity, the slavish imitation of fashions which, by their unending change, feed on the vitals of the race through their ignoble demand on the brain of its womanhood, absorbing energy, reason, imagination, and setting, so long as their diseased reign lasts, a limit to the progress and expansion of woman and, with her, of the race. We accuse of immorality the Asiatics who consume the opium we forced upon them at the point of the sword; but we fair Northerns deserve to-day, as fully as when the Roman spoke it two thousand years ago, the judgment that as a people our chief pleasures were drinking and gambling; our race courses and card tables are as essential to our happiness as the dice and knuckle bones to our forebears. Is it not more than possible that, infinite as has been the debit of humanity to the ancient non-European peoples in the past, they have yet more to confer in the future?

You may answer (she walked quicker and quicker, look

ing down at the carpet) that no sane, informed mind could regard the old master races of the East, who have led in the path of civilization, as consigned to destruction by their inferiority; that it is the dark and primitive races still leading a life of nature that it is so necessary should be removed and suppressed in the cause of humanity.

But not only does it ill become us, the latest tamed of all civilized races, to speak slightingly of any primitive barbarian; not only among ourselves is a race such as the Prussians, who were civilized many centuries later than the men of France or Spain, in no way considered by us inferior to these, but we hold, and perhaps rightly, that by the engrafting of our savage forebears on the older civilizations of Europe, though we mercilessly destroyed them for the time being and plunged all Europe into barbarous chaos for over ten centuries, that we yet vivified human life and that our savage eruption was in the end a benefit. The older civilizations were too nearly extinct, we say, by excessive civilization; a back-seat to the unclothed men of the woods and nomads of tents was necessary to vivify them. But if this were so, may not the most primitive races have the same function to fulfill towards us? Is it not possible that man, a creature of the plains and hills, naked and always in unbroken activity in the free air, cannot survive beyond a certain time when he goes about loaded with materials from all the vegetable and animal and mineral kingdoms which he has gathered from all quarters of the globe—as a mantis collects mud and shells to make a case for himself, when he buries himself deep among his little erections of mud and stone, shutting off from body and brain light and air, when he has so constructed life that half of his body social is parasitic and enervated by want of labor, and the half it feeds with crushed under the superimposed weight—is it not possible that the primitive man, individually and structurally as well as socially, may, in some future æon, have the same restorative function to fulfill towards ourselves as we imagine ourselves to have played toward older decadent civilizations?

You say that the primitive barbarian is ugly and repulsive to us: Were not our forebears so to Greeks and Romans? Were not Attila and the Huns so horrible, physically and mentally, in their eyes that they were believed to be the offspring of witches and evil spirits, nothing wholly human being possibly so repulsive? Was it not death to the Roman woman who wedded a barbarian? To have eaten or drunk or slept with him was disgrace. He was supposed even to have an unendurable smell. Was the difference not at least as great between the lovely cultured Greek and the trained imperial Roman, between Pericles and Virgil, and the naked and spear-brandishing long-haired savage, drinking blood from the skulls of his enemies, as between his modern descendant and any primitive savage on earth? Who shall say that, in destroying the child of nature with his perhaps simpler organization and untried nerves, we are not destroying that of which humanity may yet in the æons to come have need to keep the race upon the earth?

At the worst, which is fairer and more akin to the ideals towards which humanity seems to move?—the little Bushman in his open cave on the mountain brow, etching away into the rock with his little sharpened flint the picture of hunting or wild beast, and looking down in the glory of sunshine on the place below where the wild things graze, or a swell-chinned ragged woman staggering out of a public-house in one of our centers of civilization, while the man who made the drink dwells in high places? Which is lovelier here, now, or in any place or time—the troop of men and women on a South Sea island, naked and gladly disporting themselves in the water or wandering together in the sunshine and sharing their love in the open light of day, or the scene that night by night our great cities witness? Which fills us with a sense of the greatness of the human spirit—the Kaffirs on their flat-topped mountain refusing to surrender month after month, till the conquerors when they mount at last find only one or two hardly-moving skeletons—men, women and children having died with hunger—or the civilized soldier who has sworn to die, but when a tenth part of his numbers have fallen puts up the white flag, willing to take life but not to lose it?

He needs be a brave man who would dare ordain destruction to all primitive and barbarous people, who could feel so sure humanity will have no need of them on her march through the future.

But letting all those difficulties pass (she stretched out one hand with the palm extended) : supposing it were possible for us to find an individual, a class or a race, so constituted that it presented in itself all the conceivable disadvantages and deficiencies which can afflict human nature and none of the advantages ; supposing it were possible—which it never would be—to find anywhere a body of humans as diseased, as devoid of physical health and the vital enjoyment of life as a worn-out man of fashion and debauch, as stupid and ill shaped as a Bushman, as brutal as the savage, as false as the worst civilized man, as antisocial as the criminal, as hypocritical as the Pharisee, physically deformed and mentally wanting, combining in itself all the drawbacks of each form and stage of human growth and none of the advantages—you may say : "Here at least we have found at last the creature or class whom, to perfect its own growth, it is necessary society should slay and mercilessly destroy." But is this so? If such individual or race were found, would it even then be proved that the highest use which society could make of them would be to destroy them? Does not the essential element, which it is most important to develop, if human life on earth is ever to attain to its full blossoming, lie in just that very sensitiveness towards the right of existence of all other human units, that deep-seated and at last organic desire not to benefit ourselves at the cost of others, which this course of action would tend to blunt and kill? In attempting to remove the undesirable and, to us, retrograde portions of human society, are we not blunting and striking at the very existence of the quality in ourselves which is above all essential to full human unfolding? Might not an immensely more productive use be made of such undesirable elements of life, by using them as objects for the development of those broad and generous human feelings which are the crowning beauty of life? In seeking to exterminate the undesirable of the race when we find him, may not society be striking at the very heart of its own progress, inflicting a mortal wound upon itself which exceeds in deadliness any which the undesirable individuals could have inflicted on it? Is it not an act of moral suicide?

And (she stretched out her hand softly again) if even this point also were waived, if it be allowed that it might be possible to find a body of humans so perfect and impartial that they are fit to legislate for the race, and that it might be possible for them to discover persons and races so hopelessly undesirable that for the benefit of the race's growth they must be destroyed; yet there remains the second great difficulty—who would bell the cat? Supposing this body of enlightened impartial and thoughtful humans decided that tyrants, drunkards, gamblers, murderers, robbers, hypocrites and all inflicters of suffering on their kind, and stupid and blindly narrow persons were an evil to the race and should be destroyed—would this enlightened and philosophic body of persons be themselves able to carry out their edict of destruction and become captors and executioners? And, if they had to delegate it to others, would not the very persons to be destroyed be often the persons fit and able to carry it out? The debauched judge, the ignorant stupid and narrow jailer, the brutal and stupid soldier, the bloodthirsty tyrant, the very individuals ordained to destruction, may be the most impossible to get at. You may condemn Nero but you cannot compel him to destroy himself, and you may not be able to find anyone capable and willing to do so. The very conditions of lofty intelligence and wide unbiased sympathy, which would alone endow any human being with the gift necessary for impartially judging for the race, are the very qualities which might render him unfit and incapable as executioner.

But you may say that all this is merely irrelevant child's play; that no sane person supposes you could find a body of humans wise enough and impartial enough to determine for the whole race which are the retrograde elements which must be destroyed for its benefit or powerful enough to destroy them when it has so determined; that the same end is attained much more securely and quickly by simply allowing all the physically stronger elements in humanity everywhere to destroy the weaker; that, by the stronger everywhere destroying the physically weaker with a wonderful automatic action, all that is undesirable in humanity is killed out and all that is desirable remains. But is this so?

You say that, by this process through the ages of the past, all improvement and unfolding in life on the earth has taken place, and that nothing else is necessary to produce the fullest beauty, joy and strength for the race on earth.

But is this so? Has life on the globe or has mankind attained to its present position, low as that is in many ways, because the physically stronger has preyed on the physically, for the moment at least, weaker?

You say this is the great law of the survival of the fittest which leads to all beauty, strength and unfolding in sentient life; that to interfere with it in any way is to interfere with nature's one plan for attaining perfection.

You shelter yourself under the name of science. Are you not, and one-eyedly, perverting the teaching of great minds, as the priestly in all ages pervert and make falsehood of the perception of the great prophets who preceded them?

(She was whispering so loudly to herself that, in the next room, you would have thought she was speaking to some one beside her.)

You say all evolution in life has been caused simply by this destruction of the weaker by the stronger.

From every cave and den and nest, from the depths of the sea, from air and earth, from the recesses of the human breast, rises but one great "No!" that refutes you. Neither man nor bird nor beast, nor even insect, is what it is and has survived here to-day, simply because the stronger has preyed on the weaker. The law of its life and its growth and survival has been far otherwise. From the time when, in a dimly living form, amœba sought and touched amœba, and, meeting, broke out into a larger form and divided into fresh forms, life has been governed, step by step, through the long march and advance in stages of life, by union; love and expansion of the ego to others has governed life. From the insect, following that unself-conscious reason we call instinct, who climbs to the top of the highest bough to fasten there her eggs where the tender shoots will first sprout to feed them, on to the bird who draws the soft down from her breast to warm the nest, who toils to feed and warm, and hovers about before the feet of the dangerous stranger that he may be drawn to attack her and not find her young, and who draws up the food from her own crop to feed them, till love becomes incarnate in the female mammal feeding her young from her breast—this is my blood which I give for the life of the world—through all nature, life and growth and evolution are possible only because of mother-love. Touch this, lay one cold finger on it and still it in the heart of the female, and, in fifty years, life in all its higher forms on the planet world would be extinct; man, bird and beast would have vanished and the cold dim dawn of sentient existence would alone exist on a silent empty earth. Everywhere mother-love and the tender nurturing of the weak underlies life, and the higher the creature the larger the part it plays. Man individually and as a race is possible on earth only because, not for weeks or months but for years, love and the guardianship of the strong over the weak has existed. You may almost estimate the height of development in the creature by the amount of mother-love and care he stands for.

You may say that mother-love forms an exception in the rule of nature, which, for perfecting life, demands the destruction of the weak by the strong. But what of the protective care of the male, not only of his own young and his related females, but of all the most helpless of his group? It is not only the sea lion who carries about his young in the bag on his own person; but through all sea life runs the defense of the weak by the stronger. Could the ostrich breed out its eggs in the wastes, where long journeys for food are needed, if the male did not daily take his hours of brooding on the nest to keep the eggs warm and care for and watch over the young with a tenderness even greater than their mother's while she goes afar to seek for food? Could the female bird of many kinds rear and feed her young without the continual aid of the male? Nor is it only parental sympathy, but a much wider feeling for the weak, which makes possible much of the higher animal life about us. It is not only for the defense of his own young that the old stag stands ceaselessly watching for danger and raises his shrill cry when he sees it approaching, at the greatest risk to himself. I have seen upon a cliff a baboon stand defending the one defile where dogs could mount, hurling them down with his hands and glancing back every moment anxiously to see how the troop of males and females carrying their young were escaping, clinging to his post till he fell torn to fragments by the dogs, saving his race and his species, not by his vast power of destruction, but by his willingness to be destroyed that others might live. The survival of the mierkat, so small and defenseless on the barren plains where so many other creatures become extinct in the presence of danger and of enemies, is accountable only when you know that each mierkat acts for all; not for their own young only, but for each other, and, for the younger and more helpless, all labor and sacrifice themselves. When the hawk approaches, if the older males and females be gone out far to look for food, tiny creatures, themselves hardly weaned, will seize all the tinier ones half an inch shorter than themselves and in desperate anguish strive to carry them off to the hole, forgetting all fear for themselves in their passionate attempt to save those who may have no blood relationship with themselves, while the older males and females grow gaunt and thin in the breeding-time, because almost all food they find is brought to lay at the feet of the young, while mothers go away to seek food which will supply the quite small with food. It is this passionate love for one another, this endless self-sacrifice of all, this devotion to the weaker by the stronger, which makes it possible for these little delicate furry creatures with their beautiful eyes and small powers of defense to survive in our terrible barren enemy-filled plains. The panther and the lion have vanished in the terrible presence of man, and many other forms of life grow very scarce, but these tiny creatures are still surviving, aided by their passionate devotion and self-sacrifice.

Then among men in their very struggles with one another, is it always the strongest fist and the fiercest heart which aids races or individuals to survive? Has not a great love lain behind those marvelous victories of which the world's history is full, where small and relatively weak nations and individuals have survived and driven back the large and powerful—a love for an idea, for a race, for a land, which, by blotting out personal considerations, has given weakness the power to protect itself and survive? The legend of the Swiss who gathered a score of spears into his breast, and so made room for his fellows to break the phalanx and win their nation's freedom, is only emblematic of one of the deepest-seated transforming and preserving forces in human nature. The legend of the mother, which in varying form almost every country possesses, who, to save her child from the bird of prey, climbed where the foot of the bravest and strongest could never tread, to recover it, is universal because it outlines the profound truth recognized everywhere that an

almighty affection and the instinct for even self-immola-
tion in the serving of others is not merely one of the
highest but one of the strongest forces modifying human
life. Almost everywhere in the record of human life on
earth are the traces of rapine and slaughter and the suppression or destruction of the weak form by the strong;
and they have left their marks not only in the heavy and
to us hideously-protruding jaw and beetling eyebrows of
the male gorilla, dividing him from the more human female and young, but giving him that strength of bony
structure which is necessary to enable him to rend and
destroy; not only in the structure of the scorpion, all
sting and tail, so loathsome from the human standpoint
that, were it not that it bears its young about upon its
back, it would seem so unredeemably repulsive as to be
none other than a nightmare; but it may have given the
springbuck her long graceful legs to flee from the jaws of
her enemies, and have brightened the eye of the gazelle
to see in the far distance the destroyer and to aid in its
escape. It may even have rendered more intense some of
the most complex emotions in the higher animal, because
the species in which individuals were most inclined to
defend the weak at their own cost may have survived
where more purely self-centered varieties fell. It has
played its part, and a vast part, in the history of life on
earth. But to regard this destructive element in existence
as the key-note to life on earth is a strange inversion.
When we look from a hill-top on a herd of wild antelope
on the plain below us and two old males come into conflict
and desperately wound and perhaps kill one the other, the
very fact that we are so struck by the incident and absorbed in watching shows it is not the universal, the all-
pervading element, of the life before us. The care of the
young by the mother, the drawing of sex to sex, the feeding together in good-fellowship of hundreds of creatures
—all this rouses no curious remark in us, because it is
but of the universal substance of life that things should
be so. To attempt to explain and sum up life by consider-

ing this element only is like the man who should attempt to represent a great musical symphony by playing its lower bass notes alone,[1] like a man who should try to reproduce a great composer's masterpiece by striking all the discords in it without any of the harmonies into which they resolve themselves and with reference to which alone they have any meaning. From the mysterious drawing together of amœba to amœba, their union and increase, on through all the forms of sentient life, and in the life of the very vegetable world, the moving original power is always this stretching-out, uniting, creative force; shaping itself in the union of male and female, of begetting with their begotten; drawing together creatures of like and unlike kinds, bringing into all the forms of friendship and union and love, it lies at the root of existence; it shapes the petals of flowers, not for death but to call the insects to suck their sweetness and carry fertilizings to one another; it sings in the song of all song-birds calling to their mates; it blossoms into human speech; to kill, man might have been silent; but to communicate with and bind himself to his fellow, child to mother, mother to child, the sexes to reach each other, man, to reach man belonging to his social organism, man was obliged to blossom into speech. Everywhere this binding moving creative force moves at the very heart of things, growing more and more important and complex as the creatures mount in the scale of life, till it reaches its apotheosis in the artist, in whom the desire to create dominates all else, who, not from himself but by the necessity of some force within himself, is spent and must spend himself to produce that which gives infinite joy without ever being used up, over which there need be no struggle; for not-seeing the statue or not-hearing the story or not-singing the song makes others poorer. Men have so recognized that this creative (and not the destructive) power was the fount and core of life that

[1 After "alone," the MS. (in so far as it is legible) runs: "without the . . . and the air and the . . . , which alone gives it form and life," is like, etc. This sentençe is omitted.]

in all ages they have tended to call the highest intelligence they could conceive of, and therefore their supreme God, "the great Creator"; and their devils have been destroyers. It is false to say that the mighty jaw and the almighty claw, and the stomach that is never filled and is always seeking to fill itself, are the fundamental moving power in life—

> "'Tis love that makes the world go round,
> The world go round, the world go round!"

(She was speaking so animatedly now you could almost have heard what she said in the next room.)

But you may say that, granting love and self-obliteration in the cause of others plays a dominant part in the sentient life among kindred and groups, and that the mysterious instinct to create and continue to reproduce lies as the fundamental hidden power manifested in all we call life—granting all this, yet you must allow that, at least between species and species and distinct groups, a terrible conflict has always gone on, that this victory of the strongest jaw and the longest claw and the biggest belly has resulted in the survival of the fittest, and that, in the world in which this strife has gone on, we have many beautiful things—singing birds, flowers, the wonderful intelligence of man and beast—this has grown up under the struggle!

Yes, the struggle has gone on and the fittest have survived. The fittest?—to survive; not of necessity the fittest in any other sense in which we humans use the word.

The fittest has survived! Under water, half-buried in mud, only the outline of the jaw and two deep slit eyes show where the alligator lies. Age after age he has lain in the mud and slime. The gazelle has come down to the water to drink and has been drawn in by the mighty jaw; the little monkey, delicate, quick, high-witted, swinging from branch to branch and stretching its hands out to dabble in the water, has come too near, and the brown stump has moved and snapped it up; the human child has

come to play upon the bank and disappeared; the young
girl has come to draw water and only her broken pitcher
has been left on the mud to show where she was drawn
under; all have gone to fill the almighty maw and been
crushed by the mighty jaw; the creature survives. In the
ages which have passed since it came into being, many
fair and rare forms have existed and passed out of existence. The little winged creatures with large eyes and
brains, reptile in order but fitted for flitting in the air
and sunshine, whose images we find impressed on the
rocks, have gone; they may have had rare and beautiful
colors for anything we know and may have had notes
of song, but they are gone; fishes and birds and beasts
that have been, have passed forever; even in our own ages
lofty forms of life have passed and are passing away; but
the alligator survives. Not because it was more fair, more
beautiful, more complex, more brave, than the creatures
upon whom it lived or whose stay on earth it outstayed,
but because its long jaw set with serrated teeth, its dead,
solid hide, its absorption simply in seeking food for itself,
its torpid half-buried existence on mud banks and amid
slime, fitted it to destroy the complex pulsating animals
and to outlive the beautiful aërial forms which had not
its almighty jaw and its mighty stomach. It was fittest
to survive. The boa constrictor wakes in the morning,
and before night bird and beast have been crushed in its
mighty folds; it lies stupefied and torpid with the creatures it has consumed in its expansive inside. It has survived them, not because it was fairer or higher in the
scale of being than they, but because so greasily and
silently it could creep on them. The cobra strikes dead
man and beast, and survives, not because she is braver or
higher or even stronger, but because beneath that tooth
she carries that little poison bag and strikes so silently
and it may be in the dark.

If a ship full of poets and philosophers and men of science, bound for some distant place of meeting, were
wrecked on the shore of Africa and a cannibal tribe met

them, they would be consumed. The savage would rub down and oil his sides with the fat of the poet; the brain of the philosopher would frizzle before the fire; the cannibal's belly would be full of man of science and artist; in a time of famine the cannibal might survive and beget his kind, when a neighboring tribe died out from hunger for want of timely poet and thinker! Would the fact that he had eaten poet and philosopher prove he was higher than the men who filled his belly and gave strength to his muscles? The fittest to survive—but the fittest for what else? Even when nation sweeps out nation, what does it mean? Is it always the loftier, more desirable form that survives? When the barbarian swept Greece till Athens was left like an empty and bleaching skull, is it certain that the savage was higher than the race which he supplanted? In nearly two thousand years in that land of blue seas and mountains, he and his descendants have produced nothing that the world prizes or desires. The fittest survived!—the fittest for what?

You say, at least it must be allowed that, along with this struggle among sentient beings and the survival of the strongest jaw and the longest claw and the biggest belly, rare and beautiful things have survived and are among us to-day?

Singing birds are with us, insects of beauty and color, beasts of intelligence and heroic forms, and man, who, in spite of all, has instincts and powers latent within him of rare beauty, and strength, reason, imagination, sympathy and joy. Yes, this we have—but, oh, for the songs that will never be heard on earth now!—for the beauty we shall never see!—for the forms of light and glory which will never flit among earth's trees!—for the creatures of intelligence and complexity that will never tread earth's floor!—Oh, the might have been, which is forever impossible now! Much has escaped—but, oh, for that which in the long, long ravening struggle of the ages, has not escaped from the strong jaw and the long claw and the poison bag! Oh, for the forms of life, perhaps higher

than any we know or ever shall know, which in their very
first incipience were cut away and made impossible forever! In this awful struggle (a struggle waged with no
purpose of bringing the great and beautiful to life) what
has been saved, we know; what has been lost, we shall
never know. The gorilla and chimpanzee are with us; but
what if, in some hidden forest, a yet more beneficent intel-
ligent type arose, developing quite away from the predatory to a more social form, till, meeting with the stronger-
armed heavier-jawed gorilla, it was exterminated, and
one line of beneficent growth shut off forever? It is difficult to understand how what we call man ever came into
being—the manikin thing with such small physical powers
of defense and attack, whose young for years, in spite
of mother-love and male protection, could so easily fall a
prey to any wild beast, and who at its best is physically
small and powerless—unless he first, for long periods,
developed in some sheltered situations where attacks from
predatory saurians or more modern carnivora were rare;
but what if somewhere, it might be among inaccessible
mountain peaks and valleys in the dim times when man
was shaping, a branch existed in whom in time, having
to expend no great force in purely predative or physically
self-defensing directions, the germ of other faculties developed higher artistic and musical and reasoning powers,
deeper and broader powers of originality, all that for
the last many millenniums we have been slowly and with
difficulty marching towards when the conditions of life
have allowed; if this variety ever were thrown into contact
with a more gorilla-like form intent on destruction, it
must have been swept away; that one act of destruction
would have delayed the march of humanity for ages—nay,
prevented it forever perhaps from attaining certain noble
and to us desirable shapes.

If it were possible for us to land upon a planet in most
things like our own and launched on its course with ours,
it is quite possible we should find upon it a being as much
higher, and from our standpoint more desirable, than our

highest ideals are higher than ourselves; our early stage of sentient growth might have been the same, and this difference, now so vast, might have arisen merely because, once or twice in the course of growth through the æons, their highest intellectual and moral type might have escaped destruction by its lower. This is certain, that the lower and more brutal self which slumbers with each one of us to-day, with regard to which the chief difference between man and man is this, that one man's life is passed in submitting to it and another man's in struggling with and crushing it—this more brutal self, which the Christians have called inbred sin and all students of the human heart have under different names recognized—this body of qualities, which seems to some for ever to limit human growth, so ineradicable and heavy in its weight it seems—has it not gained its strength and vitality, is it not still within us in such mighty force, because age after age not merely those races but those individuals in whom its existence was weakest have been killed off by the individuals most incarnate of the lower nature and not allowed to perpetuate themselves freely, either physically or spiritually? Lies are so easy to us because age after age the lying and subtle and insincere have conquered and crushed the individuals in whom sincerity and openness were budding. It is so difficult for us to consider others justly and impartially if they have terribly injured us, because age after age the individuals striking most mercilessly at whatever limited their pleasure, without consideration of justice or sympathy, have killed out and suppressed those in whom generosity and justice were beginning to dawn. Lust, divided from all love and inborn self-forgetfulness, is so dominant within thousands of us (making the world of sexual relations, which in our ideals are the highest, often the lowest, in life), because age after age the most brutally lustful has perpetuated himself, where the less lustful and brutal has failed to rape and force the woman or kill the opposing males. Because, age after age, the individual tendency to expend force in the direction of

impersonal intellectual activity has again and again fallen
victim to the individual more concentrated on personal
aim, we to-day find the complex intellectual gift of the
thinker and artistic creator so rare and so heavily con-
flicted with by the lower opponents. Because the stronger
sex has so perpetually attempted to crush the physically
smaller, the individuals who attempted to resist force by
force being at once wiped out, sex has acquired almost as
a secondary sexual characteristic a subtleness and power
of finesse to which it now flies almost as instinctively as a
crab to the water when it sees danger approaching, the
struggles against which being the sternest that sex has to
carry off within itself if it would attain moral emancipa-
tion. Because the larger male has so long and so mercilessly suppressed the weaker and exterminated those who
refused to submit while the servile survived, we find perhaps that lowest of all human qualities, the material tendency to truckle before success and power, which in some
humans seems instinctive and in them at least is ineradicable. For it is not alone through the physical destruction
and annihilation of the weaker by the brutally stronger
that we have suffered. What has humanity not lost by the
suppression and subjection of the weaker sex by the
muscularly stronger sex alone? We have a Shakespeare;
but what of the possible Shakespeares we might have had,
who passed their life from youth upward brewing currant
wine and making pastries for fat country squires to eat,
with no glimpse of the freedom of life and action, necessary even to poach on deer in the green forests, stifled out
without one line written, simply because, being of the
weaker sex, life gave no room for action and grasp on
life? Here and there, where queens have been born as
rulers, the vast powers for governance and the keen insight the sex possesses have been shown; but what of the
millions of the race in all ages whose vast powers of intellect and insight and creation have been lost to us because
they were physically the weaker sex, whose line of life
was rigidly apportioned to them at the will of the stronger,

which governed the structure of their societies? What statesmen, what rulers and leaders, what creative intelligences have been lost to humanity, because there has been no free trade in the powers and gifts of the muscularly smaller and weaker sex?

Therefore let no man lay the flattering unction to his soul that, by rushing out and destroying what is weaker than himself, or that, by using and bending to his own purposes all that live in the society in which he lives, he is thereby aiding nature in the great and lofty and perfect life on earth. The struggle between sentient creatures and the conquest by the most cunning, the most merciless, the most consuming, the muscularly or osseously stronger, has had powerful effects on the shapes which life takes on; it may have added to the keenness of the eagle's eye, the length of the springbuck's graceful bound; it may even have added to that intensity of anguished love which makes one baby mierkat try to drag a smaller away to safety when it sees the hawk approaching, because the little people have learned by a long racial experience what the claw and beak mean, and those who have loved and aided each other most have survived—the fittest to live, not the fittest to kill in that case!—it may have sharpened the wits of all creatures who had to escape, as the poison bag of the serpent teaches great caution in the country where it prevails (we always part the grass with our foot as we walk—though it might be just as well to walk without parting!); it has left many beautiful and curious forms of life, but has also destroyed many; it has nursed into being all the vices which lie deep buried in sentient life; it has age after age killed out among advancing human creatures the individuals who, to reason, love, or any of the impersonal ends of life, sacrificed the arts of destruction and self-defense; it has hanged its Christ and poisoned its Socrates; it has nurtured in every one of us the brute which we shrink from in another when he turns it to us; it has killed out the winged reptile and a thousand noble complex and brilliant forms of life, and has saved the crocodile and the python. The only strength which it directly preserves is predatory strength, strength of reason, strength of self-government, strength of affection, all the forms of strength most prized by the human creature as it advances, are not preserved of any necessity by it. The struggle between the forms of sentient life and action within a species, and the survival of those most fit to destroy, have no more made existence what it is than the road on a mountain side makes a mountain. It has modified, in some directions powerfully modified, the external forms of life, but no more made it what it is than a hatchet used to chop trees in an orchard makes the trees; the hatchet, wisely used or by accident so used, in lopping off certain branches may make the trees bear larger or more fruit; but used otherwise it may entirely destroy the tree, and, used recklessly and by chance, might cut down the whole garden. The process of pruning itself, however wisely carried on to produce certain ends, is an entirely subsidiary process, whose end, in increasing the size or abundance of the fruit, may generally be equally attained by manuring and feeding the tree; but it fails utterly to account really for the tree, whose essential life and essence lie in its power of growth, in the mysterious power of absorbing and adding to its substance in certain directions and along certain lines and of reproducing itself. All the pruning and cutting off in the world can never account for the fundamental mystery of one bud becoming a flower, for one grain of matter in the soil or particle of gas in the air being transformed into bark, for the kernel and reality of life. Pruning is a process which creates and produces nothing new, but which, wisely used, may tend to accelerate vitality and desirable variation; which, applied haphazard, may produce mixed desirable and undesirable results; and which, used unwisely, may mean absolute destruction. Therefore let no man lay the flattering unction to his soul that, by destroying all he can destroy, and using and consuming all he can use or consume, he is aiding nature in the only way possible in perfecting the human race on earth. Let him not imagine when he prates of the survival of the fittest that he is enshrouding himself and his desires in impenetrable armor; he is only an ass masquerading in the scientific lion's skin put on hind-side before!

You say that, with your guns shooting so many shots a minute, you can destroy any race of men armed only with spears; but how does that prove your superiority, except as the superiority of the crocodile is proved when it eats a human baby, because it has long teeth and baby has none? You say the fact that you can command the labor of so many of your fellow men and gratify your desires proves that you are higher than they; it proves that your belly is large and your power of filling it great; but what, in these matters, are even you compared to the old saurians with their vast claws and paws and rough tongues, who could have licked you off the face of the earth in a moment? The theory that humanity can be perfected on earth only by the stronger jawed, longer clawed, biggest bellied preying on the smaller is a devil's doctrine bred in the head of a fool.

But you may say: If the perfecting of humanity is not to be accomplished by this destruction of one part by the other, how then is it to be accomplished?

(She was walking very slowly now, and looking before her and saying nothing.)

Is it not possible only in two ways? Is there any hope of our in any way raising and hastening the rate of human advance if we cannot do it by the killing out and suppressing of individuals?

Surely there are ways. Has not the human only now, at last command of two vast means for the modifying of life and the conscious perfecting of humanity? In that strange and lovely power which enables us to see and picture that which we have not in all parts ever fully seen, in the ideals which are clear before the human spirit, have we not the goal to be moved towards? And in our powers of reason the means to find, step by step, the paths that lead to them, have we not now reached a plane of life, in which the struggle for existence that is to perfect human life need not in any sense be one between individual lives but between qualities within the individual—a struggle within each man to be fought mainly here (she raised her little doubled-up fist and laid it softly on her breast)—here, where alone each man rules omnipotently and where alone the kingdom of heaven on earth he dreams of can be brought to pass— here, where the ideal must be formed and realized, or nowhere? Has not the time come when the slow perfecting of humanity can find no aid from the destruction of the weak by the stronger, but by the continual bending down of the stronger to the weaker to share with them their ideals and aid them in the struggle with their qualities? Is it not by the passionate persistent determination to realize within ourselves our highest ideal, and then, by that strange power which makes every man's life unconsciously a voice calling to his fellows to follow, to be able to call on those who have not yet seen so far? Is it not so, and not in any other way, that the real blossoming time of man on earth will ever come? And no man liveth to himself and no man dieth to himself. It is not by destroying and crushing.

She was walking very slowly now, with her eyes wide open, but seeing nothing—then a picture leaped out before her mind that seemed to have no direct connection with the thoughts passing there:—

She saw a great plain, and on it a woman standing, large and beautiful; a loose garment draped the lower part, but the great arms and shoulders were bare, and the long hair, turned back from the beautiful face, flowed over the shoulders; but the beautiful eyes were filled with tears and the forehead bent with pain. Beside it there was a great rush of wings and then another figure stood there, heroically large, half poised on one foot, as though just descended, and with wings half open as if ready for flight again.

She stood still. . . . After a minute she turned to her desk and, leaning across it from the side, drew her book towards her and, opening it at the end, began to write quickly on the inside of the cover, the writing running diagonally across it:—

"When the Spirit of the Ages, whose moments are millenniums, whose minutes are æons, and whose hours are a human eternity, passed amongst the worlds of space seeing how it fared there, he chanced on a planet. A wide plain stretched there, no trace of plant or shrub was on it anywhere, and burning sands stretched everywhere; but far away in the distance rose mountains; on their sides one could see that streams flowed and that the earth was green and trees waved. Alone in the center of the plain stood a woman's figure, bare and beautiful from the waist upwards, but clothed below in a coarse garment. Its eyes were fixed on the distant mountains; again and again as it looked it wrung its hands and tears streamed from the beautiful eyes. And the Spirit paused in its flight and lit on the earth beside her, and it cried, 'Beautiful one, why do you stand here weeping alone in this desolate spot, where no fair thing is, and the snake has left its track in the sand at your feet and the only footprint is the mark of the wild beast's claw? On the mountains there is verdure; surely birds are singing among the trees and the grass is heavy with flowers; why linger here in this desolate spot?' But she wrung her hands and cried, 'I cannot move; always and always I look out for one to come and deliver me and take me with him to the mountains, but he never comes.' And he said, 'Beautiful one, your forehead is high, your bosom is full, your arms are strong, your hands well knit; why cannot you move forward?' And she wept and raised the robe that was about her, and the Spirit saw that, while from the waist upwards she was fair and powerful, from the waist downward she was ill-nourished and loathsome. About her feet were iron fetters, upon the limbs were marks of unhealed stripes, old gangrenous wounds festered there, and the flesh was shrunken from the bones and the feet deep sunken in the sand. And she cried, 'My head is clear, my heart is sound, my arms are strong, but my feet, my feet, they bind me here! I wound and strike them, but they will not move; I bind them with chains in my anger. It is they, it is they, who keep me here!' And again she wept. Then the Spirit dropped his wing and drew nearer to her and whispered, 'Despairing one, no deliverer will ever come. You, you, yourself must save yourself. From those weak limbs strike off the fetters; with your strong hands bend down and heal the wounds your hands have made; remove the sand about the heavily sunken feet. When they are healed and free and strong, they, they and not another, will bear you to the mountains where you would be.' And he asked her, 'What is your name?' And she answered, 'My name is Humanity.' And he said, 'When the years have flown I shall return again and see how it fares with you.' And he smote his wings together and rose upwards: and Humanity was alone upon the plain."

She wrote quickly across the inside of the cover; when that was full she went on the flyleaf opposite; then she paused a moment; at the head of what she had written she put as a title "The Spirit of the Ages." Then she drew her pen through the words as if not satisfied. Then she threw her pen down on the table. She looked round. All the room seemed strange; the old brown walls, the little bookshelves, the lamp throwing down its light on the worn leather cover of the desk, the old exercise book she had been writing in—they looked like things look when you come back from a long visit, when all about the house is strangely familiar and yet new.

She closed the exercise book and put it in the drawer. Perhaps some day the little allegory would enlarge itself and she would write it in fit words to make others see the picture. Probably she would never touch it again because it takes time to write things for other people. But the little picture she would never forget, because the pictures one sees are actual and one never forgets them. She walked to her armchair and sat down. She knew suddenly that she was very tired; she had been walking nearly three hours; but it was a delicious kind of tiredness, like one feels when one comes home from a long walk in the open air: as if something was resting by being used. She leaned back her head into the little dent. The rain was falling now in torrents. She leaned back listening to it. It was a delicious sound. It made her feel as though great strong arms were folding themselves about her, and a great strong hand were stroking her down softly. She lay still; but after some time she drew herself up and curled her legs under her, and turning sideways half buried her face in the dent in the chair's back. She tucked one hand under her cheek and after a while closed her eyes. Her thoughts ran around in a dreamy way now. How nice it would be to be a man. She fancied she was one till she felt her very body grow strong and hard and shaped like a man's. She felt the great freedom opened to her, no place shut off from her, the long chain broken, all work possible for her, no law to say this and this is for women, you are woman; she drew a long breath and smiled an expansive smile. Oh, how beautiful to be a man and be able to take care of and defend all the creatures weaker and smaller than you are. Then she dreamed away and half asleep made one of those little stories, "self-to-self" stories, that she made as she was going to sleep, not for other people, too sweet and close, just for herself. She was a man, she thought, and she lived in a cottage about which there was bush and high forest, as at the old farm. It was night and she thought she was lying there and outside the trees were rustling as the wind moved them. It seemed she was lying on the earth, on mats in the hut, and beside her lay the woman she loved, fast asleep. She felt the little head on her shoulder, the soft hair against her cheek, and the little body within her arm; then she heard the wind blowing and the tree branches touching the roof as the wind grew strong. The little one beside her moved uneasily, and as it lay so close she felt the little body throb and knew it was the life within it that he had wakened. (She was him now, not herself any more.) And such a great tenderness came over him, and he drew her close and bound his limbs about her so that she was quite wrapped about, but the little wife upon his arms slept on, not knowing how she was loved. And then it was another day, and the little child was born so small and soft, and he held it in his arms and put his lips to its soft tiny lips (she felt the lips touch hers), and then he took it in both his hands and put it close into the little mother's arms against her breast and bent down over them,—and then it all shimmered away and she, Rebekah, was asleep.

She had slept peacefully in the chair for perhaps half an hour; the oil in the great transparent glass bowl of the lamp was burned down three-quarters of the way when suddenly she woke with a start and leaped to her feet. It seemed to her she had heard the front door close with a great bang. Perhaps it was her husband and Bertie come home; she stood to listen, but there was no sound of their voices. She was taking up the lamp to go and see, when she remembered it was the stable-boy's evening out, and that when he came back late he often came in at the front door instead of going round the back way to the yard where the servants had their rooms if he saw lights in the house. Still she took up the lamp; in the children's room they were all sleeping quietly, and when she went through her bedroom and the dining-room into the passage she found no sign of anyone having been there, and went back to the study.

Her sleep had refreshed her, but left her stupid and dull. The rain had left off and there was only the sound of a few large drops falling from the trees over the house as the wind shook them. She yawned and stretched herself and sat down in the armchair again. She drew her work basket to the side and put the lamp on the edge of the desk and went on darning the stockings that were left. She darned on mechanically, thinking of nothing much, but she remembered she must count the wash-clothes the next morning and ask the washerwoman about the three pairs of socks that were missing. And then she wondered whether she should mix on the sour dough now or leave it till the morning, and she decided to leave it. She watched the needle move in and out among the blue threads in the stocking almost without seeing them and was growing very sleepy again, when, just as she was darning the last pair, she heard a click at the gate and a step on the garden path that she knew was her husband's. She lit the fat-candle quickly and went to the hall to meet him. He was hanging up his cap but had still his greatcoat on.

"Where is Bertie?" she asked.

"That is what I wanted to ask you. Hasn't she come home?"

"No, I've not seen her."

"I suppose she has. I went to have a round with some of the young ones in the back room; and a quarter of an hour ago, when I wanted to leave, I went to look for her and couldn't find her. The curious thing is she left her walking shoes and cloak and all behind her. But no doubt she's here all right."

Rebekah turned down the side passage from which Bertie's room opened, and her husband, still in his greatcoat, followed her.

She opened the door and looked in. "She's here," she said. She walked in, shading the light with her hand. On the large old-fashioned four-poster bed which stretched right across the end of the room, so that there was just space for a person to stand at the foot, Bertie lay asleep. She was still in her ball dress, lying on her back in the center of the bed, with no pillow under her head and with one arm thrown across her forehead. The train of the white skirt hung wet and draggled with mud against the white quilt. Rebekah stepped to the bedside, shading the light with her hand that it might not fall on Bertie's eyes. Frank stood beside her.

"What on earth made her run off like that? She was dancing hard when I left the ballroom."

Rebekah gave him the candle to hold and stooped down to put a pillow softly under her head.

"What a magnificent creature she is," he said. Her right arm was stretched at her side, and the great white rose, partly faded, was fastened at her breast. "There's not another woman like her in the Peninsula, not in South Africa! And so unconscious! That's what men like. Young Smith came twice to talk about her to me this week. Did I think she'd ever change her mind and have him!"

He expanded his chest, his white shirt front showing between the parted edges of his overcoat. Rebekah was smoothing the pillow.

"Women think," he said importantly, "that men don't see through them when they ogle and flirt and try to captivate every fellow they meet; but we do! That style of woman's all very well to dance and flirt with, but when he really wants a wife and means to settle down he looks for something different!"

Rebekah had gone round to the foot of the bed and was kneeling down, taking off the little drenched white satin slippers. "What can have made her run home in these things?"

"Now I knew what I was about when I looked out a certain little woman!" he said, still holding the candle and smiling down. "There were half a dozen damsels in the Peninsula thought they were quite sure of me, but I knew where on a certain farm in the Karroo a little woman was to be found who wouldn't always be running away to balls and croquet parties to flirt with other men and forgetting all about her husband and house —and a nice pretty little woman too."

Rebekah had risen to put down the damp shoes and stockings she had drawn from Bertie's feet; he chucked her softly under the chin with his two forefingers as she passed him. "Wouldn't take 'No' for an answer, either! Smart fellow, eh? Knows what he wants when he sees it!"

Rebekah knelt down to cut off with the scissors from her chatelaine the wet draggled end of Bertie's train; if that were taken off she would be dry enough to sleep on till morning without harm, and the dress would never be any good again.

Frank had had three glasses of champagne and was in a good humor, exceedingly pleased with himself. He was an abstemious man; he took care never to allow himself more than was good for himself in the matter of drink or any other personal indulgence. Only twice in all their married life had Rebekah really seen him the worse for drink; once when he returned home at four in the morning and said he had been kept sitting up at his office to make up his books, and once on another occasion. He could drink several glasses without feeling them, but champagne always had an expansive effect on his nature, making him more sunny and talkative.

"I knew very well whom I was going to have," he said, looking down appreciatingly at the bed where Bertie was lying and Rebekah was kneeling cutting off the train; "ever since that day on Table Mountain when the rain came on and a certain little woman covered the lunch basket with her own waterproof and saved us from going home hungry, while all the other girls came running up to the rocks for us to help them up into shelter, timorous little darlings. I held a sunshade open over the head of one and gave her my hand, but all the while I was looking at a certain little woman down below tucking the covers in, with all the rain streaming off her. Oh, men aren't such fools as they seem." He laughed. "I'd always had a fancy for her since she was five and used to fight like a tiger-cat if I wanted to kiss her—'I don't love you! you're ugly! Go away! Don't come near me. You horrid, ugly, cruel boy!" He imitated the shrill agonized voice of a child, and laughed. "But that day decided me." He was holding the candle a little crooked.

Rebekah had heard that story often before; it was one of those he often told in expansive moods. She had even heard him tell it to the men in the billiard room when they were praising her milk punch.

"She looks pale," said Rebekah, rising. "I hope she wasn't ill."

"Ill—you should have seen her dancing! A freak, I suppose, to come home like this in the wet. You can't account for a woman, my dear. I've found that out long ago. Haven't I been married seven years!" He would have touched her under the chin again but she had turned to the wardrobe to get a shawl to put across Bertie's feet. "Is supper ready? They had good wine there, but really nothing fit to eat."

"Yes, I got it ready before you left. You'll find the matches and lamp on the sideboard as you go in."

He put the candle down on the dressing table and went out whistling one of the tunes they had danced to.

When he was gone Rebekah bent down to cover Bertie's feet. She stroked them softly with her hand. They were pink and dimpled as a baby's, such tiny feet for such a big woman. Then she covered them up carefully with the shawl, turning up the damp edge of the dress that it might not touch them. She put a candle and matches on a chair at the bedside, that Bertie might find them when she woke, and then she took up the light and went to the dining room.

Her husband had taken off his great coat, and sat at the head of the table, in his white shirt front and beamingly contented face above it.

"Won't you sit down and take some too? This bobotie [1] is excellent.—No, you won't? You've been off your feed the last day or two.—Oh!"—he looked up and

[1 Bobotie: curried hash.]

laughed—"I'd quite forgotten what you told me this morning! I'm to be the patriarch Jacob, eh?—'Now Jacob had twelve sons and twelve daughters'—or was it Job?" He laughed again. "Take a little soda water? That's more in your line at such times, I think.—Who'd be a woman!—You're always a bit off color the first month or two."

Rebekah sat down at the side of the table before the glass of soda he had poured out for her.

"This cold bobotie is really excellent." He helped himself again. "Had some at Brownlee's the other night, such stuff! This just wants the very *smallest* touch of cayenne, though! Is there any on the sideboard?" She rose to fetch it him. "Just bring me the brandy too while you are up—no—on second thoughts I won't; I've had enough. I'll have milk with my soda. Did the boy clean my fishing boots?"

"Yes, but he hadn't time to polish the billiard room floor. He'll do that to-morrow before you come back." She sat down again at the side of the table and leaned her elbows on it. "I don't know what's the matter with the girl. She leaves all her work for him and me. And she was so good when she first came. I liked her better than I ever liked any servant before. She is so strange now; she knocks against me in the passage, though there's plenty of room to pass. She is so rude to me, as if she hated me. I can't understand it. If I——"

He interrupted her quickly; "I'll change my mind and have a little brandy if you'll bring it me; just a tiny drop. Pour it out for me, one dessertspoonful—so! Pure soda isn't good to go to sleep on, except for a little woman in a certain blissful condition." He laughed more boisterously than there seemed need. "Isn't that the baby crying?" he said.

She listened. "I can't hear it!" But she rose and took the candle and went to see if it were all right.

He finished his supper in silence; then he rose and paced the room twice; then he stopped at the window that looked out into the back yard, and drew the blind a little aside, and looked out; but there was nothing to be seen except the dark. Then he turned down the lamp and went to his dressing room.

Now, what really happened to Baby-Bertie was this: When she and Frank got to the house where the party was to be held they found it brilliantly lighted up, the garden and veranda full of Japanese lanterns, and light streaming from doors and windows, through which came the sound of music, for dancing had already begun.

A little sitting room on the right of the entrance had been turned into a dressing room, with a large mirror and dressing table, and Bertie went in to take off her wrappers. Behind the dressing room was a small bedroom, where the maid put away slippers and cloaks of the guests as she took them. Bertie could hardly wait to take hers off when she heard the music, and as there was some one using the glass she did not even look at herself before she hurried across the hall to the dancing room. Most of the dancers were youths and girls under twenty-one, with a few of older growth. Near the window to the right as she went in stood the daughter of the house whose birthday it was, with two other young girls and a young man. As Bertie walked up to them the two young girls turned away, but the daughter of the house accepted her congratulations, and the young man spoke to Bertie. Then two men, who had seen her coming in, came towards her from opposite sides of the room; the one who reached her first asked her to dance with him, and soon she forgot everything but the light and the music and the delicious whirl as she danced. As soon as one dance was over some one asked her for the next. Sometimes one of her partners suggested that they should go and sit on one of the closed-in verandas and talk and rest, but she always said she would rather dance. She had one dance with Frank, about eleven o'clock. He liked to dance with her, partly because he liked her and partly because he knew they looked well dancing together and men envied him his pretty sister-in-law.

After that, he had gone to the back veranda to have a smoke and to chat and romp with the younger girls from twelve to sixteen, who had gone there to play round games because there was no room for them in the dancing room.

And Bertie danced on.

Once in a dance, as Bertie passed a girl she knew, she smiled and nodded to her; but the girl seemed to be looking the other way and did not notice her. The rain poured, and left off, and poured again; but she heard nothing of it as she danced.

By and by, as the band was playing a very fast waltz and she was whirling round and round with it, some one trod on her dress. The white gauze which covered the silk skirt tore from the waist to the bottom and the long gossamer flounce made a streamer behind her. She caught it with one hand and holding it together laughed and nodded to her partner, and ran away to the dressing room.

There was no one there now. She stood before the mirror to examine the torn skirt; then she began taking pins from the plate on the dressing table to pin it with. She began at the waist and pinned downwards.

The throb of the dance was still in her feet.

The rain had left off, only the sound of the great drops falling from the eaves and the branches of the trees outside interfered with the sound of the music which came loud through the two closed doors:

> "Oh the torture and the anguish
> That cannot follow thee,"

the band was playing. She hurried to get back. She had to bend down very low at one side to pin on the flounce, so that her head was halfway to the floor; then, amid the music she heard the sound of voices talking in the little bedroom at the back where the cloaks were stored. She paid no attention to them but hurried on, her face pink with bending so low in a sideward position. Suddenly a name struck her—it was Rebekah's. Two old ladies who had brought three young daughters had gone to the little back room to be out of the way of the noise and dancing and were talking together. The noise of the drops falling from the eaves and the music and dancing prevented her hearing all that was said, but she heard part. "It seems strange she should have been asked," one said. "Yes, but—the invitation three weeks ago—"; and then the music broke in with a particular loud burst—"to bring her here among our innocent young girls!"

Bertie kept on pinning; she heard "she" and "she says" and "to her." Then she heard Rebekah's name again; and then—"but perhaps her sister did not know."

Bertie was motionless with a pin in one hand, her figure still half bent down over her dress, but her head raised to listen.

She heard Mrs. Drummond's name, and then—"It was her schoolmaster."

Quickly and noiselessly she raised herself; she dropped the pin softly on to the floor; she looked round the room with her deadly white face.

If she went out by the door that led into the hall, some one would be nearly sure to meet her. Again she looked round the room. There was a large French window at the side of the room which opened in the gable into the flower garden and shrubbery. It was low, and was hooked open two inches to let in the air. Softly she unhooked it and turned it back. It made no sound; she stepped out through it. Below was a bed of rose bushes; as she stepped into the bed of rich soft mold her feet sank almost ankle deep into it. She turned and closed the window softly, and with difficulty drew her feet out of the wet earth. She stepped into the gravel path. All the Chinese lanterns had long gone out with the rain, and the shrubbery was quite dark; she walked through the bushes, keeping away from the house and near the wall till she came to the gate. She opened it noiselessly and shut it again. She was now in the great avenue. She caught her skirt and threw it over her left arm, and began to walk quickly. The drops from the trees as the wind shook the branches fell on her naked arms and shoulders and ran down her back. She began to run; the skirt slipped from her arm and the train bellying out behind her whipped through the puddles of mud and water, drawing up the sticks and dead leaves. Faster and faster she ran. She turned into the next avenue. At last she was at Rebekah's gate. She opened it softly and crept up the little graveled path to the steps. She could see there was still a light in Rebekah's study; it was shining through the window on the plumbago hedge at the end of the house. She stole up the steps and across the veranda and turned the handle of the front door without a sound; but, as she turned to shut it from the inside, it slipped from her wet fingers and closed with a loud noise. She stood still listening to hear if Rebekah was coming, but there was no sound, and she turned down the side passage and went into her own room and closed the door behind her.

She knew there was a candle and matches on the dressing table, but she did not light it. The large four-poster bed stood across the end of the little room with the window opening over it at the side; at the foot of the bed there was just room for a person to get in between the bed and the wall. She crept in and knelt up, pressing her face against the wall paper. The old, old, terrible feeling had come back, the feeling she had lost for so many years; it was here again. Something following her, following her, following her! She pressed her face closer against the wall and folded her arms over her head. She felt as if everything in her were pressing down, down, down. It was so nice to press in there between the wall and the bed, it seemed to hold one up.

If only one did not feel so cold. The cold seemed to break out from her heart over her whole body. She did not think of anything particular; she only felt so cold.

After a time she began feeling faint kneeling up there; she crept into the bed. She threw herself down on her back in the middle of the bed. After a time the faintness seemed to get better and she fell into a heavy sleep. It was so that Rebekah and Frank found her when they came into the room.

After Rebekah had covered her and left her, she slept on for a long while, a heavy, motionless sleep. Then, suddenly, she began to move restlessly and to moan. She was having a dream. She thought she was in a great round theater like a circus; it was filled from floor to ceiling with seats which rose tier above tier over each other, and all were crowded with people. She was sitting halfway down on one side. In the circle in the center of the theater there was white sand scattered, and women in white dresses were dancing there, and all the crowd were looking down at them, and she looked down too. Then suddenly she noticed that the people were not looking at the women any more, they were all looking round the theater as though they were seeking for some one; and she looked about too, to see what it was they were looking for. Then she noticed a man on the other side of the theater just opposite her, with a great red fat face, who rose from his seat. She felt a kind of horror when she looked at him. He rose from his seat, and pointed with his great red fat finger, and cried, "That is she!" And all the people from the floor to the ceiling rose to their feet; and still the man pointed with his forefinger and cried, "That is she!" Then she looked round also to see who it was they were looking at—and then, suddenly, she knew it was herself they were looking at! Tier above tier, all round that vast place, the faces looked at her, and the man pointed with his red forefinger, and cried, "That is she!" A cold sweat broke out on her (in truth it broke out on her as she lay on the bed); she tried to slip down between her seat and the one before it and hide, but she could not move. She seized the back of the seat before her with both hands and tried to force herself down, but she could not stir; she was as if fastened to the seat. And from floor to ceiling the faces looked down at her; she saw her father and her mother there and the old farm servants: old Ayah and a little yellow shawl over her shoulders, and Griet looking from under her arm; there were all the men she had danced with: high up near the roof she saw John-Ferdinand looking down at her and Veronica standing just behind him, and low down she saw Mrs. Drummond with a lace handkerchief at her lips, looking at her. Everyone she had ever known was there. Then suddenly it seemed as if the white dress of one of the dancers in the circle below got torn; a long white trail hung down from it, and as the dancer swept round and round it grew longer and longer. It skirled as she whirled, it bellied out and out at the back and grew fuller and fuller; it frilled into soft billowy waves and passed over the heads of the dancers, filling all the circle below with a sea of misty white; it rose higher and higher, unrolling and unrolling; it came to the place where she sat; it passed her and rose to the ceiling and they were all suffocating. With a wild cry Bertie sprang up, struggling; before she knew where she was she was standing on the floor with the cold perspiration streaming down her, and the four-poster iron bedstead still rattling. At first she tried to remember how she came to be standing there in her clothes on the floor in the dark, and could not; then slowly she remembered everything.

Without lighting the candle she undressed, dropping her clothes on the floor where she stood. She felt for her nightdress and crept into bed; she drew the cover up high over her head. Yes, the old, old feeling she used to have at the farm had come back to her; something following her, following her, following her, and everything in her sinking down, down, down! She drew one of the pillows from under her head and laid it against her, and folded both her arms round it and pressed it to her as if it had been a person. It comforted her a little to hold it so close; it seemed to prevent that sinking feeling. She tucked the cover in tighter over her head. If she could only keep everything out.

When she woke the next morning it was already late; she could see by the lines of light through the venetian blind at her bedside that the sun was shining, though the room was still darkened with the drawn blind. Rebekah had evidently been in early, for a tray with biscuits and coffee, which was now cold, could dimly be seen on the chair at the bedside. Bertie lay still. It pained her to see the light coming in under the bars of the blind. If it could only always be night and one would never need to see anyone.

Then she heard the sound of steps coming up the graveled path; she half sat up and raised slightly the corner of the blind; but it was only the butcher's boy coming for orders, whistling. She let it drop again. She could not bear people to come up the path.

After a time she got up and sat down in her nightgown on the floor at the side of the bed and began in the semi-darkness to put on the stockings Rebekah had put ready for her beside her boots. Slowly she drew one on; then, before she had gartered it, she drew up her knees and folded her arms about them and leaned her forehead on her arms. She sat so motionless she might have gone to sleep again.

Then suddenly she sat up and began to pull on the other. "I will go to Aunt Mary-Anna," she said. "I will go to my Aunt Mary-Anna!" She began putting on her boots and lacing them up in the darkness. Her lips were puffed and her face a little swollen. There was a dull, obstinate resolution in it; the only form of strength her face ever wore.

This Aunt Mary-Anna was a sister of her mother's and of Frank and John-Ferdinand's father. Many years before she had come out to visit her sister, and at the old farm had met a young man from the next town whom she had married. Later they had moved to a small town farther up-country, where her husband was a general agent, and where two daughters had been born to her, who were several years younger than Bertie. They had been sent to England now for some years to finish their education, and she had written many times to ask Bertie, who was her godchild, to come up and stay with her while they were away. But Bertie had never wished to leave the old farm till she had left so suddenly with Rebekah. Now it came to her suddenly that she might go to her aunt's; it was so far away from everywhere. She pictured to herself the long miles of rolling karroo, the rocks and koppies and sand and whole mountain range that lay between it and anywhere. She would go first by train and then by post cart—on, and on, and on; she would have to go for days to get there.

"I must go! I will go!" she muttered, as she laced her boots in the half-dark, with her lips heavy set.

When she told Rebekah of her plan, Rebekah was not surprised. The little mother was always writing to ask when she was coming home, and it would seem a step on her way if she went to her aunt's, which was somewhat nearer the old farm than Cape Town. So Rebekah helped her to pack her things. She could not leave the next day as she wished, because she had to catch the post cart which only traveled once a week; but three days after she left.

As she was so busy packing, Rebekah did not wonder she went to say good-by to no one. There would not be room in the post cart for all her things; so Rebekah hung her evening dress and smart gowns in the wardrobe in Bertie's room, where she would find them when she came next year to visit her again. But Bertie knew she never would.

CHAPTER VIII

You Cannot Capture the Ideal by a Coup d'État

IT was four months now since Bertie had left. Spring had come; the oak trees had broken into their delicate spring green; the arms of the dark fir trees were sending out pale shoots at the tips, and near the old summer-house in the pine woods, where Rebekah loved to walk with the children, the ground between the pines was carpeted with bluebells, and under the pines themselves the smell of the needles was sweet.

In two months her child would be born, and she was busy making clothes for the other children to wear in the months when she could not do much more than look after the baby. She never went out anywhere except to the pine woods; and if people said anything she never heard them. Bertie wrote to say she was happy at her aunt's, and her mother had written to say she might stay there till her cousins returned from their school in England.

And Rebekah was happy. It was one of those peaceful, halcyon times that come in life, when the absence of new daily recurring matter of pain makes possible that upspringing of joy which only that which morning by morning tramples it down can permanently keep out of life.

She was happy when she kneaded her bread or mixed the salads in the pantry, and when she sat at work at the children's clothes; it gave her exquisite pleasure to see the great streaks of yellow afternoon sunshine lie on the carpet, and at night it was a pleasure to lie awake and hear the branches of the trees move against the roof.

Her husband was more at home than he had been since they were first married; he stayed at home, not only when it was necessary to eat and sleep, or when men came to play billiards, but often without need he came home an hour earlier than usual from office and when she came back from the pine woods with the children she found him in the rocking chair on the veranda with a magazine or paper in his hands, smoking and smiling contentedly. And on Sunday he would stay at home the whole morning, looking at the roses in the front garden or the fernery on the back stoep, or going round to the stables to look at his horses, or would sit in the shade on the back veranda, reading.

Perhaps life would always be so peaceful and beautiful now; perhaps all the struggle and anguish was passed; all things have to come to an end, and why not sorrow too? If one walked on silently, would not everything come right at last? She sometimes even wondered if she had not fancied that life was so hard as it had been in the past, and whether she could not have made things clearer. She was like a donkey who, having drawn a load to the top of a hill, when it goes down the other side for a little way thinks it must have been all a dream, that there ever was a hillside. She was quite contented; she wanted nothing more. Even the colored servant girl was not quite so rude now, though she was dull and silent and would do little work. Rebekah had hired her for a year from her mother, a respectable woman on a mission-station, and it was as though she feared being sent home to her and forbore to press things too far. And the black boy whom they had had since they were first married, and whose only regular work was to attend to the stables and yard and to his master's boots and fishing-tackle and guns, showed a particular kindness and would, when in the kitchen, help her lift a heavy pot, clean the kitchen window and weed her garden without being asked. Sometimes she fancied she caught him looking at her almost with a pitying, questioning look, which she fancied must be because he realized that physical work was unusually hard for her.

In the branches of the oak tree that grew in the yard and overhung the house, two small birds had made their nest. She had watched them carry on the first sticks and straws for the nest; now the little hen was beginning to sit for a great part of the day and her mate carried scraps of food he found about the yard and garden to her. In less than a month the little ones would be out. When she woke in the early morning as she lay in her bed and the sun had just risen, she could see clearly printed against the window blind the shadow of their two little figures as they walked up and down on the top cross bar of the veranda or sat close together on it. In after years she knew how closely she had watched those little birds, because the memory of that time never came back to her without those two little shadows on the window blind.

She had no time to write in her diaries because when her work was done she had to lie down and rest; but, lying on her back under the pine trees or at night when she could not sleep, she read a great deal. She had got a book about lichens and roses, and she had collected some from the roots of the fir trees and the thatch of the roof and from under the rose trees in the garden, and found them all beautifully different; she had examined them under her microscope, which she had not touched for years. All the little things of life were of much interest to her again; almost as they had been when she was a little child.

One Saturday evening Frank came home earlier than usual; before ten o'clock he said he would go to bed as he was starting at sunrise for a fishing expedition to a place beyond Simon's Town. Rebekah had packed his lunch-basket, it stood ready in the hall beside his rods and tackle, so she said good night and went to her own room. She slept in the children's room now on a little bed between the eldest boy's and the baby's, because, now the new child was coming, she slept badly and moved from side to side when she was asleep and Frank said it disturbed him to have her in the same room. So she slept in the bed of her second little boy, who now slept in the bed in the corner of his father's room.

After she had lain in bed for some time reading, she put out the light and tried to go to sleep; her husband had already put out his; she could see there was no light from the crack under the door between the two rooms. At first she felt very sleepy, but the sense of weight and physical discomfort would not let her sleep; she moved from side to side. At last she piled the pillows up under her head and lay in a half-sitting position with her arms crossed over her head. She was more comfortable so. Her thoughts did not run in that clear ordered fashion in which they follow one another when one lies awake, simply because the brain is too busily secreting to rest, but in the disconnected way in which pictures and sounds succeed each other automatically when one is really very sleepy. She thought of little household things; she saw pictures of them, saw the kitchen shelf with the row of tins on it and the dust she must dust off to-morrow, saw the large bag of wash-clothes she must count; then she saw the little cups of moss she had been looking at under her microscope that day, so delicate and so minute the naked eye could not see them; then she saw a place in the kloof on the old farm deep up in the bush where some trees were growing which were covered with long hoary moss hanging down like rough hair; there were two kinds; she wondered if they were male and female of the same species, or distinct species growing side by side, because the conditions suited them both; she wondered why she had never examined them and thought she would if she ever went out to the old farm again. Then she saw the place near by, in the bed of the mountain stream, where the great rocks were piled up and the Kaffir-bean trees hung over, and where Frank had lifted her down once; she seemed to feel his strong firmly-fleshed hands holding her as he lifted her down and his eyes with a beautiful intense light fixed on hers. It made her heart, the heart of the little tired pregnant woman lying there, beat when she remembered it, as the heart of the young girl had beaten. Then her thoughts went to the man in the next room lying there on his side, with his soft light hair pressed to the pillow and his strong shoulder showing above the cover. A great tenderness swept over her as when one thinks of one's little child, as if all the heart were being drawn out of her to him. The beautiful boy, the father of all her children! It rose and surged through her, the old wave that so often, through years since their marriage when he was away from home, had made her rise suddenly at night and fetch his overcoat and lie sleeping with it in her arms, with her face pressed to the collar where his neck had been, which came to her often in the night while she lay awake beside him and which, as she listened to his even breathing, made it seem to her the most precious thing in life—a wave that swelled and swelled till it filled her with a confident hope, and she knew when he woke there would be a new heaven and a new earth for them both. To-night she only felt a great wish to be near him, to slip her arm under his and wind it softly round his waist—just to feel him and hear him breathe. She lay still for a while, then she got up softly; she could go in softly without making any noise and creep into bed and lie down behind him and put her arms around him without waking him, and, when she felt she was getting sleepy, she would creep back to her own bed. She had done it more than once already without waking him. She opened the door of the next room and closed it softly and slipped across the room with her bare feet; she had no slippers on, for fear of making a noise. The room was quite dark. It was a large room, looking out into the back yard, and in the far corner stood the large four-poster bedstead; near the window, close to the door by which she had entered, stood the little bed in which her second boy was sleeping.

She knew the room so well she felt her way without any difficulty to the side of the bed in the far corner; she put out her hand softly and touched the quilt at the foot; she felt upwards; it seemed to be thrown back; she felt higher; the bed seemed to be thrown open and no one there. She took a match from the box on the stand at the bedside and struck it; the bed was open; there was a dent in the pillow where the head had been, and when she put her hand down on the sheet it was warm. The match had burnt out, and she dropped the end on the floor. No doubt he was gone to the stables; he told her that, on several nights lately, he had to get up because he heard the new stallion fighting with the other horses in the stable; and the colored boy, though his room opened out of the stable, slept so soundly that he heard nothing. Rebekah hesitated; she thought she would climb up on the bed and wait till he came, but he was always angry when he had to get up at night, and it might displease him more if he had to talk to anyone. She turned to go back to her room. As she passed the bed of her little son her feet caught in his down quilt which had fallen on the floor; then she stooped to pick it up and pushed it in round his shoulders; then, as she was tucking it round his feet, she paused a moment and lifted the corner of the blind to see if she could see her husband. It was a dazzling moonlight night; all the veranda that ran along the back of the house and the half of the yard covered by the oak tree was in deep shadow, but over the rest of the yard the moonlight fell in a sheet of white light from the moon almost overhead. The stones in the gravel of the yard glittered; on the opposite side of the yard the rough-cast whitewashed walls of the servants' rooms and the side of the stables seemed to radiate light; even the green window shutter and the door of the servant-girl's room seemed almost black in the intense light. The outline of the oak leaves at the tips of the branches was printed in shadow on the gravel almost as sharply and exactly as at midday. Not a breath was stirring. Everything seemed to glint. Then she saw in the door of the kitchen, which formed a wing at the end of the veranda, her husband standing. In the shadow of the veranda she could see him in his gray dressing gown near the stand of ferns. Then, instead of walking across the left of the yard towards the little side passage into which the stables opened, he came straight along the veranda. Just as he came opposite the window at which she was standing he stooped and took off his slippers; he carried them hanging from the first two fingers of his right hand; he moved in past the window of the children's bedroom, and then at the end of the veranda turned up, keeping near the wall in the shadow of the oak tree; then he turned again and came out into the full moonlight, just beyond the oak tree's shadow, and stopped opposite her, before the little green-shuttered window of the servant-girl's room. He glanced back at the house quickly; then softly, with the tips of the two forefingers of his left hand, struck two short blows on the wood of the shutter which covered the glass of the closed window; light as the taps were, Rebekah heard them; she saw his white naked feet on the gravel and the moonlight on his fair hair. Then the door opened; and she saw him bend his broad shoulders and bow his head a little as he stepped down through the low door. Then it closed. She looked at the gravel glinting in the moonlight and the white-washed wall, that seemed almost to throw out light at her. Whether she stood there for fifteen minutes or for twenty or for half an hour, she could not tell; a cold blast was blowing on her and froze her; then the door opened and her husband came out. The moonlight fell full on his face. He glanced at the house, then walked quickly straight across the yard to the kitchen door. Rebekah loosened her fingers from the blind, went slowly into the next room, the door closing itself behind her, and dropped on the little bed.

At half-past four all was quiet in the house; the dawn had not yet begun to make the darkness paler along the horizon.

Rebekah sat in her nightdress in her study with her

head resting on the edge of her desk. In the transparent glass bowl of her lamp the oil was almost exhausted, as though it had burned all night. On the floor beside her the waste-paper basket held pages of paper, wholly or partially covered with writing and then torn up. At her elbow lay an envelope addressed to her husband. She sat as if asleep, but the slight irregularity of her breathing told it was not so.

When the first gray dawn was beginning to make a clearer line along the flats and even there among the trees to make the darkness less intense, she rose and took up the letter and the lamp and went into the children's room. Her teeth were chattering slightly with the chill of the morning. She opened the door in the left-hand corner of the room which led into her husband's dressing room. It was in a way the pleasantest room in the house; a large double bow window looked out into the front garden; before it stood a dressing table with a large mirror and her husband's shaving materials and silver-backed brushes arranged upon it; before the dressing table on a chair hung the clothes she had put out the night before for the day's excursion. At the back of the room was a door that opened into their bedroom, his and hers, where he lay sleeping. She put the lamp down on the table and stood for a moment with the letter in her hand. At first she laid it down among the shaving things upon the table; then she took it up and fastened it with a breastpin from the cushion on to the breast of the coat that hung over the chair. Then she took up the lamp and went back to the children's room. She was shivering violently now. She put on her little blue dressing gown and her red slippers and lay down on the stretcher between the two children's beds. The lamp, which was exhausted, flickered and she turned it out. She lay listening, but her teeth chattered. After it might be fifty minutes she heard the door from the bedroom into the dressing room open and shut. She hardly breathed; then she got softly up from the bed.

She walked up and down the room. Her steps were noiseless but her breathing short and quick; it might have been heard in the next room. Suddenly she stood still before the door; there was a sound of water running loud in her ears. Then she opened it and went in.

Her husband was standing before the dressing table in his trousers and shirt. He had just blown out the two candles by whose light he had been shaving. The blinds were drawn up to the very top; enough dawn light came in to make everything clear. He was running a red necktie under the soft collar of his flannel shirt. He raised his chin to run the knot of the tie up. Beside the shaving case on the table lay the letter with his address upon it.

She stood by, breathing heavily. She moved her hand towards it.

"You've seen it, haven't you?" she said almost thickly.

"That!—oh yes!—certainly," he said slowly—"but you don't suppose I'm going to get up at five o'clock in the morning to read letters?" He raised his chin higher and looked into the glass. "Horrid little spot this—just in the very turn—always seems to catch the razor!" He dipped his finger into a silver-topped salve pot that stood open and put a small touch on the spot.

"I knew you wouldn't read it now," she said hurriedly and softly. "I wrote on the outside you must take it with you and read it to-day on the beach when you have time—between the fishing."

He turned his face partly away from her, still appearing to look at the spot with an absorbed interest. "Really, Rebekah," he said quietly, "I thought you'd become more sensible! What on earth should I read letters for from a person who is living in the same house with me and whom I can see every day! There are going to be a lot of people there and it would be very nice for me to be sitting there all day reading a letter from my wife!" He put on the lid of the salve pot with an exaggerated slowness.

Rebekah stepped forward suddenly, her hands knit in each other.

"Oh, please read it! Please, my husband! Please! I've sat up all night to write it. I had to write it!—Oh, please—please! I haven't meant to hurt you; I've tried to be gentle!—Oh, please, please! It's something I know!—Oh, please, please read it!"

With his face still partly turned away from her as if he were looking for something on the table, he said, "Now really, Rebekah, this is too bad! You've been so decent and sensible the last few years, I'd thought you'd given up this kind of thing. You, the mother of three children and on the point of having another, to go on in this nonsensical way!"

He sat down on the chair and began to tuck the bottom of his trousers into his boots. "No, I'll *not* read the letter; and I shall *not* take it with me!"

"Oh, please read it! Please read it!" She looked at him with distraught eyes; then she knelt down between his knees and looked up at him.

"Oh, please, please, my husband! I sat up all night to write it!—I will go mad if you don't!—I can't bear it any more!—I can't—I can't—I can't!" She beat with her hands softly, softly, up and down on the gray trousers that covered closely his powerful legs on either side of her; they moved up and down so fast they seemed at last like butterfly wings fluttering; you could hardly see them. "Oh, please, my dear husband, please!" Her eyes, as she looked up at him, seemed not to see him.

He looked down at her, doubtful just what line to pursue.

Then he shook himself roughly free from her and stood up. "Really, Rebekah, you shouldn't make such a damned jackass-fool of yourself!—It's Mrs. Drummond, I suppose, you are jealous about again—with her false hair and false teeth and eyebrows getting darker every day as she grows older. It's ridiculous! It's ridiculous!" He knew he had hardly spoken to Mrs. Drummond for three months, and was glad to turn matters in that direction. "I simply won't come home at all if I'm to be met in this way." He turned and seized his Norfolk jacket from the chair. "You've seemed so awfully sensible the last years! I thought you had got over this idiotic tomfoolery." He spoke a little more gently.

She had risen and stood looking at him with her arms crossed above her head.

"Please read it!—Please read it!" she spoke in a low almost inaudible whisper; "I sat up all night to write it!—I haven't slept—oh please—please help me!—I can't—I can't——"; she beat her head softly with her two hands.

"Then why the dickens don't you sleep! If you choose to sit up all night making an ass of yourself, is that any reason you should come here howling to me? 'You know, you know,'—some nonsense you've trumped up. If you don't care anything for me or yourself, you might at least think of your duty towards the child. It can't be very good for you to be going on this way."

"The child—oh, the child—my duty towards the child!—I—don't—do—my duty—towards—the—child!" She raised a long low cry, like a stricken dog. She turned away from him.

He seized her arm. "Look here, Rebekah, be silent at once! How dare you make such a noise in this house!" His anger was not assumed now, it was real. "Do you want to wake the children, and have them running in to see what's the matter? If you've no sense of right, or shame, or decency left in you, please remember I have. You are not fit to be allowed to have children at all if you conduct yourself in this manner!"

He took up his thick gloves and the little case with extra fishhooks and thrust them into his coat pocket.

She stood looking at him silently with her arms still folded over her head.

"I hope you'll be a little more sensible when I come back; you're acting like a mad woman now!"

He turned to the door at the back of the room, banging it to behind him so that the wall seemed to shake. She heard him shut the bedroom door in the same way; then for a little while he was in the front hall taking up his fishing rods and the luncheon basket; then she heard him going down the garden path, the footsteps she knew from all others in the world, that she had spent so many scores of hours in her life in waiting for. The gate closed. Then in the avenue, just outside the gate, on the other side of the tall plumbago hedge before the window, some one met him.

"Where are you off to so early?" The voices raised in the still damp morning air came clearly into the room.

"Going fishing. And you?"

"Off for a tramp; getting too stout. Were you at the club last night?"

"No; I came home early. Had business."

"You didn't hear the latest, then?" The man's voice sank; then she could hear, as she stood there, only a scattered word here and there as they spoke. It was evidently some club story. Then a thick, jovial guffaw of laughter burst from her husband.

"Well, see you to-morrow." She heard him laugh again as he walked one way and the man the other.

She stood still. The dawn light was coming full into the room now; soon the sun would rise. She looked at her letter lying on the table; she took it up and twisted it slowly with both hands till it was a stiff twisted roll. She walked into the children's room. The back veranda and the oak tree made it still almost as dark as night there. She walked to the stretcher and lay down on it on her back, the letter still clasped tightly in her hand. It was so early that not even the bread and milk carts had begun to go up and down in the avenue. There was dead silence. Presently the birds began to twitter in the oak tree outside. She lay with wide-open eyes looking up as the dark shadows of the rafters in the ceiling became slowly visible. The letter was pressed by her hand against her body.

After a while the youngest baby woke. He raised his head and called imperiously to be taken into her bed to play, as was the custom. Finding no one took any notice of him, he laid it down again, and lifting his small legs into the air began to play with his toes.

What the letter, which Rebekah held twisted in her hand, contained, was this:

"MY HUSBAND,

"You must read this letter. I am writing it in the night. I know what has happened to-night. I know where you have been. Do not think that it is because of this that I write.

"We have lived together for years now, and we have never spoken the truth to one another, nor opened our hearts; yet we are bound together; and all we do or think reacts upon the other. You know that when I have tried to speak to you of our relationship you have silenced me. And when I have written you have not read or have not answered what I wrote.

"But to-night I *must* write; and you *must* read what I write.

"I love you, my husband. Oh! I have loved you so, you ——" (This sentence she had scratched out so that it was not legible, and went on:)

"In the years before we were married, when you were asking me to marry you, and after we were engaged, I never doubted your love for me. My fear was always that I could not love you with a love as great and intense as yours. If there was any absence of truth and openness between us, I thought it would rise from my nature. Your frank, careless nature seemed to me of necessity more truthful and beautiful than mine, which was more reserved and perhaps complex. Those letters you wrote from England and after your return from the last voyage seemed to wrap me round with a flame of love.

"Even now I wake in the night sometimes and the cry from them seems to come back to me, 'My one love, my own love, my only love—come to me!' and sometimes I seem holding your letter in my hand in the garden under the pear tree, and reading, 'My Queen, my Queen, I need you! I need nothing but you, my love!'—and, when you have wondered why I have suddenly put my arms about you in the dark and crept close to you, it has been that cry I have heard call me. It has been possible for me to go on living during these last years, because I have heard it. When I have felt my self-respect dying, and a leaden humiliation of despair creeping over me, that has saved me. I want you to know that, whatever has happened in the years since we were together, or whatever may happen in the years to come, I never have doubted, and never shall doubt, the truth of your love for me then.

"When we had been married two days, I knew I had been mistaken in thinking my love for you was not great enough; it rose in me as a wave that swept all, even my old self, away before it. When we had been married six months, to cook your food and listen for your step coming up the gravel path, to watch you sitting in the armchair to smoke, made the world quite beautiful to me. I had only one regret that I had not accepted you when you first asked me, so that we might have had the years together which I wasted away from you.

"When you went to dinners or dances I wanted to go too, because it was beautiful to see you walking about and talking to the other people, and at night the happiest time of all was when I lay awake and heard you breathe close to me.

"After we were married you began to express your love less to me in words and caresses; but that seemed to me so right. When you are seeking to make your love known you must speak of it even in crude language; but when union is complete then the silence of fellowship and trust expresses it. When I felt the need of laying my face against your knee if I were sitting near you, or something compelled me to stand behind your chair and touch the little curls at the back of your neck, and you were seldom impelled towards me in the same way as you were before we married, I thought it was because your deeper man's nature had not need for these small forms of expression when the central union was there.

"Even afterwards, when you went for a day's fishing or to a dance or dinner and suggested it might be better for me not to go too because I had a baby coming, or afterwards had it to nurse, I never thought you did not want me; I thought you were afraid I might get tired. And even once or twice when you had decided to go to a place and I said afterwards I would go with you, I thought it was because you felt I was going for your sake.

"Never, for one moment, in all that first year and a half, did it ever once come within the range of possible thought to me that you did not love me just as you had. It would have been as mentally, I might almost say as physically, impossible for me to have doubted your loyalty or dreamed that you had put another woman in my place, even in your thoughts, without telling me of it, as it would be for me now, if one of my little children climbed up in the chair behind me, to dream that it had a knife in its hand and was going to run it in under my shoulder blade and stab me to the heart.

"There are things one cannot think.

"If you had been surrounded by all the most beautiful, all the most talented, all the most brilliant women in the world, it would never have struck me to fear them. What could they all be to you compared to me; I was your nearest, I was your dearest—I was your wife!

"As I have never suspected that my feet were trying to fling down my body, so I had never suspected any hidden thought or act of yours.

"You may ask, did I not know that sometimes after men and women had married they might find they had made a mistake, that, however loyal and true was the love they had given, they might find some human creature who might have been more to them than the one they married?

"And I answer, yes, I had thought of this; it had seemed to me the great attendant tragedy that waits on human marriage. It was because of this fear that, passionately as you drew me, I wanted two years before I gave myself to you. For I said always, 'Can I give him that love which is forever till death without possibility that another shadow may fall on it and darken it?' And it was only when the greatness of your love and your need of me had burned away all doubt of myself that I gave myself to you. Even if the thought of that shadow had come to me after we were married, which it never did, I should not have feared you, for I should have known that, if either of us saw such a shadow approaching, we would have gone straight to the other and laid all before them for advice and help; and I had never doubted that two souls true to each other would have found a way to the light. But after we were married no such thoughts ever came to me.

"But, you may say, did I not know there were men and women to whom marriage was only a form, who freely entered on a lifelong union meaning some day to violate it, and who took the soul and body of a creature into their hand meaning to betray it?

"And I answer, yes, I knew that there were such things, as I knew there were thugs and assassins and slow poisoners and professional murderers,—but that such things would ever enter into my personal life and play a part there I had never dreamed.

"I have always known there were octopuses in the sea with tentacles twenty feet long which, if they caught you, would drag you down and absorb you; I have always known that there were somewhere in the world basins of boiling mud into which if a man slipped suddenly he would be swallowed up, and that sometimes there were rifts in the earth in which whole villages and cities disappeared; but I had never thought, when I was walking alone on the seashore, that a tentacle might stretch out and drag me down, or when I was walking among the karroo bushes that a basin of boiling mud might appear before my feet and I slip into it or the earth rend open and swallow me.

"These things I knew existed somewhere in time and space—but what were they to me?

"I knew of them as I knew that there were women in the streets of great cities willing to sell their bodies, and men prostitutes who fell so low that they bought them (I had even shuddered walking down a street thinking I might without knowing it have passed such an one!); I knew of them as I knew there were shipwrecks in northern seas, where men and women with frozen hands clung to spars and masts till slowly the frozen fingers relaxed their grasp and they fell back with a thud into the sea; I knew of these things, but that they could ever enter my life, or had anything personally to do with me, I had never for one moment supposed. For me, personally, they had no existence.

"I knew you were friendly with many men and women; and I liked to see you with them; you always looked to me like a great blare of sunshine among dull uncolored masses; when I saw you dance or talk with other women, how happy they must think me to be part of you.

"When you introduced me to Mrs. Drummond I rather shrank from her because she seemed to me cold and narrow, but I knew she had come out in the same steamer with you and had been very kind in helping you to buy the furniture and get the house ready for me, and I tried to be polite to her as I was to all your friends. I was glad she could play your accompaniments and when you practiced your parts in the choir; and as you both sang and went to the same church it seemed most natural and right you should walk home with her; and I was glad you had her croquet parties to go to next door, just as I was glad to economize that we might have money to build the billiard room, because both made life pleasanter for you. I knew you admired her dress; I who hardly ever notice dress admired it too, but I did not think you liked her even as well as most of the women we met, for you often said small slighting things of her that you never said of them. If anyone had said to me that you loved Mrs. Drummond as well as half the tip of my little finger, I should have laughed, because you and I were one in a living circle; outside was all the world we loved and liked and helped wherever we could—but it wasn't us.

"You must please forgive me for taking so long to tell you this, but we are talking now for all the rest of our lives and we must understand one another. You can't if you don't know how happy I was then.

"Oh, please give up just one morning to reading this; it's for all our lives.

"Do you remember that night you went out to the whist party? I was going, but you said it was damp and might rain and I must run no risks while I nursed, so I stayed at home. I sat sewing in the dining room till half past ten; then, though I knew it was early, I went and sat in the rocking chair on the veranda that I might hear your steps when you came. I had not sat there ten minutes when I thought I heard your steps coming down the avenue. No one else could have heard them, but I always did even from the corner. It seemed to me your steps stopped at the gate next door, and that I heard it open and shut; it was such a still dark night one heard everything very clearly. I thought you were taking the short cut and coming across the lawn and through the rose-hedge gate, and I went down to meet you at the gate, but as I walked I fancied I saw the figure turn up and go towards the other side of the great house. It was so dark one could only see very dimly, and there was no sound on the grass. I thought you were going to the door on the other side of the house, and no doubt were going to fetch the music you had lent Mrs. Drummond to copy two days before. I was standing at the gate, when I saw against the yellow silk blind of Mrs. Drummond's little drawing room the shadow of your shoulders and head. You were taking off your coat. Then I knew you must be going to practice the music with her and could not be back directly. At first I felt inclined to run over and sit there while you sang, but I never liked going to Mrs. Drummond's; and it was drizzling, so I went back to my needlework in the dining room.

"It was a little after half past eleven when I heard the front gate in the avenue open and your steps coming quickly up the path. I ran to the front hall. You were just going to take off your coat. You kissed me, and said you were rather late, but you had tied, so you had to stay and play a deciding rubber. Your face was flushed as if you had been walking fast. I was helping you to take your coat off, and I said, 'Wasn't it strange? I thought I saw you going up to Mrs. Drummond's more than an hour ago.' You pull_d your coat out of my hand and turned round on me and said, 'So, you go peeping, watching me in the dark!' And I laughed; I thought you were playing with me, as you often did then. I caught your arm to lead you in to supper, and said, 'See what I've got for you.' You threw my hand off so that I almost stumbled against the other side of the passage. I still thought you were playing, and I tried to catch you again, laughing.

"Then you said, 'I suppose you fancy I am always running after other women; and you do nothing but pry, and try to find out!—I haven't seen Mrs. Drummond since the day before yesterday when she came to fetch the music!' I looked up at you and saw then you weren't playing. You said, 'That's what comes of being eaten up with jealousy! You are making an idiotic fool of yourself!' and you walked towards the dining room; and then I knew you meant what you said. Frank, I walked after you, but I didn't know what I was doing. It was as if each word you said was the blow of a great iron bar falling on my head. All the words you said to me that night start out at me even now sometimes in the middle of the night when I wake suddenly; and sometimes when I am busy with my housework I suddenly hear them ringing in my ears. I ran into the dining room after you and tried to put my hands on your shoulders and ask you what it was, but you shook me off you. You said many things. You said I thought you went to service only to walk home with Mrs. Drummond; you said I followed you everywhere; you said I even asked the servants about you! Oh, Frank, Frank! I couldn't say anything, I could only look at you. You said you wouldn't have any supper and you went into the bedroom and banged the door. I ran to the door to go in after you, and then I couldn't, and I ran out into the front garden and walked up and down in the drizzle. I didn't know what it was, or what I should do. Afterwards I saw you through the window come out of your bedroom and sit down to eat your supper. I wanted to run in and beg you to tell me that you had never said those words— that it was a horrible dream, but I couldn't. Afterwards you went back to the bedroom, but I still walked for a long time. Afterwards I went into the house, and then I wrote a letter to you. You see, what had stunned me was that you had thought it possible for me to doubt you. I told you I couldn't, I didn't. I told you how I had trusted your love, and I begged you to forgive me if I had ever done or said anything that made you feel I doubted it. Of course, when you said you had been kept playing, I knew I had been mistaken and that it must be another man. I told you that, wherever you went or whatever you did, I could never doubt you, that I know your nature was much nobler and simpler than mine. I begged you to forgive me for anything I had unconsciously done.

"When I knew you would be fast asleep I went into the bedroom and put the letter on the stand beside you. I thought how you would open it in the morning and read it and turn and take me in your arms and lay my head upon your shoulder and tell me you would never think I doubted you again, and explain to me how it all happened. I lay awake at your back all night waiting for the morning, but just when the dawn was coming I fell asleep. When I woke it was not late, but you were gone and the letter was gone too. I got up quickly and put on my dressing gown, and went into the dining room. You were just finishing your breakfast. You got up and kissed me and said you had something to eat as you had to catch the early train, and began to take up your things. I put my hand on your arm to say something, but you said you had to go at once, and you kissed me quickly and went. When you were gone I saw my letter, torn very, very small, in the waste paper basket by the fireplace. I couldn't understand it that you had not spoken to me of it. I thought perhaps your heart was still too sore; and yet you did not seem bitter, you looked just as always. Though you had kissed me so quickly, you had been kind to me, even more kindly than sometimes. Then I remembered I had heard older women say that no woman understands what a man is till she has been married for some years; that unmarried women never understand men. I thought that perhaps, though you had forgiven me, the pain your man's nature had felt as though I had mistrusted you was so deep you could not speak of it as a woman would have done. I thought of my father; but he was always silent and reserved, and you spoke always to everyone you met about everything. I thought of the silent agony you must have felt all those days when something I had done had made you think I doubted you, showing no sign at all, and I felt I must learn to understand you. The only thing I could think of that might have made you think I mistrusted you was that I always stood waiting at the door for your steps when it was time for you to come home. You had liked it when we were first married; you called me your little watching bird. I thought that, when we were both in bed that night, I would creep very close to you and ask you in a whisper to explain to me what I had done. That couldn't hurt you. I walked up and down a long time thinking; then I stood at the table, breaking some biscuit into a basin for the baby's breakfast before I went to dress, when the servant opened the door; she said the servant girl from next door wanted to see me. I told her to bring her in. She came and held out her hand with a little twisted bit of white paper in it; she gave it me. She said she had picked up what it held when she was sweeping the floor of her mistress's rooms just now and thought it belonged to you. I opened the paper; inside was one of the gold sleeve links I gave you on your last birthday with your initials and mine on it. The night before I had put them into your white shirt ready for you before you went out to play whist. I gave her some money, and then I mixed the baby's food and gave it to the girl to give him; and then I walked up and down with the sleeve link in my hand, and then I went to your dressing room. Over the chair was the shirt; there was a link in one sleeve and none in the other.

"Perhaps you will find it hard to believe me (I can hardly believe it now), but in the white daze that came to me when all the world seemed to have worn away from me, though I knew you had lied to me, the only feeling I had was that in some way I must so terribly have made you misunderstand me, that you could not pursue a simple kindly human relation without having to lie to me about it. In my darkness all I could think was that you had noticed my cold shrinking from Mrs. Drummond, from the first day I met her, that you had attributed it to resentment on my part to your politeness to her, and that you had in consequence felt you could not go to see her openly but had to hide it from me. I can't understand it now, but that was how I felt. I resolved that, by great kindness and politeness to her, I would show you that I have never misunderstood your friendship for her. I remembered that, though you had often spoken slightingly of her, you had always wished me to go to see her and invite her to our house. At once I sat down and wrote to her. I told her I was going to shop in town that afternoon and asked her if she would come with her work and spend the afternoon at my house so that my baby would not be alone with the servant. It was the first favor I had ever asked of her, and I thought she would understand what it meant; and I resolved to stay away till long after your time for returning. I sent the note over with the largest bunch of roses I had ever cut from my garden, and when her answer came I spent the morning making tea cakes for her and you while I was away. It seemed to smooth my brain.

"I went in the afternoon and I did not come back till long after I knew you would be home, so that you might have a long time with her. When I came home she had gone, but you had brought two men for dinner with you. You seemed in very good spirits; after dinner you sang comic songs in the drawing-room, before you went to the billiard room. It was nearly twelve when they went. I thought you would say something to me; but you said you were dead tired, and you got into bed at once when you came from your dressing room, and lay on your shoulder and closed your eyes, and I could say nothing.

"The next morning when I kissed you in the passage before you went out, I asked you if you had read the letter. You laughed and chucked me under the chin, and said, 'Don't be a silly little woman, don't be a little fool,' and hurried out. And I saw you did not mean to speak of it; and I could not.

"I noticed that you did not go over to Mrs. Drummond as you usually did; and she did not come to our house; but I sent her cakes and flowers; and I knew one day you would take me to you and say, 'I know you have always trusted me, little woman,' and then my heart would rest. But while you held me from you I could not speak.

"One day I sent over some flowers to Mrs. Drummond, and the servant said she had gone to Somerset Strand for a holiday and would be gone some time.

"I think she'd been gone about two weeks when the post-boy brought the letters to the door. We were at breakfast, and I went to fetch them; I saw the top one was addressed in Mrs. Drummond's handwriting to you at your office, and had come by mistake to the house. I passed it to you across the table. I didn't wonder she wrote to you; I knew you did all her business for her; and there were many things she might write about. You glanced at the first sheet and said she wanted you to pay some accounts for her; and you put it in your pocket. Then you took up a half-sheet that had been enclosed. You began to read it; then you said, 'Oh, this is some woman's business for you,' and you passed it on to me. It was marked P.S., and began, 'Please tell your wife there is a woman here who makes very good *ingelegte-vis* (pickled fish) if she wants any;' and then she went on to give the price and to say how she packed it in stone jars which had to be returned to her when they were empty; and then without any break went on, 'To-morrow will be the 27th of January, that never-to-be-forgotten and best and dearest of all days of my life which first brought you to me. Do you remember?'—Then I read no more. I handed the sheet back to you. You took it, almost without looking at it or me, and tore it up and threw it into the waste paper basket behind you. Then you stood up and gathered the rest of your papers together. You didn't notice me. Then you went out; I didn't go with you to say good-by at the door. I only sat. Then I heard your feet go down the path. And then an impulse came on me to stoop down and gather together the bits of paper in the basket and piece them and read them. I knew if I waited an instant I should do it. I grasped them up in my two hands and ran to the kitchen fire and dropped them in. I didn't want to know what more she had written; I wanted to forget what I had read. I held my brain stiff that I might not realize it. Only I knew that, from the moment I read the letter, there has always been a burning pain at my heart that has never quite gone and a weight that never was there before. All the day I worked and cooked to keep myself from thinking. It was only late in the afternoon that I was forced to see what the letter meant. I did not think for a moment you loved her or could have been physically unfaithful to me by so much as the pressure of a hand, but I knew there was a friendship between you greater than you let be seen, that perhaps she loved you, and that it was your consciousness of this had made you fancy I mistrusted you. Further I would not look; I let down an iron door without a crack between that part of my brain which knew about it and the rest of my mind; and I worked without stopping. But I was conscious there was a deadened part of my brain lying behind that iron door all the while, waiting to come to life. I had talked so much to myself always about the duty of not shutting one's eyes to anything and facing all facts; and now I was trying to keep my eyes shut.

"It was two days after that you said you had to go up to Robertson and Worcester [1] on business and you would be gone five days.

"For the first two days after you left I was busy; I turned the whole house out and had the yard and out-buildings cleaned. On the third day I got a letter dated 'Worcester' saying you would be back in three days.

"The next day I was sitting sewing in the front room about ten o'clock, when a curious thing happened to me. I had had a restless feeling that I could not understand ever since I got up. But I sat sewing quietly. Suddenly a feeling came to me that I must go to Muizenberg.[2] I

---

[1] Worcester is 109 miles inland from Cape Town on the main line; Robertson is 30 miles farther, on a branch line; both are in an opposite direction from Somerset Strand. In those days there was no train to them.

[2] Muizenberg is a seaside place 15 miles from Cape Town, now connected by rail, but in those days only to be reached by a lovely veld drive; after you left Wynberg you came to few houses except Rathfelder's Hotel and some scattered farms among vine-yards and cultivated fields; for the rest, there were wild trees and shrubs.

At Muizenberg itself, where now red-brick hotels and lodging-houses alternate with tin or whitewashed shanties, and the railway whistle screams, and rows of bathing houses cover the shore, and half-clad children, not rising to the simple dignity of the nude or

had never been since just after we were married when you took me to spend a day there. I had never since thought of going there. Now, as I was glancing up from my work at the bees humming above amongst the flowers, it came to me, not as a desire, but as a pressing necessity, that I must go. I don't think I even questioned myself as to why I should go; it only seemed to me an imperative command: I must go. I had never taken a holiday by myself since I was married, nor ever left the house while you were away. I went to the back yard and told the boy to inspan the buggy and the girl to dress that she might hold the baby while I drove. I felt a kind of wild exhilaration and excitement upon me. It was only after we had started and driven some distance that it struck me how very strange it was we should be going. I thought the kind of excitement, almost fever, that was upon me must be a reaction from the many days I had been holding myself down so. Everything looked so beautiful—the green trees, the bushes with the sun shining on them. When we got to Muizenberg it was midday, there was a light southeaster blowing, the blue water was sparkling in the sun. At Farmer Peck's I told them to take the horses to the stable and feed them. They said their early dinner was over. I said I should go down to the beach for

maintaining the convention of ordinary clothing, paddle on the sand—at Muizenberg there was then one solitary farmhouse known as Farmer Peck's, with a thatched roof and mud floors, where travelers might put up their horses and obtain a simple meal. Above towered the mountain from whose crags an eagle might still sometimes be seen rising, casting its long shadow on the unsullied slopes; and below stretched the long, long curve of white sandy beach, unflecked, except where, here or there, a jellyfish or a "Portuguese mariner," thrown by the long smooth waves, decked the shore. Far out the white breakers curved in long unbroken lines, and to the right, where the sand and the curve of the bay ended, great rocks which through the ages had fallen from the crags above lined the water, and the waves ran singing in and out among them. As far as the eye could reach there was no living thing, but it might be the eagle from the crags, or the white seagulls hovering over the water, or the little dots of glittering life upon the sand.

an hour and then return to have coffee and bread. But I asked them to show me a bedroom to lay the baby down in, as he had dropped asleep. They showed me into a little room, and I told the girl to sit by him till he woke and then bring him to the beach to me. Just as I was going out through the front room I saw hanging over a wooden chair near the door a cloak. It was of soft maroon color and lined with silk and edged with fur. It struck me as familiar; then I recognized it was Mrs. Drummond's. No one else in Cape Town had a cloak like that. A feeling of heaviness came over me; I did not want to see her on the beach where I had come to be glad. It seemed strange she should have come there from Somerset Strand. Then I saw, partly hidden by her cloak, on the same chair was a man's overcoat. I was going out when something struck my eye. Out of the pocket of the coat was hanging part of a blue silk muffler with white squares upon it. I stood looking at it. I gave you such a muffler at Xmas. In the corner I had worked initials in white silk. They were there. At first I seemed dulled. I couldn't touch them, I only stood looking at them. I only felt I wanted to creep away and hide. If the girl had not been there I think I should have crept into the bedroom and hidden beside the bed. It was only for a moment, and then the feeling came over me I must run out and look for something, I didn't say to myself what. I rushed out; I did not keep to the road; I almost leaped over the bushes and stones on the way to the beach, and all the time I was crying out aloud with my teeth tight, 'It's a lie! It's a lie! It's a lie! It isn't he! It isn't he!'

"When I got to the sandy beach it was lying there all so calm and beautiful. Not the mark of a human foot was upon it, and only the great white sea-gulls were flying over the sea. I stood suddenly still as though a great hand were laid on my forehead. Had I been mad? It was all a dream!

"I stood and looked at the sea and sand and the great white birds for quite a long time, and then I began to walk

slowly to the part where the rocks lay. The tide was high
and running softly in and out among them. I got to
a little rise where the stones lay just below me. There
was not a sign of a human creature anywhere.

"Then quite close to me, just below, I heard voices.
There was a large flat rock with the water washing round
its base; on it lay a smaller rock and over the top of it I
saw two heads of people who were sitting on the large rock
and leaning back against the smaller. Of the head of one
only a little black bonnet with an aigrette standing up
could be seen, but I saw the felt hat and the row of tiny
curls and the broad thick neck of the other. I could not
doubt any more. She said something and then you answered her and bent your head a little and laughed, and
then she laughed, that little snipped-off laugh I knew. I
couldn't doubt any more. You could have heard me
breathing where I stood, only the water ran in and out
among the rocks, gurgling. If you had turned and seen
me, perhaps all our lives would have been different, because I had lost all control of myself that day. I knew
if I heard your voice again (my voice!—my voice!), I
should shriek and rush down to you. So I turned and ran.
I felt the one thing was I must escape. I gave the boy ten
shillings to inspan quickly and I got the girl and baby. I
saw the woman of the place standing in the door looking
at me as if she thought I was mad. And then we started.
We had the wind in our faces. It was the feet of the
horses that saved me. They got wilder and wilder; they
kicked up the mud and stones into the air. Sometimes as
I looked from their heads I caught sight of their feet. I
held hard; I didn't touch them, but they knew they had to
go. When we had gone some way, some colored men
working in a field ran out and tried to stop them; they
thought they were trying to run away; but I shouted to
them to let us go. When I got near to the suburbs a
policeman came up and stopped me; he said I could not
drive so fast among the houses. So I took the road down
into the flats, and we drove round miles, but we got home

at last. It was because they helped me that day that when
last year you wanted to sell one of them who had broken
his knees, I bought him from you and put him on my farm
to do nothing.

"It was three days more before you came home: I
had had a miscarriage during that time. The doctor said
I was very ill, and when you came you only kissed me and
went away, because the fever was high. They thought it
was my body caused it, but it was my brain. I was in
hell. Night and day I heard Mrs. Drummond's laugh,
and I heard your voice, that low voice I know, speak to
her. It seemed as if I was gnawing my own soul. They
said if I got out of bed and walked about I should bleed
to death; and I sometimes felt I must get up and end it
all. The third night after you came back I slept heavily,
and when I woke in the dawn such a curious calm had
come to me. You were sleeping in the spare room, and
the nurse was lying in the bed in the corner. I began to
think I could see things quite calmly and clearly, as though
they did not concern me.

"What if you loved Mrs. Drummond? What if after
you married me you found I was not what you thought,
and she was the woman who could satisfy you? What
if you had deceived me about her and your feeling for her,
because your love for her was so infinite that you could not
risk my knowing of your friendship?

"If I had had a son and he had loved another woman
not his wife, and he had come and laid his head on my
breast and told me about it, would I not have sympathized
with him and tried to help him to find a way that was
truthful and open? And should I sympathize with you
less and help you less, who were more to me than all the
sons I would ever bear? I thought it all out in the dawn,
and during the day I got a pencil and wrote to you. Oh,
I know it was tender, because I felt to you then as I can't
even now; I only wanted to help you and give myself up
for you. I told you I knew you cared for Mrs. Drummond, but I didn't tell you how I knew or what I [had

seen] because I wanted *you* to tell *me* everything. I only told you that I knew you cared for her more than you allowed to me and that I did not blame you if, after you married me, I had disappointed you and you felt you needed her friendship. I told you that if you wanted to see more of her than you could as things were, I would go for a long visit to my mother with the children, and I would ask her to come and keep house for you while I was away. I should tell everyone before I went that I had asked her, so there would be no scandal; and if, when you had been with her two or three months, you wished then I would stay away forever, you could sue me to return, and, when I did not return, you could get a divorce, and no one would blame you. And then if you and she wished to marry I would write to her husband, and I would beg him to act as I had done, and make it possible for you to be happy together. I told you how much I loved you, but that the joy of helping you to what was best for you would cover my pain and heal it at last. Oh, I know I wrote tenderly, because I never felt so tender to my little baby when it lay sucking at my breast as I felt to you that day. Even to Mrs. Drummond I felt no bitterness; if you loved her, why should I judge her! For three days I kept the letter in my breast, because I didn't think it fair to give it you while I was lying in bed, because you could not have spoken as you would. Even after I got up I kept it for three days. I always seemed to feel a hot place where it lay in my heart; I thought you would understand all when you read it.

"I could not give it you myself, because my breath got so short when I came near you; so I gave it the servant to give you on Sunday morning while I was still in bed. After breakfast when I got up I went to the billiard room where you were practicing with the balls.

"I waited a little, and then I asked you if she had given you my letter. You said yes, and kept on playing the balls as though you had hardly heard me. I asked you if you had read it, and you said yes, and went on playing.

And then I asked you if, when I went to visit my mother, you would like me to ask Mrs. Drummond to come and keep house for you. And you burst out laughing; you said I must be very hipped to think of such a thing; that Mrs. Drummond would run up enough bills in a month to run our house for a year; you said I must be completely hipped to write such nonsense. You kept looking at the balls as if all your thoughts were with them. You said I seemed to have Mrs. Drummond on the brain; that the only excuse for me was that I was ill. You said that if there was only one woman in the world, and that woman Mrs. Drummond, you wouldn't marry her. That any man who had the settling of her business for her, and the sending to England of cheques for her dresses, would have only one feeling about her and that was pity for her husband; and then you laughed again. You asked me why I wasted my time writing such nonsense, and you went on playing. And then it was suddenly as if something broke in me, and I lost my self-restraint. I cried out I knew you loved her, I knew everything; and I begged you to tell me the truth; and I threw myself down at your feet and I clasped them and I told you I was quite willing you should get a divorce from me, and I would go away and take care of the child and would love you all my life just the same, and I kissed your feet and cried out to you, 'Please to tell me the truth,' and told you I loved you. I begged you only to speak the truth to me, nothing else. And then you pushed me from you and swore; you said I must be mad to talk such nonsense about a divorce and leaving you. You said even my illness did not make any excuse for my making such a miserable exhibition of myself, and then you went away.

"You may say, why didn't I tell you exactly what I had seen and knew. Oh, didn't you see I couldn't? It was *you* who had to tell *me!* I would have taken your last chance from you! Would you have been any greater, would you have been any better, because I had forced your hand? Then I saw what you wanted was not truth between us, but just to be left alone to lead your own life.

"I was ill and had to go to bed again; and you never referred to what had happened; and I never did. But you knew that, if you wished it, you could be free and that I would not keep you.

"It was about two weeks after that that something else happened. I was about again, but hadn't done any work in my garden. I hadn't seemed to care what happened to it. But one morning the sun was shining and I had a feeling I wanted to put it neat. I took my mat and sat on the ground picking up the weeds and rubbish that had blown in. I was tired, and was just going back to the house, when I saw a quantity of dried leaves and bits of paper gathered among the forked roots of my large rose tree, and I sat down on my mat by it to clean it out. I was scratching the rubbish out with my fingers and the trowel when I pulled out half a sheet of note-paper yellow with the mud and rain and a little bit scorched at the bottom as if it had been thrown into the fire. I threw it down with the other leaves and rubbish before me, and then I saw my name on it. It was written in a clear round hand that I knew was Mrs. Drummond's. It was a letter dated three months before, therefore before I saw you go to Mrs. Drummond's that night. It began, 'My Friend'— but from what came next I saw it was to you. You and she had evidently been discussing me. She spoke of marriage generally, and then quoted with inverted commas what you had said about our relation to each other, even our physical relation. She began to comment on what you had said, then came the bottom with the last line burned off. I did not turn it over to read what was on the other side. For a little time I sat as if I was dead. Then I took my trowel and cut at it. I chopped and chopped it till it was the finest fragments; I chopped at it till it disappeared into the ground and there was not a sign of it left.

"I had believed, older women had told me, that a man

never talked of his wife to other women, that he might be unfaithful to her, that he might humiliate her into the dust at his own feet, but that, as long as she was his wife, he never allowed any other woman to speak of her, as long as she was a part of himself he put his hand out over her and covered her as a man covers the nakedness of his own body. I had never doubted it. I think it is because many women believe this that they stay on with men when their hearts are breaking: they say, '*Am I not still his wife?*'

"Afterwards, Mrs. Drummond came back and you never went to her croquet parties and seldom saw her. I knew it wasn't only when I was by you avoided her, because she often came over when she expected you would be home and seemed always restlessly looking for you. But oh, I didn't care; nothing mattered. When she looked at me there were little contractions in the inner corner of her eye that come to some women when they look at another whom they hate; but nothing mattered to me. I knew I would have given you up to her if you had really loved her.

"One night I was putting the children to bed and you were smoking on the veranda with some men. I came to your dressing room to put your clothes ready for the next morning, and I could hear what was said. They were discussing Mrs. Drummond. One man laughed and said she was ten years older than she professed to be. The other talked of her husband, and laughed about the way she always professed he was longing to come back to her, but he never returned. And you laughed and said you had heard she was bald at the top of her head and had two wigs, one to wear by day and the other at night, so that if she were taken ill suddenly no one might find out. And then you all laughed. Oh, don't think it comforted me to hear you laugh at her. The only thing that could have saved me would have been to believe you loved her with such a mighty passion that it swept all before it, even me! It made me see the thing I was trying to press from me with both hands that I might not see it. The less your love for her, the lower I fell, and you. Was it for this you had put me from you!

"After that, when I was expecting Frank [her baby] I became very weak; the doctor said my heart was going, that I was bearing too quickly and working too much. Oh, it wasn't the childbearing or the work or the miscarriages; a woman can bear all and do all if the arms of a man are tight about her. I had loved so to bear for you and to work for you. Now nothing mattered; I couldn't read, I couldn't think! Oh, it isn't only the body of a woman that a man touches when he takes her in his hands; it's her brain, it's her intellect, it's her whole life! He puts his hand in among the finest cords of her being and rends and tears them if he will, so that they never produce anything more but discord and disharmony, or he puts his hand on them gently, and draws out all the music and makes them strong. Oh, it isn't only her body a woman gives a man——" (This paragraph Rebekah had not finished and had scratched out.)

"Some time after that, but just after Frank was born, you said you must go into town by the early train; you had always gone by the late one because you said you hated the crush of the business people and the children going to school; but you said you had more business. You always seemed angry and irritable if you thought breakfast would be late; I thought your work was troubling you. You seldom noticed me or the children, and seemed always absorbed. One night the girl was out, and I brought the tray with refreshments to the billiard room myself. One of the men was hanging up the rest as I came in, and his back was to the door; he was laughing, and he said something about 'that young inamorata of yours who is so faithful to you in the train.' He turned and saw me and took up his cue and began to play. I took no notice of what he said; I did not even know to which of the men in the room he was speaking. I took it as some man's joke; but afterwards I remembered.

"One evening you decided suddenly to go the next day to Simon's Town, and you had some papers at the house you said it was necessary should be in your office the first thing in the morning. I said I would take them in for you, and you gave me them before you started in the morning in the leathern handbag you always carried with your initials on it. I thought I would make sure they were in time, and I hurried to catch the early train. I had just taken my seat in the carriage when a girl put her head in as if she were seeking for some one and went on. In a few moments she came past again, still looking in at the windows. She was just going by, and then it seemed she caught sight of something. She looked up at me and stared, and then, just as the train was moving, jumped in. She was a stout girl of about fourteen or fifteen, but wearing very short dresses and with a satchel of school books on her arm. She sat down opposite me, and as she stuck her feet out across the carriage you could see the great thickness of her legs. She had a great head of short curly black hair, very tousled and standing out at the sides, with a red jellybag stuck on the top. She had large, round, dark eyes, and beautiful white teeth; and, though her mouth was very large, she would have been good looking if her round face had not been covered with pimples with little blackheads. As she sat opposite me she stared at the bag on my lap and then up at me; and then she tossed the end of the jellybag from one side of her head to the other and stared again. I felt she was coarse and unpleasant, but I soon forgot about her. When the train got to Cape Town she jumped out and ran up the platform at once; when I came to the gate she was standing there watching the men from the smoking carriages as they came up. I passed her and went out of the station. When I was crossing over to the other side of the road I happened to look back and saw her standing before the station, staring after me. I hurried on to the office and forgot all about her. I gave the bag in at the office and went to Adderley Street to do some shopping. I had finished and was going slowly down the street to the station, when suddenly something struck my brain; it seemed as though a cold hand had grasped my heart, crushing the life out; in a moment I knew everything just as I know it now. I knew what the man meant in the billiard room; I knew why you went to town by the early train; I knew why the girl stared at your bag and at me. I had no ground for knowing it; one moment before I knew nothing, I was thinking of my purchases. It flashed out on me as a moving picture in a street flashes on your eye; you see all parts of it almost in a second. It was like when one makes a story; one does not think, all the characters flash out before you in a moment speaking and acting—you *see* them!

"When you came back that night you were as usual, and the next morning you went to Town by the early train. I tried all day to put the thing that had flashed on me away from me; I tried to say it was a fancy; but deep in my heart I *knew* it wasn't. You came back at midday for dinner because it was Saturday; at dinner you said I was looking very pale, and you said I ought to take the children and the servant and go into the pine woods for the afternoon; you said you were going to the flats to see a friend, so you would not be at home. I thought it kind of you to think of how I looked; almost gladness came to me. At three o'clock I took the children and the servant and went; you were still reading the papers on the front stoep; you said as soon as you had finished you were going and would lock the front doors; the stable boy was at the back and could look after the yard entrance. When we got up to the old summer house and had been there for some time the girl found she had forgotten the basket with the baby's feeding bottle, and I said I would go back and fetch it. When I got there the stable boy was sitting before the back gate cleaning harness, and when I went into the house all the front doors and windows were locked, and I thought you had gone out. I had got the bottle and was just going out of the dining room into the passage that leads to the kitchen and billiard room, when I heard a noise of laughing and shouting. I went into the passage; at the far end the door of the billiard room was open and I saw two figures chasing each other round the table; the one seemed to me to be you, and the other the girl I had seen in the train. I walked straight down the passage to the door of the billiard room. You had caught her by that time; she was lying on the floor on her back; her legs were under the billiard table but her head out, and you were kneeling on the floor at her head bending over and tickling her. Your back was to the door. She was gasping with laughter and kicking with her feet against the underside of the table and crying between the gasps, 'You horrid man—I'll pull your mustache again—like I did the day before yesterday!' And you said, 'Will you! Will you! Will you!' and kept on tickling her. The soles of your feet were turned to me as you knelt, and I saw your beautiful broad shoulders and the curls above your thick neck as you bent over her. You said something in your soft thick way between your half-closed lips; only she could hear it, and she laughed louder. Then I turned and ran; I ran as I have never run in my life. I threw down the basket in the kitchen and my cloak caught the door and closed it loud behind me; I ran across the yard and up the side passage by the stable boy and up through the woods and up the mountain. I climbed and climbed; when I got to the blockhouse I dropped on my face, but as soon as I had breath I got up and I climbed till I climbed so high there were only the crags of the mountain above me where the gorge comes down to the silver trees. Then I lay on the ground. I was deaf and blind. I heard nothing of the outer world; only inside my brain I heard always—'The father of your children!— the lord of your body!—the owner of your life!' When I called your name aloud, 'Frank!—Frank!' —that was the answer that came back to me. All the time I ran up the mountain and all the time I lay there, the only thing I saw was your broad back and the curls about your neck and the girl's legs with the rim of the red flannel petticoat that showed as she kicked and laughed.

"When it was dark I felt my way down the mountain back to our house. It was half past eight when I got there, but you had not come back. I went to bathe the children. Afterwards you came in; you were very friendly and in high good spirits. You came into the bedroom and stood by the bath, and said how nice and fat the baby was growing, and squirted him with water; you didn't notice that I said nothing. But afterwards, when we were at supper, sometimes as you ate you glanced up at me from under your eyebrows; as if you had heard the door slam or the stable boy had told you I'd been home. You didn't say anything, but, just as you got up from the table, you half turned and said quickly, 'Oh, by the way, there was a girl here this afternoon, the station-master's cousin or niece or something of the kind. She had some lace her aunt had made to sell, and she wanted to see if you would buy it. I told her you were out and she must come again when you were here; it wasn't in my line!' and then you laughed your little laugh and went out of the room.

"Perhaps you'll say again, why didn't I speak to you directly and tell you what I had seen? Oh, I couldn't, don't you see I couldn't! If you had sworn at me, and spoken as you spoke before, I would have died, and my baby was six weeks old.

"The next day was Sunday and you stayed at home. and you played with the children. But I was in hell, wandering in the dark.

"On Monday morning you went to catch the early train as usual. I was washing the baby; and suddenly the feeling swept over me that I *must* follow, that I *must* see you meet her. I hadn't a definite plan of saying or doing anything, just the feeling I must go. I laid the baby down on the bed and put on my hat and without dressing I ran down the avenue after you, till I got to the place where the second avenue turns to the station; then

I stopped. An awful wave of humiliation swept over me, and I turned and came home again.

"All the week you were the same as usual, only in better spirits; you sang and whistled more. Late the next Sunday afternoon you said you were going to visit a man and would go straight from his house to church and I need not expect you back till nine o'clock for supper. About an hour after you left some one came to say the old Malay cook we had when we were first married was very ill and wanted to see me. I went and stayed with her nearly an hour. When I came out it was beginning to get dark; so I didn't take the short cut through the woods; I went the long road past the station. When I got near the station it was almost dark; I saw, without noticing, a man's figure standing near a gate in a hedge in the road. It had never struck me it was you, as you had gone in the opposite direction. As I got nearer I saw in the dusk a woman standing inside the gate, leaning over it and evidently talking with the man. As I was almost opposite the gate on the other side of the side road under the fir trees, I saw suddenly that it was you and the girl I met in the train. You were saying good-by to her, and you had her hand; you were holding it between both yours, and you drew yours slowly and softly away till her hand fell, as you used to say good-by to me at the farm. You turned away and walked slowly up the road in the other direction, and I took the turn towards our house. That night, when you had gone to sleep, I lay awake behind you, thinking and thinking.

"It seemed to me I might have been unjust, in the bitterness of those last days. I had understood that you should love Mrs. Drummond with her refined face and her graceful figure and her beautiful dresses and her many tastes in common with yours and her years almost the same. It had seemed quite possible to me you loved her with great love; I had been able to make so many justifications for you in my own mind—this had been so different. I had envied Mrs. Drummond when you sat on the rocks with her and called her 'my friend.' *This* had only filled me with a creepy horror, that had passed from her to you. Now, when I remember how you stood at the gate drawing her hand through yours, the thought came to me that perhaps I had been unjust. What if it were that very sensitiveness and refinement, which Mrs. Drummond and I had each in our own way, which ultimately repelled you from us when you came close to us and made you feel you could not permanently love us? What if your nature required just that animal element, without thought and without self-restraint, to draw out its depth of loyalty and love? What if the round pimpled face, and the loud laugh, and her stare which filled me with horror were the things your nature needed to draw you permanently? Was there not a whole side in your laughter-loving, sport-loving nature which was nearer her than to me or Mrs. Drummond? Was there not even a likeness between your rounded face and figure and hers? Might not she much more easily be mistaken for your child or your sister than I? And must not like seek like? Had I any right to think there could be nothing beautiful and tender in your feeling for her because I could not have loved her? I even said to myself that perhaps I had been wholly unjust to you. What if after all there was nothing of sex in your feeling for her, if you simply longed for young light-hearted society and romped with her as you might with your own boys, when they were older? What if you concealed it from me simply because you thought I could not sympathize with or understand your feeling? Was not what I had thought the terrible sex-desire of a man, who had already brought a child into life, for a child less than half his age, merely a paternal joy in young life? Was it not the same desire to gambol with a young creature which made you squirt the water in the baby's face where I only wanted to kiss it and sing to it? Was it not the same feeling that made you care only for awkward gamboling young puppies, while I cared for older more matured animals? Was it

not perhaps I, who had thought myself large and able to
sympathize with others, who was really small and narrow,
measuring you by my own little standard? I thought so
long lying there behind you, that at last I had persuaded
myself it was I who was wrong in not giving you a larger
generous sympathy. Oh, can't you see I had to! If a
woman loses her feeling of honor for the man she has
given herself to, then she'd better be dead! Her love for
him is like a little lamp that she carries in her breast, that
she must shield with both hands from every wind that
blows, because if it goes out it means death to her.

"The next day I sent the servant to the station-master's
wife with a letter to say I had been out when her niece
called with the lace, but if she would come again that
afternoon at five I would be glad to see it.

"At five o'clock I had spread the table in the veranda
with cakes and preserves, and soon after five the girl
came. She looked hard at me as she was walking up the
path; she handed me a bit of paper with a small bit of
crochet lace in it. I asked her to sit down at the table and
I made her tea. I offered her six shillings for the lace;
I knew it was only worth one, but I wanted to show her
I felt friendly. I tried to talk to her about flowers and
fancywork, but she hardly answered me. She sat eating
cake, picking the plums out with her fingers, and looking
every now and then at the gate. At last she asked what
time you generally came home. I told her you would be
home soon. A curious half smile came over her mouth;
it was as though she thought I knew nothing of your
friendship with her and I was unconsciously playing into
her hand. It was a look—a little of triumph, almost of
scorn.

"When she saw you come in at the gate she drew herself up and all her face changed. She looked full at you
and smiled, all her white teeth showing when you said
good-day to her. I showed you the lace and told you
what I gave for it, and went away at once to make you
fresh tea. I was gone a quarter of an hour; when I came

back with the tea she was sitting alone eating dates; she said you said you had to go out again at once. I picked her a large bunch of roses because she said she had none in their garden, and I asked her whenever she wanted some more to come any afternoon and fetch them.

"When you came home to dinner you did not mention her, but when you were undressing in the evening you said, 'What on earth made you give six shillings for that bit of lace? It wasn't worth one; but it's your own money if you like to squander it.' You didn't say anything more about her.

"Twice the next week she came, about five, to fetch roses. I always gave her tea and cake, and never mentioned your name to her. The first time when you came home you stopped and said a few words to her, and then walked on into the billiard room; the second time you hardly spoke to her, and went straight in. She waited very long, but you did not come back. Then just as she was going down the path to the gate you came to the dining-room window and looked out. She was just shutting the gate. You said, 'What monstrous legs that girl has! she'll be a tower of fat and deformity before she's twenty-five.' As I was putting the tea things together you said, 'What on earth do you have that great lolloping larrikin of a girl here for? If you want to have her, I wish you'd take her into the drawing-room and keep her out of my way.'

"The next day you said you wanted breakfast at the old time, as there was no need for you to go in by the early train. For nearly two weeks after that the girl never came again. Then one afternoon I saw her coming up the path: she looked very heavy and sullen. I went in and got her tea. She did not keep on eating cake as she generally did; she crumbled it up in her lap and kept her eyes fixed on the ground or looked up staring at me. She said not a word, only moved her head sullenly in answer to my remarks; and I felt as if she had some purpose in coming. I cut a large bunch of roses for her;

she seized them and, hardly saying good-by, turned to go. When she got to the gate she turned and flung the roses all over the path. 'We've got flowers of our own,' she said; 'we don't want yours!' Then when she had got outside the gate and had shut it she turned and leaned her folded arms on the top. I was standing before the veranda on the path. She looked full at me with her eyes very wide open, then she burst into a loud artificial laugh with all her white teeth showing. 'You think you've got him all to yourself, do you? You think because you've taken him away from me you've got him! He doesn't care two straws for you! He'll go after another girl; I expect he's got one already!' She opened her mouth wide and laughed, and then she went away.

"Then I knew you had deserted her, and there was no use my trying to do anything. I have never tried again to have anything to do with a woman who was your friend.

"And after that the dark closed in about me. It wasn't faith in your love I had lost—it was all faith in life. I didn't care for anything any more—not for the children, not for the house, not for books, not for nature; I only wanted to die. I did my work because I must; but the only time I felt glad was when I thought of death; it seemed that then there was a faint stirring at my heart like hope. And sometimes in the morning, just when I woke, there used to come a feeling to me that somewhere, somehow, sometime, something would come to help me, some person, some man, some woman, some book. Sometimes in my dazed state I have even gone out and looked up and down the front avenue as if I thought some visible human being was coming to help me. Nothing goes on always in this world; it seemed I couldn't be left always in my despair. Life can't go on for ever letting a human creature seem alive, who really is dead.

"And at last help did come, but not from a man, or a woman, or a book. You had gone away for three weeks to the Eastern Province by sea, and it was the day after you left. I was sitting in the rocking chair on the stoep with a newspaper on my lap, open, but I was not reading. As I looked mechanically at it my eye caught certain words. It was a small wine garden to sell just beyond the suburbs. It gave the price and the agent's name. I read it once or twice mechanically. Then suddenly I grasped it and began to think. I got up and began walking up and down with the paper in my hand. I had thought that, if once I could find some man or woman to whom I could tell everything and who would hold my hand tight and let me creep close to them I should be saved. But this did it. I had the money my father gave me when I was married; it would almost pay for the ground, and I could raise a mortgage for the rest of the money to work the farm with.

"I thought all the morning, and in the afternoon I went to see the agent and the farm.

"He would not give me the deeds till he had seen you and you had given your consent, because I was a woman. But I paid him the money and he gave me possession at once. I put my old Malay cook and her husband and son there, and for three weeks I and the children lived there. They played in the sun on the grass, and I worked. I climbed on to the roof and pulled out the old thatch and helped the man to rethatch the shanty. We cleaned and planted; before you came back it was almost in order. The seeds I had planted were coming up, and the vineyard was clean. I could not study, and I dared not feel; but I could still [work]; it was my hold on freedom and life; and it has been so to me ever since.

"Frank, you must forgive me that I write to you in detail; I know it will tire you. But it is for all our lives. You must understand where I stand, and how I stand there, because now the silence between us must end.

"I need not write fully about the things that have happened later; they have always kept on happening, and I think you have suspected that I suspected them. Sometimes for a little time nothing happened, and then a hope rose in me that things had changed; but they always did happen at last, and I have realized what we have to deal with is not an isolated event but a permanent condition. Such little things—but they always keep on happening.

"Do you remember two Xmases ago when we were walking down Adderley Street to buy the children presents? I was walking just a little in front of you looking in at the windows when I heard a rustle of silk skirts and some one running down the pavement behind us. I glanced back and there was a woman with a red dress and black bonnet with red roses in it; she had just caught hold of your arm from behind and called out 'Hello!' You turned quickly towards her; I heard you say three words in a low voice: I could not fully catch them, though I think I know what they were, and you glanced at me. In an instant she let your arm go, and stood looking at me with her head a little on one side with that half-curious, half-contemptuous smile I saw first on the station-master's niece's face, but which I have seen since so often. Then she laughed softly and drew her skirt up tight about her and crossed to the other side of the street, and you came quickly to my side. I think you must have noticed that I saw her catch your arm, for presently you said, 'I wonder who that woman can have been that came up to me just now? Seems she mistook me for some one else!'

"I said, 'Have you not seen her before?'

"You said, 'Oh, I may have. Rather expect she's one of the actresses that came over on the steamer with me last time I came from Port Elizabeth!' And then you began talking about the toys in the window. All these years they've kept on happening. Once you sent me a note from the office to say you had to make up the quarter's books and you wouldn't be home till very late; I mustn't sit up for you. At four o'clock you came home in a cab. Your face was swollen with tiredness and you dropped on the bed and went to sleep at once. I kept the house very quiet the next morning because I thought after your hard work you needed sleep. At nine o'clock your clerk came and said he wanted the key of the safe to get out a document. I said I didn't like to wake you because you had sat working so late making up the books. He looked at me surprised and said, 'But we made up all the books last week!'

"Another time, perhaps you remember it, I went into Town to buy new oilcloth for the billiard room. I thought I would ask you to come with me to choose it. When I got to the office it was closed up. The caretaker said you had given the clerks a holiday to go to the races, and had closed at eleven o'clock. I bought the oilcloth and went home. In the evening you were an hour late for dinner. I went to the door to meet you. I was just going to say that I wished I had known you were going to the races, because I had never seen any and would have gone too, when you said you were afraid you had kept dinner waiting but there had been such a succession of people in the office all day you'd had no breathing time. You said your head ached and you did not want dinner, only a cup of coffee on the veranda. I could not understand why it was you should wish to hide from me you had gone, but the next day a woman came (it was Mrs. Drummond, but Rebekah did not say so) and asked me if I had been to the races. I said I had never been to races. She said she thought I must have been, as some one had said they had seen my husband driving in a carriage with the girl who kept his books and two others, but that she had felt sure it must be me and some of my friends; and she looked at me to see how I felt it. A few days after I met a man in the avenue who stopped to say good day to me. He asked if I had been at the races the week before: I said I had not. He laughed and said, 'You should look after your husband a little; you shouldn't let him be so gay!' And he looked at me with a curious inquiring smile. One of the strangest things to me has been how not only women, but men, men who call themselves men, come close to you and prod their fingers into your wound to see how much you feel; it is like when wild animals gather round the wounded one of the herd and prod it with their horns when it falls wounded. It came to this at last, that I felt as if nothing mattered to me if people didn't come and talk to me of you and show me that they knew. There was a cow at the farm one day whose side was torn open by a barbed-wire fence so that her entrails hung out; she tried always to turn that side away from the other animals, and they seemed always trying to come round to it, till we shot her.

"Perhaps you will say if life has been so [cruel] to me, why haven't I left you and gone home to my father? Oh, you know I asked you to divorce me or send me away if you wished, and you said nothing. I have often asked myself why I didn't get up and go. Is it perhaps the spirit of those old ancestresses of mine who for millions of years have followed the man over steppes and through deserts and across mountains, with stripes and burdens, always following, following, following,—which to-day cries out in us, 'Follow—follow—till he sets you free!' I do not know how it is that I, who would bear binding to no other human creature, feel an iron chain about my heart binding me to you. Often I have said, 'Why do I not get up and go!'—and then something cries out in me, 'If he should need me!—If he should want me!—If I am good for him!' When I have thought of leaving you against your will, it has been as if I left my little child while it cried for me; something begins to bleed inside of me.

"When I went last year to visit my mother at the farm even my brain seemed rigid. But when I saw the places where I had been when I was a little child, when I saw the long moss still hanging from the tree in the kloof and picked up the Kaffir beans that had fallen from the trees and saw the old great pear tree under which I used to play, I walked about alone and cried for joy, and my heart came back again to me soft, like before I married. I felt as if something went out from me and clasped itself about everything. I wanted to read and to think again; and when I had been there a month such a strange tenderness to you sprang up in my heart. It seemed all my fault that I had not wound my arms about you and made you talk about things to me, and so we should have got to understand each other. At last I had only one desire, a hunger to see your face and to hear your voice. And when you wrote a letter in which you said you missed me and the children and would never let us go so far away again, I packed up my things and came home a month sooner than I had meant. I thought when I came back the past was going to be past, that what I had wanted for so long was going to happen, because deep hidden in my heart there had always been a hope; I see it now.

"And when we came back all did seem better; you spoke kindly to me almost as you spoke to other women, and never spoke roughly to me before the children and servant; but you wouldn't let me come near enough to you to speak of anything. I was glad you had Bertie to go out with, and when I knew this child was coming I was glad, almost as when the first was coming; the other two had been so terrible.

"After Bertie was gone things seemed just as bright; you still cared to stay at home and seemed happy here with us. I thought I was making you happy; I didn't want anything more; it seemed I could let an iron curtain down between me and the past; I could be quite satisfied just to live peacefully and attend to you and the children and feel you near me, and nothing ever happening. Oh! I asked so little, so little!

"Now to-night what has happened has made me feel we must speak the truth to one another. I have been afraid of you all these years; I have been afraid if I wrote or spoke to you and you answered me as you did years ago, something would break in me. But to-night I am not afraid.

"Do not think that, because what happened in the yard to-night would give me the legal right to freedom in any court, therefore I write to you, who have been silent so long. In the eyes of the world it might seem a grosser and more brutal thing—but not in mine. When I saw you and Mrs. Drummond on the rocks at Muizenberg, and when I picked up the letter beginning 'My Friend,' in which you discussed marriage and me, my youth died in me, and it will never come back; this is not so great. When I saw you in the billiard room that day you did not inflict such anguish on me as when in the last years you have often sat talking with women in the same room with me, bending perhaps over a young girl, plain it might be, with the same passionate light in your eyes begging for a return of sexual feeling, which you once turned on me, not caring that I was present to see, or the glances other women directed to me; and when, just because it meant nothing permanent and she might pass out of your life in a few days, it has inflicted deeper humiliation on you and me and the bond that bound us. It is the lightness of the attraction which could come between your manhood and my womanhood that is the measure of our degradation.

"I do not know whether other women feel so, but I can understand, I can almost sympathize with, a wave of black, primitive bestial desire surging up at some moment in life in a nature otherwise pure and lofty. I can imagine it for an instant sweeping all before it, so that the creature itself cried out in the pain of a grasp it cannot comprehend, which drives it forward to action it abhors,—the resurrection of that long-buried animal past, when man on earth knew not of love and loyalty; and I can understand that the creature, man or woman, should shrink with horror from the force within them while they fell before it. There are lands where, in the course of centuries or scores or decades of years, the earth rends and opens and sulphurous fumes desolate it and darkness covers it; and yet men live in it and love it and it is still a fair land, except at that rare and terrible moment when the convulsion falls on it; but a land that always trem-

bled, that was never still, when from every smallest crack
the fœtid fume rose, and a fine, almost imperceptible,
fall of ashes covered it: the very dogs would leave it—
no man would live there!

"Do not think that I am taking a mean advantage because to-night you have weakly committed yourself into
my hand; it is not what you have done that makes me
speak; it is because something has happened in me that
never happened before. I feel that to-night the end has
come, and you and I must speak openly and sincerely to
one another. I am not afraid of you. I am not a woman
speaking to the man who owns her, before whom she
trembles; we are two free souls looking at each other. If
you will not read this letter, then you shall hear me speak.
But that long life of silence and repression and deception
ends here. You must hear me.

"It seems to me that there are just three possible
courses open to us.

"The first is, that you should get a divorce from me.
As I told you years ago, when I thought you loved Mrs.
Drummond, if you wish for one I shall do all I can to
make it easy for you. I will go to my parents; you can
demand my return, and, when I refuse, divorce me. Then
all blame will rest upon me. I have my farm and I can
work. I will support the children, but for your sake, for
yourself, I think you ought to. This seems to me the best
plan; then we shall both be free to lead our lives—such
as they can be now.

"The second is, if you do not want the disgrace of a
divorce (I know you will fear it; I do not fear it; it will
not touch me), that we should separate. I can go on my
little wine farm; it will not attract much attention; you
can come sometimes, if you will, to see the children. We
can each lead our own lives; but it will not be so right as
if the tie were utterly severed and openly.

"Then there is a third. If, if it so happens that you
still think you love me and do not wish me to go from
you, then there is yet one course open for us. You must

meet me, fairly and straightly, as one man meets another, and speak to me as one speaks to one's own soul. You must tell me what you feel, what you desire and wherein you think I have failed, as I have told you in this letter. There must be no subterfuge or concealment between us. Then, if you still wish to possess me, I will live with you; as long as you are loyal to me I will be loyal to you; I will bear children for you. I will forget the past; never by a word or a sign shall I recall it.

"Oh, Frank, Frank, I have loved you! Oh, even now I love you, as you have not known, as you never will know! Only once in all the years we have been together has it ever seemed for a moment to have gone out. We were sitting at dinner at the time you were still friendly with the station-master's niece. You were eating with your eyes fixed intently on your plate, but evidently not thinking of what you were eating. As I looked up at you, as I looked at your mouth and your jaw, a wave of horror swept over me. It was not as if you were the man who was myself, but any other man whom one might see at a restaurant for the first time. The horror and shrinking swept over me so I rose and left the table. If I had continued to feel so, then I must have left you at once. But it passed almost immediately and remained only as a terrible memory. It may have been some thought that was in your mind, written on your face for the moment, which affected me so, but, except then, never in the darkest moment has my love died. You have never been to me as another man.

"Frank, I have tried to blame myself; I have sought, as a rat in a trap seeks a way of escape, to find out I was wrong and you were right. I have tried to understand you. I do even now see there may be elements in your nature forcing you almost irresistibly to certain courses of action that I cannot rightly understand, because those forces are not in me. I see that I must be unjust to you if I measure you by my standard. Can love and marriage and the relationship of human to human have the same meaning to you and to me, when in everything else we differ? Sometimes I have lain awake whole nights thinking over it.

"You care for wild animals. You will spend days in the blazing sun or the cutting winds, you will creep on hands and knees over rough koppies or through the mud of vleis to stalk a buck or a bird you have fixed on. When you get near it you shoot it; when you get to it, you pick it up and turn it over in your hand, or you kick it over with your foot. That is the end; you have got it. You sometimes care so little for a buck you have spent half the day in stalking that, rather than carry it back on your shoulder to the cart, you will give it to the man that is with you. Only if one who is shooting with you should say his gun brought it down, then it becomes of importance to you, and rather than let him have it, you would battle over it.

"I have cared for wild animals too. I had a wooddove that the Kaffir boys had caught and crushed in their stone trap; I bought it from them with the only sixpence I had, and I nursed it and cured it. It made a nest in the garden, and sometimes when I woke in the morning it was fluttering round my bed or sitting on the rail at the bottom singing and waiting for me to wake. I had a raven they shot in the land and broke its wing and leg. I tied splints to it, and, though it could never fly, it lived; and when I went out in the morning into the yard a thrill of joy used to come over me when I saw it hop out of the wagon house with its one stiff leg and its head on one side coming to peck at my skirt that I might pick it up and let it ride on my shoulder. I also had a passion for wild animals; but it has been to possess them and know they knew me and wanted me.

"If you have a spare day, you go fishing, and you stand on the rocks from the morning to the evening, sometimes soaked with spray to bring a few fishes to land. I have seen your eye gleaming and your whole being intent as you have seen your float move or have reeled one to the shore. And yet, when you had them, when you had put your fingers through their gills, your interest in them was ended. You threw them into the basket with the others. Only if it were a very large one, and you wanted to take it home and weigh it and tell your friends its size, would you often care to take it home. I have known you to give a whole basketful to the colored boys on the beach because they were not worth carrying. I would not. I would not endure the labor you go through in catching them for anything but to save my children or someone dependent on me from absolute hunger. Yes, if I were standing in the water and a fish should creep up to me and glide between my feet and over them, not fearing me, I should stand still shivering with delight every time its beautiful body touched me. I have always dreamed of having a tame fish, one that would come to me when I called and lie with its slow palpitating beautiful belly on my hand in the water and let me feel it.

"Only once I tried to capture a thing, when I was six years old, and I saw for the first time one of those great purple butterflies with the golden eyes on their wings. It seemed so beautiful, I desired it so passionately, I think I would have committed a crime to have it. I ran after it all the way to the great dam and through the mielie lands, though I knew I should not go so far, and when it sat on a karroo bush I fell down on it and caught it. When I stood up and looked it was crushed, and the fine fluff was clinging to my hand. I lay down on the ground and cried beside it. You see, what I had really wanted was not to catch it, but to have it, and I thought I could if I caught it. I don't think since then I have ever wanted to catch anything that has tried to escape from me, an animal or a human creature. I have understood that what I wanted from living things was what they could *give* me, not what I could take from them. The supreme moment to me is not when I kill or conquer a living thing, but that moment its eye and mine meet and a line of connection is formed between me and the life that is in it. It knows and understands me and we are united by something within us. Then it is mine; and I want it.

"There is the same difference between us in everything. If I have a few hours to spare on an afternoon, I like to go to the blockhouse on the mountain and lie down and see the town below me and the Bay and the mountains and the bush. I lie and look at it till I feel it all belongs to me. And my little life, which sometimes seems so small when I am shut up in the house alone, grows great and beautiful. And I have my half holiday.

"And if you have a free afternoon, if you have no animal to pursue, you go to the cricket ground or play croquet; you strike or chase the balls; even if they are not alive, you have the pleasure of trying to do it better than another man; and, if you cannot play yourself, you watch others do it; you are pleased so there is winning, conquering, taking—sport!

"If you have a dog, you like it because it is thorough-bred and wins prizes at shows or hunts well, and you flog it when it makes mistakes. The dog I have loved best was a terrier of no full breed. For six years it slept at the foot of my bed; and even now, when I wake in the night, something in me cries out to feel it creep softly up in the dark and lie between my arm and my side with its little head on my shoulder and its little heart beating against my side; and if there were another world where we could see again the things we have loved here, one of the first things I should ask to see would be those eyes which when I woke I used to find watching me, when it lay with its two paws on my chest waiting for me to wake.

"And, sometimes, I have asked myself, if we feel so differently with regard to everything in life, is it not also inevitable we should feel differently about love? What if for you a woman is only 'sport'? What if there is something irresistible in your nature which compels you to feel that the woman who has once wholly given herself to you is a dead bird, a fish, through whose gills you have put your fingers?

"Long ago you met Mrs. Drummond secretly and got letters from her; you were careful I should not see and seemed to care much for her, but as soon as I said that I would go away that you might have her for six months in the house with you, and that if you wished it you could divorce me and marry her—then you cared nothing more for her; when she waited at the gate for you, you tried to avoid her; when she asked you to her parties, you never went; when she waited about for you and sent you presents and you knew you could absolutely possess her, she had no more value for you. Only two years ago, when the old Major was so attentive to her and was always coming to see her, you too went to see her and took her out till he left off coming, and then you left off going to her too, till last year, when there was gossip about the young bank clerk who came so often to see her; then you went to church with her and brought her home and went to her croquet till she left off having anything to do with him; and then you left her too. You liked to meet the station-master's niece and go to town with her while it was secretly done, but when I asked her here and you could have seen her every day in your own house, then you avoided her and you got to dislike her following you and waiting for you. Hasn't it always been so, you haven't cared for any woman for long?

"I have sometimes thought that perhaps if I had been another kind of woman—not if I had taken more care of your house and the children, not if I had been more eager to satisfy the wants of your nature, not if your touch had been more precious to me—but if, when you came home, you were never quite sure who you would find had been taking tea with me; if, when I went for a walk in the woods, you never were quite sure that it was alone; if, instead of showing all my letters and telegrams to you, you had noticed that I tried to prevent any falling into your hands; if I had carried on a long correspondence with a married man, whose letters you never saw or mine to him, and met him when you were from home; if, at

balls and assemblies, you had seen me sit with men of
my own age and men much younger bending over me,
and you had seen my cheeks burn and my eyes grow bright
with a color they never wore for you,—then perhaps you
would have been able to keep on loving me! I have
thought that perhaps the only woman you could have
kept on loving all your life would have been a woman
of whom you were never quite sure, that there must be
at least a flutter in the bird's wings, a possibility of its
again taking flight, to make it of value to you!

"If I am mistaken in this, tell me so. But if I am
not, if you know it to be true, why should we not both
face the fact plainly? If it is not possible for your nature
to keep on caring for a thing that absolutely belongs to
you and yields no excitement of chase, is it not as unjust
to demand it of you as it would be to demand of me with
my nature that I should desire to kill things simply because they were alive and I saw them move?

"I sometimes think that why you were attracted to me,
when I was a little girl and you first saw me, was simply
because I always ran away from you to hide in the bush;
if I had hung about you and wanted to play with you,
you would have driven me away; but when I climbed into
the top of the willow tree and you set the dogs to find
me and stood at the bottom of the tree declaring you
would stay the whole day if I did not come down and
play, and I refused, then you liked me. I believe that
afterwards it was the fact that I noticed no man, that I
had accepted none of the proposals made me that drew
you to me. You loved me then. When you lifted me off
the rocks, when I hurried in late to breakfast and you
rose and drew out the old wooden chair for me, as you
looked down at me, the light upon your face seemed to
me God's light shining out upon my life; when I think of
it even now, I want to push everything from me and run
to you and creep close to you—even now. After we were
married I never saw it again on your face for me—my
light; but I saw it shine on your face for others. In a

ballroom I have seen you stoop to pick up a fan dropped by a young girl you did not know and who did not know you; as you have handed it her, her face has burned softly crimson and then white and she has gone away fingering the fan softly, and I know at night she has dreamed of the face with the light upon it.

"I have seen it play on your face as you helped a woman much older than yourself into a carriage; I have seen it come for a girl you were saying an ordinary good-by to at a railway station, and my heart has beaten with the feeling that when you turned to me it would shine on me also, but it has been dead when you turned and said, 'Are you ready, Rebekah?' I have seen you on a sofa beside a girl not young, not beautiful, bending over her, with the light upon your face so clearly that every person in the room has noted it and in a way quietly smiled, and the woman has thought she had won you wholly and looked up at me with the scorn of the victor; but the next week or the next month it has been just so for another woman. What is it but the old, old lure-light, the decoy-light, that through the ages has led woman on, crying to her, 'Here is light! Here is warmth!' and when she has followed it up hills and down valleys and, reaching it, stretches out her hands to warm them, she finds a few white ashes.

"If the fish could see it, is it not the same light that burns with deep intensity in the eye that watches him rise slowly to take the bait? What is it but the *ignis fatuus* which leads woman on to surrender and toil and bear for man, the very memory of which, even when it has gone, binds her to him so that she cannot break the tie? Oh, now, even now, when I know what it means, something in me cries out to see it once again, my light, for me, just once before I die!" (She scratched out this last sentence.)

"Sometimes, in hours of great darkness, it has come to me that perhaps there is nothing strange in our fate; that perhaps in all these houses with their tender gardens and their little front gates, and between all these men and

women whom one sees walking smoothly to church together and going out to dinner and sitting on the stoep,
there lies the same ghastly reality that the strange joy
which fills the heart of the man and the woman we see
walking alone together as they plan their future home
and life, from whom we turn away when we meet them in
the pine woods lest we should trespass on the beautiful
solitude—that perhaps in the end it all comes to this—
that the love and fellowship which we are taught to look
to as our end in life, which compensates us for all that
larger world of duties and actions, which we dream of
from our earliest girlhood as that which is to consecrate
our lives, means in the end only this—an hour's light, and
then a long darkness; the higher the flame has leaped, the
colder and deader the ashes.

"If I believed this always, if it came to me otherwise
than as a nightmare, I would not live; because human life
would be false at its core. Even the animals know what
love is; the eagle mates once and never again, they say,
if its mate dies; the singing birds mate with a companion
whom they tend and follow; even those beasts whose
union is a moment of sensuous life have no deception;
the moment after, both are free; the wide world is before
them; the very polygamous beasts do not win their partners by protestations of eternal love; each is free to form
another union when it will. Is man the creature whose
love is a falsehood by nature; who has one decoy song,
crying, 'My love is eternal,' which in the anguish of
child-bearing and the years without freedom she is to hear
no more? For in spring the bird may call to a new mate
and she to whom he cried last year answers to a new call;
is woman the only creature for whom there is no spring,
and no fresh call when the old song is dead? Is the
passion cry with which the man follows one woman for
weeks or months or years, chanting that his love ends only
with death, with no refrain to say that its death hour is
possession and that its life is long because it passes on end-

lessly to others,—is this always a conscious or unconsciour lie?

"Sometimes I have believed this—but it is only in a nightmare. When I wake from it I know that the loveliest thing that has blossomed on the earth is the binding of man and woman in one body, one fellowship, and I know that all the failures are only the broken steps which Humanity builds in stairs she is shaping for herself to climb by, which she will have to rebuild better in the future. All man's love cry is not delusion, and the dreams we have dreamed in our girlhood will have their realization though it may never be by us.

"And, when I see this, the feeling comes over me that, oh, somewhere, the woman must exist whom you could love; perhaps some young girl or some older riper woman, who, if you could meet, would draw out all the tenderness and beauty and self-devotion of your nature which I have never been able to touch, whom you would be loyal to, not for her sake but for your own, because she was yourself. And sometimes it has even come to me that perhaps, at a future day, I might be that woman, that perhaps we may yet meet each other and understand each other, and all the past ——"

She had scratched out the whole of this unfinished paragraph. When she wrote next it was with another pen and more hurried and illegible.

"Oh, can't we speak the truth to one another just like two men? Can't we tell each other just what we think and feel? If you can't love me, tell me so; do not be afraid of hurting me. If you feel you cannot love one woman long and that only a succession of women can make you happy, I will try to understand. I will try to be a man with you. Oh, nothing can be so terrible as this awful silence that has been between us through these long years. It is that that has crushed me, always to hold myself down with an iron hand. I do not ask you to love me, only to speak the truth to me, as you would if I were another man.

"O Frank, my love, my husband, I have loved you, I have loved you! You will never know how I have loved you! If there were any woman you loved more than all the world, I would do everything in my power to bring her to you. If you had a little child that was yours and not mine, I would take it to my heart and love it as if it were my own. If you, if you don't love me, but you want me still to live with you, I will do all you ask of me; but, oh, we must speak the truth to each other, we must speak the truth. It is this life of lies and subterfuges which we have been living which is dragging down both our souls to hell."

Here she seemed to have paused a long time and paced the room, for the handwriting when she went on was suddenly quite changed and almost illegible.

"O Frank, my love, my husband, please help me! I want to do what is right and I cannot see the way! I am like a little child that has lost itself in the wood and it is dark everywhere. Oh, please take my hand and help me. You are much stronger than I; you are the only human being who can help me. Take my hand in yours and let us find the path."

Here it ended suddenly.

This was the letter held twisted in a roll in her hand as she lay looking at the shadows among the rafters. The baby had grown tired of playing with his toes and had dropped asleep again, and there was no sound in the room but the even breathing of the still sleeping children.

Then Rebekah stood up and went out onto the back veranda. Dressed still in her blue dressing gown, with only the little blue slippers on her bare feet: she walked up the side passage of the yard, past the closed stable-door, and out at the back gate.

There the early morning sunlight was shooting down a clear light through the young green oak leaves and playing delicately on the ground; below and beyond, where the pine trees began, single shafts of light fell through the tall branches across their stems and on to the moss and pine needles, wet with the early morning dew. Rebekah stood with her back to the outer wall of the stable gazing into the woods, but her eyes were sightless. Then she began slowly walking up and down close to the wall. Her feet made a little pathway among the weeds and the bits of dry straw that had blown there from the yard gate. Presently she leaned the crown of her head against the roughcast whitewashed wall and looked downwards. She watched the little weeds at her feet and the bits of straw against the wall. Then something rose and surged through her; from her feet it seemed to mount till it reached to her brain and swept all before it. She would go into the house and gather them all in her arms, those children born of lust and falsehood, and they and she and the unborn would pass away together! For an instant the impulse seemed to gain upon her with fearful force. Then slowly her will took command again and she annihilated it. But in years that came, when in some chance newspaper she had read of a woman in despair who had taken her children out of life with her, to her it was no impossible nightmare; she knew the steps by which a woman's soul may pass, till it stands looking down into that awful abysm.

She stood motionless, but with her head pressed to the wall, so that tiny fragments of the rough plaster clung to her soft brown hair. She tried to think; but, like a mockery, from a voice outside herself, broke in the old proverb she had read first in the little brown history, "You cannot make a silk purse out of a sow's ear!" She began to walk up and down again. "You—cannot—make—a silk purse—out—of—a sow's—ear!" And still she paced up and down trying to think.

A colored man, passing through the woods early to look for his master's cow, paused for a moment in the distance to look at the little figure in its blue dressing gown with bare slippered feet pacing up and down, with its low bent head—and then wondering passed on.

At last, as she walked, that quiet onlooking self, which,

except in moments of rare anguish of body and soul, can always regain the mastery, woke in her. She walked along slowly. The question came, "Why are you agonizing here? Are *you* the only creature in the world who has suffered wrong? If life has no value to you, are there not others weaker than yourself to whom you can make it of value? Because in your anguish you are alone and no hand comes to help you, can you put out your hand to none? Are you the only woman in the world who has suffered?"

She raised her head; as she looked up she saw for the first time the green and golden glory of the light through the young oak leaves and the bright shafts shooting through the dark branches of the pine wood and the soft moist earth below. She raised herself and stood looking at it; it seemed as if a soft dew were falling on her mind.

"When all hope is dead in your own life, is there yet nothing left to live for? Are there not others?" She stood looking at the morning world, like a soul come back from a long journey; then she walked in at the little gate. The door of the stable was open now and the stable boy had evidently taken the horses out to exercise. At the end of the passageway she turned into the yard. The milkman had evidently been, for the milk can stood in the stand at the kitchen door, but there was no sign of any other creature moving except two sparrows walking in the sunshine on the gravel of the yard. The green wooden shutter of the servant-girl's bedroom was thrown open; but the door was still shut. Rebekah passed across the yard to it, then she stood for a moment and glanced back at the sparrows and the sunshine; and then she knocked at the door. At first there was no answer, and she knocked again. Then a voice called out in Cape Dutch, "Who is there?" And Rebekah said softly, "It is I," and opened the door. She stood for a moment before she stepped down the one step that led into the room.

Before the window on the side of her single bed the servant girl was sitting. She was half dressed: her short black wool, with difficulty parted, was combed out to stand in two solid masses on each side of her head; her small dark face, with its puckered forehead even a little blacker than the rest, was raised as Rebekah opened the door. She had on a red striped flannel petticoat and a pair of crimson satin corsets, embroidered with white flowers; above the corsets, from a mass of frilled white lace, showed her puny black arms and bare shoulders; on the bed beside her lay a white nightdress heavy with bows: on the other side lay the serge dress she was just going to put on. The girl placed a closed fist on each of her hips, and raising her chin in the air looked at Rebekah through her half-closed twinkling eyes.

"Wat wil jij hè?"[1] she said, throwing her chin yet higher.

Rebekah stood silent; all she had determined to say passed from her. The girl threw back her head yet farther and burst into a laugh, intended to be defiant but with an undertone of fear, all her white teeth showing between her thick dark lips as she sat with her fists on her hips.

Then, as Rebekah looked at her, Rebekah knew that it was with that girl even as it was with herself that day.

Softly she turned and went out; she closed the door behind her. Almost on tiptoe, softly and quickly, she ran across the yard, like one who fears something that is following them and tries to escape.

She disappeared through the back door.

It was late that night when Frank returned. He had had a successful day's fishing. The friend with whom he had driven had put him down at the gate. As he walked up the path he saw the front door open and the lamp burn-

---

[1] Literally, "What do you want?" But the pronoun "jij" is in Cape Dutch, the only language of the colored people of the West, and is the most extreme insult when applied to a superior. It is used only to children or servants. Even equals avoid its use as much as possible.

ing on the stand, but Rebekah was not there to meet him and take his bag.

He set down his things on the hall table and went into the dining room. The lamp was lit, his supper was laid ready, his soda water was cooling in the window, but no one was there. He passed into their bedroom; it was dark; but in his dressing room a light was burning and his change of clothes hung ready for him over the chair, but there was no sign of anyone stirring in the house though it was not yet eleven. The servants were, of course, in bed, but it was the first time in all his married life, except when Rebekah was in childbed or suffering from a miscarriage, that he had come home at such an hour and found no one to attend to him.

He washed and changed his fishing clothes for the light-gray lounging suit; then he opened the door into the children's bedroom. That room also was dark, but from the crack under the door he saw there was light in Rebekah's study. He felt no particular wish to call her just then, so he went to the dining room and sat down to his supper. He enjoyed the chicken and bobotie and even took three glasses of wine; but as he finished a sense of the strangeness of things came over him that he did not like. He took a cigar and lit it and went on the front veranda to smoke. After a while he sat down in the rocking chair, but he felt restless. When his cigar was half done he threw it away and lit another. Perhaps, after all, it would be better to go and see Rebekah now and have it over; it was most unlikely she would speak about anything that had happened in the morning; she never did if you gave her time—she was an awfully sensible woman if only you gave her time—gave her time! He took his new cigar between his first and second finger and lounged away to the study door in an almost exaggeratedly easy style, as though he were preparing himself for a certain attitude of mind.

He opened the door without knocking and walked in easily.

"Hello, old girl!" he said, and seated himself on the edge of her desk with one knee thrown over the corner and the hand with the lighted cigar resting on it.

"Had a good day!" he said, "the best I've had this season!—Thought everyone was dead in the house when I came home, it's so quiet." He raised his cigar to his lips. "Hope Wilson came and fetched those two cues to mend. Don't like giving the other fellows my favorite cues!" He looked at the smoke from his mouth rather than at her. "Think I shall go to bed soon; I'm awfully tired!" He expanded his chest and raised his shoulders as people do who yawn, but no yawn came. He knocked some imperceptible ashes off the tip of his cigar with his little finger.

Rebekah, who had been sitting in her chair when he came, still sat there leaning back, with her head a little raised. Now she leaned forward a little and laid her hand on a large sheet of open blue foolscap paper on the desk on which there were some lines written in large clear characters.

"You must take this," she said slowly, "whether you wish to or not"—she was looking full up at him—"and to-morrow I want your answer."

He put his cigar back into his mouth and looked at her. He had an unpleasant sensation that she was looking at him as if she were looking at a tree or a wall—or any other man—not at *him*. The little sensitive almost imperceptible contraction about her mouth and eye, that he was always accustomed to see when she looked at him and spoke, seemed not there.

"Last night," she continued, "when I wrote that letter that you called a book and would not take, I said there were three lines of action on which I was willing our future relationship to each other should be based—now there are only two!"

He took the cigar from his mouth as if to speak, but something stopped him.

"They are there," she said, moving the paper towards

him. "They are short, and will not take you more than sixty seconds to read." She rested her fingers on the paper as she spoke. He had an unpleasant sensation as he looked at her that she was growing physically taller and larger at the moment.

"Either," she said, looking at him, "you must procure a legal divorce from me; in which case, both you and I will be free and may marry again, or not, as we wish. I would take the children to my farm or to my parents; if you wish it, I will support them; if, as I hope you do, you feel it is your duty, you can assist in their support. Under any conditions, we shall be free, and I think this is the best course; it is the one I prefer." She let her fingers drop on the paper. "If, on the other hand, you do not like these conditions, if you are afraid of what the world will say, then there is another course." She looked at him, but, as though absorbed in her own thought, she hardly seemed to see him: "I will, if you wish, continue to live in this house. I will look after your children and I will attend to your material wants; I will provide for my personal needs as I have already done for some years; but you will understand that, from to-night, you and I will never be anything more to each other than any man or woman who pass each other in the street for the first time. You will be free to lead your own life, to think your own thoughts, to form your own friendships; but you will understand that I also am equally free. Last night I gave you the choice of a third course; to-night there are only these two. You can let me know your decision to-morrow before twelve o'clock." She pointed to the paper on the table.

He looked down at her. For a moment he thought of bursting into a fit of rage such as had always silenced her; he would say he was shamefully treated, swear at her, and violently close the door. But that intuitive perception, which in him took the place of reason and was almost preternaturally keen where his own interests were concerned, told him it would be useless now.

He looked down at her curiously. "Oh, it's all too ridiculous, Rebekah. What do you mean? You are a tired little woman"—he spoke gently—"your condition makes you take these silly little fancies into your head! You need a good night's rest. How you live, with so little sleep as you take, I don't know! I'd be a washed-out rag!—I'm jolly tired too to-night," he said slowly, rising from the desk and drawing back his shoulders. "I've had a long, tiring day of it. I can hardly keep my eyes open."

She rose too. "Take that paper," she said quietly. "I have put it down in writing to avoid any mistake. I have kept a copy." She folded it up and held it out to him.

He was going to speak; he looked into her face, and a sense of something that seemed almost preternatural and inverted came over him. It was as if a man called to his own dog, who had followed him for years, and it walked by with its head down, no quiver even in its tail, and turned a dead eye on him. He took the paper from her, holding it a little in one hand, while in the other he held the lighted cigar. He moved almost awkwardly from one leg to the other.

"Well, I'll take it, of course, as you want me to," he said; "but you know it's absolutely ridiculous! You're tired to-night, that's what it is!" He tried to smile, but it died away at the corners of his mouth in a kind of twitch. "Of course, you must know it's all nonsense. I'm just taking it not to upset you to-night." He put it in his pocket. "I'm really awfully tired! I think I'll turn in. I suppose you're going to sit up a bit?"

He turned towards the door; when he had opened it and was going out, he began to recover himself; he turned and looked back at her with the door in his hand.

"Oh, this is all very well, you know," he laughed, but with his mouth a little on one side; "we know what'll happen before to-morrow morning! It won't be dawn, a fellow'll just be having his first sleep and he'll feel a tickling at the back of his neck; some small individual shedding tears upon it and combing out little curls with her fingers—kissing them too!—Eh?" He laughed again. "Happened before—hasn't it?"

Rebekah was still standing by the desk, staring at him.

"It'll be all right in the morning!—Eh?—Good night!" He shut the door behind him. When he was on the other side, the smile died out. Deep in his heart he knew it would not be all right in the morning. He had seen that look on the face of women before, and he knew what it meant. Without the shadow of a doubt he knew that the quicklime had ceased to act, that the net was broken, that the bird was out! He walked through the dark bedrooms into the dining room and took the paper from his pocket and read it under the hanging lamp. There were only twenty lines in a neat round hand, stating two alternatives. He walked up and down the room once or twice with it in his hand; then he put it in his pocket and walked to the window, lifting the corner of the blind a little. The window of the dining room looked out into the back yard as the window of the bedroom did. The white moonlight was flooding the yard; when he looked across it to the servant's room it seemed to him that both door and window stood wide open. He put his face close to the pane. The door of the servant's room was exactly opposite the dining room window, and as the moonlight fell in at the open door it seemed to him that the green box which had always stood just inside the door was not there.

He drew a soft, almost noiseless, indrawn whistle, and let the blind fall. He paced the room twice; then, glancing round to see that the door into the bedroom was closed, and listening to hear if there was any sound, he went out into the back yard. At first he walked as if to go to the stable passage; then, glancing once back at the house, he walked to the door of the servant's room and looked in. It was empty. A great splash of whitewash lay on the earthen floor where the patch of moonlight fell in through the door; the room held nothing but a bare iron bedstead standing in the center, and there was a strong smell of fresh whitewash. So that was it!

A flush of anger rose to his face as he turned quickly and walked to the house. Was it that devil of a stable boy? He had given him ten shillings twice, just to keep quiet in case he had noticed anything. Was it the girl herself who had talked?—you never could trust a nigger, do what you would for them! Had Rebekah noticed anything for herself? He walked into the dining room and took another cigar from the mantelshelf and bit off the end, throwing it into the waste-paper basket, but he did not light it. It had all come of being too soft hearted! He ought to have sent her away two months ago, when she first told him, instead of listening to all her nonsense. If her mother did cut up rough about it he could easily have settled it with money. It was all nonsense about her coming to talk to Rebekah about it—she would have had nothing to gain! And now Rebekah knew! He had been an absolute fool—that was what he had been!

He bit the end of his cigar again, forgetting what he had done, and began to pace the room once more with the unlighted cigar between his first and second fingers. After a while he lit the cigar and began to smoke, blowing clouds of smoke, and his brain began to work smoothly and quietly. He faced the entire position now that there was no escape. Whatever the girl might do and wherever she might go, it really did not matter, now Rebekah once knew! At the worst, if she did turn up again, it would only be a matter of a few shillings a week:—A dirty, beastly, little nigger!—but perhaps it would never be born? There flashed through his mind the rate of infant mortality among the colored population which he had seen in some paper:—at the worst that could be all set right with money; there was no need to think of it.

Then he walked, smoking more slowly and looking down. After a time he went and stood still before the mantelpiece, deep in thought. Then he sat down at the little desk in the corner where Rebekah wrote her orders and kept her accounts. He took a sheet of paper and wrote:

"DEAREST WIFE,

"A certain little person was so cut-uppie to-night that I quite forgot to tell her I have to start for Caledon before five o'clock to-morrow. I have to go and see about some farms; the man will be waiting for me at the hotel with his cart. I shall be gone from a week to ten days. I won't wake you and the children, as no doubt you will be asleep when I start. I'll write if there's any chance, but it's not very likely, as it's an out-of-the-way part. Expect me when you see me. Take care of yourself and the children.

"Your loving husband,
"FRANK."

He put it in an envelope and closed it and put it in his breast pocket. Then he turned out the lamp and went to his dressing room. He put the few clothes he would need into a small portmanteau and stood it out of sight behind the door; then he undressed. He listened for a moment near the door of the children's room, but there was no sound, so no doubt she was still in her study. He took up the lamp and went to the bedroom, set it down on the stand at the bedside, and then, before he took off his dressing gown and opened the bed, he sat on the bedside with his legs stretched out and folded across each other; and for a long time he sat looking down at his bare feet. Then he took Rebekah's paper out of the pocket of his dressing gown and read it again. An angry flush rose to his face and dyed it red at the top of his forehead. "And in that case, both you and I would be free to marry again." How could Rebekah write a thing like that! She, whom he had always looked upon as the type of all that was pure and womanly, to talk of giving herself to another man! He crumpled the paper in his hand. NO, there would be no divorce. It was impure, it was unclean for her even to talk of such a thing. It was enough to kill all a man's faith in women! He rose as if to pace the room, then he sat down again. But of course there was no need to consider that—the scandal—the gossip—and, what would be gained by it? He fell to considering the other proposition. After all it was not so bad! If she said she would do a thing, she would go through with it. She would be always there to look after the house and children; no one would know anything; if there was one thing you could depend on Rebekah for, it was to hold her tongue. A more placid look came over his face and all signs of anger died. Even if she carried out what she said she would, it would not be bad. When a woman has borne four children and had several miscarriages, she's not just what she was when you married her, and after seven years of marriage it would be nonsense to pretend there was very much romance:— a slight placid expansion, almost like a smile, spread over his lips and drew back the corners of his mouth; it was the look of deep, inward contentment with himself and the world that made people call him the best-tempered, jolliest man in his club.—She was not the only woman in the world! A dreamy smile played over his face, as if he were recalling past events. If only he got away for ten days, and avoided discussing matters while they were hot; that was the great thing. At the end of that time when he came back—well, if it had to be discussed—his forehead contracted a little at the thought—it would be quite a different matter from discussing it now. Give her time, give her time! Rebekah was a sensible woman if you gave her time and didn't take her on the hop while she was warm. He sat looking down at his feet. Who could tell but that, after a time, she—then he stopped, and knit his forehead; he knew that, as between him and her, things were at an end forever. He got up and threw his dressing-gown over a chair. It was all a damned nuisance! But it was no use worrying about it any more. He got into bed. At the head of the bed a little silk satchel hung in which Rebekah always put the daily papers for him to read after he got into bed. He took out the evening's sheet and began to read the account of the last cricket-match at Sea Point. He ran his eyes carefully down the row of figures, noting who had done well and who had not, but his thoughts wandered, and when he had gone twice over the figures he stuck the paper back in the holder; he turned the lamp out and drew the cover up over his shoulder and turned his face on one side.—After all, the great thing was just to give her time! Things would all settle themselves somehow! In ten minutes he had gone to sleep.

When her husband had closed the door of her study, Rebekah stood silent for a moment looking at it. Then she sat down in her armchair and leaned her head back against it. She folded her hands over her head and looked up at the dark little ceiling. She drew a long breath; but it was not the ceiling of the little room she saw as she sat there staring upwards. It was as though a vast dome were reared over her, as though a dark pall, which for years had been stretched out just above her, were folded up and removed and she looked up into almost infinite space. So wide, so still, so peaceful; and she was alone there!

After half an hour she stood up; as she turned out the lamp and lit the candle to take to the room, a curious sensation came to her, as if she were a little child again. Even the candle she had lighted and held in her hand seemed like candles used to long ago. At the door of the room she turned and looked back; she seemed to have come from a long journey and to be seeing it all again— the little statue of Hercules in the corner which she had bought when she first married, her shelves with the books, the cabinet with the fossils in it that she had loved so; she saw them all as she used to see them. It seemed as if some great crease of anguish which had lain in her brain for years had smoothed itself out.

She closed the door and went to her little stretcher

between the boys' beds. She had not slept for thirty-six hours. She undressed and put out her light, and in a few minutes was in a deep unbroken sleep.

When the stable boy brought the coffee to her door early the next morning, he told her that his master had called him before daylight to make coffee and to drive him to Town, and he gave her a letter his master had left for her. She opened it before the window and read it. A relaxation passed over her lips as she finished it: it was not bitterness, it was not disappointment; it was a placid recognition of the inevitable which always repeats itself.

He did not return till the eighth day. A nurse met him at the front door. She said Rebekah had been confined four days before of a seven months' child. She had had a bad time, and, until the day before, her life had been despaired of. The child, she said, was very puny, but it was alive. She had driven out to her farm twice, once the day before he left and again the next day, and the jolting might have been too much for her, otherwise there was no explanation of her illness. He could not see her, the nurse said, but he might see the child. She took him into his own bedroom. Rebekah lay in the children's room, where she had been taken ill; she had refused to be removed into the large room. From the small bed in the corner the nurse took up a pillow and uncovered on it a tiny morsel of flesh, eyebrowless, hairless, with a small wizened face. He had been proud of his other children; they had all weighed ten or twelve pounds, and people had called them prize babies; he had even boasted of them to men at his club. For this sorrowful, tiny thing he had a feeling of horror, almost of loathing; he turned away from it quickly. He told the nurse as Rebekah was so ill he would go to an hotel in Town, to save giving trouble in the house; but he asked her to let him know at once if she were worse or there was anything she needed, and he would himself try to come out in the evening to hear how she was.

He went to his dressing room and filled his portmanteau with the things he would need in Town, then carrying it in his hand he walked through the dining room. The room looked dusty and unused. On the table in the corner stood her work basket, on the top of which lay one of his white shirts on to which she had been sewing a new wristband; the needle was stuck upright into the work with the thimble balanced on the top, as she had left it the last day when she was taken ill. As he looked at it, a sensation of what was perhaps the sharpest pain he ever felt in the course of his life over anything that did not touch him personally ran through him. He passed on quickly to the front veranda and down the garden path. All her lilies and roses were in bloom, and as the sun shone on them the mignonette and verbena sent up a strong scent; the trowel she had been weeding with lay in the soft mold near the garden gate. He hurried out quickly and shut the gate and walked down the avenue.

After all, it was not his fault if she chose to go driving out two days running in a jolting cart. She had said she was not going to the farm again till after the baby was born—and she might yet get well again! As he passed the little suburban chemist's shop at the corner, he went in and bought two bottles of scent of a kind he knew she liked when she was ill, and ordered the chemist to send it up at once to the house with a cut-glass spray. After he got into the train he resolved to go and buy three books he had heard her say she would like and a little ring they had seen in the window of a jeweler's shop in Adderley Street the last time they were out together, which she had admired. She so seldom noticed jewelry or anything of that kind; and he had never given her anything since they were married. When he got out he went to the bookseller's and ordered the books to be sent out at once; then he walked up the street to the jeweler's; just as he was going in he stopped; after all, the ring would cost seven or eight pounds, and she might not really care for it; anyhow, he could get it later. Then he walked on to his office. It was too late to settle down to work before lunch, so he soon went out. On the way to the club he met a friend who condoled with him on his wife's serious illness and they went in and had a drink together—a thing he seldom did— and they had a short game of billiards together before lunch. After lunch he felt better and went back to his office.

When the office closed he went out to the suburbs to hear how his wife was. The nurse met him at the door; she said Rebekah had been sleeping quietly the greater part of the day, that the fever had quite left her and the doctors thought the danger was passed. She had asked to see the baby—a thing she had not done yet. He said he would not come in, and walked down the avenue again. After all, she was *not* going to die; she would have had to be ill and have the baby some time; perhaps it was just as well it came when it did! It would be a week certainly before he could see her, and then probably a fortnight before they could discuss things. It would be very different from discussing everything while it was still fresh! After all, how much better it was to let things slide! Men made half their own troubles by walking up to things and grasping hold of them. Perhaps it was just as well everything was as it was!

A little lower down the avenue he met an old friend, who asked how his wife was and condoled with him and asked him to come in to dinner. All the family were very kind and sympathetic and after dinner the two elder daughters played and sang for him.

CHAPTER IX

Cart Tracks in the Sand

UP-COUNTRY, in the red karroo, was the town [1]
where Aunt Mary-Anna lived, red karroo to right
of it, red karroo to left. A river-bed [2] ran below the town,
in winter full of dried mud banks and reaches of gravel
and bare stone, but, in the summer rains, coming down
red and full, the dark sand-laden water lying level with
the banks and bearing on its waves trees and stumps, the
carcasses of drowned animals, and even sometimes at long
intervals a human corpse.

All round the plain were flat-topped mountains, some
broken into jagged points, but still bearing the marks, in
their flat structure, of what had been the shores of seas
and lakes, the remains of whose mammoth amphibious
beasts lay still within the stratified shale, turned in the
course of the ages to stone themselves.

There were three churches in the town and a great
square full of sand with shops and houses round it, where,
in the early morning, buck wagons drawn by long teams
of oxen rolled slowly in, laden with produce from the
country, skins and pumpkins and firewood, bags of meal
or mielies and sometimes butter and garden growths; and
the little market master held the morning market. There
the townsmen gathered to hear the latest news and send
round the latest gossip, till by eight o'clock they had all
gone home to their breakfasts, the wagons had rolled
out and the square was left empty and silent enough all
day, crossed occasionally by customers making their way
to the different shops or business men going home to their

[1 Cradock.]   [2 Fish River.]

292

meals, and, at eleven o'clock, by streams of men coming to the hotel at the corner where they went to have their morning drink of soda and brandy and to smoke and chat for a while on the hotel stoep.[1]

Three times a week the post cart with its dusty wheels and horses came in, blowing its bugle and bringing its news from the outer world, and everyone hurried to the post office to get his letters. And twice a week came Cobb and Co's great coaches, swinging on their great leather straps; and their teams of six horses, bearing passengers to and from the Diamond Fields,[2] drew up before the hotel door, when for two hours the town was alive and excited with the new arrivals; then the horses would be put in again and pass away in a cloud of dust and the town would be left to its silent monotony.

There were two croquet clubs in the place frequented by the members of two churches which formed the two great cliques; there was a courthouse where occasionally the members of one church gave a dance which the other church thought wicked and never went to, and once or twice a year some traveling showman would arrive and give an entertainment there. Every year the members of each church had a large Sunday-school picnic to which all the members of that congregation went; and sometimes a lady would give a high tea and invite a few friends, for no one dined late there.

In the upper part of the town there were rows of little flat houses, generally kept shut up and empty, where the Dutch farmers stayed when they came in once in three months to the Lord's Supper ("Nagmaal") and now and then to the Sunday services in the weeks between. But on Monday they all went out again, and the houses were left empty, and the town to its English inhabitants.

During nine months of the year, while the winds blew, clouds of dust whirled along the streets before thunderstorms; when the gusts came, great clouds of sand rose from the market square and met the still mightier clouds

[1 The Victoria Hotel.]   [2 Now Kimberley.]

raised from the wide sandy plain; and the town was shrouded in sand.

It was a dull narrow little life enough, lived there among the flat-roofed houses, far removed from the currents of life and thought of the great world beyond.

Yet, if some summer morning you rose at half past four and went out to the koppie at the end of the town and climbed its round black ironstones, and stood looking down at the little town with its long rows of houses and the little brown huts of the Kaffir Location sleeping at your feet in the still blue morning air, while the damp of the night yet rested on everything and nothing moved or stirred, except where here and there a Kaffir servant might be seen hurrying from the Location to the town, her shawl drawn tight about her to shut out the chill morning air; till by and by, from some of the chimneys in the town, long blue curls of smoke began to rise, standing upright and almost motionless in the still air; then suddenly the bleak moist stone on which you stood turned golden at your feet; a shaft of light had shot across the plain and struck it; another came, and the little ice plant in the crevice of the rock at your feet glittered in every crystal drop; then another, and the whole plain was golden and the roofs of the little flat houses glinted—then the town was beautiful.

Bertie's aunt and uncle lived in a street leading out of the square, so close to it that from the front windows you could see half across it. It was an old dingy house, a foot lower than the street and the water furrow above, with a little strip of flower garden six feet wide and a low paling before it.

Her uncle's business place was on another plot across the square. He was a general agent; he held auction sales, conducted cases in the little Magistrate's Court, drew up wills and managed estates, and speculated on his own account. He was thin, silent, and rather hatchet-faced: he was regarded by his fellow townsmen as a clever business man, though he was said to have lately burnt his fingers in some speculation and to have lost on a company he had fitted out and sent up to the Diamond Fields; he was hard in business matters and said to love money; but he was a leading man in the church of which he was a member and was regarded as one of the principal men in the town. More than twenty years before he had married Bertie's aunt, whom he had met when on a visit from England to her sister, the little mother at the old farm; and had brought her to his little up-country town, where they had lived in the same house ever since, with the same furniture and the same strip of flower garden, and where their two daughters, now in England, had been born. Her aunt was not unlike the little mother in feature, but tall and thin and much less pretty, and with a cold measured manner. Her head, like Bertie's, was small compared to the size of her body, and three rows of short faded white curls hung on each side of her head. In the chapel she was the leader at prayer meetings and all religious gatherings and was one of the most esteemed women of the town.

Besides her uncle and aunt, there was no one in the house but Dorcas, the tall heavy-faced Kaffir servant, who always wore a red handkerchief bound across her head and helped in the kitchen.

Once Bertie might have found the dingy, flat little house with its three inhabitants lonely. Now she loved it.

On the first day when Bertie was unpacking her clothes her aunt admired her mantle, and Bertie had begged her aunt for her old silk shawl and out of it by the next Sunday had made a mantle exactly like her own, and had remade her aunt's bonnet and retrimmed it with lace from one of her own ball dresses; so that when Aunt Mary-Anna appeared in chapel everyone thought it was a new mantle and bonnet. Some said that if the general agent were really in business difficulties she should not purchase such expensive things, others that perhaps they were presents from a rich niece in Cape Town, but everyone admired them.

The next week Bertie got from her uncle a large roll of flower-covered chintz that had been lying in his sale room for months and with it made covers for every chair and sofa, till all the old dingy furniture blossomed out in pink roses. And the next week, when her aunt went to a farm for three days, she bought with her own money some cheap wall paper and, with Dorcas to help her, repapered the passage and the front parlor, she standing at the top of the ladder and Dorcas at the bottom; and she took up the carpet in the parlor that had lain there for twenty-four years and cut it down the middle and resewed it so that the worn center came to the sides, when, by placing furniture over the worn patches, it looked like a new carpet; so that when Aunt Mary-Anna returned she was filled with surprise and delight; and the house looked as if the general agent were refurnishing.

Early in the morning Bertie was up making curry and hot rolls for breakfast; for dinner and supper she made sosatie [1] and bobotie [2] and pumpkin fritters and puffs and grilled chops, as she had learned from old Ayah; and the hatchet face of the general agent, who for twenty-four years had suffered from bad cooking, seemed to be perceptibly filling out. When she had no cooking to do, she rummaged her aunt's old wardrobe and boxes and, from ends of lace and bits of old material, shaped little caps and aprons, and, by unpicking and cleaning and reshaping old dresses, made her aunt's wardrobe full of wearable dresses.

"I really don't know how we ever got on without you," her aunt used to say. "You must never leave us, or, if you do, you must promise to remain for eight months after the girls come home, so that they may learn from you."

Even her silent uncle praised her food, and, as he passed through the kitchen where she was stooping over a pot,

[1 Sosatie: roasted curried meat.]   [2 Bobotie: curried hash.]

stirring its contents, would say, "Our little cook must not burn her face too much, though I know it's something good she's going to turn out"; and Bertie's cheeks would flush a deeper red, more with pride and happiness than from the heat of the fire.

Even Dorcas liked her; she coaxed her so gently, and, when Bertie had given her a white silk handkerchief to tie in with her red one on Sundays and had shown her how to arrange it round her head and had made her a cotton blouse with red butterflies on it, Dorcas would do anything for her.

"I am very, very happy here," she wrote to Rebekah; "I should never like to go away. Everyone loves me."

After the first Sunday when Bertie appeared in church, the ladies of the town had called to see her, and her aunt said it was necessary she should return their calls with her; but after that she refused to go out. She accepted no invitations to picnics or parties and declined to join the croquet club. At first her aunt tried to persuade her to go out; but when she found she really did not wish to go and that Bertie's staying at home gave her more time to attend prayer meetings and classes and to fulfill her duties as leading woman in the church, she gave way; and the only times when Bertie was ever seen out were when she went twice to church every Sunday and once on a week night, and when she now and then went out shopping for her aunt. The mothers of the place all praised her and held her up to their daughters as an example of devotion to hard work and duty.

When she first came the young girls of the place felt to her much as the ducks in a farmyard might to one that had wandered in from the open. They all said she was not nearly so pretty as the men said, that she looked proud and her curls were not natural. But when, after some weeks, they found she never crossed their paths, when she had lent them the patterns of her dresses and had helped two of the prettiest girls in the place to make bonnets for themselves exactly like her own, they all said she was nice and much the prettiest girl that had ever come to the town, that her curly hair was beautiful, and that they thought her aunt unkind to keep her so much at home.

The young men had not many opportunities of seeing her except in church; two, who had always gone to the other church, began to attend there, and two who had sat in the center moved into a wing so that they sat opposite the general agent's pew. On Sunday and week nights such as knew the general agent and his wife hurried to the church door and tried to walk home with them. But Bertie seemed always to manage to walk between her uncle and aunt; and if they spoke across to her as they walked she said "yes" or "no" and seemed not to see them. And if she went to a shop to buy anything, and the young shopman spoke to her of the weather or the dust or of anything but business, she answered him quickly and softly and went out.

Even the magistrate's clerk, who wore a black coat and carried a little walking stick, and said there was no one in the town he could associate with, and never took notice of any girl, called three times formally at the general agent's after Bertie came; but as she did not appear, he had to content himself with sitting opposite the general agent's pew.

Bertie was very happy all day. If ever, as she worked, a thought came to her she did not like, she put it from her quickly, saying within herself: "They all love me here! I will never go away! They will always let me stay."

Only at night when she had gone to bed and put out the light and was just dropping off to sleep, suddenly the old dream which she used to have on the farm when she was a little child used to come back to her—she was running down the road in the dark and on, behind her, came something with heavy breath; she knew its tongue lolled out and she heard its steps, and as she ran it came nearer and nearer!—till she woke shrieking; and Rebekah used to hear her and come from her bed and lie beside her and sing "London's Burning! Fire! Fire!" till she went to sleep.

Now it often came back to her; she would wake with the bed trembling beneath her and would sit up wringing her hands, before she remembered where she was. Then she would lie down quickly and pull the cover close over her head and take a pillow and hold it longways against her and clasp it tight, with both arms around it, so that it seemed like something living she was clinging to.

One day at breakfast her uncle brought the post in and gave her a letter. She read it, sitting behind the coffee-urn at the head of the table.

"I hope you have no bad news, my dear," Aunt Mary-Anna said.

"Oh no," Bertie said, "it's from mother." But when breakfast was over she hurried to her own room and knelt down beside the bed and laid the letter open before her and read it through. As she read her cheeks darkened slowly to a red as deep as the darkest of Rebekah's roses in the garden at Cape Town. She buried her burning face in the letter and knelt motionless. What the letter said was this:

"MY DEAR BABY-BERTIE,

"I am glad you are so happy at your aunt's, but I wish you could come home by Xmas-time. John-Ferdinand and Veronica come over and spend every Sunday with us and generally drive over once a week, so I'm not so lonely. But Veronica is going to have a baby at Xmas-time and I shall have to go and stay with her for some weeks. Of course, old Ayah can stay and look after the house and your father, but come if you can, unless your aunt very much wants you and you want to stay." Then came much farm news that she read without noting; then came the P.S. "Veronica is looking so well. . . . She has a lovely color and her face is getting quite round. . . . You would hardly know her."

After a time Bertie lifted her face from the letter; it was growing slowly white; she put it in her breast and went to knead the bread in the kitchen.

After dinner, when her aunt was asleep and her uncle had gone to his business, she slipped out and went to a shop across the square. There she bought the finest muslin and lace and embroidery the town held and needles and thread even finer than those she generally used; then she slipped back to her own room and all the afternoon sat cutting out and sewing. She got up early the next morning as soon as the sun rose and went back to her work, and at night she sat sewing at her bedside till one or two o'clock. Her aunt noticed that now, as soon as her work was done, she went to her own room, but thought she was doing sewing for herself.

Slowly the scores of little tucks and the fine embroidery shaped themselves. At the end of a week there were two tiny armholes. Again and again she would stop in her work to put her fingers into them and fill them out. At the end of a fortnight the long white robe with its delicate invisible stitching was almost complete. At night, before she put it away, she would lay it out on the bed, putting a pillow at the top and filling it out so that it almost seemed there was something inside it; and she would stand across the room looking at it. One day it was finished. She packed it in white tissue-paper with a few little bits of fresh lavender put in it. She tied it with pink ribbons and packed it into a handkerchief box with red rosebuds on the lid; then she carefully folded brown paper round it and tied it with string across and across. When her aunt went to sleep after dinner, again she stole out and went to the post office and stamped it and sent it off. After it was gone she was always picturing how it traveled: it would take seven days to reach the farm; it might have to wait two days at the post office in the village if no special messenger came to fetch it; then on Sunday morning it would get to the farm; some one would open it. She never would let herself think any further; she began picturing the journey over again.

The poet, when his heart is weighted, writes a sonnet, and the painter paints a picture, and the thinker throws himself into the world of thought, and the publican and the man of business may throw themselves into the world of action; but the woman who is only a woman, what has she but her needle? In that torn bit of brown leather brace worked through and through with yellow silk, in that bit of white rag with invisible stitching, lying among the fallen leaves and rubbish that the wind has blown into the gutter or the street corner, lies all the passion of some woman's soul finding voiceless expression. Has the pen or the pencil dipped so deep in the blood of the human race as the needle?

After that the summer began to grow hotter, every afternoon clouds of dust wheeled along the streets and over the plains; and now and then a thunderstorm broke at four o'clock and laid the dust for that day.

The week before Xmas the post brought no letter for Bertie, but her aunt came into the kitchen where she was shelling peas and said she had had a few lines from the little mother, who could not write to Bertie because at six o'clock on the day she wrote Veronica had had a fine little boy. Mother and child were doing well. Bertie went on shelling the peas and got dinner ready; after dinner she went to bed with a sick headache and did not come to supper, but early the next morning she was up kneading the bread and said she was quite well. Some days after that came the news that Rebekah also had a little son, born prematurely, and that she was very ill; then news that she was better. Then a long time passed when nothing happened.

Slowly the summer heat began to die and the nights to become cool, sometimes almost sharp. All the housewives were busy plucking fruit and drying and preserving. Bertie had made rows and rows of bottles of peach and quince jam which lined the shelves of her aunt's pantry;

and now she was making watermelon preserve. Her
aunt's daughters would be out in five months, and everything was being got ready for the teas and suppers when
they came.

Then a curious experience began to come to Bertie.
It was as though a weight seemed always resting on her;
it might be the change to the autumn's coolness, but something heavy seemed always pressing on her. She tried to
shake it off; but from being a vague feeling it grew till
it almost took definite shape. Sometimes if she went out
to a shop or to carry a message to her uncle's office, if
girls she met passed her and she wished them good
day they returned her greeting, but, if she did not, they
seemed to pass without seeing her. When one of her
aunt's women friends called and she went to open the door,
they did not smile, but asked gravely if her aunt was in.
It might have been her fancy, but it seemed to her that
when her uncle and aunt spoke to her they did not look
at her, and they spoke more seldom. A curious silence
seemed to have settled down on the house. One morning,
when her aunt was having her breakfast in bed and Bertie
sat, as she always did, at the table behind the tray, she
looked up suddenly and saw her uncle, who sat at the
other end of the table, looking at her intently over the
top of the newspaper he held. The moment he saw she
had noticed him he dropped his eyes and raised the paper
so that only the top of his head was visible over it; and
several times, when she came into a room where her uncle
and aunt were, they were talking together in a low tone,
but stopped at once when she came in.

On Sundays after church there were still some young
men about the door, but, if the general agent did not speak
to them, they did not force their company as they used
to, and the three walked home alone together. One Sunday the magistrate's clerk, who had never waited near the
door like other young men, walked straight up to them
and forced his way in between Bertie and her uncle and
walked next to her, talking to her; but there seemed some-

thing strange in the way he walked and talked, looking round at all the people they passed, as if he were challenging them to see where he walked. That afternoon, when her uncle and aunt were sleeping, Bertie sat alone in her bedroom with her hands in her lap; it seemed to her all the while that a lump kept rising in her throat and she wanted to cry, though she could not tell why.

The autumn was closing in fast now, the leaves were falling from the trees in the street and filling the furrows and covering the sidewalks in the lower part of the town. In the gardens everything but the winter crops was drying out.

One afternoon about five o'clock Bertie sat in the little parlor that looked out across the garden into the street; she sat sewing before the window on the little low chair on which she always sat, and her aunt sat opposite in a high-backed cane rocking chair, knitting. For nearly an hour they had sat there with no sound but the click of Aunt Mary-Anna's needles to break the silence. The sky was becoming slightly overcast as though it was going to rain, and the light was already beginning to grow duller in the little low room. Suddenly Bertie leaned forward and laid her hand, with the threaded needle in it, on her aunt's knee.

"Aunt Mary-Anna," she said quickly, in a low, slightly thick voice, "have I done anything to displease you? Are you angry with me?"

"No, Bertie, no," she said, knitting quickly. She dropped three stitches but knitted on without noticing them.

"I was so afraid I had done something to displease you," Bertie said, looking up at her.

"No—you have done nothing to me, Bertie." She knitted on without looking at her. "And yet," she said, after a pause, "it is perhaps quite as well you spoke, because I have been wishing to speak to you. Your uncle and I think"—she waited a little—"it is perhaps quite as well you went home. In fact, your uncle wrote yesterday to your father, and posted the letter to-day, to say you would be leaving this by next Thursday's post cart, and they must send to meet you at the town next week."

Bertie sat upright in her chair, looking at her aunt with wide-open eyes.

"But I can't go home, I don't want to go," she said, in a low thick voice. "You said I could stay here with you. Oh, what have I done?"

For a moment Aunt Mary-Anna knitted on blunderingly, then she stopped and looked at Bertie. "There is no need for us to discuss the matter, my dear. You have been very kind and of great use to me, and your uncle and I will always be grateful for the many ways in which you have helped us. But we both think it best you should go home now. You have been here nearly six months and your mother may be wanting you."

"But you said I could stay! Oh, please let me stay! I don't want to go! I can't go back there!" She laid her hand again on Aunt Mary-Anna's knee and looked up at her with large wide-open eyes.

Aunt Mary-Anna hesitated. Then she drew herself up. "Perhaps I had better tell you the truth, Bertie. It is as well you should know it. People here have been saying very strange things about you." Bertie looked up into her face with eyes that seemed to grow wider. "Your uncle heard something first in the town, and he told me; and afterwards the minister's wife called and told me the same thing. She said she felt it her duty to tell me what people were saying. It is the common talk of the town now. I don't believe a word of it, neither does your uncle; and I have told everyone so who has spoken to me. And after you have gone I shall deny it everywhere. But with my two girls coming home, you will understand, Bertie, that, as it is something regarding your conduct as a young girl, I could not have you staying on here with them. It may be all perfectly untrue, my dear"—there was something almost of kindliness in Aunt Mary-Anna's tone—"but a woman's character is like gossamer, when you've once dropped it in the mud and pulled it about it can never be put right again. With a man it's different; he can live down anything. People say, 'Oh, he was young, he's changed.' They never say that of a woman; the soap isn't invented that can wash a woman's character clean."

Bertie leaned farther forward, looking at her. Her aunt moved restlessly.

"Of course I don't believe a word of it; it's just silly talk of what happened when you were a schoolgirl of fifteen. I know there's no truth in it. But that doesn't make any practical difference. You are one of the best girls I ever knew." Bertie leaned yet more forward and laid her hand on her aunt's knee.

"But if it is true?" she whispered.

Her aunt drew herself up suddenly and looked down at her wide eyes. Bertie stretched out both her hands; it seemed as if she would have caught hold of her aunt's hands. "I'll tell you—I'll tell you everything ——!"

Aunt Mary-Anna rose quickly. "Really, Bertie, I am astonished at you! I will beg of you to tell me nothing. If there is any truth in what they have been saying about you, the least you can do is to keep quiet about it. I have asked you no questions, and you should at least leave me the power of denying it. You have cost me trouble enough as it is. Your mother and Rebekah did very wrong in letting you come here, knowing I had young girls."

"Oh, they don't know! No one knows! I have only told one person about it!" Bertie rose and stood before her. A blind look was in her eyes as though she saw nothing; she moved her hands aimlessly. "I was so young," she wailed suddenly. "Oh!"—she moved her hands.

"Will you lower your voice, Bertie! Do you want Dorcas, who is in the kitchen, to hear everything you say! If you want to tell anyone about it, tell your mother and your sister."

"Oh, I can't! They must never know! They think I'm a baby still!—Oh, I can't go home! I never can go home!"

"You must go home," said her aunt quietly, "and not later than by next Thursday's cart."

At that moment there was a sound at the front door and of feet in the passage, and then the general agent flung open the door of the little parlor. Beside him shuffled a little figure. He ushered him in. Aunt Mary-Anna turned quickly to the door; but Bertie still stood motionless before the window, where the quickly fading light fell full on her. She had a little crimson rosebud fastened at the throat of her white dress, which made her face of a more deadly paleness under its cloud of brown curling hair, and the eyelashes of her drooping eyes seemed printed on her cheeks. Aunt Mary-Anna stepped forward to greet the visitor, whom she had evidently met before. She shook hands with him and asked him if he had arrived by that evening's coach from The Fields.[1]

He was a small man of about fifty, with slightly bent shoulders and thin, small limbs. His face was of a dull Oriental pallor, and his piercing dark eyes and marked nose proclaimed him at once a Jew; above a high square forehead rose a tower of stiffly curling, gray, upright hair. He spoke with a strong foreign accent. The general agent introduced him to Bertie. She gave him a cold dead hand without looking at him and then turned slowly to the window and with her back to the room stood looking out, her hands hanging lifeless at either side. The Jew took his seat on a small chair in the dark corner between the sideboard and the wall, and twisted his feet into the legs of the chair. The general agent begged him to stay to supper; he assented shortly and sat looking keenly about the room, now at Bertie's figure as she stood

[1] The Diamond Fields were in those days known simply as "The Fields."

before the window, and then at the furniture, at the hanging lamp and the old piano and what-not and then back at Bertie. Her aunt asked her to go and get supper ready, and she left the room without looking round. Presently her aunt came into the kitchen and asked her to prepare the best supper she could, as their visitor was a man with whom her uncle had business dealings and wished to entertain as well as possible. She carried a lighted lamp into the parlor, where the general agent was inquiring from his guest the state of affairs at The Fields and the condition of the country through which he had passed, to all which inquiries the Jew answered shortly and looked keenly about him. He was a money lender and diamond speculator whose home was in London but who had come to South Africa several times since the discovery of diamonds, and he had lent the general agent a large sum of money at a high rate of interest with which the agent had financed the diamond-digging venture that had failed. He knew it was to attend to this matter that the Jew had broken his journey from The Fields to England at the little town, and that, if the Jew pressed for immediate payment, it meant his insolvency, and he talked with unusual fluency and suaveness; but the Jew did not trouble himself to make conversation, and when the general agent ceased to speak there were long pauses.

When Bertie had prepared the supper she went to her aunt's bedroom, where her aunt stood before the glass putting on her best cap and collar and arranging her curls. Bertie who stood in the doorway said that all was ready, but that her head ached and she would like to go to her room instead of going to supper. Her aunt ran her curls round her fingers and said without looking back, "You will do nothing of the kind, my dear. The least you can do for the few days you are still here is to allow no one to see that anything unusual has happened. You will at least come to the table if you do not care to eat." Then she added, as she patted her curls, "You will also please note, Bertie, that you need not refer again to anything that passed between us this evening while you are here. Your uncle has taken your seat in the post cart that leaves on Thursday. He has not mentioned to your parents why you are going; he simply said that as your mother seemed to need you we could not think of keeping you here longer. One thing I should like to say to you, Bertie: never attempt such confidences as you were desirous of making to me this evening. If a woman has made a mistake there is only one course for her—silence!" Her aunt still looked into the glass and Bertie withdrew softly from the door.

At the supper-table Bertie sat in her usual place behind the tray at the head, with the great coffee-urn before her. Her aunt sat on the right side of the table and the Jew on the left and her uncle at the other end.

The Jew ate hurriedly and absorbedly, as people do who have lived through much of their life alone: he bent low over his plate, shoveling in the frikkedel [1] and gravy with his knife and seldom looking up. Once or twice as he ate his eye passed from his plate to the end of the table where Bertie sat silent, her cheeks so pale they were almost sallow and her eyelashes almost resting on them as she looked down at the plate on which she toyed with her food.

When the supper was almost done, in answer to some remark of the general agent's as to the color of diamonds, the Jew took from an inner breast-pocket a small parcel wrapped in oilskin and carefully tied. He removed the oilskin and took out a small brown paper parcel, from the inside of which he took a small round japanned box. He opened and poured carefully into a plate a little shower of white, yellow-tinted stones, which glittered softly in the lamplight. He put the plate between himself and the general agent and began touching the different stones with his bent forefinger, describing their various qualities and values. The general agent's wife leaned forward to see

[1 Fricadel: minced meat ball, "rissole."]

them. He passed the plate over for her to examine them more closely. When she had handed the plate back to him, the Jew looked up to the end of the table where Bertie sat. "And ze young lady, vill she not see too?" he asked.

Bertie lifted her eyes heavily. He passed the plate up towards her; she put it down at her side, looking at them with her indifferent drooping eyes. "They are nice," she said slowly, and was going to return the plate, when the Jew bent forward. "Vitch zinks she is the best now?" he said, with his head a little on one side.

Indifferently, with her finger Bertie touched a small perfect octahedron stone. "This," she said, and handed the plate back to the Jew.

"Ha-ha! Zat is very good! It is small, but it is ze best. Ze young lady has a good eye."

He put the stones back into the little box and returned it to its wrappings and put it into his breast-pocket. Then they rose. The general agent invited him to return to the parlor; but he said he must leave. He shook hands with Bertie and her aunt.

In the hall, when the general agent and helped him on with his coat, he turned to him for a moment and said, "Ze young lady, does she live viz you?"

The general agent explained that she was his wife's niece and only on a visit, and was to leave in two days. The Jew made an appointment to meet him at his office the next morning to discuss business. The general agent opened the door for him and wished him good night; the Jew shuffled out into the street, and the door closed behind him.

It was a glorious night. Up above, ten thousand stars were throwing down their points of light brighter than any diamonds and making dimly visible even the outlines of the houses in the dark town. The Jew began to shuffle through the thick sand in the street and the yet thicker sand of the square. But he saw neither the bright lights above him nor the dark earth about him.

Far away, across the mist of fifty years, he saw again a little garret room under the eaves in a North German city, where a small dark-eyed boy and girl played together when their parents had gone out to their work and had locked them in. He saw again the little garret window, through which they crept out on to the roof where the tall chimneys rose. Again they played at being storks, and, with tiny fragments in their mouths of the brown bread their parents had left them to eat during their absence, pretended to feed tiny imaginary storklings in an imaginary nest between the chimneys; again he heard the little girl's cry of admiration at his courage and of terror lest he should fall when the boy walked to the extreme edge of the roof to peer down into the street below; again he held fast the skirts of the little girl as she crept back through the window lest they should sweep against the box of mignonette their mother had planted there and break them. And then it was later, and a boy of seventeen and a girl of sixteen whose parents had died in Germany were living alone in London in an East End garret whose roof sloped to the floor at one side. Again it was early morning and the boy with the black curls hanging into his neck and an old black bag over his shoulders paced the streets of Bloomsbury; again he felt the nip of the fog-laden London morning air in his nostrils, and again he felt the fresh young blood coursing through his veins as the boy raised his cry, "Old clothes! Old clothes!" and raised his eyes anxiously to the grim rows of houses to see if from door or window came an answering beck or nod. And then it was evening and the bag was full, and, up the flights of stairs in the East End lodging-house, the boy was mounting three steps at a time. Then he saw the door open and the pile of clothes on the floor and the girl in the fading light at the little sloping window bending over her work, till she raised her dark soft eyes with their curled lashes to greet him, and they prepared their evening meal of fried fish on the little stove in the corner, and to save light and keep warm sat down on a heap of clothes before the stove and ate it together from one plate; and when it was ended sat talking of the prices she had got at the shops for the clothes she had repaired, and the things he had in the bag. When she grew tired, she laid her head on his knee, and, staring at the small bed of coals, he talked of the future, of the time when their savings would have mounted and they too would possess a tall house in Bloomsbury. He talked of the jewels he would buy her and the carriage they would keep, and she talked of the food she would see he had and the things they would do for their aunt and her children in Germany who were the only relations they had. And all the while, as he saw the pictures, he saw also dimly Bertie's face at the head of the table, with the thick curling hair above the low forehead and the large eyes with the curled lashes that had waked the old pictures.

He struck his foot against the lowest step of the little hotel stoep and swore and shuffled up them. In the bar the men were gathered drinking and talking; he went in and sat for a while listening, now and then putting in a remark to see if no news as to the general agent's monetary position was to be gathered, and then he went upstairs. When he had undressed and put his oilcloth-wrapped parcel under his pillow, he got into bed and blew out the light. His long day's journey on the coach had tired him, but he could not sleep. First his thoughts traveled over the news he had heard of the general agent in the barroom; would it, or would it not, be best to push him? Then his thoughts traveled back to the Diamond Fields, to the man he had left at the River Diggings to buy claims for him, to New Rush [1] and his claims there. Then they led back to London, to the tall grim house in Bloomsbury, where hundreds of houses, equally yellow and dull and deadly in their exact likeness to one another from attic to basement, filled the long weary street in which he had lived alone for twenty years, with only Martha, his grimy broad-shouldered housekeeper, and later on her weak-eyed short-witted son, with a gait like his own, to keep him

[1 Now Kimberley.]

company. He wondered irritably if the woman was not burning too many coals and using too much food during his absence and whether Isaac always remembered to lock the area gate; and then he saw Bertie sitting at the agent's table, with her large eyes and her drooping lashes and the curly hair that had brought back the past. He tossed wearily. He lit the candle and looked at his watch; it was half past eleven; then he blew the light out and tried to sleep again. But when the clock struck twelve he was still lying staring up into the dark.

Then the Jew rose; he lit the candle and took from under his pillow the parcel of stones. Carefully he opened it and, examining the stones, selected the one which Bertie had touched that evening. He held it in the palm of his hand, looking at it by the candle light. Softly he touched it with the forefinger of the other hand, caressing its soft soapy surface as a mother might the hair of a child with which she was to part. He extended his arm, holding it close to the candle, and drew back his head that he might look at it from a distance; then he put it down on a fragment of the brown paper and wrapped it carefully in it; then he cut off a piece of the oilskin and folded it in that; then he tied the tiny parcel carefully and put it in his purse. He refolded the large parcel and put it with his purse under the pillow. Then he got quickly into bed and was soon asleep.

The next morning the Jew visited the general agent's office; he discussed their business; he asked at what rate the general agent would be willing to pay if he left the money due now in a few weeks for another two years, and what securities he could give; but he gave the general agent no definite answer as to whether he would accept his terms or not, but said he should hear from him later in the day.

As he was turning to go the Jew took from his purse the small brown parcel and handed it to the general agent.

"Ze young lady, she liked zat stone. Vill you say I

have ze honor to present it to her viz my compliments?" Then he went out at the door without waiting for thanks.

When the agent went home to dinner he gave Bertie the gift. She opened it with no sign of pleasure. At his request she wrote a note of three lines thanking the Jew. After dinner, when she had gone to her room to finish her packing, Aunt Mary-Anna turned to her husband. "Why did he give it her?" she asked.

"How can I tell?" asked the general agent.

She looked at him. "Is he married?"

"For all I can tell he may have a wife and half a dozen children in Hamburg or England or wherever his headquarters may be!" But he divined her meaning as the slowest people who have lived together for twenty years will do without words.

"The idea did just flit across my mind also," said the general agent, answering her thought, "but it's ridiculous. No doubt he admired her; she's the kind of woman every man finds attractive. But Jews don't marry Christians, even supposing him to be unmarried. A Jew will eat sucking pig, he will be a Christian in all his manners and customs, but when it comes to legal marriage, he's a Jew. It's a ridiculous idea, and he's leaving to-morrow."

"It's very strange he should give away a valuable stone like that to a girl he has only exchanged three words with!"

"Not at all. You never can account for what a Jew will do. I've known a Jew give thirty pounds for a Sunday-school picnic for Christian children, when he would have wrung ten shillings out of a starving man who owed it him: a Jew has whims like a woman." He went back to his office.

That evening Bertie had finished all her packing; her large box stood ready locked and tied to go by transport wagon, her small portmanteau and hat box were standing ready at the foot of her bed, to be put in the post cart the next morning. Her aunt had gone out to a mothers' prayer meeting, and at four o'clock Bertie took a ball of cotton and a crochet needle and went to the low rocking chair before the parlor window where she sat every after-noon. For a time she crocheted, then she rested her hands on the ball in her lap and looked out of the window across the four feet of garden, with its faded geraniums and pinks and across the little green paling into the street. After a time she leaned her forehead on the window ledge. The world was so large, so large, why was there no place for her? Her thoughts went back to Rebekah's house among the oak trees at Cape Town and the old farm with the blue-gums, to John-Ferdinand's homestead almost showing over the nek; and she felt a hand laid on her heart. She thought of the whole world, of the Far East that Rebekah taught her of when she was a little girl, of India with its swarming millions and Juggernaut cars and palm trees, of China with its pagodas and little bells: there, there, far away, if one could only get there, one would be lost among all those millions, there one would be free. Why, why was there no place for her in the world where she could go and no one ever find her! Slowly the tears gathered in her eyes and fell upon her lap. Only a few hours and she would be in the post cart, and then a few days more and she would be at the farm, and John-Ferdinand and Veronica would come over to see her. She moved her hands passionately in her lap. Then the front gate clicked. She sat up and dried her eyes. Dorcas had answered the knock and opened the parlor door and ushered in the Jew. Bertie rose to meet him; the tear stains were still upon her cheeks, but she held out her hand passively to him. He asked if her aunt were in, as he had come to say good-by. Bertie said she was out but would be back in a very short time: she was expecting her every moment. The Jew sat down on a small stiff-legged chair to her left, and Bertie sat down passively in her low seat. She made no effort to speak, but turned her face towards the window, so that only her profile was visible to the Jew.

For a few moments he sat quiet, then he said, "It looks it vill rain to-night! It grows dark."

"Yes," said Bertie slowly. And then there was a long silence. The Jew sat watching her with his keen eyes, his feet twisted round the two forelegs of the chair.

"You are not vell?" he asked at last, bending forward.

"Yes—yes—I am quite well, thank you." She still looked out of the window. The Jew watched her.

"You vill go away to-morrow?" he said presently.

"Yes," she said slowly.

"I go on viz ze post-cart. You viz it too?"

"Yes," she said, without looking at him.

Then there was a long silence and the Jew thought of something to say.

"You vill like zat you go to your home and your family again?"

Bertie turned her face slowly from the window. "No," she said slowly, and then turned it back again. The tear marks were clearly visible on her cheeks. The Jew felt curiously perturbed.

"Vat is it zat you cry?" he said suddenly, bending forward low; "your uncle, your aunt, are zey not good to you?"

"Oh yes, yes, they are."

The Jew waited a moment and looked at her motionless figure.

"Ven you shall vish to stay longer, shall I not speak viz your uncle zat he let you stay?"

"Oh no, no!" Bertie started and looked round at him. "Don't, don't say anything to him!"

"Ven I speak to your uncle he shall let you stay. He shall hear vat I say!" A little gleam of conscious power crept into the Jew's eye.

Bertie had half started up, moving her hands quickly; the ball and crochet needle fell to the floor. "I don't want to stay here," she said. Then she sank back into the chair. Suddenly she bent forward to the Jew: "I want to find work, some place where I can work. You— you have been all over the world; don't you know where I could get some work?" Her hands interclasped themselves in her lap. "I can do nearly anything," she said, with her eyes now wide open and fixed on him, "that a woman does with her hands. I can cook and sew, and I can trim hats; I could take care of a baby or house. Wouldn't anyone at The Fields want me? I could do anything. I wouldn't mind working hard." She looked full up into the Jew's face.

"Ze Fields is not ze place for you!" he said. His eyes swerved from her face and fixed themselves on the hands in her lap, rounded and dimpled and so small for her large body. "You are for ze joy, ze life, ze beautiful clothes, ze beautiful zings: you are not for ze hard work!"

"Oh, I can work!" she said, bending closer to his knees. "I could do anything. If your wife wanted some one to help her, I could do all she wanted. I wouldn't mind going to another land, I would like it. If I could only——" They saw the shadow of Aunt Mary-Anna's figure fall across the window as she passed it. The gate clicked and she opened the front door. Bertie drew back and sat upright in the shadow of the curtain. The Jew rose to his feet as she entered the parlor. He said he had done himself the honor to come and wish her good-by and to thank her for the very good supper he had had the night before.

Aunt Mary-Anna thanked him properly for the diamond he had given Bertie and asked him to stay to supper again. But he declined, as he had business. He shook hands with Bertie without addressing her, and her aunt conducted him to the front door.

It was half past one that night. Bertie lay in the bed in the dark. She had slept for an hour after getting into bed, but since then had lain awake. Again and again she tried to draw the pillow to her and pull the cover over her head; but no sleep came. She lay now looking up into the dark. She heard the clock in the dining room strike the half hour. Every moment brought nearer the time of her going, and then the journey, and then the arrival at the farm. Again and again she went over the steps that always ended with the arrival of John-Ferdinand and Veronica from their farm. She listened to the deadly stillness in the house and felt the inevitableness that drew her on; she must start the next morning, she must arrive at the farm, she must see them all. She turned on to her side; the curls on her forehead were damp with a chilly sweat. The clock struck two. Then she threw back the cover and stepped out of bed. In her white nightgown she walked to the door and opened it and walked softly with her bare feet across the little passage and opened the kitchen door. From the large uncurtained window a great square of dazzling moonlight fell on the stone-paved floor, making every crack visible in the stones where it lay and lighting up dimly the whole kitchen, so that even the pots on the wall and the legs of the table and chairs were visible. On the floor before the fireplace, wrapped in her brown blanket, Dorcas the Kaffir girl lay, with only a fragment of her red handkerchief showing at one end of the living brown roll. Bertie glided softly across the floor and knelt beside the roll with one knee on the floor and one raised.

"Dorcas! Dorcas!" she called softly.

Dorcas did not stir.

"Dorcas, please wake!" She touched her softly. "Oh, please wake, Dorcas!"

Dorcas gave a low guttural sound; her head protruded slightly from the blanket like a caddis worm creeping out of its case; but her eyes were fast closed.

"I'm so lonely, Dorcas! Oh, please let me hold your hand!"

Dorcas snored and turned slightly on her side. Bertie put down her hand under the blanket and took the thick coarse hand of the Kaffir woman and held it tight in her own. "I'm so lonely, Dorcas!" But Dorcas moved heavily and then lay motionless. Bertie shivered; after a while she withdrew her hand and rose softly and glided with her naked feet back to her own room.

At half past four the post cart driver had inspanned his

horses and had drawn up before the post office on the square and was blowing a great blast on his bugle, while the cold sleepy postmaster was dragging out the bags. Twenty minutes later he had drawn up before the general agent's door and blew another blast. Bertie, who had long been up and dressed, went to her aunt, who was still in bed, while the general agent, who had risen hastily and put on his slippers and dressing-gown, carried her hat box and portmanteau to the front door. When Bertie got to the door the four gray horses were champing their bits and moving their heads in the sharp morning air; the colored driver was fastening her hat box and portmanteau on to the back of the cart, while before the front seat the post bags were packed higher than the splashboard. On the back seat of the cart sat the little Jew wrapped in a fur-lined coat whose turned-up collar hid almost all but the sharp eyes and nose that looked out above them. The general agent stood shivering on the doorstep, with his hands in the pockets of his dressing-gown, and was remarking to the Jew that it would be warmer as soon as the sun rose. All the square and the street had been drenched with a heavy night dew, and the moist trees and houses looked damp in the still morning air. The Jew moved his head in greeting to Bertie, who had a thick gray veil drawn over her face; and, when the man had fastened on her luggage at the back and had climbed into his place on the front seat with his legs hanging over the post bags and had gathered up the reins, the general agent turned to Bertie and helped her into the cart to her seat on the back bench beside the Jew. He passed her up her little hand bag and asked the Jew to take care of her, as far as their path lay together, and asked her to write and tell of her arrival as soon as she got to the farm; he raised his arm to shake hands with the Jew over the side of the cart, and the Jew told him he would hear from him from the Bay in a few days' time.

The driver put the bugle to his lips and blew a loud call, then he drew the reins closer and the horses made a great turn and swept out of the street into the square. The general agent looked after them for a second and then went back into the house and closed the door. As they crossed the square and swept out at the upper end past the hotel, Bertie raised her veil a little and looked out over the back of the cart at the square with the sleeping houses and the church like a great damp white angel watching over it.

Then they passed out of sight and there was no trace of them but the deep tracks of cart wheels across the damp sand of the square.

CHAPTER X

How Griet Sat on the Stone Wall and Watched the Gnats

IT was a rich yellow afternoon. All the valley was filled with a haze, through which you saw the outline of the hills and the trees and the flats through a sheen of gold. The air was so thick it seemed you might have cut it with a knife, and yet so clear you could see the farthest object through it, and so warm and balmy you had only one wish, to sit still in it and breathe it.

On the kitchen doorstep old Ayah sat working, hemming a yellow handkerchief that was pinned to her knee. Every now and then she would rest her hands in her lap and look away up the valley, and then sigh deeply and take a pinch of snuff and say slowly, "Ach!—ja, God!" and then take up her sewing, till her hands fell to rest again.

Away off, on the stone wall that ran from the wagon house, which broke off suddenly and left a large gateless opening for carts and wagons to come through and then was continued to the sod wall of the garden, Griet sat. She had a piece of blue sewing in her lap, but it was tucked in between her knees; her little bare heels tapped slowly against the wall as she swung them to and fro, but her head was thrown back as far as it would go, and she was looking up into the air where dozens of gnats were wheeling their flight above her; she turned her head slowly from this side to that, following them, and sometimes pretending to snap at them. Presently she glanced round to see if old Ayah was watching her, but the afternoon was too balmy and peaceful for old Ayah even to trouble herself with other folks' concerns. So Griet went on looking up.

Suddenly she closed her mouth with a snap and threw her chin down on to her breast. Her eye roved far off across the flats, not where the road came over the nek from the town, but round the hill from the next farm. She bent her head a little on one side to listen, as for all the long generations of the past her foremothers had listened on the great pathless plains for the coming step of the antelope that meant food, or of the enemy that meant war—death. Then she raised her head and looked. Yes, there, coming through, moving among the mimosa trees, whose branches seemed white with thorns everywhere now their leaves had fallen, was the yet whiter tent of a cart. Griet looked round; but old Ayah had observed nothing. She took up her sewing and bent devotedly over it. The cart went out of sight at the drift and then came out near the dam, clearly visible now. Griet looked at it, wrinkling her little flat nose scornfully, and then bent down over her work, sewing on diligently, and began humming the verse of a hymn to herself.

Then the cart came out at the kraal just below her. On the front seat sat John-Ferdinand; his broad felt hat covered the large dark eyes that looked out gravely above his close-curling pointed beard. Behind him on the back seat was Veronica in a light print dress, her face shaded by a large mushroom-shaped straw hat bound round with white muslin. On her arm lay the baby, wrapped in a white shawl. Griet did not raise her head but bent low over her work as the cart passed her into the yard. It came so quietly that old Ayah, who was growing a little deaf, did not notice it till it drew up a few feet from the kitchen door. "Child of sin!" she cried to Griet, "why did you not let me know people were coming, that I might have had coffee ready? Go pick up chips to make the kettle boil quickly; there are always eyes enough in your head when there is nothing to be seen but, when there is, you are as blind as an earth-snake!"

Meanwhile John-Ferdinand had fastened the horses' heads to the horse post, showing he did not intend to stay long; and, when he had helped Veronica out with the baby, they walked into the house, Griet walking slowly to the wood pile beside the wagon house, where she carefully searched among the piles of mimosa cuttings for the very greenest and sap-oozing chips. With these drawn up in her print dress in front, she walked slowly to the house, flaunting her little short skirts superciliously with each step and wrinkling her nose slightly as she passed the cart.

In the little whitewashed dining room, when John-Ferdinand and Veronica entered it, the father was still sitting at the table in his shirt sleeves with his spectacles on his nose, his volume of Swedenborg open before him; but he seemed to have been half asleep as he took his glasses quickly off his nose and wiped them before he rose to welcome his visitors. The little mother had heard the sound of their voices and ran in from the bedroom, where she had been lying down, her little pink print dress still crumpled as she had lain in it. "Oh, I am so glad to see you," she said. "Why didn't you let me know you were coming this morning when I sent the boy over for the sour dough? I should have had the cakes ready."

"We did not know we were coming," said Veronica.

The little mother tripped away into the kitchen to see if the kettle was on. Veronica had seated herself in the chair in the corner near the door; her face, which had been painfully long and straight, had filled out so that it was a long smooth oval; there was a warm rose color in her cheeks, and her blue eyes, though still with deep-set orbits under the high arched brows, were fuller and had a light in their pale blueness they never wore in her maidenhood. She removed the shawl and hood from her child's head and laid it to her large white bosom, against which it pressed its little fingers and thumb, while she drew across it a small lace handkerchief, partly concealing it. John-Ferdinand stood somewhat awkwardly beside her, while the father, still rubbing his glasses, asked if he would not outspan.

Before he had answered, the little mother had hurried

back. "The boy came again from the town this morning. It will be three weeks next Thursday since the day they wrote she was leaving. I can't understand why your uncle doesn't write; he must have got our letter asking why she didn't come! I haven't slept all this week. Your father says if she was ill they would have written, but I——" She looked suddenly from John-Ferdinand to Veronica: "You haven't any news, have you?"

John-Ferdinand looked down at his wife. "Yes, aunt; that is why we came over; we have a letter from uncle," said Veronica.

"Oh, she's ill! She's dead!" cried the little mother, wringing her hands and dancing before Veronica like a little child.

"No, dear aunt; no, she's quite well. They are well."

John-Ferdinand put into his wife's hand a letter and walked quickly past her into the front room and out on to the stoep. The father sat suddenly upright looking at her; and Veronica, with her right hand, took the letter from the envelope. The little mother stood before her motionless. "It's from her uncle," Veronica said slowly, unfolding the letter; "he asked us to come over and see you about it."

Then, partly reading and partly explaining, Veronica begin to give the contents of the letter. The general agent wrote that she had left, as he said she would, by the Thursday's post cart, and he had not doubted she had arrived home safely till, on the day before he wrote, thirteen days after her leaving, he got letters from the farm saying she had not come; on the same day he had also received a letter from Bertie without any date or address saying she did not wish to return home, and that she had of her own free will and at her own request gone away with the Jew who had been her fellow-passenger in the post cart. She said she did not wish anyone to follow her, but that she would write shortly to her mother and Rebekah when she had reached her journey's end. Where that would be she did not say——

'Has she married him—married him! A Jew—a man we know nothing of!" cried the little mother. "Oh, if Rebekah were here!"

"I don't think she has married him, dear aunt," Veronica said, holding down the letter; "from what her uncle writes I should say she has gone to live with him but is not married."

The little mother stood transfixed, but the father rose and tore the letter from Veronica's hand to read it himself. With a faint helpless little cry the mother ran out of the room and to the stoep where John-Ferdinand stood looking into the dark green of an orange tree. She stood before him, stretching out her hands to him. "Oh, please explain to me, please explain! I can't understand. Oh, it's so terrible! Tell me what it is!"

John-Ferdinand took her hands in his.

"My dear aunt, it is our Father's will. We cannot understand the strange and terrible dispensations that come so us in life. We can but submit."

"But Bertie! my little Bertie!" she cried. Then she tore her hands from his and ran back into the dining room. "Oh, where is she? Where is she?" The father stood with the letter in his hand, still reading it, unconscious of anyone's presence. "You must go to fetch her back! John-Ferdinand must go, Rebekah must go."

Veronica had taken her breast from the baby, who had now fallen asleep, and was drawing her dress back over it. "My dear aunt, in the part of the letter he is reading now, Bertie's uncle says he has no idea where she and the man have gone; it may be to the Diamond Fields, to the Free State, to the Transvaal, to England, to South America, to Cape Town; and he says, very wisely, that we should make no fuss and not make public inquiries and let the thing get into the papers. He knows the man slightly, who, he says, is very wealthy and is sure to be kind to her; and there are other people to think of, his children and Rebekah's and mine. A thing like this, if it is once talked of, is never forgotten, never. For Bertie's sake, for all our sakes, it must be kept quiet."

The father held the letter in his hand. The little mother looked, almost silenced by the whiteness of his face.

"You see," said Veronica slowly, "whatever has been done is done. For Bertie's own sake, for the sake of the innocent who would suffer with her, we must not act hastily. She is over twenty-one and of full age; she has a right to do as she wishes."

"I will start to-night. I will go to her uncle and learn all he can tell me," the father said; "we must bring her home." The mother flung herself upon his breast with her arms about his neck: "Oh, she was my little baby— she was such a child!—she knows nothing!"

Twenty minutes later John-Ferdinand and Veronica, with the baby in her arms, walked through the kitchen. There was nothing they could do for the old people, and they felt it better to leave them. Old Ayah, who had just come back from the milk room with fresh cream and butter, apologized that there was no tea. Not only had the chips burned faintly under the kettle, but Griet had absently put two beakers of fresh cold water into it before she slipped off to her old seat on the wall.

John-Ferdinand helped his wife and child into the cart, loosened the horses' heads from the stake and turned the cart round; then, mounting the front seat, drove slowly away. As the cart passed through the gap in the wall, Griet on her perch seemed deeply absorbed in her sewing and did not once raise her head to glance at it, but as soon as it was once well through and passing down beside the kraal, she threw down her work and, extending her arms with the thumbs sticking outwards towards the back of the car and the fingers pointing inwards towards herself, raised a low snort of scorn and disapproval. Then she sat still watching it as it passed slowly down the rise among the thorn trees.

In the house a strange stillness reigned. In the little

whitewashed dining room, with the afternoon sunshine playing on the wall, the father sat with his shirt-sleeved arms stretched out on the table and his head resting on them; his volume, which had fallen, was lying on the floor at his feet.

In the bedroom on the great bed on which her children had been born the little mother lay, with closed eyes, sobbing noiselessly, while old Ayah laid rags damped with vinegar and water on the forehead and wrists. As she bent she sighed deeply with sympathy; not that the little mother had yet told her what happened, but she felt that some bad news had come which had some connection with Bertie, and she had a vague feeling, for which she could give no reason, that the bearers of the news were somehow to blame for it.

Griet watched the cart till it had passed the great dam and the last glint of its white tent had been lost among the thorn-trees beyond; then, seeing that no one called her and a dead stillness reigned everywhere, she fell to her old occupation and, with her head back as far as it would go, watched the gnats as they buzzed above her in the warm yellow air.

CHAPTER XI

How the Rain Rains in London

THE Jew beat his feet on the pavement. It was eleven o'clock and a rainy night. Up and down the street the rain was falling; it made a wall so dense it almost shut out the light of the few gas lamps that glimmered through that long Bloomsbury street. The rain drops hung in beads round the hat of the cabman whom the lamps of his cab made dimly visible as he sat on the front seat.

The Jew went up the house steps and rang the bell loudly; then without waiting he rang again. There was a sound in the passage and then the door opened a few inches. The Jew kicked it wide. Inside, a figure could be seen holding a lighted candle.

"Vhy ze davil can you not come ven I ring? And vhy you not light ze hall lamp?"

Then he turned down the steps and opened the cab door, helping Bertie to alight. She was thickly veiled and wrapped from neck to feet in a fur cloak. The Jew led the way up the steps into the hall.

On the large, new, empty hatstand the candle was standing, and the woman who had held it stood on a chair lighting the hall lamp. There was an overpowering smell of paint and varnish and oilcloth everywhere. In the back of the passage behind the stairs a moving figure was dimly visible.

"Isaac! Isaac! Vhy you not come and bring ze zings in?"

From the back of the hall the figure shuffled forward slowly. It was a youth of about seventeen, with a high, narrow, sloping forehead, above which rose a tower of strongly curling hair like the Jew's but of a pale sandy color, though further, except in the shuffling gait, there was nothing to recall the Jew. He had a long straight nose slightly crooked, the tip of which was so sharply a four-sided square that it almost suggested that the point had been artificially cut off instead of being the work of nature. He had weak, bleared, blue eyes, and walked with his shoulders bent and his head stretched forward as if trying to see. He shuffled past Bertie without seeing her.

The Jew nodded at the candle. "You take ze lady upstairs to ze room," he said to the woman; and he followed Isaac out to the cab.

The woman who had descended from the chair took up the candle. She was a woman of about forty; her grizzled dark hair, drawn into an untidy knot at the back of her head, hung over her forehead till it almost touched her heavy eyebrows. She began without a word to mount the stairs, and Bertie followed her. She was short and broad-shouldered, and Bertie noticed, as she followed her, that the wrist of the hand in which she held the candle was almost as thick and strong as a man's and a little hairy. Her shabby black dress had a three-sided rent at the back and hung down, almost touching the stairs as she mounted. On the first landing she stopped and opened a door, and Bertie followed her into a large room. Here the smell of new paint and new furniture was even stronger than below. There was no light in the room, but the woman led the way with the candle. Bertie saw the glittering of a great cut-glass chandelier hanging from the roof in the center of the room and of chairs and sofas and mirrors everywhere. The woman opened a small door in the folding-door which cut off the room from the one behind it, and Bertie followed her in. Here a great coal fire was burning, the warm light making visible the great bed and large drawers and wardrobes with glass doors. On the dressing-table the woman put down the light. Drawn up before the fire there was a sofa covered with purple velvet. Bertie sat down on it. For a second the woman glanced at her curiously, then went out and closed the door. Bertie took off her hat and laid it on the head of the sofa and unbuttoned her fur cloak, but did not take it off. In a few moments the Jew and Isaac came bringing up the luggage, which Isaac set down within the door and went. The Jew came up to her. "You like ze fire?" he said, looking down at her. "I vill tell ze woman zat she bring you some supper." He took a little bunch of keys out of his pocket. "All ze drawers, ze wardrobes are your sings in; ven you vant zomezing you vill open zem!" He put the keys on the mantelpiece. "I vill go down now to my office—it below—and see some letters of business, and vill come up soon." He stood looking at her anxiously, shifting from one leg to the other. "Ven you want anyzing you will ring?—You are tired?" He looked down at her. "I vill tell ze woman zat she bring your supper soon," he said; then he went out and closed the door.

When he was gone she opened her cloak yet further and threw it partly back; once she glanced round the room and then she looked back at the fire. She was very tired. For two weeks the Jew had delayed their journey at Madeira that the repairs and furnishing might be completed before they came. She had only landed that day, and the journey in the damp chill air, to which she was unaccustomed, had made her very heavy. After a little she leaned back on the purple velvet pillows and drew up her feet, and lay with one arm over her head and the other hanging at her side, looking at the fire. How soft the velvet cushions were!

In about ten minutes there was a knock at the door and, no one answering, it was pushed open. The woman looked in; she was carrying a silver tray with the supper set on it; she put it down on the dressing-table. She looked at Bertie; from her slow even breathing it was evident she was fast asleep. After a moment the woman walked toward the sofa from behind and, coming to the top, bent down over it. The firelight was shimmering on the silk linings of Bertie's open fur cloak and cast a ruddy soft light on her face; she bent over Bertie a little; like her son she was near-sighted and saw nothing clearly till she came close. She bent her face low over Bertie and noticed the roundness of her snowy throat and the fullness of the little rounded chin, and looked at the long curled lashes on the pink cheeks; she put out one thick unwashed grimy finger, almost as if she were going to feel the cheek to see if its soft curves were real; then she turned and went softly out of the room with a not unpleased smile about her mouth as she closed the door.

About half an hour later the Jew came up. When he left Bertie he had gone down to a room on the ground floor; originally it had been the back dining room of the house, but the Jew had bricked up the door between it and the front room, and for nearly twenty years it had been his home. Here he lived and ate and slept when at home, while the rest of the house, which Martha attended to, had been let to lodgers. There was a stretcher on one side with a folded grimy quilt; a little iron stove was in the corner with a black kettle on it, on which the Jew made himself hot water without the trouble of calling anyone. In the other corner was a large sofa; the table was covered with papers and documents; an old cracked lamp, blackened with age, hung over it, and the paper was a faded yellow, grimed with the smoke and wear of twenty years. When all the rest of the house had been renovated and refurnished, this room alone had been left untouched. Here for twenty years he had eaten, drunk, slept and sat up to work at night and the mustiness and the grime were home to him.

When he went into it that evening he took off his new black coat, hung it behind the door, put on a short black jacket, greasy and shiny, and sat down at the table to his papers. Most of them were bills for the decorating and furnishing of the home. There were long bills from silversmiths for cutlery and plate; there were yet longer bills from the Bond Street dressmakers, to whom he had sent Bertie's measurements with orders to supply her with a complete lady's outfit with which to fill the drawers and wardrobes in her room; there was a lengthy bill from his agent, who had been obliged to compensate the lodgers turned out of the house without the full month's notice. He added up the costs and sat looking down at the large total they came to, with a certain gleam of satisfaction. Yes, it had cost well.

Then, before he went on to the other papers, the Jew rose. He put off the little jacket and put on the black coat, and for a moment looked into the little cracked, eight-inch looking glass that hung on the wall, to see that his front hair stood up straight; then he went up the stairs to Bertie's room. After knocking twice and getting no answer, he opened the door and saw her still asleep on the purple sofa. Very softly he closed the door and walked on tiptoe to the foot of the couch. She was still fast asleep with the firelight playing on her. Very gently, to make no sound, he knelt down on the floor, loosened the buttons of her little shoes, drew them off and placed them on the floor. He ran his hands very softly, so softly along the curves of her feet, so tiny for the body. He looked at them for a moment, he put down his face as if he were going to press the soles against it, as women press the feet of little children. Then he rose and went to the bed and fetched a large down pillow. She was lying so low in the pillows that her feet almost hung over the end of the sofa; he slipped the cushion very carefully under them to raise and support them. Then he went to a wardrobe and discovered a large white fluffy shawl. He heaped it softly over her feet, tucking it in at the sides of the pillow. He blew out the candle, that its light might not add to the glare of the fire; then he stood looking at her for a few seconds with his hands curved before him; and then he went down to his room and his greasy coat to go on examining his letters.

When Bertie woke the next morning it was half past

[? eight]. She raised herself on the sofa. Someone had been in and built the fire, for it was burning still. She stood up and threw from her the fur cloak in which her arms had been all night. A curious dull gray light came through the two windows at the other end of the room (it seemed hardly like daylight) and a far-off roaring sound, like a million sounds breaking into one. Bertie listened to it for a minute and then walked towards [? the windows]. Her little stockinged feet sank noiselessly into the soft pile of the carpet as into moss by the rocks in the kloof. She drew up both blinds and stood before a window looking out. A gray damp was everywhere. It seemed to ooze out of the walls of the buildings opposite, to ascend from the ground as much as come down from the sky. Opposite were the backs of houses in the next street, all built of the same dead yellow-gray brick, and all oozing. There were rows of windows all alike. Out of two windows on a top floor a line was stretched and a shirt was hanging out on it, but it was not drying; the water dripped from its sleeves as they hung down. Up above, in what looked like a loft, a window was open and a boy's face looked out, then the window closed. Down below, between the tall houses, tiny back yards with high walls were crushed. She pressed her face against the window to look down into them. In one were a few broken flower pots lying in the wet, and a great gray cat was stealthily walking along the top of the wall, drenching wet but seemingly accustomed to it, for it did not try to climb down. There was a pungent curious smell that seemed to burn in her nostrils, something like when they burned harpuis [1] bushes on the lands at home. Bertie wondered what it was; she shivered; she looked out for a moment longer, and then turned back to the room. There all was beautiful. The soft double-piled carpet had pink roses in it; on the great brass bed was a blue embroidered satin quilt. There were two great mahogany wardrobes with two mirrors in each and two chests of

[1 Harpuis: resin.]

drawers with brass fittings; the dressing-table had another large mirror and there was another over the mantelpiece that reflected the whole room; besides the velvet sofa there were two armchairs and a table with a purple velvet cover. Bertie walked about softly, touching the things with her hands: how wonderful and beautiful it was; and it was hers, all hers. She ran her finger along the edge of the brass bed, of the tables and chairs; even the white marble of the fireplace seemed beautiful to her; she had never seen it before. She thought of the little stained deal wardrobe in the best bedroom at home, and the little deal dressing-table with the muslin on it; and a curious kind of pain came to her. She took the keys from the mantelpiece and began to open the drawers and wardrobes. In the drawers were piles of linen so delicate she hardly liked to touch it roughly; she laid out on the bed a nightgown with so much of fine lace and soft ribbons falling about it that at first it seemed to her it must be an evening dress. In the wardrobes hung gowns in silk and muslin and velvet and lace. She took them down and looked at them in turn. Then she came to one: all her life she had dreamed of having a dress made of thick black silk, with large blue daisies with white centers embroidered in raised work all over it at intervals. Her mother had had such a bit of silk in a patchwork quilt she had brought from England with her. Once on board ship the Jew had asked her what sort of a dress she would like best, and she had described it made of such stuff, quite plainly and with a long train, and a fine lace scarf to throw over the shoulders and hang down in front. In the wardrobe were the dress and the scarf. She put the dress on and hung the scarf about the low body so that the long ends hung down, and then she walked up and down in it. There were three mirrors where she could see herself in the dress; it was as beautiful as she had thought. Then there was a knock at the door and the woman stood there with a tray of breakfast; on the tray was a note from the Jew saying he had had to go to his office in the City before she woke but he would be back for lunch at one. Bertie sat in one of the purple velvet chairs with her breakfast beside her on a little table, and ate it luxuriously. She was hungry; she had not eaten since early the afternoon before. Then she leaned back and fanned herself. There was a black fan with daisies on it that was attached by a silk cord to the side of the dress, and she fanned herself, not because it was hot, but to use it. When she was tired of looking at the dresses she went into the next room. It was a large oblong room with two windows; the great cut-glass chandelier hung from the center of the ceiling; on the mantelpiece and stands there were vases and candlesticks with cut-glass pendants that glittered; the couches and chairs were covered with crimson-colored velvet, as rich as the purple in the bedroom; the carpet was as soft and deep; the velvet curtains at the window were lined with rich satin and had cords and ball-fringe, as heavy as the curtains in the picture of Queen Victoria that hung in the front room at the farm. Bertie touched them and rubbed her cheek against them. How wonderful and soft they were! She walked about touching all the things. She rang for Isaac to make a fire in the room and then she went and stood at the window and looked out at the houses in the street; all the houses were the same, high and yellow and dark, and the rain dropped from them. Far down at the end of the street she could see a square opening; cabs drove up it, and a postman with the rain dripping from him walked quickly up the street knocking at all the houses. She shivered and turned away and went back to sit by the fire. At one she had put on a beautiful white woolen dress made like a Greek robe, and the Jew took her down to lunch in the great dining room below stairs; it had an immense sideboard and pictures of fruits and hunting, and the great mahogany chairs were so heavy she could hardly lift them. After lunch the Jew went away again and she looked at her dresses.

At four he came and told her to get ready and he would take her for a drive. The carriage came to the door; the coachman had a livery, but had an overcoat over it; Isaac had the same livery and overcoat and sat beside him. She and the Jew got in; it was still raining, but it was close and warm inside in her furs, and she looked out through the windows at the damp people hurrying by. The Jew took her to many shops. At the milliner's she asked the price of a hat. "Zat is nozing! Zat is nozing! Take vot you vill"; and he made her buy three hats. At other shops she bought gloves, sweetmeats, flowers, lilies and orchids that cost sovereigns a bunch, though she thought only a few pence. At one jeweler's the Jew bought her a diamond bracelet and emerald earrings. She bought ornaments and knick-knacks, all kinds of things she had never seen before. When they got into the carriage at last, the front seat was piled so high with parcels that they kept falling down. When they got home the Jew went to his room to work till dinner, and she unpacked and rearranged her things. She rang the bell and made Isaac go and call the Jew to see how she had arranged the flowers about the drawing-room, and she pinned a buttonhole into the Jew's coat. At dinner she wore a low white dress with roses wreathing on the bodice. It seemed to her at first extravagance to wear such a dress for an ordinary dinner; but there were none commoner. The dinner was laid out with much silver and cut glass, and there were many courses and three kinds of wine. She had only seen things something like that when there was a grand dinner-party at Cape Town. The Jew had ordered the best cook that money could buy through his agent. Bertie would not take wine, she wanted lemonade, and Isaac had to go out and get it for her; but she ate three helpings like a child of some wonderful cake with cream and almonds in the middle. She made the Jew pull crackers with her, and when a yellow crown came out of one she made him put it on, and she put on a bishop's mitre. When they went upstairs her train was so long she nearly fell over it, and she told the Jew he would have to carry it for her. When the Jew had taken her up to the drawing-room he soon went back to his little office, and she sat by the fire and looked at some of the purchases, and then listened to the roar of the city till she got tired and cold and went to bed. All the next morning she tried on her dresses and cloaks and hats. The Jew could not come back to lunch, and had ordered hers to be sent up to her; but he came at four o'clock to take her out in the carriage. She asked him to take her to a shop where they sold materials for fancy-work, and she bought work of every kind, and work-boxes and a work table and a work basket, and all the evening while he wrote in his room she sat by the fire knitting him a silk purse. When he came up at eleven o'clock she was bending over her work with a flushed face, and asked him if he liked the pattern. He could hardly get her to go to bed she was so interested in her work.

The next day it rained too heavily to go out at all; she sat all day working, finishing the purse, and began a pair of slippers. The day after she was so busy working at the slippers she said she did not want to drive. But in the evening, when the Jew came from his office at bedtime, she was sitting before the fire with her work in her lap staring into the blaze.

Suddenly she looked up at him. "Do you think by this time they have the letter I wrote?" she asked.

"Vhy, no," the Jew said, looking down at her. "It takes long."

She sat still looking into the fire. "But don't you think I ought to write and send them my address?" she said presently. "I told them I was well, and you were kind to me, and I was happy; but perhaps they want to know just where I am." She waited a moment. "Perhaps they are anxious."

The Jew looked down at her with his bright eyes. "Vhy you vish to tell zem vere you are? I give zem ze address of my partner in Zous America, zat zey may sink ve are zare. Do you vish zat zey come here to fetch you?" He looked keenly at her.

"Oh no, no!" Bertie said, raising herself. "Oh no, I never want to go back to Africa! I am so happy here with you; you are so kind to me. I—only—sometimes —I am afraid they are anxious. I—I am afraid of that."

"Ven zey sink you go on to Zous America as soon as you come here it will be nine ten months before zey come to you here; do you vish zey come soon?"

"Oh no, no, I want to stay here. You won't let anyone take me back to Africa, will you?" She raised herself.

"No, no!" he said.

She took up her slipper and began working again; but soon the Jew said it was time to go to bed.

Every morning the Jew went to the City at eight and Bertie had her breakfast in bed, and in the morning she tried on her dresses and did fancy work, and at one Isaac brought her lunch up on a silver tray to the drawing room. The Jew had made her understand he did not wish her to go to the lower floor when he was not there, that her world was the first floor. After lunch she lay on the bed and tried to sleep, and then before the Jew came she dressed herself again, and if he was early enough and the weather not too bad they went for a drive in the closed carriage. When they came home she dressed again for dinner and did her hair and they went down to the dining room and had dinner, with the silver and glass and the massive furniture about them, and then the Jew went to work in his little office and she sat in the drawing room. Though it was summer, it was a wet summer, and however warm the day might be she kept large fires burning night and day in the drawing room and bedroom. The light of the fire was the only thing that gleamed.

One afternoon, when it was raining too heavily to go out, she asked the Jew what was in the floors above her, and, as she wished to see them, he took the keys and opened the door. There were three floors with the garret, but there was nothing in any of the rooms. They had been painted and papered and decorated, but they were quite empty. She said to the Jew it would be nice if they furnished them. The Jew asked what they should do with them. She looked round and said perhaps when he had visitors; but he said he never had visitors, and they locked them up and went back to the drawing room.

The next day when the Jew came home it was pouring with rain. Out in the streets as he drove up he saw an organ-grinder and with him a boy of eleven standing in the rain turning their barrel organ. When he went upstairs he found the front window of the drawing room wide open and Bertie standing before it, the rain beating in on her white dress as she threw out to the man and boy little balls of crystallized fruits and sweets wrapped in paper. She had just wrapped a box of chocolates in her lace pocket handkerchief and thrown it out to them when the Jew came up. "Catch! Catch!" she called, flinging it. The Jew came up to her. "Oh, look at that poor little boy! Do give me some money to give them! They've been playing so beautifully. It makes one's feet jump. I've been dancing all round the room by myself while they played. And I haven't anything to give them but sweets."

"Look, look how wet you are!" the Jew cried, pulling down the window. He touched her dripping sleeves and bodice with his finger. "You must not talk viz people in ze street. Bad people zat will come and steal all ze sings!" The Jew turned quickly and went downstairs. He sent Isaac to tell them that if they ever came again he would send the police after them, and Isaac was to be always on the watch lest they or others should return. When he went upstairs again, he impressed on her that never again under any condition must she open a window and speak to anyone in the street; nor under any condition must she ever speak to anyone to whom he had not introduced her. In Africa you could do these things, but not in London. She listened to him quietly. "You like ze music?" he asked. "Oh yes," she said, "dance music I like. It makes me dance all over. I'm never tired when near dance music."

The next day, when they returned from their drive and

Bertie came back into the drawing room, there was a grand square piano, the most richly toned that money could buy, standing between the window and the door. With a little cry of joy she sprang towards it and flung her hat and gloves upon it and opened it. The Jew, who was following her closely, looked on with delight. She drew out the rich music stool and seated herself on it, still wearing her fur cloak. She opened it and began to play. "I can't play very well, you know," she said, half turning to the Jew, who stood beside her, "not real grand music, but if I hear a thing I can always play it; and they always got me to play for them at dances because I kept the time so."

She started a waltz, swaying her head gently from side to side.

"Oh how beautiful! It's a lovely piano! I never saw one like it." Then she paused and began a reel. "This is the 'vastrap,'" she said, half turning her face to the Jew, who stood beside her, and nicking her head at the end of each part where the final step came. "It's what the Hottentots dance; I learnt it from hearing them play it on the concertina. When Rebekah used to set me to practice my scales, I used to try to practice them, and then suddenly I used to find I was playing this!" She was smiling and nicking her head all the while she talked: "You should see their old velskoens [1] flying when they dance, all full of holes!"

She played louder and louder and with more emphasis. Then suddenly she put her arms down on the notes and rested her head on them. She was motionless. The Jew stepped closer and put his hand on her shoulder; it was quaking. "Vat is it?" he asked. Her shoulders were slowly convulsed, and then wild suppressed sobs broke that seemed rending her shoulder.

The Jew moved from one foot to the other with his

---

[1] Velskoens (skin-shoes) are the home-made shoes of undressed leather generally worn by Hottentot or Bushmen servants at the Cape. The vastrap is a kind of wild Highland fling danced by them.

hands extended, as an old hen might shuffle whose chicken was in a convulsion she could not understand. "Vat is it?—Vhy——" He bent over her. "Are you not vell?"

She made no answer, the sobs growing wilder till her whole body seemed convulsed by them.

"You are tired? Ve have go to too many shops zis afternoon?" He put his hand on her, then he hurried downstairs to get her a glass of wine. When he came back she had left the piano and had thrown herself on her face on the sofa in front of the fire in her bedroom and had buried her face in the pillows. She was sobbing, but more slowly. He pressed her to take the wine; but she said she could not, her head ached and she would lie on the sofa and try to go to sleep. He covered her feet with a rug and built up the fire and stood looking at her as she lay extended, with questioning anxious eyes. She did not move again till just before dinner, when she dressed herself and came down and said her head was better.

After that she seldom played on the piano, and after a while not at all. As the summer passed it grew damper and duller, and she often declined to go out driving when the Jew came home. He never took her to the parks or places where she could see fashionable people walking about, but always offered to take her to the shops. Generally she said she needed nothing; but whenever she went out she still went to the flower shops and brought back the carriage filled with flowers, with which she decorated her drawing room and bedroom; and she went to the confectioner's after and brought back boxes of sweets, which she munched all day as she sat before the fire. She seldom did fancy work now; she had made all she could think of for the Jew, and the great sofa cover she began lay untouched day after day.

One evening the Jew came back later than usual and found the drawing room door locked and the other door on the landing which led into her bedroom locked too. She came quickly to the door and opened it. He asked her why it was locked. She had a large fire burning and the room was bright with it. "I don't know," she said, resting her hand on his arm. "I nearly always lock them now when you are away. I don't know what it is"—she drooped her head lower to his—"but I feel so lonely. I'm so afraid," she said softly.

"Afraid? Afraid of vot?" the Jew asked her looking up at her.

She still kept hold of his arm. "I don't know," she whispered softly, with the other hand shutting the door; "but I always feel as if something was following me, as if something was coming upstairs after me. I can't go to sleep because I'm afraid it'll be just behind me when I wake, so I keep the doors locked.—I'm so lonely," she said, after a pause. She took her hand from the Jew's arm, and they walked to the fireplace.

"Ven you are alone," said the Jew, "vy do you not call Marzer zat she comes and sits viz you? I vill tell her."

"Oh, no, no!" Bertie said hurriedly. "I don't want her." She stooped to the Jew and said, almost in his ear, "It's *her* I'm afraid of! Her wrists are so large!"

"Did she ever zay zomesings to you zat you not like?" the Jew asked, his eyes flashing quickly.

"Oh no," Bertie said, "she's never spoken to me once; Isaac brings the things up. And when she does the bedroom I come in here. But I see her looking at me. Sometimes, when we come up from dinner, I see her looking up the stairs after me! But!—but," Bertie hesitated, "it isn't her fault; it isn't really her I'm afraid of; it's—I sometimes feel as if something was just behind my left shoulder, and when I look back quickly it seems I'm just going to see it—but I never do! It's always my left shoulder." She glanced round.

The Jew looked at her with a curious questioning face. He thought for a little and then he proposed that, whenever she felt lonely, she should ring for Isaac and let him come and sit on the chair just inside the door. She said she would feel safe then; she was not afraid of Isaac. After that day Isaac had orders to come and sit with her whenever she rang. But the Jew always impressed on him he was to answer no questions she asked, nor to carry out any letters to post for her, nor to give her any money.

The first day when Isaac came up she tried to talk with him once or twice. But the convulsions he had had as an infant, while they seemed to have left his brain more or less intact (for he could do his mother's shopping, making better bargains than she could, and showed an exceeding keenness where money matters were concerned), seemed to have broken the full relation between the brain and the organs of sense; he could not tie a shoe lace except very slowly and not exactly, and, when he spoke a word, it was only slowly and after much consideration that the brain carried the order to the tongue. Bertie found he did not easily answer her and after the first day made little effort to speak to him. Every day she rang he came and sat on the chair just inside the door in his green livery with silver facings and buttons, one hand spread open on each of the knees he kept close together before him, and with his head stretched a little forward, the blunted tip of his nose always turned to the fireplace at the far end, his faint blue eyes fixed and striving to see everything where Bertie sat before the fire—as a worshiper at the far end of a cathedral looks to the altar with its lights and incense and flowers and its slowly raised chalice which announces a sacred presence. He watched, breathing slowly while she dozed in her chair. His breath became a little quicker when she rose and moved or stirred the fire; his eyes were fixed on the bedroom door when she went in to change her dress, and when she came back he noted everything she had on—the little diamond earrings, the belt, the comb in her hair—and when sometimes she drew her chair, so that as she sat before the fire he saw nothing but the little crown of brown curls on top of her head, he watched that. He watched with an intensity of interest when she put a sweetmeat between her lips and sucked or broke it. She always shared her chocolates and crystallized fruits with him; but he never ate them while he sat there; and his mother could never get him to go and do her shopping; he was always waiting in the kitchen passage for Bertie's bell to ring.

When he had been three days she proposed that he should help her move the furniture. She put the tables where the sofa had been and the sofa where the chairs had been, and they moved the piano. When the Jew came back that afternoon Bertie showed him quite excitedly the changes she had made and asked him whether he did not think it nice. During the next few days they moved everything in the room; at the end of a week all the furniture and all the pictures had been turned round and everything had been in the place of everything else; then she began to get tired of moving them, and after a few days they remained where they were.

As the summer grew older it grew damper and more oppressive. She generally refused when the Jew offered to take her out in the carriage; she liked better to rest in her armchair close to the fire, eating sweets.

One afternoon he was driving her down towards the Strand to a place where he had heard Persian sweets were kept. There was a block in the large street and they had to turn down Seven Dials. So many vehicles had come that they had almost to stand for some moments; she rubbed the damp from the window-pane and looked out. There was a low dirty shop at her left, in the window of which were boxes with rabbits and kittens and some cages with birds. Next to the shop a door stood open that led directly up a flight of stairs; in the open doorway were five children in ragged clothes with matted hair and no shoes on their feet, the eldest holding an almost naked and very dirty baby of a few months old in her arms. The rain beat in through the open door upon them as they pressed on one another and looked out into the muddy street from which the pouring rain had driven them.

"Oh, do look at them," she cried to the Jew, "so dirty and so ragged, and no shoes on their feet! Oh, do give me something to give them."

The only thing the Jew had never given her was money. He gave her two half-crowns, and as the carriage moved on she opened the window and threw them in at the open door; but the carriage was already moving on, and the Jew said she must shut the window to keep the rain out.

That evening, when the Jew came up at half past nine, instead of finding her dozing in the armchair, she was sitting back in it with her eyes wide open staring interestedly into the fire, so absorbed that she did not turn, as she always did if she were awake, to nod or say some word to him when he came in. He sat down in the straightbacked chair near her; but she sat with her soft eyes unusually bright staring at the blaze.

Suddenly she asked him, but rather dreamily without looking at him, what the price of cocoanut matting was.

The Jew stared at her. "Vhy," he said, "you vant some?"

"No," she said slowly, "I don't want any; I'm only thinking."

He told her the price. She was dressed in a red silk dress, and about her shoulders hung a cream lace scarf; she looked very beautiful leaning back there, and the Jew thought she had almost a smiling look about her face, which she seldom had now.

"And what is the price of whitewash?" she asked slowly, presently. "At the farm we used to pay three-and-six for lime, but up at my uncle's it used to cost four shillings."

The Jew gazed at her. "But vot do you vant ze lime for?"

"Oh, you see," she said slowly, her Cape drawl becoming intensified, as was always the case when she tried to make anything but a very short speech or to explain anything, "I was just thinking, if someone gave me thirty pounds and said I could have that house and all those children that we saw in the door to-day and said I must put everything right, how I would do it: I don't know if I could do it with thirty pounds, but I think I could. You see," she said, interfolding her hands in her lap, "I would first get a big bath and wash them all and cut their hair quite short, and I'd buy that blue stuff for threepence a yard I saw the other day and make them all blouses or frocks, and I would make them warm petticoats. The boots and socks would be dear"—her voice got more dreamy—"but all the other things I would make myself. —I'd put alum-wash all over the floors and ceilings first, and then I'd whitewash.—How many rooms are there, do you think, in a house like that? It's not high, like this." She turned her head and looked at him. "I should think there were four, eh?—I could do it for the thirty pounds, I'm sure, and buy new furniture, but it's the cocoanut matting I'm not sure of. For fifty I could do it! Cocoanut matting is such a help. It keeps a house clean. I could whitewash, myself," she said, after a pause; "the stairs one could have planed down; they are so very dirty. That second little girl would be very pretty if she was clean, and the boy too."

She had looked away from the Jew back into the fire. He had never heard her talk so much before; he said not a word and sat staring at her, as he always did when they were together. Presently he asked if she was not sleepy, but she said it was early yet, and he went back to his office to work, and she sat looking at the fire. She had not untied the ribbon round the packet of sweets that lay in her lap and which she had brought with her after dinner to eat. The next day, when she drove out, she asked him to take her that way again; she leaned out when they came past the house, but the door was shut.

As the summer grew old it rained rather less, but the air grew heavier and more dull. Bertie now refused to drive out at all, and sat by the fire. She ate less and less but was growing very stout. At night, when the Jew woke, he somehow often felt the bed shaking, and when he looked at her she was crying. Sometimes she seemed to be crying in her sleep; but when he roused her and asked her what it was she said it was nothing, that her head ached. She began now seldom to ask Isaac to come and sit in the drawing room, and she cried nearly all the time. From the time the Jew left in the morning till he came back in the evening she sometimes cried. She shut the door so that no one could hear her, and walked about the rooms wringing her hands and crying. She did not know why she cried except that there was always a pressure on the top of her head and that everything was pain to her. She would be quite quiet and she would go and look out from the front window at the long row of yellowish drab houses opposite with their tiers of windows one above another, and she would fall at once into a passionate crying that nothing would stop for hours. If she was standing near the window and happened to stroke down the great soft velvet folds of the curtains, it would make her cry, or unfolding a dress, or opening a packet of sweets. Everything she saw or heard made her cry. When she woke in the morning and heard a voice outside say, "Old clo'! Old clo'!" it made her draw the cover over her head. At dinner sometimes, just as she was going to eat, she used to burst out wildly crying and the Jew could do nothing to comfort her or stop the crying. She left off having Isaac to sit with her—she said she was not frightened—and passed most of her time lying on the sofa in the bedroom before the fireplace, with a white shawl over her head. The Jew bought her one day the most astonishing collection of things—jewelry, hats and knick-knacks—and sent them home all at once. When he came home in the evening she put her arm on his shoulder and thanked him, but the next morning he found them still all piled on the sofa in the drawing room, and some of the parcels were not even opened. When he asked her if she were ill, she said no, and when he asked if she wanted anything she said no. The only thing she ever complained of was a feeling of pressure on the top of her head. She wept so persistently that there were sometimes not six hours in the twenty-four when she was not weeping either waking or asleep. Sometimes the Jew lit the candle and, raising himself on his elbow, watched her weeping in her sleep till the pillow under her face was wet, the great tears bursting from under her eyelids. He had never dreamed that a living thing could weep so.

At last he sent for a doctor, an old Jew he had known for years. He examined Bertie carefully and said there was nothing organically wrong with her; she wanted change and excitement and above all exercise. He ordered she should live no more on milk and biscuits but should take a glass of wine with her meals and a glass of stout before she went to bed at night to make her sleep. He said she was right in not caring to drive in a closed carriage, that every day for at least an hour she must walk, and walk quickly. The Jew thought over it all and made plans. That evening when he came home he told her to dress in her best dress and jewels; he would take her to a theater. She rose from the sofa and began at once to take her dresses from the wardrobe. She tried on ten before she decided on one to wear; it was a white heavy satin; with it she wore a small diamond and emerald necklace the Jew had given her, and a star in her hair above her forehead.

They had an early dinner, and she talked and laughed and drank the two glasses of champagne instead of the wine she always took with her meals. Afterwards when the carriage was waiting and he went to fetch her, he met her fully dressed on the landing outside the drawing room and was stricken dumb with her glittering beauty. Only the tiny feet, which hardly supported her large body, and gave her the slight uncertain swaying movement as she walked, took from her absolutely regal grandeur. He covered her with her cloak and took her to the carriage. She talked and laughed all the way. The Jew had taken a box. He placed her where she saw the stage well, just below her, but he drew the velvet curtain a little so that she was sheltered from the audience, and he sat between it and her and watched.

They were playing already, and for a little while she kept asking questions. In Cape Town there was no theater, and she had only seen two domestic little plays very badly set. In the first act there was a harvest scene. Men and women in country dresses appeared tossing hay and a wagon came on the scene, and behind a hayrick a young man declared his love to one of the pretty hay-makers in a sun-bonnet and asked her to marry him. Bertie was so deeply interested she leaned forward pressing before the Jew and resting her elbows on the edge of the box, looking down.

Then the curtain fell. When it rose the lights were turned down in the theater, but on the stage it shone brilliantly; the crowd of women had returned who were haymakers in the last scene. Robbed of almost all their clothing, their lower limbs made more obtrusive with flesh-colored tights, some wearing a few yards of spangled gilt about their waists, some only with bandages of silk drawing between their legs, the trousers cut away even from the hips, the women leaped and flung their limbs in smooth contortions. She sat gazing at them. Presently she put her head closer to the Jew's. "Aren't they women?" she asked, "the same that were here a little while ago?"

"Yes," the Jew said; "now zey dance."

Bertie's hand shaded her face away from him as she looked.

"Why do they do it?" she whispered.

"Zey get money, zey pay zem for ze dance!"

A moment after Bertie had drawn herself back in her seat into the shadow of the box. When the Jew looked round at her he thought he saw tears on her cheeks; when he went near her he found she was shaking con-vulsively. He asked her whether she felt ill. She only sobbed for answer; the tears were pouring down her cheeks. He asked her whether he should take her home. She nodded and sobbed, "Yes, yes!" He wrapped her up and led her out. As she passed down the corridor she sobbed aloud, and the attendants looked curiously at her. When he got her into the carriage she sat back with her head in the corner, her white lace scarf wrapped completely over her face, sobbing heavily.

"Are you sick? Are you tired?" the Jew whispered.

"No, no!" she said, but sobbed louder, while he looked at her anxiously. His attempt at amusement seemed to have failed utterly.

When they got home she went straight upstairs and into her bedroom and, dressed as she was, flung herself face downward on the sofa before the fire. In half an hour the Jew came up with the glass of wine the doctor had said she must always have before she slept. The fire was burning low and she had not lit the lamp, but he could see her lying motionless and silent with the shawl still over her head. He touched her arm and asked her to sit up and take it. She raised herself, but, just as she was going to take it, threw herself on her face on the pillows, sobbing, "Why don't their mothers fetch them home?"

"Vot?" said the Jew, bending over her with the glass in one hand.

"Why—don't—their—mothers fetch—them—home?" she cried, her face half choked in the pillow; "they are women!—they are women!—and—the—the men—they—they—they——" She sobbed incoherently.

The Jew put his hand on her softly. It was the first time she had ever tried to explain to him what she was crying about; was it always something so unintelligible?

"Vitch men? Vot men?" he asked. The ballet-dancers and the men in the front rows of the stalls had completely passed from his mind. She made no answer, but sobbed more quietly.

"Come, drink zis!" the Jew said coaxingly, as one speaks to a little child. "It vill do you good. Ze doctor says you are very veek! Here——" He drew her with his hand. Slowly she sat up; he put the glass to her lips and she drank the contents; then she rose, a sudden dead quiet having come to her crying. She stood in the dull glowing light of the fire in her white satin dress, and she folded her arms on the mantelpiece and leaned her forehead on it.

"Do you feel better?" asked the Jew.

"Yes," she said. Then in an instant the wild sobs convulsed her again. "And—some of them—were—so young!—and—no—no—no one——"

The Jew bent close to her, but could not distinguish the word in her sobbing. "You are very tired," he said gently, "shall I light ze lamp and you go to bed and rest?"

"No—no—I—like the dark!"

She still kept her forehead on the mantelpiece.

"Shall I not take off your shoes?" said the Jew; but she shook her head and sobbed a stifled "Thank you."

As she stood there quite quiet again and there seemed nothing for him to do, the Jew said he would go down and write for an hour and then come up again. And when he came up she was in bed and asleep.

The next morning, before he went to business, he told her that it was the doctor's order she should walk every day for an hour; that at eleven every day she must be ready and Isaac would walk out with her till twelve. He begged her to be careful never to speak to anyone; he impressed on her that London was not like South Africa, and that if one spoke or even looked at anyone terrible things might happen. He spoke long to Isaac, telling him exactly the path they were to go: down the street through the square into Oxford Street and along it, but never farther than Oxford Circus; then to come back, to walk close behind his mistress, to speak to no one, and, if anyone came to speak to her or stared much at her, to stand close behind her, and to come and tell the Jew everything as soon as they returned. "Ven one should look at her, Isaac, ven one should walk after her, you vill tell me, Isaac," the Jew said, his keen eyes fixed on Isaac; and though Isaac only nodded and said nothing, the Jew knew it would be done.

At eleven Bertie dressed herself very carefully in her smartest walking boots and cloth dress and walking hat. It was the first time she had walked, and she was even excited when she and Isaac started, Isaac in his best livery with gilt buttons walking behind her, carrying the waterproof goloshes and umbrella the Jew said he must always carry.

She enjoyed the walk and when the Jew came home told him of much she had seen, and asked questions about the cabs and omnibuses. She dressed herself carefully for dinner that evening, ate well, and did not cry all the night; and the Jew thought her cure had been found.

For some weeks she went every day. The early autumn was coming in drier and warmer than the rainy summer. The air was sometimes hot and oppressive, but she went every day.

For some time she dressed herself very carefully when she went out, and noticed closely all she saw and looked in at the shop windows; but after a while she became careless and walked more slowly and looked more down on the pavement. There were four things she always noticed, one a large place with its windows full of books. Before Rebekah married she had once bought some secondhand books, on the outside of which a yellow card was pasted with the words "Mudie's Select Library, New Oxford Street." The first day she looked in at the window and saw the books it came to her with a strange thrill how Rebekah had sat under the orange trees and in her bedroom reading from a book. Always, without missing, every day she stopped at that window. She read the names of the books over and over, without thinking what they meant, and went on.

Another thing was far down the great street; there was a dark house that stood far back from the pavement, and out of huge doors upstairs men were nearly always throwing into carts or wagons below brown stuff with a smell like malt. She never passed without looking at it. She disliked the strange dank smell. She never asked what it was, but all her life it came back to her with sickening remembrance of the long walks.

The other thing she always looked at was a shop window a little lower down. It was full of filters of all kinds, and there was a little fountain there that played with three small balls. The water came up like a tiny geyser and threw the balls in the air and always as they fell the water caught them again and threw them up. Every day she looked at them. The first day she had looked with interest; afterwards it became a terrible compulsion—she must look. She knew just how long it would be before they fell and how the water would catch them up again, but she had to look. She felt a kind of sick shrinking; yet she always had to watch them always do the same thing,—they were always the same, like the curtains in the drawing room and the chair before the fire and the sofa in the bedroom, always the same. They all made the dull feeling in the top of her head worse.

At first she had looked at the streams as they passed her, men and women, old and young, all pressing onward somewhere, up and down—people in omnibuses, people driving, people walking; and a strange feeling always came to her that they were not really people, but like the people from the photographs which you look at through the two glasses, who move when you pull a string and shake their heads and jaws. And sometimes the thought would come to her that they *were* people; that they were people living just as people lived in Africa, with their homes, and relations, and people they visited, who had children and felt and laughed; that each one was real and alive, just as much as the people she had known. And sometimes a strange feeling used to come to her that she must go up to someone and put her head on their arm and say, "Talk to me, please talk to me!"

But after a while she left off noticing the people. She took no care about her dress any more, put on anything that lay nearest and walked all the while looking down at the paving-stones. She got to know them all; after the

very large one came the small ones and then one cracked
across. When she came home, often she remembered
nothing and had seen nothing but the paving stones and
the window with the balls and perhaps Mudie's and the
malt place. Often, if it was at all damp or chill, she
would not go at all though she knew the Jew wished it.

One day, a dull brown day with no rain, but the thick
sky just above the roofs of the houses and damp autumn
thickness everywhere, when Isaac came at eleven to tell
her he was ready, she was lying dozing on the sofa in the
bedroom in the pink silk dressing-gown she had worn
since she rose. She did not take it off, but pinned it carelessly round her waist with two pins to shorten it, but so
[? carelessly] that it showed here and there a glimpse of
her white heavy-laced petticoat. Over it she put on the
great fur coat she had thrown over a chair when she
returned the day before and which reached almost to the
bottom of her dress. She took from a wardrobe, almost
without looking at it, a steel-blue French bonnet and
without looking in the glass placed it on her roughened
curls and tied it under her chin; she took up a pair of
gloves, but, instead of putting them on, thrust them into
her coat pocket. She did not trouble to put on her walking
boots, but followed Isaac out into the street still wearing
her little high-heeled patent leather shoes with paste
buckles; she followed him heavily and when he dropped
behind her she walked, looking down, hardly seeing the
shop with the filters or noticing anything as she walked.
When they got to the end of the walk they turned to come
back down the same side of the street. For a moment or
two she stood passive, looking into the great plate-glass
window of a shop where tiers of new autumn hats and
dresses were displayed. She looked vaguely at them for a
moment, conscious only of the heavy gray sky above.
Then she looked round and saw, standing close beside her
also looking in at the window, two ladies. The elder
one was about forty, older than Rebekah and rather taller,
with her hair, which was already partly gray, turned back

from her forehead instead of being worn turned down at the side as Rebekah wore it; her eyes were blue, but there was the same full high forehead, the same delicate sharp marked nose dominating the face, a delicate strong rounded little chin and the sensitive strong mouth. She was dressed in a sealskin jacket with a little brown bonnet and skirt, just as Rebekah might have dressed. The girl beside her was about sixteen with very light hair and the exquisite pink and white skin which Northern women often have; her large blue eyes and her dreamy mouth were smiling as she looked in at the window.

Bertie looked at them, and an irresistible impulse came over her; she put out her hand and laid it softly on the sleeve of the sealskin jacket. The woman glanced down quickly, as everyone glances at being touched in London. For an instant she looked at Bertie and took it all in— the beautiful round white face with its fringed eyes, the little fifteen-guinea French bonnet tied a little askew on the natural curls, the ninety-guinea sealskin coat with the edge of pink silk showing below it, and the points of white petticoat with priceless lace that had tipped here and there in the mud; she looked at the little house-shoe with the paste buckle and the ungloved hand with the rings. All her face hardened. If she had asked her why she touched her, Bertie would have spoken; but she turned and said to her daughter, "Dear, we must go now." The girl who had noticed nothing smiled and turned from the window. Bertie stood looking after them with her head on one side as they disappeared into the crowd. Then she turned and walked back. She walked so slowly that it sometimes seemed to Isaac she was going to stand still. When she got home she went upstairs to the bedroom and lay on the sofa before the fire.

From that time the Jew found it impossible to make her go out for a walk. She said she was tired or was cold. Some days she lay in bed till twelve o'clock and sometimes till five. If she got up earlier, she generally half dressed in a loose dressing-gown and lay on the sofa in the bedroom or sat in the chair before the fire in the drawing room with a great shawl wrapped round her. She ate more than she had eaten, and she never cried now; she drank two or three glasses of wine for dinner and with her lunch, and the Jew brought her up something before she went to bed. But as the time passed the Jew grew anxious; he almost wished she would have the old wild fits of crying. Her face grew whiter and whiter and stouter, till under her little round chin a double chin was gathering. She never spoke unless he spoke to her, and, when he brought the carriage, only if he insisted on it would she put something on and drive out with him. She never complained of her head any more, and she never asked Isaac to come and sit with her; she said she was not afraid. Nine months before she had looked much younger. Then she was like a girl in her early teens, and now she looked ten years older than she was. Her face was still very beautiful, but it was the heavy pallid face of a woman who might be thirty or more. She never asked if there were letters from her friends or referred to the Cape.

Again the Jew called in the old doctor. He said again she ailed nothing organically; she needed change and fresh air, and advised the Jew at once to take her to the seaside. The Jew was obliged to start for Hamburg on business at the end of the week, but before he left he went to St. Leonards-on-Sea and took rooms for her, and the next day he took her and Isaac down.

The rooms he had taken for her were in a house facing the sea, kept by a widow woman who was a cousin of Martha's and whose husband had owed the Jew money. He had been kind to her and started her in this house. He had hired all the rooms from her for the time of Bertie's stay, stipulating that no other lodger should be taken; but the rooms really reserved for Bertie's use were the drawing room on the first floor and the bedroom opening from it, also a tiny closet on the first floor just outside her door where Isaac was to sleep. She had been almost excited when the Jew told her she was going to the sea; she had begun at once to pack her boxes, and had laughed several times.

They got there late in the evening when they could see nothing, and Bertie was still in bed when the Jew left the next morning. He gave many parting instructions to Isaac never to leave his mistress for a moment, and to tell him when he returned if anyone had spoken to her or come to sit by her on the beach.

When Bertie had had her breakfast and was dressed, she called Isaac and walked out on to the esplanade. As far as the eye could reach, long rows of gray houses, three or four stories high, rose on the right hand; almost as far as the eye could reach the solid stone pavement stretched, and to the left, under a gray sky, was the gray sea, breaking with a soft "sushing" sound its dull water on the long beach of rounded boulders and gray pebbles. She stood looking at it for a little while, then she began to walk along the stone pavement with the tall gray houses to her right and the sea to her left, and Isaac followed her. Here and there were still a few bathing houses and a few people bathing in the gray water, as the air was still and warm though so dull. On the stone pavement here and there were bathchairs with invalids in them being pushed by men, sometimes with other persons walking beside them; and there were nurses wheeling babies in perambulators, or little groups of children down on the pebbles playing. In only one spot the long endless line of pavement was broken, where in the middle of the esplanade stood a little group of shops under one roof— a fish shop, a chemist's, a green-grocer's, a flower shop. She stood for a while looking in at the windows. She wanted nothing. Then she walked on for half a mile, then they turned and walked back again. After a time they came to where a great square of houses all exactly alike opened on to the esplanade; but here there were more people, and she turned back and walked up the pavement again to the point where they first turned.

After an hour and a half they went back into the house; she took off her walking things and walked about the great empty drawing-room with the windows looking out on the esplanade and the sea. She looked at a glass bowl with some goldfishes on the side table and at two little Dresden figures holding vases on the mantelpiece; and then she went into the bedroom and drew down the blind and lay covered on the bed till lunch time.

Every day she and Isaac walked out on the broad pavement, with the sea on the one hand and the rows of houses on the other; every day she stopped at the little building in the middle of the pavement with the little shops; she noticed how the fish was crimped at the fishmonger's, and the large Persian cat at the greengrocer's; then she walked on another half-mile and they turned. She began to know the stones as she had known them in Oxford Street, the large stone with the cracks and the place fifty yards on where there was the bluish stone. Sometimes she looked up at the houses, the tall stuccoed houses stories high, and then would come the strange thought to her that they were real houses, houses where men and women lived like at the Cape. They were homes. Once she noticed specially a man with a tall silk hat run up the steps and open the door with a latch-key; he was going home to lunch just as Rebekah's husband might go home; once she saw three girls come out with tennis racquets, laughing and talking; they were going to play; and once she noticed a mother come back with some little parcels, and the children upstairs waved at her from the window till she went in and the door shut. They were real houses, with real people; it was not a nightmare; they were all real; it was she and Isaac walking up and down, up and down on the pavement, that were so strange.

One day the sky had changed from gray to a dark heavy leaden blue; it seemed to rest just on the roofs of the gray houses; and the sea was very dark when Isaac came at eleven to ask whether she would walk; he said he thought it would rain, but she walked to the front door and Isaac followed her, carrying her umbrella and cloak. They passed the shops and came to the place where she generally turned, but she walked on. They passed more and more houses, still in an unbroken row, with the stone pavement stretching on with the pebbles below and the gray muddy sea breaking softly on them. She walked on till there were no more people on the pavement and the row of houses to the right was growing smaller. The esplanade itself grew narrower. To Bertie it seemed they walked for miles; then both houses and esplanade ended. At the end of the esplanade some steps with iron hand-rails led down to a curved pebbly beach and the houses died away, leaving a bit of cliff-like rise with gorse bushes upon it. Away in the little bay there were stakes sticking in the water and what looked like wickerwork baskets showing in some places; there were no human creatures in sight except some men loading two carts with pebbles from the beach, and higher, near the houses, some men digging what seemed to be the foundation for a new house. She stood resting her hands on the top of the iron railing that ran along the end of the esplanade; her eyes looked far out across the dull gray waters, to where, some sixteen miles off, a small gray headland jutted out into the sea, strangely clear in the humid blue water-laden air. Presently Isaac touched her on the sleeve: "It is going to rain," he said. She shook her head without moving her eyes from the distance. A few more large drops fell on her, and he opened the umbrella, but she put out her hand to keep him from holding it over her and went down the steps. She sat down on the pebbles with her back to the wall of the esplanade; she drew up her knees and folded her arms round them and sat looking out across the gray water of the little bay with its stakes and baskets, away to the gray headland dimly visible in the blue moist air. Isaac came down the steps too and stood on the pebbles a few yards from her. Quickly as the rain began to gather in about them, the few large drops became a thick haze, coming partly from the sea

and partly from the land, that grew damper and damper.
After a while the outlines of the distant headland vanished and from all sides the rain was creeping up. Slowly
it blotted out the distant landscape, and then the posts
standing out in the water in the little bays near by and
the baskets vanished. The men loading the pebbles from
the beach had turned up the collars of their coats and
driven away. The men digging the foundations had put
their tools together in the trench and were walking away.
Isaac moved from one foot to the other, looking at Bertie,
the rain beginning to run down him. The water was beginning to gather round the brim of Bertie's fur hat in
large drops and to run slowly down her fur cloak.

After a while the gloved hands she kept clasped round
her knees were soaked, and the small streams ran down
from her cloak and dress and made little puddles in the
pebbles and earth about her. The wall of rain closed in,
so that nothing farther than a few feet away was at last
visible. And the water streamed down the steps. Then
she looked at Isaac and saw him shivering where he stood
three feet away from her, holding her closed umbrella and
waterproof as the rain ran off him.

She rose. "Let us go home," she said. She climbed
the step and they walked home along the dripping parade
on which there was now no one, seeing nothing farther
than two feet before them for the blinding drizzle. When
they got into the house she undressed and went to bed and
had her meals brought to her room and did not get up
again that day.

The next day she got up, but the rain was falling; she
went to the drawing room windows after breakfast, but
the gray rain was falling on a gray sea, and the great
stones of the parade lay wet. She shivered and shuddered and went to her bed and drew the down quilt over
her head and slept all day.

The next day and the next it rained and she did not go
out. But the next morning the rain had left off. It
was gray but no rain was falling. Before eleven o'clock

she rang the bell and Isaac came. "Isaac," she said, standing before him and looking into his face, "is there any country here? I want to go into the country." She spoke very slowly that he might catch each word.

"Country," he repeated.

"Yes, country. I mean a place where there are no houses and people. In my country where I come from we call it veld."

Isaac looked at her. "No houses, no people—country," he said slowly. He seemed to be considering, then he said slowly, "Yes, I can show you. Come." And Bertie went into the bedroom and got ready, and they went out together.

He led her in the opposite direction from the one they always walked in, past many shops and hotels and busy streets and a little fishing quarter where the fishermen's nets were out drying on the beach and little children played, then up a hill where there were little houses about and the town lay at your feet, and into a hollow where there were still more houses. Then they climbed another rise; the path went up among rough grass and some gorse bushes along the cliff. Isaac walked on before, Bertie climbing after him in her dark puce-colored silk dress, holding it high above her laced white petticoat to keep it from the mud into which their feet sank as they climbed. Then the path ran along the top of a cliff. To the right was the gray sea, with many little fishing boats out on it; overhead was the drab sky; the footpath was full of white chalky mud which clung to their boots. Then they came to a broken fence partly of brambles. Isaac helped her to get through, and they walked on a little farther. Here was another hollow leading down to the cliffs and the gray sea. There were a few bushes and small trees growing below. Near by, a few yards from where they stood, was a great building which was closed and seemed unused; it had a red roof covered over with a fine yellow lichen that stained it everywhere. Far off there were

more houses. Suddenly Isaac turned round and stood
still; she also stood still.

"This—this," said Isaac slowly, "is country."

She looked about her.

On the slope about them everywhere there were the
marks of cows' feet, which had sunk deep into the soft
soaked turf. Some of the footprints were full of clear
water, in some blue flowers had been growing which
raised themselves stooping and half crushed. She looked
round at the gray sky, at the damp bushes, at the barn a
few hundred feet off with its red roof, damp with yellow
lichens, and at the mud and grass at their feet. The high
heels of her little shoes were sinking deep into the grass as
the cows' hoofs had done. She drew her skirt tight about
her and stood looking.

"Let us go back," she said, and turned, Isaac following
her.

She led the way through the hedge and along the path
upon the edge of the cliff, Isaac patiently following her.
They passed the fishermen's houses and the streets with
shops and hotels and got back to their own quarters with
its long hopeless row of gray tall houses and its long endless pavement and gray sea breaking on the round gray
pebbles and shingles. Bertie went straight up to her
bedroom, took off her little wet shoes, and curled herself
under a great shawl on the bed, took only a glass of wine
with a biscuit for her lunch and did not rise till late in
the afternoon.

That evening the Jew came. He had only returned
from Hamburg that day.

He asked her whether she would like to stay longer
where she was, but she begged him to take her back with
him the next morning; and the Jew chuckled much to
himself as he lay in bed that night thinking her life with
him could not be so unbearable if she were so glad to
return to it.

When Bertie got back, for the first two or three days
she ate more and was a little less pale, but then she sank

back into her old life. It was duller and damper now, so she never went out. She kept the blinds nearly always drawn down, but great fires burning night and day and lamps lighted if the fog were a little dark. She wore always one dress, a crimson velvet gown, loose and long, which had cost forty guineas. She put it on in the morning and wore it till night, never changing it for dinner. When the point-lace about the neck and shoulders grew soiled she did not remove it, but threw a lace scarf over it.

All day she sat deep in the armchair before the fire or lay on her sofa in the bedroom. For lunch she took nothing but a glass of ale with biscuits and at dinner she ate little, though she took some glasses of wine; yet her face and figure grew quickly heavier.

She never referred to her friends in Africa or spoke of her letters to them; a complete silence seemed to have fallen on her, and, unless it was quite necessary to answer some question the Jew put to her, she never spoke.

One evening as the Jew sat in his room writing, he looked round to see Isaac standing behind him and asked what he wanted. For a moment Isaac paused, drawing his power of speech together. Then he said slowly, bending his face near to the Jew's, "The—lady likes—cats!"

The Jew started up. "Cats!" He looked at Isaac.

"Yes," said Isaac slowly. Then knitting his hands together as if for a great effort, so that the knuckles cracked, he said, "I was—cleaning—the window—she came—she saw a black cat on the wall—she said, 'Catch it for me; I—like—cats!'"

The Jew stared at him; no one had ever before heard Isaac attempt a description. The Jew had a horror of all living creatures except storks, and cats he shrank from especially. "Cats?" he said, "cats?"

Isaac nodded, "She—likes—cats."

The Jew looked at him doubtfully. "Can you get her one?"

"Three," said Isaac slowly, "kittens."

For a moment the Jew hesitated, then took from his pocket a ten-shilling bit and put it into Isaac's hand.

"You vill get zem, Isaac. Zey vill be small and not to make a noise!"

Isaac nodded.

The next morning while Bertie still lay in bed, eating her milk and biscuit, someone tapped at the door. In answer to her question, the door was slowly pushed open a little and a basket thrust in; then the door was closed.

A little wheezing sound from the basket made her leap out of bed and go to it.

Half an hour after when the Jew, who had just finished his breakfast, went up to say good-by to her, he was astonished to hear shouts of laughter through the closed door; not knowing Isaac had already brought the kittens, he was astonished at the door to see Bertie kneeling on all fours in her white nightdress; on the hearthrug before the fire, one kitten was lapping milk from a saucer before her, one was mounted already on her back, and one, as she knelt with her head down, was leaping up at the long loose braid of curly hair hanging over her shoulder and trying to hold it with his paws.

She looked up laughing, "Oh, aren't they lovely! One's climbed right on my back—look how this one plays with my hair; it means to climb up by it!" She half raised herself, taking the one off her back. "There are two black and white and one gray and white; look, its eyes are quite blue; the other two are browny!" She stood up, still holding one in her hand. "Oh, did you get them for me? It was so kind of you ——" She rested her hand on his shoulder; standing in her white nightdress she looked like a tall white angel beside his little dark figure; the top of his head barely touched her chin. Then she stooped to pick the others up and gathered them all three in her arms, pressing her face against each. She asked the Jew whether it would be possible for him to let her have the carriage in the morning, as she wanted at once to go and buy some things for them. The Jew was very busy, but he returned at eleven o'clock and took her out.

She bought three exquisite little china bowls, decorated, one with a rose, one with holly and one with larkspur. She bought three rolls of ribbon exactly to match the flowers on each bowl and three tiny real silver bells. When she got home she tied on each its bell with a ribbon to match its bowl and gave each one the name of the flower on its bowl, Holly, Larkspur, and Rose.

When the Jew came home at night, she rushed to the door and brought him to see them all drinking milk in a row, each out of its own bowl with its own little ribbon and own little bell.

At night she put their basket close by her bed on a chair where she could put out her hand and feel them. But the next day she was not satisfied with the basket, and drove out with the Jew in the afternoon to order a cradle she had thought of. It was of white wood, in three little compartments, all joined together and on rockers, with three little hoods, one over each compartment. The next day the cradle came and she spent three days lining it; from early morning when she rose till near midnight she was lining and draping it; she made the kittens tiny down mattresses and down pillows and tiny blankets and sheets, each with the kitten's name embroidered in silk in the corner; she made three little satin quilts with the flower of each kitten embroidered on it in silks; she edged them all with real lace. When the Jew came up to bed she took him into the bedroom and showed him the three little kittens lying before the fire, each in its own division in the cradle with its head on its own little pillow and tucked in under its own little quilt. "Isn't it lovely?" she said, peering down at them; "just like little babies, eh?" She bent over them and smoothed their little sleeping heads softly with her hand. The Jew looked down at her with astonishment.

"Do you like babies?" he said after a time.

"Yes—of—course," she said slowly.

"You see"—she raised herself—"you can put your foot on the end of the rocker—like this—and rock them all at once if they want to wake." And she stood rocking them softly with her foot. The next day she made three little silk bags and hung them in a row by the drawing room fireplace, and in each was a tiny silk handkerchief, embroidered with a kitten's name, with which to wipe their mouths after they had drunk milk.

For two or three evenings after they came she dressed herself in white for dinner and carried all the kittens down in her arms. They walked about the table and had three little china plates set at the end into which she put tit-bits.

The Jew turned cold with horror when they walked to his end of the table and put their whiskers into his glass and even their paws on the end of his plate, though he said nothing. She fed them with tiny morsels of chicken held between her lips and gathered them all up into her breast to carry upstairs again.

For nine or ten days when the Jew came home she sat for half an hour telling him all they had been doing—one had climbed on to the piano and broken a glass vase and one had been found asleep in the folds of the window curtain. Sometimes she asked the Jew to drive her out in the carriage as she said change of air was good for them, and she held them to the closed window to let them see the fog and dark of the street; but after that the excitement began to die down. When she had had them three weeks she had dropped back into the old life; she still fed them three times a day, but generally she put the food all in one bowl; their ribbons were unchanged for three or four days; they slept in any compartment of the cradle, and she never took them down to dinner; they went if they chose. Sometimes she stroked them as they climbed about her, and she let them sleep in her lap; but she spent her day silently dozing before the fire or watching it with wide open eyes.

One rainy evening, just before dinner, she sat dozing before the fire in her red velvet gown with the lace scarf

twisted about her throat. The Jew was in his little office
downstairs, working at his books; the French cook who
came in every day to make the dinner was busy dishing
up with Martha in the kitchen, and Isaac was in his little
room in the basement, dressing to wait at table, carefully
brushing his hair before the little glass upon the wall to
see if it were perfectly straight—as he always did before
he went into Bertie's presence. Then there was a knock
at the front door. Isaac not being ready, his mother went.
In the doorway stood a tall handsome man of about thirty,
whom she knew well as the son of the Jew's only surviving
cousin, with whom thirty years before the Jew had
quarreled hopelessly because she had insisted on marrying
a wealthy Christian; but he had partly made up the
difference with the son, whom he sometimes asked to his
house and often gave money to. It was supposed by the
few who knew the Jew's affairs that, in spite of his being a
Christian, the Jew might yet make him his heir, as he had
no other near kin living; and Martha had never regarded
him with favor. He asked if his cousin were in, and
stepped into the hall. He stared round in astonishment
at the change which had passed over the place since he
was there last, glanced at the double-piled carpet on the
stairs and at the glass and silver on the lighted dining
room table visible through the open door. The Jew,
hearing sounds in the passage, came out of his den as his
young cousin was taking off his overcoat and hanging it
in the hall.

The young man turned and shook hands with the Jew.
He apologized that he had not been able to see him for so
long but for the last year he had been traveling abroad.
As he spoke he glanced round and in at the dining room
door; and at that moment Isaac passed them with two
dishes for the dining room.

"You have made things very comfortable here, I see,"
he said.

The Jew gave him no explanation and asked him into
his den, but when half an hour had passed and the young

man made no sign of going, he asked him whether he
would not stay to dinner and went up to the drawing
room to see Bertie. She was lying back in her arm chair
with one kitten asleep on her shoulder and two playing
with a worsted ball on the hearthrug.

"It is dinner time," he said.

"Yes, I don't know why Isaac has not rung the bell,"
she said slowly.

The Jew looked down at her. "My cousin is here; he
comes to dinner too."

"Yes," she said, slowly stretching herself and preparing
to rise.

"You vill not dress you a little?"

"No," she said heavily, "this will do." She put the
kitten down on the floor and ran her fingers indifferently
through the brown curls above her forehead but without
looking in the glass. Then she turned and walked slowly
towards the door, the Jew following her. She went
straight to the dining room and took her seat at the table,
while the Jew went to his den to where his cousin waited.

When he brought him into the dining room, "This is
my cousin," he said, pointing his hand towards him, but
he gave Bertie no name. Bertie half rose, and a look of
surprise came over her face. She merely bowed her head
slightly and sat down again. (She had expected to see a
man of the Jew's age and type. But the visitor was quite
six feet high and nothing suggested the Jew but the
brilliancy of his dark almond shaped eyes with long lashes
like her own and a slight curve in his finely shaped nose.
His forehead was broad and smooth, shaded by smooth
wavy black hair; his jaw and chin were powerful and well
shaped, and the voluptuous fullness of the much arched
lips did not take away from their strength; they also closed
firmly.)

The Jew showed him to a seat on the right side of the
table opposite to Bertie, where Isaac had set a place for
him. Between him and Bertie, somewhat obscuring her,
was a silver stand full of flowers; but across it he was

able to note the full voluptuous beauty of her figure even
in the loose velvet gown, the richness of the curly hair
above the flower-like white face and the perfect shaping
of her arms which the wide drooping sleeves of the old
dressing-gown made visible almost to her elbows.

Isaac handed round the soup. The Jew began to
discuss the Stock Exchange in Paris, where his cousin had
been spending some months, and Bertie, with eyes fixed
on her plate, ate silently. It was not till the third course
had been reached that the Jew's cousin, leaning forward a
little to the side to escape the vase, said to her: "These
flowers are very beautiful. One hardly expects to see such
flowers at this time of the year."

"Yes," Bertie said slowly, without raising her eyes
from her plate. Then the Jew asked him another question,
and it was only when they were finishing dessert that the
visitor once again addressed her; there were oranges on
the table and he was explaining the signs by which he
knew these came from the South of France, and he described the orchards there. "Perhaps you know the South
of Europe?" he said, leaning forward and speaking to
Bertie again.

"No," she said slowly, hardly raising her eyelids and
head.

The Jew glanced sharply from one to the other, but
Bertie had not raised her head nor glanced at the visitor
and was passively picking her walnut out of its shell.

The Jew's cousin at once reverted to a business topic.
He saw at once Bertie had not been born in England, and
it puzzled him to guess where she came from; he had
thought his question might lead to an answer.

Soon Bertie rose; she bowed slightly towards them at
the table without saying anything and slowly moved
towards the door. Without seeming to do so the Jew's
cousin noted everything—the queenly body, the small
lovely round head and neck, the long trailing untidy velvet
gown, the slight swaying motion in the walk, the little
hand hanging at her side with three rings on it.

When she had gone out he glanced at the Jew for a second to see if he would refer to her, but the Jew passed the wine bottle to him and told him how much he had paid per dozen when he bought it. When they had emptied their glasses he took him to his den; the young man stayed three hours longer than he had ever done before, but the Jew made no offer to take him to the drawing room, nor did he in any way refer to Bertie or explain her presence.

When, he had left, the Jew went upstairs. He found Bertie as always in the chair before the fire; the kittens had gone to bed and she was lying back holding a large fan to screen her face from the hot blaze. The Jew stood for nearly four minutes beside her on the hearth rug. Then he said, still looking into the blaze, "Vell, vot zink you of my cousin?"

She laid the fan down and stared into the fire.

"He's not like you," she said.

The Jew looked keenly at her. "He is young," he said. "He is handsome?"

"Yes," she said slowly, "he is handsome—but," she added yet more slowly, turning her head towards him, "he's not so nice as you."

The Jew waited a moment. "Do you not like him?"

She waited; then she said, dreamily looking at the fire: "On the farm where I lived once, they caught a tiger, one of the large leopards, and Rebekah went to the cage every day to feed it; she wanted to make it love her, but I was afraid of it ——" She paused as though she had lost the thread of her thought, then she said, remembering, "And one day after dinner, when she was going to feed it, it nearly caught her hand and bit it off; my father just caught it in time and after that he sent it away to be sold."

"Vell?"

She looked up. "Oh, I'm frightened of him, like I was of the tiger, too. Rebekah, my sister, wasn't frightened. She never was frightened of anything."

"Vhy are you frightened of him?" the Jew asked, looking down at her.

"I don't know," she said slowly. "I think it's his eyes —his teeth are so white when he eats."

"He is no good," the Jew said. "I give him much money; I have sent him to ze University. He has always no money; it is ze pleasure, ze gamble, ze horse race, all ze bad zings he likes."

Bertie looked passively at the fire. She seemed to have nothing more to say; and presently the Jew went down to finish his work and soon she went to bed.

During the next ten days the Jew's cousin called three times—once in the afternoon, when Isaac answered the door and told him the Jew was out; once in the evening just before dinner, when Martha opened the door for him and he exchanged a few words with her before she showed him into the Jew's room—the Jew did not ask him to stay and he soon went; the third time he came Bertie had been staying in bed all day, as she often did when the fog was bad. Martha and he had a long talk in the hall and he left a gold coin in her hand as he went out.

It was three days after that visit, on a heavy drizzly night, that he called again about nine o'clock. Bertie was sitting fast asleep before the fire upstairs; Isaac was in his little room; the Jew was in his den working; when there came the sound of a tap against the window in the area, and presently Martha, without a light, came out of the kitchen door, went up the area steps, unlocked the gate and led the Jew's cousin down into the kitchen where a candle was burning; she put her finger to her lips when he began to speak. "The boy is in his room," she said, "but he may not yet be asleep; he is very sharp—be quiet!" She slipped off her own shoes. "You had better take off yours." He hesitated. "You can get them again when you go."

He sat down on the kitchen chair and removed them. "There is no possibility of his returning to-night?"

"Not till to-morrow night."

He rose and with his boots in one hand prepared to mount the carpeted stairs. Martha followed him. He looked back at her. "You are sure she expects me?"

Martha nodded her head and pointed to the door under the stairs to signify Isaac was there; then she whispered to him, "Remember, it's the door facing you on the first landing, the door at the side going into the bedroom." As he passed the door of the Jew's room he glanced at it, but it was closed and the light from the hall lamp was too strong to allow any light to shine from beneath it. Martha, standing at the back of the hall behind the stairs, motioned with her hand for him to put his boots down by the hat stand, but he shook his head, hung his hat on it, and carrying the boots in his hand went softly up the thickly carpeted stairs. At the door of the drawing room he paused, drew on his boots, drew off his soiled gloves and removed his overcoat; then he knocked softly. Bertie, dozing before the fire with the kitten in her lap, was half roused by it and sleepily called an answer; she fancied it was the Jew bringing her wine and biscuits. He entered, hung his coat over a chair near the door, and walked with long light steps across the room to the fireplace. It was not till he stood beside her on the hearth rug that she turned her head and saw him. She started, partly raising herself. He held out his hand to her, but in her startled surprise she did not see it.

"I am afraid you will have thought me very late, but they wouldn't let me come before." He bent a little towards her. "It was very good of you to let me come." She turned her head to see if the Jew were coming; she thought the Jew must have asked him to spend the evening with them. He noticed her glance at the door and said, "I have shut it." He turned and drew a chair on to the hearth rug, not two feet away from her, and sat down on it, carelessly leaning his elbow on his knee and bending a little towards her. She saw how spotless his black coat was and his white cuffs, and noticed his white hands with their long delicately rounded finger-nails.

"I don't wonder you are very lonely here all by yourself," he said softly. He put out his hand with its white fingers and nails and stroked the kittens sleeping in her lap. She was sitting upright with her right elbow resting on the arm of her chair; the wide sleeve of the crimson gown had fallen back; her left hand rested near the kittens; she moved it a little that his hand might not come near hers as he touched them.

"I suppose you are very fond of them," he said, looking up into her face.

"Yes, I like them," she said.

He thought his eyes had never been so near the face of a woman which had looked at him in a manner so absolutely passion-dead. "It's a shame all your affections should be showered on them," he said softly. "One envies them their resting-place."

He looked up into her face, then he withdrew his hand and raised himself a little. He looked down at her. "How beautiful!" he said. "You know, that was the first thing I noticed about you!" In a moment he had placed his full-curved lips upon her arm halfway between her elbow and her wrist.

With a half-suppressed cry Bertie rose; the kittens fell at her feet. "How dare you! How dare you!" she cried, standing at her full height before him.

He also rose. "I hope I have not been too hasty," he said; his mouth drew back a little. "After the kind message you sent me, I think"—he put his hand out towards her—"that perhaps——" He smiled.

"Oh, I never sent a message to you; you are so terrible to me; I can't bear you! I can't bear you! Go, go, please go!"

He looked at her shrinking face with its wide open eyes, and at that moment his quick ear caught the sound of steps on the stairs outside the door. In an instant the truth flashed on him. There was a sound at the door. In an instant his eye glanced round the room; then without a moment's hesitation he glided past her; the door that led into her bedroom stood open behind her; with two long steps he had entered it and closed it slowly behind him; as he did so the drawing room burst open and the Jew with Martha behind him stood there.

The Jew glanced wildly round the room. "Vere is he?" he cried to Bertie, who stood before the fire. Before anyone could reach him he turned on Martha: "You vitch, zere is no von; vhy did you lie to me?" He turned to the fireplace where Bertie stood crying, "Oh, I'm so glad you've come, I'm so glad you've come!" But Martha took the overcoat from the chair beside the door and, holding it up high to her shoulders, called the Jew; he turned and looked at her. For a moment he stood transfixed; then he stepped near her, looking at the coat. Bertie had run up to him: "Oh, he is horrible! Why did you let him come? Why did you let him come?" She put her two hands passionately on the Jew's arm; he was still staring at the coat. At that moment the street door closed loudly; the Jew's cousin had evidently made his way through the bedroom door on the landing. "Oh, you must never let him come again! Never—never— never!"

The Jew turned an ashen gray face slowly to her. "No, he will not come here again," he said. A few drops of sweat stood out on his forehead; his face was shrunken; it was the face of a man of eighty. He looked at her. "Come!" he said. He grasped her wrists, one in each hand, and drew her towards the door. "Come!"

"Oh, you are hurting me!" she cried. "What is it? What is it? Why do you look at me so?"

He had drawn her out of the door on to the landing; the kittens, suddenly awakened from their sleep, ran after her, climbing on to her train. On the landing he turned her round so that she was below him and he above, and pushed her slowly backwards down the first stair. It seemed impossible that the iron force with which he held her wrists resided in his little shrunken body.

"Oh, let me go!" she cried. "What is the matter? Oh, what is it—what is it?"

He pressed her down step by step; the kittens, trying to hold to her dress, slipped down the stairs behind her. His eyes were fixed on hers. "I—I—" he said from between his closed teeth—"I took you—you told me—you had no home—I——" He grasped her wrists as he pushed her down.

"Oh, you are going to kill me! Oh, Martha, Martha, ask him to let me go, ask him to explain to me! Help me, help me, Martha!" They were halfway down the stairs now. Martha stood close behind the Jew with the man's overcoat over her arm. "Oh, you are going to kill me!" she whispered. "What is it? What have I done?" Then understanding something, she cried: "It was not my fault that he came. You asked him! Oh, I hated him, I hated him so!"

Then something in the Jew's face silenced her; the only wish she had was to escape from him. They had reached the hall now. He pushed her towards the door; she offered no resistance. He loosened one of her wrists and, with the hand that had held it, he pulled from her fingers the three rings she wore, so roughly that the flesh of her fingers was torn. Then he turned and took from Martha the coat. He raised it and put it over Bertie's head and shoulders; quietly, almost gently, he opened the door and, taking both her wrists, pushed her out backwards. She offered no resistance; she gazed at his face in a kind of frozen horror.

"Go," he said. "Somevere he vaits for you."

He shut the door.

For a while Bertie stood stupefied, with her face to the door and the man's coat thrown over her head and shoulders, on which the rain fell heavily. Then she felt dizzy and sat down on the step and leaned her face on her hands. It had happened so quickly it seemed dreamlike; only the pain in her wrists and fingers told her it was real.

At last she rose and turned to the door as if to knock at it. She heard the sound of voices and steps in the hall, and a terror seized her. If the Jew had been alone she would have knocked till he opened and thrown herself at his feet, and, if he kicked her, have cried till he listened; but she feared Martha's face behind him. She walked down the steps, looking back to see that no one was following her, and then a little way down the street till she came to a place a few doors off where a short street opened from the long one and led into a square. She walked down it. The rain was falling softly and steadily on her head. There were a few lamps almost deadened by the rain, and in the center of the square one saw dimly the outline of high iron railings and trees. At the corner of the square she stood still. Just beside her, in the first large house looking into the square, one of the blinds had not been pulled quite down. She stood close to the area railing and looked; it was a large dining room or sitting room; there was a great table; at the other end, with his back turned to it as though sitting before a fire, was the head of an elderly man; at the table, near him, bending over her work, was the head of a woman with grayish hair and a white cap; two young girls and a boy were reading at it. There were books lying on it. The light inside was so intense and bright, seen from the dark outside, that she could see the pattern of the paper on the wall with a large gilt figure and the bottoms of the picture frames. She pressed close to the railing, looking in. Then from the other side of the quiet square some one came walking with long loud steps. She did not know it was a police-man, but she felt as if he noticed her, though on the other side of the square. She walked away a little distance and stood beside the railings shutting in the trees and plants in the center of the square. She moved her arm in and out of the tall railing and rested her head on it. A shrub hung over the railing above her, but it did not shelter her; the rain fell on her back.

Suddenly a hand touched the sleeve of the man's coat;

she started and looked around; some one brought his face close to hers. It was Isaac.

"I saw—all," he said. "I was behind the stairs. They think—I sleep."

"Oh, Isaac, what have I done? Why did he do so?"

Isaac waited. "She," he said slowly, "let him in at the kitchen.—I saw—she took him up. She told *him*"—he made the curious motion with his thumb with which he always signified the Jew—"he came with his latch-key himself—she said he often came to see you."

"Oh, but Isaac, it isn't true, it isn't true," she said; "if I go back and tell him all the truth won't he believe me, won't he let me in?"

Isaac shook his head strongly. "He," he said slowly, "killed—all—the cats!"

Bertie shivered.

"It's—no—use," he said slowly.

"But where can I go, Isaac?—I've no money." She wound her arm about the railing again and rested her head on it.

"I know," he said. He took a black bundle from under his arm.

"Put it on," he said. It was a black lace shawl which she had left hanging in the hall, when last she went out driving, because it got wet.

"Put—it—on," he said. He took the man's coat that covered her and held it for her to put her arms in and slowly buttoned it before; then he put the shawl over her head.

"Come!" he said. "I know—a place. Come!"

He opened the umbrella he had brought and held it over her head. He paused to pick up the train of her dress, which was hanging in the mud, and helped her to put it up. She was so faint and cold she asked him nothing. She walked close beside him.

The rain was pouring down heavier now. For a little while they walked through dimly lighted squares and streets: then they got to the fuller light of Oxford Street.

The shawl covering her head and shoulders prevented the strangeness of her coat from being very apparent.

Isaac called the first cab he saw and put her in it and got in beside her. She sat very close to him, almost pressing to his side. She clung to him as a drowning man clings to a rope, frail and worn it may be, but which is all that holds him to life. She felt faint and almost dizzy. When they got to a railway station he helped her out. When he had taken tickets he took her across a platform and got with her into a third-class carriage. She sat in a corner with her head thrown back into it. Only once she bent forward and said to Isaac:

"Don't you think he would ever believe me, and let me go back?"

Isaac shook his head. "No—no," he said.

When the train stopped and they got out they were still in the suburbs of London, but the air felt fresher and lighter. A slight mizzle was yet falling.

Isaac walked close beside her with the umbrella. They went down a long rise among houses and then up, still among small houses closely packed together.

"Where are we going?" she said at last.

"To a woman," he answered; then added, "She—lodged in our house—I know her."

As they passed the houses Isaac went up to one or two and peered at the numbers, which were hardly visible to his short-sighted eyes in the dimly lighted road. At last he stopped at one. Two or three steps led up to a little porch. He left Bertie standing on the pavement and went up and knocked. When he had knocked twice and waited for some time the door opened. In a very narrow passage the light of a dim gas lamp showed a woman of thirty in a shabby black dress, with a small, much worn and pinched face.

She recognized Isaac and asked him what he had come for. He took her to the back part of the passage and talked in a low voice. The woman peered towards the figure of Bertie out in the street, and they had some discussion; he took out his little red purse and slipped two pounds into her hand, and then went down the steps and brought Bertie in.

The woman stared at the tall figure in its strangely cut overcoat, and the black shawl, so draped about the head and face that little was visible. Isaac pointed to the woman. "She," he said, "will show you." He put his head nearer to hers and whispered, "I will come again—soon—when I can." Then, without shaking hands or saying good-by, he turned and shambled out at the front door, shutting it behind him.

The woman looked up at Bertie with her sharp pinched face. "You've no luggage, I suppose?" Bertie shook her head.

The woman took up a bedroom candlestick from the little shabby hatstand, lighted it and began to climb the very narrow flight of stairs, motioning Bertie to follow her up. Once Bertie's foot caught in a hole in the stair carpet. On the landing the woman stopped, opened a small door on the right and went in. Bertie followed her. She set the candlestick down on a chest of drawers with a soiled white cover. There was a single bed in the room, also with a white cover, and some other articles of furniture. She looked at Bertie as if expecting her to remove the shawl; then she went to see if there were water and a towel on the small wash-hand-stand.

"You don't want anything to eat, do you?" Bertie thanked her and said she did not; and the woman turned to go out. "You ring if you want anything," she said, pointing to the bell, and went out.

When she had gone Bertie turned and, without removing any of her wraps, threw herself down on her face on the bed. After a little while she seemed to feel the wraps strike her damp, for she stood up and took off the overcoat and shawl and threw them over the foot of the bed; then she took off her small red satin shoes, soaked through with the rain, and threw herself down again with her arm over her head.

In twenty minutes the woman came again to the door and knocked and, getting no answer, opened it. She came in and stood at the bedside, but Bertie was fast asleep. She took up the light and looked down at her, afterwards not unkindly, but shook her head, and put the light down again on the drawers and laid near it an old calico night-dress she had brought to lend her.

Then she went out, but Bertie still slept on heavily without stirring. It was nine o'clock the next morning before she woke. For a little while she looked about her in surprise and then sat up on the bed. It was a small room, with a common wall-paper with a dull yellow-brown ground covered with diamonds of dull blue transverse lines. Besides the bed and drawers there was a small wooden washstand and a yet smaller chair; over the little unpolished fireplace was a yellow mantelshelf, and above it hung a picture in a yellow polished oak frame of Queen Victoria when she was a young girl. The paper on which it was engraved was yellow with age and under the glass were large swelled marks all over it as if at some time tears had fallen on it and blistered it; there was a little window with a green blind, and below it, through one round hole in it as big as a shilling, two streaks of sunshine came; both fell on the torn strip of carpet beside the bed and showed the dust and dirt which had almost caked it over and obliterated the faint pattern.

She sat for a moment, then she got slowly off the bed and went to the window. She raised the blind and looked out. It was a long curved street running up the side of a hill with little gray stucco houses built exactly alike and touching each other all the way along; each house had a little portico with mock pillars before the door and two or three steps leading up to it, and each had a little bow window on the right side of the steps. Some had a few pots of geraniums in the window, and some had none; that was all the difference between them; and one house far down had one tiny tree growing in its little area. The air of the suburb was clearer than it had ever been in

Bloomsbury. The late autumn sunshine was brighter than any she had seen since she came to England, though it was December. She let the blind drop and sat down on the side of the bed.

Presently the door opened and her landlady came in carrying a small tray with some tea and bread and butter. "I've been in twice already," she said, "but you were fast asleep." She put the tray on the drawers.

"I haven't any money to pay you for it," said Bertie slowly.

The woman looked at her. "Oh, the young man who came with you gave me a couple of shillings" (she did not mention it was two sovereigns), "and I said I'd do for you till he came again.—You'd better drink your tea before it gets cold." She glanced down at Bertie's hands. "You seem to have hurt yourself," she said. There were blue marks round her wrists and the skin torn a little on two fingers where the Jew had torn the rings off.

Bertie said nothing, and the woman went out and closed the door. She had four children to support and four lodgers to attend to. When her husband lived they had hired the garret floor at the Jew's house in Bloomsbury, but he had died of drink a year before and left her with the children to support. Isaac had been sent with her when she moved into her new house, purely because she owed the Jew money and he wanted to know exactly where she was; and twice he had been sent again to collect the installments, so he knew the place well. She had no time to think of other people's affairs, the pressure of life was too hard on her, but she fancied Bertie must have had a room in the Jew's house and been turned out because she had not paid rent, or perhaps some man had deserted her. Isaac had told her she had lived for six months in the house at Bloomsbury.

Bertie stood up and drank some of the tea, but the mouthful of bread she bit seemed to oppress her and she took no more; she sat down on the bed again with her arm across her eyes. She seemed to see the farm, the great dam in the flats by the willow trees, with the little ducks wading in and out among the weeds, and below, where it ran out, the Kaffir girls sitting in the sun and beating the clothes on the stones and laughing. She saw the orange trees before the door and the flower garden beyond and old Ayah working at the milk house and scolding the maids and Griet dancing about pretending to put the rooms neat. She saw all the thorn trees in the flats beginning to burst into their yellow blossoms ready for Xmas; she saw her father and her mother. Oh, she would go back to them, she would go back to them; it didn't matter what they said.

And then she saw, fleetingly, pressing it from her as quickly as she could, the little parlor in the bush, and John-Ferdinand's face with its great dark eyes, and Veronica's, and she saw the little face—she could not go back! She could never go back! Then she heard the voices of the women talking in the little back room at the dance and she had the feeling of running home through the avenue, and the suffocating tightness across her chest; and the people that looked at her as she came out of the church at her aunt's. No, no—she could never go back, never—never—never! Oh, what should she do? Where should she go?

She stood up and began pacing the room. Oh, if only the Jew had killed her, if she hadn't got away! "If I were dead! If I were dead!" she cried, wringing her hands and pacing up and down. The wild uncontrollable weeping that had left her so long returned to her. "If I were dead! If I were dead! O God! If I were dead!" All thought went from her as she paced, wringing her hands. "Where shall I go? What shall I do? If I were dead!" By and by the woman came up and listened at the door. She had heard the pacing from below and fancied she heard cries. It was no affair of hers, so she went away again, and the pacing and crying went on.

At last Bertie stood still suddenly before the mantel-piece and leaned her head against it. Where was she?

What was she doing? Everything in her brain seemed to stand still and be a blank; she did not cry. She raised her head and looked about her; it seemed as if she suddenly saw again, after being quite blind, the little lodging-house bedroom with the streaks of sunlight coming in through the hole in the blind. It did not come from under the blind any more. She leaned her elbows on the fireplace and looked at Queen Victoria as a girl. She noticed all the fly-blows on the frame and the large teardrops swelling on the yellow paper under the glass. Was it her wedding dress, or do queens wear those coronets and veils flung behind at any time? The "Queen Victoria" and the date printed below were quite faded. It must be twenty-five years old. Then she suddenly began wringing her hands and crying again. She paced the room quickly. That little ray of sunshine shone right on a hole in the dirty little strip of carpet.

Then suddenly a barrel organ, which a man had drawn up before him, struck up *Polly is my sweetheart, Polly is my darling*. She stood quite still and listened to it. When it had finished it played *My Grandfather's Clock*—"And it stopped short—Never to go again—When the old man —died!" It ate into her brain and made the pain at the top of her head worse. After a while it went away and played lower down the street, and then again lower down. And then it went away out of all hearing.

She lifted the blind and looked out into the street; it was perfectly empty and silent—not a thing moved there. All the houses were alike, so exactly alike. A horror of pain came on her, just as when she looked at Queen Victoria's picture or at the ray of light. She pulled the blind down. She went to lie down on the bed with her shawl wrapped right round her head and was quite still.

At one o'clock the woman brought her up a plate with some meat and cabbage, and Bertie got off the bed when she had gone and ate it all, and then lay down again. About three the woman came to fetch the plate. Bertie got up.

"I want to ask you something," she said.

The woman stood still with the plate in her hand at the door.

"Couldn't you help me to get any work to do?"

"What can you do?"

"I could cook or sew, I could be a servant."

"Well, you couldn't get a situation unless you had some reference. I don't know what they do in your country—the boy told me you came from some place far over the sea—but here no one takes people without references. You've never been a servant before, have you?"

"Oh no," Bertie said slowly.

The woman looked keenly at her. "Well, you'd get nothing to do in *those* clothes; you'd have to get something quite different. Why don't you go home to your friends? It is much the best thing you can do."

"I can't. I haven't any friends in this country."

"Well, you know your own business best. I couldn't help you to work; I do all my own. The young man said he'd come again; and perhaps he'll help you."

She looked at Bertie's curled hair, swollen baby-pretty face, and the red satin slippers, still wet from last night's soaking, which stood at the foot of the bed, and went out; and Bertie lay down: there was nothing else to do.

Just before dark she drew up the window blind and looked out again. There were more people in the street now; every now and then men passed up, principally clerks; and other men who had come home from the City walked up to one house or the other. The sky was dull and clouded over again as if it were going to rain and a wind was whirling down the road in gusts.

Then down the street from the top of the hill came a curious figure, a man who looked like a Chinaman. He had a curious straw hat on his head with little bells all round tied on to it; on his head was a drum, which he hit with two sticks fastened to his shoulders; before his lips he had a curious wind instrument fastened, which he played with his lips by moving his head; in his hands he had bones and a pair of cymbals. He stopped before the window when he saw her standing there and played all his instruments together, making a kind of band. Seeing she had nothing to give him, he went on and the darkness gathered down.

Presently the woman brought her up a candle and some tea and bread and jam, but she said she wanted only the tea, and undressed and went to bed in the landlady's nightgown. But when the woman went upstairs to her bed room at eleven o'clock, she heard the crying and sobbing going on in Bertie's room when she stood close to the door.

The next day it rained heavily and Bertie lay in bed all the morning; the woman brought her dinner up at one o'clock. "You really must try to eat something," she said; "you've taken nothing since you came but that little bit of dinner yesterday." She told Bertie she was going out on business in the afternoon, but that, if she rang the bell, her little daughter was at home and would bring her anything she wanted. Bertie took a few mouthfuls of the food and then turned on her shoulder again and slept till three o'clock. Then she was stiff with lying so long, and she got up and dressed, but soon lay down again. She had no wish to cry any more; she was in a torpid state.

About four o'clock the landlady's little girl knocked at the door and opened it; she said a man had called and had asked to see Bertie.

Bertie rose quickly. So Isaac had not forgotten her.

The little child said she had asked him into the front sitting room downstairs, and if Bertie went there she would find him. Without looking into the glass to arrange her tumbled hair, Bertie went down the stairs; to the right of the passage was a door opening into the little sitting room, which was unlet just then, as there was no lodger who could afford to take it. It was a very small room, with a few geranium pots in the window and a discolored pair of lace curtains, keeping out the little light

that came in from the dull rainy world outside. In one
corner was a little what-not with a few China pigs and
other animals upon it. There was a low horse-hair sofa;
four horse-hair chairs stood about the room and an armchair with a broken spring in the seat stood in the corner
next the window. Over the mantelpiece was a mirror
with fly-blown gilt frame and bits of green tissue paper
pinned about it, and before it stood two vases with hanging cut-glass ornaments, several of which were missing;
a small Japanese umbrella was opened in the fireplace
and the room was almost filled by a small square table that
stood in the center, covered with a faded red tapestry
cloth. At first when Bertie slipped in she saw no one;
then a figure rose from the broken horse-hair armchair
in the corner. It was not Isaac; Bertie started and looked
at it. It was the Jew's cousin who rose lightly to his full
height and stepped towards the table. He had another
overcoat on, open in front, and she could see the points
of his sharply curled mustache as he moved towards her
and held out his hand. She stood silent on the other side
of the table and did not take it.

"I am not surprised you are astonished to see me, and
not at all surprised that you should be angry with me,"
he said softly, still bending across the table, "but I felt
that I owed it to you as well as to myself to explain to
you about all the terrible trouble I've got you into. I'm
so very, very sorry."

Bertie stood still, with her arms drooping impassively
at her side.

"Please go away," she said.

"Oh, don't ask me to do that! Don't be so unkind!"
he said gently; "I've taken such trouble to find you! I
feel I must do something to put things right. Please sit
down." He put a chair round the corner of the table for
her. Still she stood. "It's all that terrible old woman
and the damnable lies she told! You really must let me
explain to you; it won't take long.—Please sit down!"

Bertie drew the chair he had set for her further, so that

not only the corner of the table but the whole width was between them. He sat down also and leaned his elbow on the table and looked at her. The rather dim light was behind him but it faced her.

"I always knew she had a spite against me, but that she would do such a thing as this I didn't dream. I used to lodge in the first-floor rooms you had and she used to carry my cousin all sorts of tales about me—the hours I came home and the people I had; but I never dreamed she could do such a thing. One day, when I came to see my cousin, she met me in the hall and talked about you." (He did not mention that he had called specially, knowing the Jew was out, to see the woman and find out who Bertie was and what her relation was to the Jew!) "And she told me how lonely you were, no one coming to see you, and that you had come from another country. I told her how much I admired you, and she told me you had wished that my cousin should bring me upstairs, but he refused it. In fact"—he bent forward a little more— "she implied that you felt lonely and would be glad to meet me. I sent a message to you to tell you how delighted and honored I should be if I could see you. The next time I saw her she told me you would send me word the first time my cousin was away on business. Of course I quite understood how lonely you must be shut up there with no one but that old man to speak to ———"

"He was always very kind to me," Bertie said slowly, drawing herself up a little.

"Oh, of course, of course! Who could have been otherwise!" He moved his head a little and looked at her; it was a little difficult to explain to a woman who spoke and showed herself so little. "She came to my rooms and told me my cousin had gone to the country for twenty-four hours and you would be willing to receive me; naturally I came. She assured me he was away and would not be back till the next morning. Of course I never dreamed she was lying and that all the while he was sitting in his office downstairs.—Shall I shut the door?" He half rose.

"No," Bertie said, putting out her hand to keep it open behind her.

"You really must forgive me!" he said in a low voice. "I have suffered just as much as you have in a way. I am his only living relative, and it has always been supposed that when he died I should be remembered. That was just what the woman didn't like; she thought if I were out of the way it would be better for her and that boy. I've no doubt she was afraid of you too in the same way!"

"If I went to him and told him all, do you think he would let me go back?" she said slowly.

"Oh no; it would be quite useless. I made inquiries and I find that yesterday every stick of furniture went out of the house back to the dealers, and he's sold the lease. The new people take possession on Monday. I inquired at his office, and I find he sails for South America to-night. The boy and the old harridan are to go to Hamburg in a few days. It would be no use your trying to communicate with him; he's not a man who forgives."

Bertie stood up and turned to the door.

"Oh, don't go! Please don't go yet! If you knew what trouble I had taken to find you." He rose also. "You didn't think I went off and left you without a thought that night! I waited about outside; I knew how violent he was. I saw you come out and go round into the square. I followed you, but you know I'd been so deceived—I didn't know what further plot there might be. I saw Isaac come to you, and I followed you all the way here. I could not lose sight of you." He lowered his voice a little and bent his head towards her. "You must let me help you a little; you must let me take care of you. She told me you had no friends in this country— you must ——" He put out his hand a little, almost as if he would have stretched it and touched hers.

Bertie, who had half turned and stood looking at him,

shrank and drew herself together, and went out at the door.

He looked after her; under the red gown the sinuous movements of her body were visible and he noticed how beautifully the little head was set on the little neck. She beckoned to the little girl, who was sitting at the head of the kitchen stairs, to follow her, and went up to her room.

For a moment the man stood doubtful; then he rang the bell.

The landlady, who had just returned, answered it. She was astonished to find the tall handsome man, from his dress and voice evidently a gentleman of a type her house seldom saw, standing in her little front parlor. He told her he had come to call on the lady who was staying there, who was a friend of his; he hoped she would pay her every attention. He took from his pocket a card with his name and address upon it; under it he had slipped a sovereign. He placed both in her hand. He would call again soon, he said, but if by any possibility the lady should leave she would kindly communicate with him at once. At that moment the little girl came down carrying over her arm an overcoat which she said Bertie had told her to give the gentleman. He said he could not take it then, and asked them to hang it on the stand in the passage; he would fetch it when he called again the next day. He gave the little girl half a crown, and asked the woman to order anything Bertie might need and charge it to him. Then he opened his umbrella and walked out. The woman stood on the step for a moment watching the fashionably dressed figure in its overcoat and silk hat, and then went to the kitchen to prepare a good supper for Bertie.

It was three days after that Isaac stood at the same doorstep and knocked. It was a Sunday afternoon, and a soft mizzly rain was falling. He stood on the doorstep in his overcoat. He had not been able to get away before. His mother had kept him constantly employed and near her while the furniture was moving. Now she had gone to make some arrangements for their leaving the next morning for the Continent, and he was free. In the pocket of his greatcoat he carried a little square parcel; in it was a very tiny leather bag with gold coins, about which were wrapped a tiny roll of five-pound notes; all were carefully wrapped up in a bit of thick cloth and tied with string. He had kept his left hand in his pocket and on the parcel ever since he had left the house. He had been collecting the sum ever since he was a little boy of five and the Jew gave him halfpence when he swept his office or cleaned his boots. Gradually the pence had become shillings and the shillings pounds, and at night, when his door was locked, he got out his little hoard from behind the loose plank in the wainscoting, where it was kept in the inner of two little iron boxes. He liked the rustle of the bank notes even better than the gold. He was going to say good-by to Bertie, and then, just as he was going, he would take out the parcel and put it in her hand. After he was gone she would see what was in it. His money had never seemed so valuable to him before.

After some moments the woman opened the door and looked at Isaac with the raindrops dripping from his hat.

"I want—to—see—the lady," he said slowly.

"She's not here."

He waited. "Has—she—gone—for a walk?"

"No, she's gone. She went away this morning."

Isaac looked speechlessly at her.

"Where to?" he said at last.

"A gentleman who's been here three times to see her came this morning. They went away in a hansom cab."

"Where—to?" asked Isaac.

But the woman said she did not know.

CHAPTER XII

Fireflies in the Dark

IT WAS a still, hot night. Outside among the roses and lilies of Rebekah's garden the fireflies glinted. In the large bed of carnations, where the white blooms shone out like dim stars in the half-dark, they flitted everywhere.

There was little change about the house or garden since that time five years before,[1] when her youngest boy was born. Only the window of her study was now a door; its inner door, that led into the children's bedroom, was walled up, so that you could reach it only from the garden; and, between the billiard room and the little rose hedge, a new square block of buildings had been raised, not connected with the house. It contained two rooms; the large front room looked out into the garden through windows and a wide glass door; in two of its corners were little white beds in which the two youngest boys slept; by day all the children played in it and at night learned their lessons there; in the room behind, Rebekah slept with Sartje—a little, yellow-brown, frizzly-haired girl she had adopted five years before as a little baby and treated in all ways as her own child, except that it was taught to call her mistress. The two elder boys slept in the main building in the room which had once been the nursery and which opened out of their father's bedroom.

To-night the French windows and glass door of the

[1 See end of Chapter VIII for the birth of her youngest son, Bertie. The children, in order of birth, are Charles, Frank, Hughie and Bertie. Sartje, mentioned a few lines farther down, is her husband's daughter by the colored servant-girl.]

large room stood open and the heavy scent from the flowers in the garden came in with almost cloying sweetness on the night air. In the center of the room on a large square table a lamp burned; about it hovered a cloud of insects and little night flies and moths, and curious creatures with long hard wings, and little flying beetles. Some hung about the opal shade of the lamp, others had stuck fast to the transparent glass bowl, while others walked slowly about on the brown tablecloth.

At the farther end of the table the children were gathered. The eldest, a tall fair-haired lad, with delicate features and eyes that would exactly have repeated his mother's had they not been so pale, was bending over a drawing pad on which he was working with colored pencils. On the table was his brother, a year younger than himself, but already as tall and very powerfully built, his face and figure repeating, with a curious exactness, his father's. He rested his elbows on the table, with his chin on his hands, and looked down from under his fair almost white eyelashes at his brother's pencils as they moved. Close to the left elbow of the eldest boy stood the third— dark, round-headed, with straight, short-cropped hair and curiously alert, dark, very round eyes; he was standing on tiptoe, trying, with his elbows on the table, to raise himself high to see well what his brother was doing. At the other elbow stood Sartje, the adopted child, whose small head of woolly hair and glittering narrow eyes hardly showed above the edge of the table, but who also was trying to get a glimpse of the work. Only Bertie, the youngest of the boys, lay already in his little white bed in the corner, his cluster of brown curls spread out on the pillow, his delicate rosebud mouth and tinted cheek and round eyes shaded by long lashes recalling the aunt who had never seen him and whose name he bore; but there was a still dreaminess in the eyes that hers had never known. Before him on the white quilt lay one of the lesson books of the older children in which he had been looking at pictures; but now his little elbows rested on the quilt, and his small hands were raised, the finger tips of one hand playing softly with the other's, and he was whispering as he looked at them, as though telling them a story. Between the face on the pillow and the little dark wizen face of the girl, who stood trying to look at the picture, there was a likeness; her forehead was drawn up with wrinkles, like an old woman's, as if from some pre-natal and inherited anxiety, while his was smooth as a white tablet; but both had the same low, broad outline; in both the hair grew directly up from the forehead in a long, straight line; her lips were blue and pouting and her black eyes twinkled between narrow lids; but both had the same perfect oval outline of face and the same rounded chin indented by a dimple—the likeness between a figure carved delicately in alabaster and the same cast roughly in brown clay; but it was there.

"I say, man," said Frank, the second boy, looking down at his brother's work over his hand and filling out his chest as he spoke, "it's just wonderful how you do it all out of your head! When I am a man and rich, and you are an artist, I'll buy your pictures to hang all round my room." He took one hand from under his chin to flick away a moth. "Get away, Sartje! Get away!—I say, get away!—You are not to come too close to me, touching my arm.—Get round the corner."

Sartje got back to her first position close to the eldest boy, and slipped her hand on to his knee.

"When you've done this," said Frank, again resting his chin on his hand, looking down at the work, "you must draw a picture with fellows playing cricket in a field, all the fellows we know. I want to show the boys that you make them out of your head. That Grey boy says you take them out of your books; he can't say that if it's fellows he knows."

"And you'll make me catching the ball, won't you, eh?" said Hughie, laying his hand eagerly on his brother's arm.

"*You* catching a ball!" said Frank, biting a thumb

nail as he spoke and without looking down at the small child. "Why, you can't catch anything! You just pick up a ball when it rolls to your feet—and then you fancy you are a big boy and can field! Why, you can't even talk plain! You lisp worse than Sartje or Bertie—just like a baby."

Hughie's face flushed and his eyes flashed over the top of the table. "I—I ——" he cried; then, suddenly realizing the undeniable truth of the accusation, he slunk down from his tiptoes and almost disappeared behind his side of the table. "I thall be theven nexth birffday," he said softly, after a moment's pause, but whether because he wished to change the subject or at least to prove that the charge of babyhood was unfounded, no one asked him.

"There won't be time to draw another picture to-night," Charles said, moving his head back to look at the effect of his work; then he bent low over the pad to add the finishing touches. "I want to write to grandmother to-night and tell her that mother thinks we shall be able to come and visit her at the farm the month after next," he said, without raising his head.

"Oh Goy! Won't that be fine!" Frank slapped his legs with his left hand. "Just the time the fruit's all ripe!"

"And you'll tell her to make muth peath thjam, eh?" said Hughie.

"Pugh!—you can't tell people when you are going to visit them what they must make before you come," cried Frank, blowing out his lips. "She'll think you are an awfully greedy boy."

Hughie slunk down again till his head almost disappeared behind the eldest brother's arm.

At that moment a firefly, which had flitted in through the open door, settled down on the drawing pad. With a shout of delight the two elder boys stretched out their hands and, interlacing their fingers, raised over the firefly a small dome with their hands, leaving only one tiny opening between the fingers at the top.

"A peep show! A peep show!" shouted Frank. "Does anyone want to pay a penny for looking in, and see a live candle walking about?" He put his own eye to the opening. "She's just walking over the tree you made; I can see it quite plainly by the light."

The elder boy put down his own eye to examine also, and Sartje and Hughie were both allowed to climb on to the table and peep in.

At that moment the door of the room behind opened and Rebekah stood in the doorway. She had changed little in the five years; but the drawn lines that had gathered about the eyes and mouth had grown faint, and there was a repose about the face that was perhaps not rest but calm.

She was dressed in the black dress covered with little silver stars which years before she had made after the fashion of Mrs. Drummond's because she thought her husband would like it and which had always hung in her wardrobe. During the last five years she had not gone out in the evening; but to-night there was a concert in Town given by artists said to be the best who had yet visited South Africa. As Frank had said he was going, she had taken a ticket for herself for the seat next his and was going with him.

Generally her hair was brushed down in smooth waves at each side of her forehead, but to-night she had fastened it back and bound it up high with a silver fillet, and she had a little silver belt about her waist. The children, who had never seen her in evening dress before, looked round at her as she came in.

"Oh, how beautiful! How beautiful!" Charles cried, raising himself slowly from his seat and standing before her; while Sartje and Hughie ran to her and began feeling with their hands the little silver stars upon her skirt; and Frank, climbing slowly down from the table, stood with his hands in his pockets looking approvingly at her: "I say—but you *are* a swell!"

She laughed.

"You are like Titania, the Queen of the Fairies," said Charles softly, twirling his pencil between his fingers. "Where did you get it from, mother?"

"I made it when you were a baby," she said, moving forward, while the two little ones clung about her.

He looked at her with his head a little on one side. "I'd like to do you so—like that"; he moved his pencil round and round softly. "Only you know, I couldn't.— Perhaps ——"

"Let *me* see too!" piped a small voice from the bed in the corner. Rebekah turned and threw the red silk cloak she carried on her arm (the same Bertie had worn the night she went to the dance) over the foot of the bed, and walked to the bedside.

Bertie hardly looked at the dress, but wove his small arms round her waist and drew her down to him. "Tell me a story!" he whispered, creeping close to her.

"Ah yes, finish the one you were telling last night," said Frank.

"I'm afraid there is no time," she said, drawing out her watch.

"Oh yes, there is. I heard father just now calling for the hot water for his bath; he won't be ready soon." She sat down on the side of the bed.

"Tell," said Bertie.

Rebekah raised her little black slippered feet on to the bed and leaned her head against its iron frètwork, while Bertie crept closer under her arm. The two elder boys sat down on the floor between the table and the bed with their knees crossed; Hugh clambered on to the bed's foot, while Sartje sat flat on the floor close to the side of the bed where Rebekah's train hung down so that she might count the stars upon it softly as her hand passed over them.

"You were just where the Robber Baron had put the two pilgrims in a dungeon and the young girl was coming down the stairs in the dark," said Charles.

It did not take Rebekah very long to finish the story;

to tell how the girl, finding her father was going to starve the prisoners to death, had taken his keys from him as he lay in a drunken sleep; and how, having opened the dungeon, she took the prisoners to a secret gate in the castle walls, gave them food for the journey and directed them to a path through the woods by which they might escape to freedom.

The children listened intently; there was a moment's silence when she had finished. Generally they asked questions and there was a free discussion of the story when it was done; but to-night Frank burst forth suddenly, "Mother, I want to say something to you: I'm never going to walk with Sartje again; never, never! In the streets or anywhere!"

Rebekah glanced down at him without raising her head. "Why?" she asked slowly.

He puffed out his full cheeks a little and pushed forward his red lips. "Because, when we came back from singing lesson yesterday, the boys at the corner house came out and laughed at us. They said, 'Walking with a nigger-girl!—Walking with a nigger-girl!—Walking with a black nigger!' I'll never walk with Sartje again; never, never, never!"

Rebekah lay quite silent for a moment; she seemed looking at the wall opposite; then she said, very slowly, "It was very cruel and very evil to speak as they did, and it is also not true. Sartje is not a black nigger any more than she is a pure white child."

"She *is* a nigger!" Frank burst forth, looking down glumly at his hands. "Father calls her that. I heard him say it to a man the other day—a black nigger; and that she and Bertie have to have their meals here and only come to table when father is away. I know it!"

Rebekah started as he began to speak, then she lay back motionless, with her eyes fixed on the opposite wall as though she saw nothing.

"She's a black nigger," Frank repeated, half under his breath, "and I'll never walk with her again!"

Sartje, not understanding what was said but feeling she was being discussed in some way not wholly to her advantage, sat pressing the back of her head into the folds of Rebekah's skirts as they hung down from the bed, and looked out at the boys with her thick lips a little pursed.

Rebekah, still leaning her head back against the ironwork of the bed, had half closed her eyes and thrown one arm across her forehead; while Bertie, with his head tucked under the other, was softly stroking it where it was bare from the elbow to the wrist.

"Do you know, boys," she said suddenly, after a pause, "sometimes I have had a dream. I have dreamed that as we are living here in this old world, just as we have always lived, suddenly there has arrived among us a strange, terrible, new race of people, coming from I know not where, perhaps from the nearest star."

She waited.

"I have dreamed they were like us in body and mind, but with terrible white faces; our skins are tinted, but theirs were white as the driven snow, and their hair like thick threads of solid gold.

"They talked and laughed just as we. Mothers brought their little babies into the world and trained and cared for them, and men and women had friends and relations that they loved, and when they died as we die bitter tears were shed into the new graves. When they were struck their bodies felt pain, and when they were insulted they resented it; they lived, living and fearing and hating and hoping, and in the end their bodies turned to dust like ours. They were human; but there was this difference between them and us—that, of many things, they knew what we did not, and they could do things we could not.

"We, here on earth, have been so proud of our little cities and our little inventions, our ships and our books and our telescopes and our laws and our manners, and we have thought we were so wise and knew right from wrong, but, suddenly, when these terrible white-faced strangers came among us, all changed. The cities we had taken ages to build they shoveled away in a few days, and in their places raised palaces so large that our cathedrals went into their cellars. They had learned how to grasp the force of the tidal wave and of the very movements of the earth, and to use it as they would. Where we with difficulty dug holes a few hundred yards into the earth, they with their wonderful machines cut in miles, as though it had been cheese. They had machines that drew great currents of cold air down from the higher regions to cool the tropical plains, and they could send vast currents of warm air up to heat the mountain peaks. They sent currents of warmed air and water to the poles to make perpetual spring there, and cooled the equator with water from the poles. If they wished to speak to one a thousand miles off they spoke and were heard, how we could not tell; and when they wrote they did not use their hand, they set something against their brains and the thoughts registered themselves. To go to the other side of the earth they had no need to use our little trains and ships; they passed through the air, and the highest mountain peaks warmed by hot currents from the plains were their resting places. They had instruments so delicate you could see the blood beat in the leg of a gnat no bigger than a pin's point; and others so strong you could see a pebble no larger than a thimble lying on the moon's surface, just as we now with our telescopes see the extinct volcanoes. They laughed at our dirty habit of putting diseased matter into our veins to save us from disease and of pouring poisons into our stomachs to mend all parts of our bodies. They had found out what it means when you say a thing lives and grows; they knew what passed on in our bodies, and when anything went wrong they knew how to go back to the cause to put it right. They called us savages. In their laboratories they shaped the most rare and delicious foods from gases and primitive atoms—foods such as we can get only when they have been drawn from the earth and air and combined in the living laboratories of the plants and animals. In every mouthful of food they ate they knew just how much of each substance the body needs was in it, and what the effect would be; they did not eat in the dark whatever came, as we do. The bloody flesh of our fellow creatures which we feed on, the roots we dig out of the ground too, the milk drawn out of the bodies of other living beasts, they thought as horrible and unclean as we think the grubs and entrails on which the Bushmen feed. And our clothes—the skin of dead creatures which we fasten over our hands and feet, the jackals' and bears' and skunks' skins which we hang about our shoulders with the tails flying and think ourselves so grand in, the feathers of birds and the dead birds which we mix with grass straws and fasten on our heads, the shreds of hair and wool from animals' backs, the threads from the insides of little worms, the torn decayed fiber of plants that we beat into clothes and are so proud to carry about everywhere on our bodies and think others savages if they have not got them—they thought disgusting.

"They were so civilized they knew the body of a human being was more wonderful and beautiful than any covering matter made out of dead animals or decayed plants, and when they wore any covering it was only for warmth or to fasten on their wings. What they wore were beautiful scale-like things, woven as we weave glass out of sand, but soft and of many colors, fitting each human being's body as perfectly as their own skins; so that, when a man was fitted out for flight with wings on, he looked as a dragon-fly looks when it is hovering over a pool. They thought our clothes and the way we hid our bodies from light and air uncleanly; and they turned their heads from us, as we turn our heads from natives dressed in skins and rubbed with fats."

The two elder boys were leaning forward with their arms upon their knees and their lips apart following each word, and Hughie had knelt straight up at the foot of the bed, his eyes fixed on his mother's lips as she still lay with her eyes shut and her arm across her forehead.

Bertie had still one arm tightly about her waist; the hand of the other was softly stroking down her arm but moving more and more slowly; and Sartje on the floor had drawn the folds of the bead-net train about her shoulders and was holding it fast at her chin, pretending she was a lady sitting in church with a black lace shawl on. The children were all quite silent when Rebekah paused for a moment. Then she went on:

"But it was not only about such things as clothes and food and houses they knew more than we. They had beautiful and wonderful things we have not even dreamed of—musical instruments more wonderful and sweet than ours, as our organs and violins are better than the gorra-gorras which the Bushmen and Hottentots play on. If you listened to their music, it was as if all the stars were singing together; it filled the earth and sky.

"The pictures talked and moved.

"Also, because their knowledge was different from ours, their laws and their ways of life were different. Things we had thought right they called wrong. They laughed at the things we believed, and called us ignorant and superstitious savages. They jeered at us when we put water on the foreheads of little babies to save them, and laughed when some of us said bread and wine could be changed into blood and meat because a man spoke a few words over them, just as we laugh at the Kaffir witch doctors who mumble over bones and make charms. They didn't feel sorry for us because we were ignorant; they only laughed at our books and our pictures and all that we made and did. They thought our bodies uglier than theirs, though we thought we were just as beautiful. They would not ride in the same airships with us nor breathe the same currents of air; they called us 'The Inferior Races.'

"Perhaps we were. But, in the world that had been ours, in which we had tried to grow and learn and make things a little more beautiful, *they* said there was no place for us unless we could serve and be of use to them. They broke down our little countries and our little governments and our little laws; they took all the earth. They said, 'Work for us; that is all you are good for; we will let you go on living if you are of use to us.'

"Here and there one tried to teach us and help us to know what they knew; but while one tried others cried, 'This is sentiment; you are taking them out of their place; they are an Inferior Race.' They wondered why we lived in the world at all, or what we had been made for."

"And we? What did we do then?" asked Charles softly, leaning farther forward as she lay still.

"We ought to have driven them right out into the sea! If I'd been there I'd have shown them!" said Frank. "What business had they coming here when we were here first? It was our world!"

Rebekah lay still an instant. "We could not really fight them," she said slowly: "we could die, but could not fight them. Sometimes thousands of us did gather together. We said, 'It is better to die with arms in our hands than to lie here like dogs and be trodden into our graves.' And we gathered together our little guns and our little cannons, the things we had once been so proud of, and we came on in thousands; but we could not really fight them. From high above in the air they saw us and poured down blasts of poisoned air upon us so that we died by hundreds and by thousands, as locusts die when you spray poison on them, without knowing where we were struck from. Sometimes they shot streams of liquid metal at us, and we fell as corn falls in the harvest. We could not fight them—we could only die. And sometimes, if by a strange chance we managed to take the life of one or two of their men, they called us murderers—but our dead lay in heaps.

"Thousands of the bravest of us fell so; whole nations were swept away from the earth and were forgotten. We could only fight to die.

"But to some of us a much more terrible thing happened. We did not try to fight and were not killed suddenly; a more awful fate overtook us.

"Because they despised *us*, we began to despise *ourselves!*

"If you pull up a tree suddenly by the roots and throw it down on the ground with all its roots exposed (the roots through which it has sucked its life for so many years), for a little while the leaves may keep green and the sap run up the stem; but by and by the leaves will wither, and the tree dies. Even if you try to transplant it and stick it up carelessly in a bit of ground, if you do not spread out the roots in the new earth and press down the ground carefully on them and give it much water for a time—it dies.

"So, when they took from us all our old laws and our old customs, when they told us all we had thought right was wrong and all we had known foolishness—and when they made us believe them; when they did nothing to teach us their wisdom and make us grasp their freedom— then we despised ourselves; and so we died.

"We did not die suddenly; we faded and faded, as the leaves fade on an uprooted tree and grow browner and browner till they drop off and are blown hither and thither by the wind, till you see them no more. So we died by millions. And the strange white people said, 'See, they are an inferior race; they melt away before us!'"

"And we, did we all die so?" asked Charles, bending yet more forward, his eyes fixed on his mother's shaded face.

"Not all," she said, after a little while. "Some of us, perhaps not always the bravest or the most beautiful, but the wisest of us, said, 'We will not fight their weapons, only to die! Neither will we fade away. This world also is our home. We also are men. We will not die. We will grasp the new life, and live!'

"And we did not despair; and we did not despise ourselves. We learned all the terrible white-faced strangers had to teach, and we worked for them. We worked—

and we worked—and we worked—and we waited—and we waited—and we waited——"

"And then, what then?" asked the boys together, seeing she said no more.

She lay quiet for a moment. "I do not know," she said. "The dream ends there."

Then suddenly she moved her arm from her forehead and sat upright. Bertie, whose large eyes were slowly closing, drooped his head softly over into her lap.

"You see, boys," she said quickly, glancing down at those on the floor, "when we talk of the dark peoples and the inferior races, it has often seemed to me, it is as with those terrible white-faced strangers of my dream.

"But we have not the excuse they had when they scorned us and tried to set their heel upon us. They came from another planet, and might say, 'Those earth men and women, what are they to us? Except that we are parts of the same Universe, what connects us with them?'

"But we cannot say so of any men or women living.

"Once, on this old Mother World of ours, there were no creatures living such as we see to-day. I do not know, but I think there was a great silence. Then the time came when there were living things in the seas and in the air. Fishes began to swim and shell-fish fastened on the rocks near the shores and tiny living creatures by myriads moved everywhere.

"And then there came a time when there were four-footed beasts and great birdlike creatures—the old monsters whose bones we find now everywhere turned to stone in the rocks, but who are nowhere with us on the earth to-day.

"And then there came a time when on the earth walked beasts and in the sea were fishes and in the air were birds and on the trees climbed four-handed animals, many of them such as we know to-day:—but still, there was no man!

"And the ages passed. And then a strange little creature began to lift itself up and look round on the world.

It tried hard to set the sole of its hind limb flat on the ground and to straighten out its hip, so that the fore limb might be free to carry the helpless young, and to pick the fruits and dig out roots. And then at last the time came when between its thumb and forefinger it could pick up even a very little stick; but yet there was no man!

"And then the ages passed. And there came a time when the creature's foot stood firm and flat on the earth, and he could grasp the very smallest particle between his forefinger and thumb and hold it tight. He had found that if you rub two sticks together sparks will fall. And at night, when he and his fellows sat together over their fires, they made many sounds which each one understood; they talked!—and then, there was MAN!

"Perhaps not just man as we know him: not man of the many thoughts and the many words and the much possessing; but still, man!—the man whose little arrowheads and tools of flint we still find everywhere from the north seas to the equator, whose bones lie mixed with the bones of the animals he killed and the shells of the fishes he ate in the caves where he took shelter—caves from which he went out with his little flint and stone tools to hunt and fish. And the woman, perhaps with just such ringed stones as those I picked up and have now in my study, went out to dig for roots and insects, with the stones fastened on to the end of her stick, and to look for grass seeds and berries, with her baby tied upon her shoulders and with a skin. And at night, in the firelight, as she sat waiting in the cave for the footsteps of the man who was to bring game, while her baby lay on the floor beside her or still hung on her back, she crooned to it the first little human love-song; and perhaps, as she sat waiting, she took a bone from the heap from which they had eaten and, with a sharp stone, began to carve on it those pictures and patterns which we find on the bones to-day, pictures like those the Bushmen have left in their caves, and patterns like those the Kaffir women ornament their pots with. And when the man came in with the game and they had cooked it in the embers, they threw fragments to the lean long-legged creature who lay near the cave entrance. And when they had finished they lay down to sleep beside the blaze; and the creature kept watch at the cave door ready to bark as no wild thing ever barked if the steps of animals or men came near:—then there was man, and woman, and child, and dog—there was home! Nowhere on the earth was there the civilized man that we know—but there was *Man* and *Home!*"

The boys leaned forward watching her intently. She had again leaned back with her head against the iron fretwork, looking upwards, hardly seeming to think of them, but her hand was on Bertie's head.

"And then again, the ages passed; and here and there, in this old earth of ours, men learned something more. Somewhere women found that, if you shaped vessels of clay and baked them in fire, they would stand great heat, and they learned to work in them. Somewhere men found that, if you put some kinds of earth into a great heat, you could smelt it, and they made iron and no more used bones and stones for weapons. Somewhere men found, perhaps in many parts of the earth, that if you hollowed out trees and guided them with sticks you could move on water— and there were boats. Sometimes, when female creatures were killed and their young caught, the women brought them up, and in time these had young and there were flocks and herds; and the milk of asses or camels or cattle made it easy for men to live without that terrible search for food every day. And in time women learned it was better to plant grasses and roots, and water and tend them, than to seek for them every day, and then there were gardens. And the men did not always hunt; they tended the tame beasts and defended them, and the women built houses and wove the threads of grasses and fibers of leaves into coarse cloths, and then there were rough clothes. And in time men found it was better to gather into large bodies and build their houses near together and have their gardens joining, so that they might defend them and tend them together, and then there were villages. And, when they found it was best that strong wise men should lead them all, they chose chiefs, and there were tribes and a government. And at last in many parts of the world there were half-civilized men and women such as the Kaffirs were when we found them, with flocks and herds, and houses and gardens and lawns—but still, not just the civilized men we know.

"And then, as the ages passed, in different parts of the earth men went further. Here and there on different parts of the earth men learned to do better than hollow out trees for boats; they made large vessels with sails. Instead of mud and straw or skin houses, men learned to build them of stone and baked bricks. Women learned to weave many kinds of clothing. Then men learned to set down their thoughts in writing, so that what one generation knew was passed on to another—and then there was civilized man!—man with his palaces and temples and laws and cities and books—books, sometimes written on stone tables, sometimes on mud tablets, sometimes on leaves or bark or skin, but still books where the thought and knowledge of mankind might be stored and each generation begin where the last left off—and there was civilization.

"Now it has spread from country to country. There are civilized men all over the earth, and we are proud of belonging to them. We despise the men who have not the material things we have and who have not learned to read and write, who have not the command of the stored-up knowledge of the ages; we despise them as the half-civilized Kaffir and Hottentot despised the Bushman.

"And yet—and yet—Englishman and Frenchman, Chinaman and Greek, Hindu and German, Zulu and Japanese, Roman and Hottentot—if we go far enough back we all have to come together and stand before that cave door. The lady in her white satin with her jewels and broidered handkerchief, the king with his crown, the judge in his ermine, the poet and the thinker, the millionaire and the beggar, the warrior and the slave—we all stand huddled there; and, as we peep over one another's shoulders and bend to look in, we have still to whisper to what we see there—'Father!—Mother!'"

Her voice sank almost to a whisper.

"Perhaps you will say, 'Yes, we know we were savages once, but what we are so proud of is that we are not now. We are right to despise the people who do not possess the things we possess and have not the knowledge we have. We are right to despise them and call them Inferior Peoples and to treat them as it would [? not] be right they should treat us.'

"But have we really any right to fill out our chests so proudly? Is it really our civilization—yours and mine—made by us?"

She sat up. "Look at this little book!" She took up from the quilt the little school book which Bertie had dropped there and held it up half open with the leaves turned to them. " 'It is our book,' you will say, 'written and printed in English by Englishmen'; and perhaps you feel a little proud that even small English boys of ten and eleven can read it and understand all that is in it when the great chiefs and leaders of many barbarous nations could not. But how much of it have we made? Look at these little black lines and dots!" She held the book more open towards them. "You will say they are only the alphabet, something so simple that even babes like Bertie and Sartje can learn them. Yes, and any fool can learn a thing when once it has been invented and another teaches him how to use and understand it—but who made them?—not we!"

She dropped her hand with the book upon the bed. "From the old cave days men made pictures of birds and beasts and men on cave walls and stones and trees and bones; and at last a time came when they found these pictures could be made to speak to others. Sometimes I think I see a man carving figures with a flint on the stem of a tree; the sunlight about him is the sunlight of a day scores of thousands of years ago. He is drawing the pictures there, so that the friends whom he has lost in the chase may know he has been there, and he is the first man writing. As the centuries passed some men went farther; they learned to give each picture a meaning: a raven meant death and a serpent meant life, and a circle meant time, for instance; and then they would write long sentences in pictures, saying what men feel and think as well as what they say. And then the time came when men found that, by turning the pictures into short signs, by leaving out many lines they could write quicker—and so men wrote thousands of years ago in Egypt and Assyria and China. Then a time came when somewhere men found out the greatest thing men had discovered since they found out how to make fire; some men found out that if you used the signs not to mean words but simply sounds and put them together you could express at once and easily everything the human brain could put into words and the human lips utter—then there was the alphabet as we know it. For thousands of years men in Asia and Africa and on the shores of the Mediterranean labored; the Phœnicians passed it on to Greece and Rome; and so to-day we read and write with it. Look at these little lines!" She held the book up again, where in parallel columns were rows of Roman and Arabian numerals. "You will say they are only figures that any simpleton can read and even calculate with.—Yes, but each one of them has a history thousands of years old, since that time when our little first fathers and mothers first began to count upon their fingers and were proud when at last they could reach five. Countless millions of men have counted and thought and invented that these little simple signs might exist; and, if the Arabian figures had never come to us from Asia, some of the work we are most proud of doing could never have been done. Look at this!" She held open a page on which was a picture of the solar system. "Perhaps you think it very clever that little lads like you can tell the names of all the planets and how far they are from the sun, and tell much about the movements of the stars; but thousands of years ago, on the great solitary plains in Asia, dark-faced men through long nights lay and watched the stars, and in solitary towers night after night they watched how the heavens shifted and what rose and what set, and how the seasons of the year were marked; and, but for the labor of these solitary watchers, whose names we shall never know and whose very nations have passed away, the telescopes and observatory and calculations of which we are so proud could never have come into existence; they laid the foundations down; we raise the walls! The very paper of which this book is made:—You will say, 'At least that is ours made out of rags spun in English mills and beaten into paper in English factories.' But, when I hold these paper leaves between my fingers, far off across the countless ages I hear the sound of women beating out the fibers of hemp and flax to shape the first garment, and, above the roar of the wheels and spinnies in the factory, I hear the whir of the world's first spinning wheel and the voice of the woman singing to herself as she sits beside it, and know that without the labor of those first women kneeling over the fibers and beating them swiftly out, and without the hum of those early spinning wheels, neither factory nor paper pulp would ever have come into existence. If I tear one sheet of paper out of this little book and there were some being wise enough to tell me its whole story, with all the lines and dots and marks upon it, and what they mean and how they came to be, and how the leaf itself came into being, the whole story of the human race on earth would have to be told me, from the time our little forefathers and mothers rubbed two sticks together and made light. This little book!— this little book!—it has got its roots down, down, deep in the life of man on earth; it grows from there. It is not your book, it is not my book, it is not the African's book, or the Asiatic's book, or the European's book; it is THE WORLD'S BOOK!"

She dropped it again softly on to the quilt and leaned forward with her elbows resting on her slightly raised knees, so that Bertie's head within her lap was entirely hidden.

"Do you know what a *parvenu* is, boys? He is a man who becomes suddenly very rich. Often he keeps horses and carriages and houses and lands, and he swells himself out, and tries to make people believe he has always had these things; he would like to make people believe that the grand old house he lives in was built by his own ancestors, that the pictures on the walls were of his relatives, and that the beautiful old library was collected by him. He is proud of the things with the existence of which he had nothing to do and which he only enjoys because a fortunate chance has given him money—and men call him 'upstart'—and perhaps they are right, because the lowest and most foolish sort of creature is one who is proud of the things which reflect no sort of credit on himself.

"I sometimes think, boys, that we, people like you and me, have to be very careful, lest we also become *parvenus*.

"For this one thing we have always to remember, because the moment we forget it, and speak and act not remembering it, we shall act like fools. It is this: We must always remember that, only the other day, as we count days in the life of men on earth, not even so many centuries ago as a savage would count on the fingers of his two hands—so short a time ago that perhaps the lichens which are growing on the rocks that have fallen from Table Mountain were growing exactly as they are to-day —our forefathers, yours and mine, were savages wandering naked in their woods and on their steppes, staining their bodies with colored juices, wearing as their only covering the skins of wild beasts, and building for themselves huts of mud and straw.

"There were civilized men on the earth then. The Hindu had already built his great palaces and written his great books; the Chinaman had long wrapped his body in soft silken robes, and in delicately furnished rooms was sipping his tea out of China cups so delicate we cannot even now imitate them.   The Medes and the Persians and Egyptians and nations whose names we do not know had had their great empires and their civilizations and had passed away; but we all the while lived the life of naked savages.

"Even the Greeks had gathered their learning from Asia and Africa and had already written their great books and carved their great statues and reared their great temples, while our forefathers were dancing naked round their wood fires at night.   The Romans had built roads and cities and made collections of laws; they looked upon our savage Northern forefathers as *'something hardly human'*; *'more like beasts than men'* one old writer called them.   And if a Roman woman had married one of your ancestors and mine, the time was when they would have buried her alive as one who had eternally disgraced her race and people.   And if they captured one of our ancestors and took him to Rome to follow one of their triumphal cars, he stared about him in the streets with the same stupefied wonder at all he saw, as a Zulu from the heart of Zululand, if he had never left his kraal, would stare if you set him down in the streets of London or Paris.   Perhaps they were wrong to despise us so; there are ways in which a Zulu chief may be higher than a learned professor—but we were savages!

"For you see, it was not only with regard to clothes and food and houses and the material things of life that we knew less than some civilized peoples.   When our forefathers were still sacrificing human beings to their gods under the oak trees, and their priests, like the Kaffir witch doctors to-day, were 'smelling out' the people who should be killed; and when our forefathers dreamed that heaven was a place where men forever drank mead out of the skulls of their enemies—already—long ages before— the great teacher of Asia had sat under his Bo-tree, and had sent out to the earth his message of love and peace. And when our poet sings to-day,

> 'He prayeth well, who loveth well
> Both man and bird and beast . . .
> He prayeth best, who loveth best
> All things both great and small . . .'

he is only seeing over again what the man in Asia saw thousands of years ago. And our great men to-day are only slowly finding out bit by bit, as they climb along that path which we call science, what men of Asia saw years ago when they cried, 'All life is one!' "

Her voice sank into silence. She seemed dreaming to herself rather than talking. Then she said gently, "You know there are people who, before they eat, bend their heads and say a thanks. But for me, when I read a beautiful book or a great poem or see lovely pictures—and even when I have been very happy walking along and thinking—then it comes to me that I want to raise my hand to my forehead and salute, as the soldiers do when their officers go past. I want to say—'To all the great dead, to all the men and women who have been before me whose names will never now be known, without whom I could never know what I know, or understand as I understand or think as I think—Be Thanks!'

"And sometimes even when I am walking in my garden and I see the peach tree covered with blossoms in the corner and the roses and lilies growing all round, and the grapes hanging from the gable, and all the small flowers sending out their scent, the feeling comes to me, and I want to say—'To all the gardeners that have been before me—to the little old first mother, who scratched earth and put in roots and grasses—to Chinaman and Persian and Egyptian and Babylonian and Indian, and men and women of races whose names I shall never know, without whom I should never have this beauty—Thanks!' And sometimes as I work there I feel as if they were working beside me and the garden belongs to them and me. And sometimes

I think perhaps in years to come, when I have long ages been dust, some woman working in a garden more beautiful than any I can dream of now will stretch out her hand and say—'To all the gardeners that have been before me——' and I, so long dead in the dust, will live in her heart again."

There was a moment's silence. You could hear Bertie's slow, even breathing from her lap.

"You know, up-country on the great plains, where the camel thorn trees grow, there are ant heaps as high almost as a man. Millions of ants have worked at them for years, and slowly and slowly they have grown a little and a little higher. Sometimes I have fancied, if a little ant should come on the top of one of these heaps, and should rear himself on his hind legs and wave his little antennæ in the air, and should look around and say, 'My ant heap, that I have made! My ant heap, from which I see so far!—My plains—my sky—my thorn trees—my earth!' and should wave his little antennæ and cry, 'I am at the [? beginning] of all!'—and that then suddenly a gust of wind should come! The ant heap would still be there, the ant heap on the top of which he chanced to be born; there would still be the trees and the plain and the sky; but he would be gone for ever.

"I have sometimes wondered: Isn't it a little bit so with us, when we walk about so proud on the top of our little heap of civilization? Because the most that any man can hope for, and the most that any nation can hope for, is this: The man, that, in the one little hour of life that is given him, he may be able to add one tiny grain, so small perhaps that no eye will ever see it, to the heap of things good and beautiful which men have slowly been gathering together through the ages;—the nation, that, when its time to pass comes as it comes to all, it may have added to the things good and beautiful, which humanity lays up through the ages for the use of all, one layer, perhaps one thin layer, but that so well and truly laid that all coming after shall say—'It was nobly done!' "

"Mother, mother," whispered Hughie, "why are your eyes so big?" He was kneeling forward with his knuckles on the bed, staring intently into her face; but she did not seem to see him.

"You will hear people talking often of Inferior Races and of how superior we are—the people who may be speaking; but for me I know this, that, if you took from me bit by bit all I have gained and learned from other races and other peoples in whom my blood never flowed, I should go back and back, and you would find me at last only a little cave mother with her baby tied by a skin on to her back, peeping out at the door of the cave to see if the man with his bone hook or flint arrows was coming home with game, while a dog who was not yet quite able to bark howled at the door. And when I think of all I have and all I know, the only feeling I have is—'Pass it on! Pass it on!'"

She lapsed into silence and the boys sat watching her.

"When I was a little girl," she said, stretching her arms out upon her knees, "I could not bear black or brown people. I thought they were ugly and dirty and stupid; the little naked Kaffirs, with their dusty black skins, that played on the walls of the kraal, I hated. They seemed so different from me in my white pinafores and my little stiff starched pink skirts that rustled as I walked. I felt I was so clever and they so stupid; I could not bear them.

"I always played that I was Queen Victoria and that all Africa belonged to me, and I could do whatever I liked. It always puzzled me when I walked up and down thinking what I should do with the black people; I did not like to kill them, because I could not hurt anything, and yet I could not have them near me. At last I made a plan. I made believe I built a high wall right across Africa and put all the black people on the other side, and I said, 'Stay there, and, the day you put one foot over, you heads will be cut off.'

"I was very pleased when I made this plan. I used to

walk up and down and make believe there were no black people in South Africa; I had it all to myself.

"But one day—I must have been about seven years old then—there was a war going on against the Kaffirs near where we lived, and a white man who had just been to The Front came to see us. He sat talking to my father and mother in the front room and drinking coffee, and I sat on my stool in the corner, by my mother's work table, and listened. He told how many black men had been killed and only two white men hurt, one by falling off his horse. I did not mind that so many black people had been killed— they were only Kaffirs! Then he told about a fight he had been in the day before. It was a big fight. The white men had their cannon and all their soldiers on the top of a hill, and the Kaffirs came out below from the bush; there were hundreds of them; they had hardly any clothes or guns, only assagais,[1] and they came on naked up the slope; but before them walked a young Kaffir woman. Her arms were full of assagais. As the men threw their assagais she gave them new ones; she called on them to come on and not to be afraid to die. She walked up and down before the front row, and called on them to come on. The guns fired and the dead lay in heaps. When she got close up to the mouth of the cannon she was blown away too with the others. He said hardly any escaped, only a few got away into the bush again. But I felt I was suffocating. I ran out quickly to my pear tree in the garden and walked up and down. I couldn't bear any more. I saw the woman walking with her bare arms glistening in the sun and her red blanket tied across her as I had often seen Kaffir women, and, with the assagais in her arms, calling the men to come on and not to be afraid to die. I walked up and down; at last I lay down on the ground and cried. After that, often in the night when I lay awake I thought I was the young Kaffir woman, and I called the men to come on—and then the cannon fired.

"And once, when I was an older child, about nine, I

[1] An assagai is the spear used by the Kaffirs in war.

was sitting at the kitchen door on the lowest step feeding my chickens, and my mother and old Ayah were standing at the top, talking. I don't think they noticed me: they were talking of a Kaffir woman who used to live on the 'arm before I was born. I didn't quite understand everything they said—you know children often don't when grown-up people talk, and yet in a way I did understand everything. They were talking of a trouble which had come to her—I know now it was the greatest trouble that could come to any person—and they said, when she couldn't bear it any more, she took her two little children and climbed the mountain to the very top where the precipice stands so high. And when she came to the place where it curves out, she tied her two children under her arms and jumped down. They talked of how all the morning they looked for her and wondered she did not come to work, and then another Kaffir woman said she had told her what she was going to do. Your grandfather and all the men went up, and there they found her, just where the precipice curves out, with the two children tied to her, quite dead.

"They did not know I knew what they said; but the next Saturday, when I had no lessons, when breakfast was done I went up into the bush. I told no one I was going; and I climbed up past where the tiger traps were, and then on where there was no path. And when it was nearly midday I got to the foot of the precipice where it curved out. The trees were all about and at the foot of the precipice were rocks that had fallen down with lichens on them and black ground between. I sat down on one of the stones. I knew that was where she fell. I thought perhaps if she knew it she would have liked to think that, so many years after she was dead, a little white child came and sat there and felt sorry for her. I had made up a little poem about how beautiful the world was, and how sad she must have been when she went away from it. And I sang it when I sat there. It was all I could do. And twice after that I came there, and often when I saw a

Kaffir woman walking past I used to wonder if perhaps her husband was going to bring home a new wife, and if she felt as sad as that other woman did; and once I ran far down the road after a traveling woman I saw going by with her baby on her back, and gave her my slice of bread and jam, because I didn't know what might happen to her some day.

"And so you see," she said, "as I grew older and older I got to see that it wasn't the color or the shape of the jaw or the cleverness that mattered; that if men and women could love very much and feel such great pain that their hearts broke, and if when they thought they were wronged they were glad to die, and that for others they could face death without a fear, as that young Kaffir woman with the assagais did, then they were mine and I was theirs, and the wall I had built across Africa had slowly to fall down.

"It's natural," Rebekah said, "that we should love those who are like ourselves. A little child feels very lonely if it has not another child of its own age and size to play with. And perhaps the greatest longing a human being can have is to find another being who feels and thinks as they do; and when they meet they are like two drops of water that run into one as soon as they touch. But, even if people aren't like us at all, deep down there is something that joins us together; and if you shrink from them at first, if you are very kind to them and try to help them, it's wonderful how you get to love them."

She had dropped her right arm at her side, and the fingers of the hand were moving softly among the frizzled curls of Sartje's head which she had pressed back deep into her mistress's skirts, her drowsy eyes already full of sleep and dreams.

"And so, when I hear people talking of superior races and inferior peoples, and of keeping other races and peoples down, I hardly understand. Because, if I find people who seem to know a little less or to see a little less than I do, I always feel I want to say to them, 'Oh little earth-brother and sister, climbing with me that long climb out of the dark, through the cave doors and on we do not know up where,—if it should happen that I have climbed on to a step a little bit higher than the one you stand on and can see a little farther—here is my hand— let me help you up.' "

For a moment she sat silent, her eyes looking straight forward almost as full of dreams as Sartje's. "Out there in my garden," she said softly, "there are flowers of all kinds growing—tall queen-lilies and roses and pinks and violets and little brown ranunculuses—and I love them all. But if the tall queen-lilies were to say, 'We must reign here alone, all the others must die to give place to us,' I do not know, but I think I might say, 'Is it not perhaps then best *you* should go?'

"And perhaps the next day there might come a blighting frost; the rose bushes would live on and the little violets hidden at their roots, and even the little brown ranunculuses sheltered by higher branches, would be alive; but the lilies—the tall white queen-lilies—would all be dead!

"I am glad there are all kinds of men and animals living on the earth where I live, that I and men like me are not the only creatures. If the time should come when there was only one kind of creature left, then the blooming time of the gods' garden would be done, and I would be glad to creep away under the dust and sleep."

She put Bertie's head down softly on the pillow, and slipping down herself, stood on the floor beside the bed, rousing Sartje from her half-waking slumber and causing her to sit upright on the floor.

"One thing I tell you, lads," she said quickly, in a changed voice, looking at the two boys who themselves were now rising from their curved-knee position on the floor: "it is this—I hope, I believe, I know, the day will come when you will regret utterly every slighting, every unkind word or act, that you have ever given place to towards Sartje, and when you will be deeply grateful for every kind or generous thing you have done towards her.

Sartje is not a black child any more than she is pure white. It is not her fault that she is not white, any more than it is your virtue that you are not half black. Sartje is alone in the world. Her mother does not want her; her father does not know that he has even such a daughter in the world. She has no one but us to take care of her. I shall not ever ask one of you to walk with her again. She shall walk with me."

"Mother, mother," said Hughie, sliding down from the bed and catching hold of her skirt, glad that the conversation had suddenly taken a turn in which he could find a part, "*I* will walk with Sartje! And," he cried, filling out his little chest and striking his fist against it, "I will walk with her in the big street; and if the boys laugh at her, *I* fthrow them wifth stones!"

Rebekah put her hand on his short, dark hair. "No, you wouldn't; you'd just be like Rover; when little dogs come out and bark he goes past, he doesn't see them. You'll be mother's big Rover!"

For a moment his face fell; then he said approvingly, "Yesth, yesth, I *am* big Yover!"

"Well, and I'm sure," said Frank, pursing out his lips and pressing his double-chin against his white collar as he looked downward at his hands, "*I* don't mind walking with Sartje, if it's in the pine woods or somewhere where people can't see. But I'm not going to walk with her in the main road or on the road to the station." He pursed out his lips yet further.

Sartje, now wide awake, was paying no attention to anything that was said, as she was busy spreading out Rebekah's train in a great wide [? circle] on the floor.

"You mustn't think I don't understand, laddie," she said, putting her hand for an instant on his shoulder; "I am your mother and three times older than you, and I ought to be much wiser; but when I go down the Government Avenue, and the colored girls sitting there laugh because they see I don't wear stays as other women do, it's as if a knife ran into me under my ribs. I know I'm right; that in years to come people will wonder women could be so mad and foolish as to deform themselves. And yet, when these women laugh at me, I am so full of pain I can hardly walk down to the station; and when I come home I feel I want to creep on to the bed and cry. I've tried to like colored women and do all I can to help them, and then they jeer at me! I don't want for days to go out again. If I, your mother, who should be so much stronger and wiser, feel these things so, what right have I to expect that little boys like you can bear them? You would be heroes if you could."

Frank had raised his chin from his collar and both boys were looking her full in the face. She looked at them a little wistfully.

"You know, laddies," she said softly, "you are always talking of being *men,* and how fine it will be when you are grown up. It is a finer thing to be a 'man,' than either of you can know now. But it's not being able to lift a great weight or strike a great blow or crush things beneath you that can ever make you that. The thing that really matters is this: that, when that day comes, as it must come to you at last, when your bodies lie still and dead, whether it be in a palace or a poor man's hut, on a solitary Karroo plain or in a crowded city, whether you have been rich and famous or poor and unknown—what matters is this, that, if one should stand beside you and look down at you knowing all the story of your life, they should be able to say, 'This strong man's hand was always stretched out to cover those feebler; this great man's body never sought good or pleasure for itself at the price of something weaker.' Then, though no eye could see it, you would lie there, crowned—the noblest thing on earth, the body of a dead man who had lived the life of a man! No strength and no size and no beauty of body can ever give you that."

The two boys stood with their eyes fixed on her face; but Hughie, who stood close beside her, pulled down her arm and peered anxiously up into her face; but there were not tears there.

At that moment, through the window, came the sound of the opening of the front door of the large house and there was sound of a step on the gravel. Rebekah turned quickly and took from the foot of the bed the red silk cloak which Bertie had worn to the dance five years before. She put it on and drew the hood over her hair.

"Oh, little Yed Yiding Hood! Little Yed Yiding Hood," cried Hughie, clapping his hands. Then, throwing himself on all fours on the ground—"Now I'll be the wolf!—Boo-hue-hue!" He careered round her while Sartje, pretending to be greatly appalled, leaped on the bed and buried her face by Bertie's, who still slept on. Rebekah whisked her train out of his [? hands] in affected fear, and stooped to pin up the skirt under her cloak. There was the pleasant scent of a good cigar, and, in the open doorway the children's father stood.

He wore a gray cap and his overcoat, hanging open, showed a large expanse of white shirt front. He had grown stouter in the last five years, his face somewhat redder and the flesh stiffer. One passing him now in the street would hardly have noted him as a handsome man, but he had still a fine fully developed presence. But the latent vigor which had given him charm as a young man was lapsing into a placid self-content which made almost an impression of sluggishness.

"Well, what's the row about?" he said good-humoredly, taking the cigar from his lips as he looked down at Hughie, who was still on all fours. "I'm afraid I've kept you waiting," he said to Rebekah; "but when I'd had my bath I found unless we hurried we'd miss that train; so I took things leisurely. We should have been half an hour early if we'd gone by that, and now we shall be three-quarters of an hour late"—he took out his watch; "but it's such a long programme, it's rather an advantage."

"I didn't at all mind being kept," Rebekah said; "I will be with you in a minute."

He put the cigar back in his mouth and blew a long whiff of smoke. "Well, I'll wait for you at the gate. We've still twenty minutes to get to the station." He called good night to the children and went down the steps.

Rebekah turned to Sartje: "There is a candle burning in my room; go in and go to bed at once. There are three peppermints on the mantelpiece which you can take to go to sleep with. And you two big boys, go and get your mattresses and bedding from your own room and spread them here on the floor, so that if the young ones wake and cry before I come back you can be here to hear them."

"Oh, a bivouac! a bivouac!" shouted Frank. "We'll be Red Indians sleeping in a wood."

"We'll have a make-believe fire with twisted papers, and sit round it," said Charles.

"Yes, and you can go and find the box of chocolates in my top drawer, and put them on the fire for chops," said Rebekah; "but mind you give the little ones some— Sartje too. You must all be in bed by nine o'clock. I'll kiss you and tuck you all in when I come back."

Hughie ran to fetch the chocolates, and the two elder boys prepared to rush off to fetch the bedding. As Charles passed her he laid his hand softly on her arm. "Mother," he whispered quickly, "you know I will never mind walking with Sartje?"

"Yes, I know, dear," she said softly, "but for her own sake I will not let her. Thank you." They exchanged a swift glance; then he ran out and she turned to the bed. For an instant she put her lips on Bertie's forehead and spread his curls on the pillow; then she went out through the glass door.

She stood on the top step for a moment, drawing on her glove. The night was very dark now and absolutely still; the scent from the flower beds rose up almost over-poweringly, and the fireflies seemed to flit by in dozens among them as she walked slowly past the beds to the gate. In after years the sight of a firefly brought always back that night to her, with a sense of the coming dawn after the dark.

Frank stood outside the gate smoking. He pushed it open and closed it. He was always polite to her now, sometimes almost attentive. When they had walked a few steps they passed Mrs. Drummond's gate.

"I met her to-day," he said, inclining his head in the dark to the house, "sailing out of the booking office, as I went in to get our tickets. Hadn't seen her for months. She says her husband's come. Goes away in a week on a long journey into the interior—rather a short visit after twelve years' absence!" He laughed. "He must have found her much younger than he left her; the story goes now that she goes to bed three days in each month ostensibly for her health; really, to have her face enameled."

"I think it is going to rain to-night," Rebekah said quickly, looking up at the sky.

"Why didn't you say so sooner, and I could have told the boy to come with the trap and fetch us?"

"Oh, it may not," she said, looking up again, "but it's so still and there were so many insects out to-night."

Here they turned out of the main avenue into the short cut through the woods. The footpath was narrow, and he walked before, she following, holding tight her skirts.

"By the way," he said, "you don't want to buy that gray horse of mine, do you? He's too broken winded for hunting any more, but he'd do well to draw that milk cart, or fruit cart, or whatever it is, on that wonderful farm of yours."

"No," she said, "that old horse I bought from the Malay for ten shillings because he was going to shoot him has turned out wonderfully. We feed him on warm bran and meal and give him two raw eggs a day, which he can eat without teeth, and he's got as fat as a young horse and takes the cart to the station twice a day."

"Philanthropy turned out well this time, eh? I really must go and see this wonderful farm of yours. Growing quite a millionaire, I suppose! Sixpence for cabbages, sixpence for grapes, mounts up!"

"Well, it pays all my expenses and Sartje's, and keeps the man and woman at the farm, and we owe nothing."

"Oh, I'll give you credit for making it pay," he laughed. "By the way," he said, when they had gone a few steps further, "I think I shan't put off my trip to the Eastern Province till you and the children return. I've practically made up my mind to go to-morrow. I know the captain going with this boat and there are some people I know going, so I might as well go now and perhaps have a week's shooting when I've done my business; it'll be the close season if I wait till you come back."

Rebekah fell to no speculation as to why he had suddenly changed his plans since the morning; she had long ceased to look for the real reasons of his obviously superficial explanations or to have instinctive perceptions about anything that concerned him.

"Yes," she said, "and it will be cooler now than later. I suppose you will take the black trunk and your small portmanteau."

"Yes," he said, "you might see about packing them to-morrow, as the boat will not leave later than four."

The path here got so intricate and uneven, that they walked in silence till they got out into the road at the station. When they got to the hall in Town where the concert was given they found it far advanced. Their own seats were in the front row but one, and the place seemed crowded. No place seemed vacant but the chair on Rebekah's left.

Rebekah felt very tired. She had been up and at work since six that morning, and she almost wished she had not come. Then four men on four violins began to render a passage by Beethoven. In a few moments she was leaning forward breathless and motionless like a little child who goes to the pantomime for the first time. It was the first music belonging to her own world she had ever heard: she did not see the men or their instruments, but had the joy one feels as one rides alone across a solitary Karroo plain in the sun and hears nothing but the rhythmic beat of the horse's feet.

Then it ended; and a woman, the great singer of the troupe, in a tight white silk dress, wearing many bracelets, stood on the platform; she shook out her dress and bangles, and bowed to the audience, and unfolded her music and began to sing. A wild burst of applause shook the hall when she finished, and again she bowed and smirked towards the audience and sang. Rebekah leaned back wearily, speculating why it was that one woman, with her song and her tight silk dress, should at once be able to produce an atmosphere as trivial and suffocating as an afternoon tea where women are discussing their neighbors' dresses and concerns.

And she fell to planning a new kind of concert room— quite round, with seats rising tier above tier and the music coming from the center or one end, but all so arranged you could not see the players or the audience, high partitions shutting you off from your neighbors, and each seat so long that it was a couch on which you could lie down and lose every consciousness but that of sound; a dim soft light coming from veiled lights in the roof. She was a little distressed as to arranging the lights for the performers, so that while the sound was not impeded the light was not visible, and she was lost in this when her husband touched her to say he was going out.

The interval had come; almost all the men streamed out to the refreshment bar and the hall was left almost entirely to women. As she glanced back to look at the clock her eye fell on a man who had not gone out and sat in the seat beyond the empty one next to her. But beyond the fact that he had a closed music book upon his knees from which he had evidently been following the music, and that he was a stranger and not South African, he left no mark upon her thought. She sat back still trying to arrange the lights in the concert hall. As she sat dreaming her eye fell unseeingly on the hand which rested on the music book on the man's knee beside her. She started and looked at it consciously. She knew it; it was strangely familiar. It called back sensations of her childhood and of her past life; she looked up curiously into his face to see who he might be. But he was a man she had never seen before. His skin was bronzed like that of one long habituated to the open air; his beard was dark and close-clipped; his dark hair curled close to his head, and, though he did not seem more than thirty-five, was slightly tinged with gray. She knew no such man. She glanced back at the hand again, and the same strange sense of familiarity came back to her, only it seemed to have been a hand smaller and softer. Long afterwards she knew that the hand it reminded her of was her own.

She sat back in her seat again, looking at the empty stage and continuing her plan, till the people who had gone out for the interval came streaming back again. Frank, when he came back again, spent the rest of the interval in looking round and telling her who of their acquaintances were or were not there.

"So Mrs. Drummond didn't come after all," he said in a low voice, fixing himself back in his seat.

"Perhaps she is in the gallery," Rebekah said indifferently.

"Hush—no! that empty chair next you is hers; that's her husband sitting beyond you."

Rebekah looked round quickly. So, he was the man whose little statue had stood for ten years in the corner of her room, whose notes on the margin of the book she had read and re-read with the text, and whose comments she had herself put notes to—this was Mrs. Drummond's husband!

The time was long past when any mention of Mrs. Drummond affected her as rough matter touching a naked nerve-point; she had no living interest in her. But no creature which has ever crept into the core of our life, and fed on the bleeding macerated tissue it has created there, ever becomes for us again a matter of complete indifference. Anything connected with them makes in us a faint adumbration of pain.

Then the music began again, and she forgot him or was only faintly conscious of his presence.

Just before the concert ended, as the woman in white satin was for the last time raising her voice on the stage, there came the sound of pouring rain on the roof. It fell in torrents that almost drowned the woman's voice. People looked round anxiously, those who had not ordered carriages questioning how they were to reach the station or their homes in town. And before the last notes of the woman's song had died, everyone rose and crushed towards the doors, eager to capture any stray cabs that might be waiting outside. From their seats in the front row it was long before Rebekah and Frank reached the entrance hall. By that time many of the audience had left in some conveyance, or had walked away in the rain. But the hall was still crowded with people waiting for the chance of a returning cab or a diminution of the rain.

Rebekah made her way to the front door and looked out. The rain still fell in torrents, and, except a couple of private and pre-engaged carriages, whose owners, knowing they were secure, were leisurely making their way out, there were no conveyances in the street.

To the left of the hall, where a veranda jutted out, the motley crowd which gathers outside the doors of places of amusement when the hour of departure arrives—colored men and boys, white loafers, colored and white women in gaudy finery or squalor—had taken refuge from the rain and were standing under it, laughing or swearing as they tried to force their way to inside places for shelter. She turned back into the hall.

"I suppose," said Frank, who stood buttoning his coat, "we had better wait till the worst is over."

"I can't," she said; "the children are alone, and I shall miss the last train. I will run down quickly to the station at once."

"Well, I shall stay in town to-night. I'll have plenty

to do in the morning if I'm to be off at four. You'll probably find some one at the other end who's going the same way as you are."

She was trying to twist her dress about her to start, when some one, who stood pressed close behind them, accosted Frank. The hall was dimly lighted by one small lamp; she could not see that when Frank, in replying, held out his hand, the speaker seemed not to notice it.

"Let me introduce you to my wife. This is Mrs. Drummond's husband," he said rather hurriedly.

The man who stood close beside her bowed, without holding out his hand. "You will excuse the liberty I am taking," he said, "but in these close quarters I could not avoid hearing that you were not going out to the suburbs to-night. I have a closed carriage waiting here; if your wife would do me the honor, I should be glad to put her down at her door. I believe the house is next to the one in which I stay."

Before Rebekah could speak Frank had accepted the offer; the man pushed his way out to call the carriage to the curbstone, and Frank, seizing her by the arm, hurried her towards the door: "Of course you must go. It's no favor—you'll get soaking wet before you get to the station." He hurried her across the pavement.

The man stood holding the door of the carriage open; when she had taken her seat, he stepped in and took the seat opposite to her; Frank closed the door and was about to pull up the window, when from the crowd under the veranda there rang out a long, reckless, gurgling laugh. It was unmistakably a woman's. In an instant Rebekah sprang forward and stretched her arm through the window, trying to turn the handle of the door.

"Let me out!—Let me out!" she cried, shaking the door with her left hand as the handle refused to turn. Then the door burst open and she leaped out.

"Rebekah, what are you doing?" Frank stretched out his hand to detain her.

"It's Bertie!" she said hoarsely, evading his hand, and

ran across the sidewalk, now deep in water, towards the veranda, her long train and cloak fluttering out behind her. The man inside looked out. Frank drew up the collar of his coat and drew the lappet of his cap closer over his ears and leaned in at the door, gaining shelter from the rain.

"I must really ask you to excuse my wife," he said. "She's really a most sensible and practical person generally, but there's one thing about which she's unhinged—a sister of hers who cleared off to England some years ago with a Jew; she and her people spent a small fortune trying to find her. Sent some one all the way to South America to look for her—found she'd never been there, been in London—stayed with the Jew for some time, then gone off with another man. The last they heard of her she'd landed in a brothel in Soho—never been able to hear of her since. My wife's possessed with the idea she'll turn up here some day. It's insanity. I've known her to leap up at three o'clock in the morning and rush out in the avenue because she thought she heard her step. She's fancied she heard her laugh now in that crowd, and's gone to see. Of course you won't mention what I've told you to anyone, but since you saw what passed I thought it was best to give you an explanation."

The man pushed past him and got out. "Are you going to help her look?" he asked shortly.

"Oh no; she'll find out her mistake in a few moments and be back." They stood looking towards the dark little crowd under the veranda. "It wasn't her, of course," said Frank, "though the laugh did sound a little like her. What I can't get my wife to see is how much better it is for everyone she shouldn't turn up!" He drew the collar of his coat yet higher, but did not like to shelter himself in the cab while the man was standing in the rain. "I don't believe there's a disreputable place in Cape Town or Simon's Town where my wife hasn't had her looked for. She was a very pretty girl; the prettiest woman I've seen yet; but she wasn't much good, I'm afraid." Frank stood with his back closer to the carriage. "Won't you get in again? You're getting awfully wet."

The man appeared not to hear him; his face was turned towards the veranda.

"Of course," Frank said, moving a step nearer him, "I need not ask you not to mention to anyone what has happened to-night, or repeat anything I have said; having seen so much, I thought it was better to be frank. People know, of course, that there was some sort of a scandal when she went away, but, as far as I know, nothing definite—and things get so soon forgotten, if they're not talked of."

The man turned his shoulder towards him.

Then they saw Rebekah coming through the rain. She was walking slowly; her train dragged behind her in the mud, and the light from the carriage lamps made the water glisten on her red cloak and hood as she came near.

"I am too wet to get in," she said slowly; "I will walk down to the station."

She turned to go.

"Don't be ridiculous, Rebekah!" said Frank. The water from his cap was running into his neck. "If you walked you would probably miss the train and have to stay in town all night." He seized her arm and half lifted her towards the step; the man was holding the door open. "Don't," Frank whispered, "don't let us make any further public exhibition of ourselves." He raised her into the carriage, and she dropped on to the back seat. The man got in and Frank closed the door. He put his head in at the window, "I shall likely not get out till half past two to-morrow; but if you have the black trunk and the portmanteau ready, I shall be in time to get on board by four. Good night!" He withdrew his head and told the driver to move on, and then turned to hail a cab which was fortunately passing at the moment.

Rebekah sat drawn into the corner of the carriage, her head leaning back. The man opposite her drew up the window and sat silent till they passed the station. Then he took off his coat and leaned forward towards her.

"Your cloak is very damp," he said. "Will you not take it off and put my coat round you? It is hardly damp."

She shook her head and declined almost inaudibly. The reaction from the few moments of intense excitement and the long tiring day had left her almost exhausted. She leaned her head farther into the corner; she was not conscious of the pressure of her damp clothes or anything but the soothing motion of the carriage.

Presently, without speaking, he folded his coat and laid it down on the floor. "Set your feet on it: put them into the folds," he said shortly and quickly. He bent for an instant and moved the long wet train of her skirt farther from her.

"I have always found," he said in a short sharp business tone, as he raised himself, "in twelve years of travel and roughing it, that the secret of health lies in always keeping damp material from the feet, and, where that cannot be, in covering them. When we are civilized we shall wear no covering for the feet in warm climates." His tone was markedly short and businesslike, precluding an answer, and he turned his face to the window. Little could be seen through the rain-speckled glass, and, as they got out into the suburbs, lights were few and far, and the landscape was dark outside, but he still appeared absorbed in watching it. For nearly three-quarters of an hour they drove on slowly, the carriage moving through the mud of the drenched roads. Rebekah sat motionless, as if she were asleep.

After a time they got more completely into the country, where the trees grew higher and thicker, and later turned into the avenue that led to Rebekah's house. Then, for the first time, he turned from the window and leaned back in his place. They were almost within a stone's throw of her gate when he leaned forward.

"You will forgive my intrusion," he said slowly and

distinctly, "but, when you had left the carriage, your
husband told me you had gone to look for a friend whom
you had long lost and hoped to find." He paused. "I
should be intruding unforgivably," he said, bending a little
more forward and speaking yet more slowly and distinctly, "but, that once in my life I found that which to
the world seemed lost and worthless, and which, to me,
became the good of life. If"—he paused, and then spoke
a little more dryly—"I could be of use to you in helping
you to seek, I should feel it an honor. I have a week to
spend here; and I have nothing to do. Unfortunately, as
the world is to-day, a man has facilities of search in some
directions that a woman has not. If you could make use
of me, I should be glad. There is no house, however bad,
which I could not enter to seek."

Then he drew himself up quickly and the carriage
stopped at Rebekah's gate. Again he leaned forward
slightly before opening the door and said in a short
whisper, "If, thinking the matter over, you come to the
conclusion I can be of use, will you set down on paper de-
tails that may be a guide to me? Send me a photograph,
anything that would help me to identify. What you in-
close in an envelope and address to the house next door
will find me."

He opened the door quickly and got out. Then he
turned to help her. It seemed to her afterwards he had
almost lifted her out and stood her on the ground. Then
he turned sharply and opened the gate. She passed
through it: he closed it, said shortly, "Good night" without extending his hand, and turned and got into the carriage. She walked slowly up the path, and, when she got
to the top step before the door of the new rooms, turned
round and stood still. Then it struck her she had not
thanked him for his offer or for driving her home. She
still stood on the step. She heard the carriage, which had
stopped before the gate of the next house, drive away;
and there were steps going up to the house.

Then she turned and went in. The two boys lay in

their beds on the floor; a few moths were still hovering round the lamp or lying dead on the table, and on the two little beds in the corners the small boys slept. She walked past them to her own room. She took the lamp from the drawers and set it down on the dressing table; then she dropped her wet cloak and dress upon the floor. Without removing any other article of her damp clothing she sat down before the dressing table. Out of the drawer she took the notebook and pencil with which she kept her household accounts and opened it on the table. She leaned her naked elbows on the edge and rested her face in her hands, thinking for a little while; then she began to write. Slowly she put down the items, numbering each one—color of hair, height, walk, size of hands and feet. Sometimes she paused to think: then she took from her neck the gold chain and locket. There was a picture of Bertie as she was just before she left. She closed it and folded it in paper, and tore out the leaf of the pocketbook on which she had written and folded it and laid it beside it. Then she sat still, looking at them; after a time she folded her arms on the edge of the table and leaned her head on them. When she raised it she unfolded the locket and put it away in the drawer, and tore up the page she had written and left the fragments on the toilet cover. Then she got up almost stiffly and removed her damp clothing; and when she had her nightgown on went round to tuck in each of the sleeping children.

CHAPTER XIII

The Veranda

THE next day Frank left, and four days passed; on the fifth Rebekah went to the farm to work all day and took Sartje with her.

When she returned at five o'clock she expected to find the boys home from school, playing cricket in the yard; but it was empty. She walked round to the front garden. Then she heard the sound of voices and the high ring of Hughie's laugh. She walked to the rose hedge and looked across.

Croquet had gone out of fashion and what used to be Mrs. Drummond's lawn was now a tangle of long grass, with here and there a yellow flower; the late afternoon sunshine shining across it made it an intense green, the oak trees casting flickering shadows in some parts. Under the largest of the oak trees was a collection of heads bending down over something among the grass. The children were forbidden to go in without invitation, but she recognized the heads. She walked quickly to the little gate. It moved stiffly on its hinges now; the little path that had once been so deeply worn was now almost imperceptible. Frank seldom used it, nor did anyone come from Mrs. Drummond's but now and then a servant to borrow something.

Rebekah stepped over the knee-deep grass. Lying at full length on his back under the oak tree, with his hands clasped under his head, was Mrs. Drummond's husband. Little Bertie in his white embroidered dress sat at his head, bending over it, dividing with his tiny fingers the short stiff curls along the top and stroking them; Hughie

434

knelt on the left, his fingers planted on the man's chest and his eyes fixed on his face; the elder boys sat close to him on the right with their backs turned to her. He was speaking, and all were so intently listening they did not hear her steps.

Hughie saw her first, just as her shadow fell across them. "Mofther, mofther, it's about a baby chimpanzee was sticking fast, and the man——"

"He asked us to come, mother," said Charles, standing up; "our ball came over from the yard, and he said we could come and look for it."

The man raised his head and rose quickly to his feet: "I hope I have not tempted them to break bounds," he said; "they have been entertaining me so well."

"Mofther," cried Hughie, running close up to her and trying to touch her chin with his hand, "justh when he was going to take the baby chimpanzee the big mofther——"

"He's been in a real big island," said Frank, "for more than two years, with no white people, and he dressed just like a nigger with only a cotton cloth about him, and once he went down a river on a log——"

Rebekah loosened Hughie's fingers, that were still trying to attract her attention by holding her chin. "I'm afraid if you once began telling them stories, you did not find them very easy to get rid of."

"Oh, I haven't done all the entertaining. Charles here"—he rested his head on the boy's shoulder—"has been telling me things that interested me more than my stories did him."

A delicate pink flush came into Charles's face. "I didn't think you'd mind, mother," he said quickly. "I tried to tell him about the ant heap and the dark people. He's been in Central Africa himself, and seen the great ant heaps and the camel thorns——"

"Mother," broke in Frank, "he says we can come again to-morrow and he'll tell us a story about a war they had in Africa, and how he found a little boy with three Bushmen arrows sticking in him!"

Only Bertie was silent. He had risen gently and had caught hold of the man's forefinger, which he stood holding tightly.

"My fear is Mr. Drummond will feel as the Britons did when they invited the Picts and Scots to come over the wall and couldn't get free of them," Rebekah said.

"Oh no, he won't," said Frank. "What time shall we come to-morrow?"

"I shall be here about four; then I shall whistle for you, if your mother will let you come."

"Oh yes, like the Lap did for the reindeer you said; and we'll all come trooping like a lot of reindeer."

"Do not let them trouble you, please," she said; "send them back when they tire you."

"Children and animals do not easily do that," he said.

Rebekah turned to the children. "You must come home for your tea now." She held out her hand to Bertie. He loosened his hold of the finger, but turned to the man and stood looking up at him.

"Don't you seeth, he wanth to kissth you?" said Hughie.

The man stooped and lifted the child up and pressed his mustached lips softly against his; when he set him down Bertie walked to Rebekah and took her hand, but looked back as he walked. All the children shouted "Good-by." The man replied, "Till to-morrow!" Rebekah said "Good night," and they walked away to the gate in the rose hedge, Bertie holding her hand and stumbling over the grass as he walked with his head half twisted round to look at the man who was standing under the tree and watching them.

When they had gone he lay down in the same position as before and was completely lost among the grasses.

At tea all the children talked at once. Hughie said when he was grown up he was going to travel all over the world with the man. Frank said he had promised to show him a real boomerang and explain how the savages

used it. Charles said he had invited them to go to his
room on the other side of the big house where all his
things were, which he was packing away to send to the
museums in Europe—fossils and dried plants and photographs and collections of insects and savages' implements.
Sartje whispered to Rebekah to know if they went whether
she might go too. Only Bertie sat silent in his high chair,
eating his bread and milk with large intent eyes.

The next afternoon the children heard the whistle and
went. In the evening they came back full of the stories
they had heard and the things they had seen.

"And, mother," said Charles, twisting his arm about
her, "he makes up stories like you. He has a little white
box all full of manuscripts, and he let me read a little bit
of one. It was beautiful. I could quite understand it."
But she did not question him about it.

The next day the children waited in the front garden;
but there was no whistle calling them, or the next day
either. Rebekah thought, as the week was nearly ended,
perhaps he had left. On the third day they had gone to
school at their governess's down the avenue, and Rebekah
was at home alone with Sartje, who was dressing her dolls
on the back stoep. Rebekah went into the pantry to put
the shelves neat. She was dressed in a blue cotton dress
with a dark blue cotton overall pinafore that she always
wore at her work in the morning. She resolved to
turn out the whole pantry. It was not really necessary;
there was sewing that needed even more to be done; but
she felt she did not wish to sit still. She stood on a chair
before the dresser taking down piles of plates and dishes
and dusting them one by one, before she put fresh paper
on the shelves. It all looked so bald; the sunshine coming
in through the pantry window and dancing on the yellow-
washed walls and yellow-white shelves. She counted the
plates in piles of eight and put them up again; was it
worth doing, was anything worth doing? She began
taking down the jugs from the next shelf.

Then there was the sound of a knock at the front door.

Often the carts with ferns and greenery to sell came up
the front avenue at that hour and knocked at the front
door. She called to the girl in the kitchen to go and see
who it was. The girl came back and said it was the
gentleman she had sometimes seen next door, who had
called and wished to see her mistress for a moment. The
girl handed up his card. She said he had declined to come
in and was standing on the veranda waiting. Rebekah
stepped quickly down from the chair, waited a moment,
then hurried out through the kitchen and went round to
her bedroom in the new building. Quickly she tore off
the dark blue pinafore, and before she took off the dress
went to the wardrobe and took down the white embroidered gown she often wore in the afternoon. She
turned to the glass; her hair, brushed down at either side
of her head and coiled in braids at the back, was a little
ruffled in front with her morning's work. She caught up
the brush and began to smooth it, making the dark waves
show undulating and glossy. Then she paused and laid
down the brush. If it had been an ordinary tradesman
who had called, she would have gone just as she was; if
it had been a formal caller, she would have dressed carefully. She hesitated. Why should she try to show herself
to this man looking better than she often looked? Why
should he not see her at her worst? For anyone else she
would have dressed, but not for him. She turned to the
chair and put on the blue pinafore and walked slowly
back by the way she had come. In the front passage the
door stood open; the man was standing with his back
to it, looking out across the garden from the top of the
veranda steps. As she came out he turned and raised
his hat; he looked down very fully at her as she stood
beside him.

"I hope I have not disturbed you by calling so early?"
he said. She answered quickly that he had not. He
looked again across the garden.

"What an astonishing blaze of color!"

"There's a pleasure," she said, "if you have a very small space, in seeing how much will live in it."

"Yes," he said, looking somewhat abstractedly at the garden. "I've sometimes thought that a life itself might be lived more satisfactorily a little hedged about with narrow conditions which compelled one to expand oneself in that circle—there's such a thing as being dissipated with too large an horizon and too much liberty to expand in it."

"If the hedges are too close round, they may kill the plants," she said quickly.

"Yes, that is so!—The reason why I called," he said, glancing down at her again and then looking back across the garden, "is that, though you did not write to me nor give me permission, I thought perhaps you would forgive me if I tried to go on with the search you made the first night we met. I got a photograph and the information I needed next door, without mentioning your name. I have been to all the places, places where I don't think you could easily have entered, where there seemed possibility of news. The last two days I have spent at Simon's Town. Once it seemed to me there I was upon a track; but it disappeared again."

"Thank you," she said; "but I have no hope really."

"Do not say that," he said, glancing down at her and speaking as one would to a little child. "When we fix all our desires in one direction, I think one is almost bound to find what one hungers for at last. I have always had that feeling. I will not detain you longer; if I hear anything I will let you know."

He touched his hat and began to descend the steps. But she walked down with him. He stopped as they passed a tall pink rose bush. "How strange that is," he said; "one quite white rose where all the rest are pink."

"That bush has always done so," she said.

He bent down over it. "That's rather strange. I thought it might be some injury or growth that caused it. May I take it home to examine it?" Rebekah cut it with her scissors that hung from her belt. He held it, examining the stem and the back of the flower. "It's particularly healthy and perfect," he said, as he walked to the gate, still looking down at it.

"You said you would be leaving in a week," she said. "Your stay is almost ended, is it not?"

"No," he said, "I shall be here for three weeks." He opened the front gate and went out, hasping it on the inside.

"Thank you for what you have done," she said.

"Oh, it's my concern now, as much as yours." He bowed and turned down the avenue.

Rebekah turned and walked up the garden path. The roses had never been so red before and the lilies and carnations so white. The sky above was a dazzling radiant blue, and the light poured down over the flowers and drew their scent. She stood by the pink rose tree; it had the most delicate scent. In the pantry she put the jugs and dishes quickly back on the shelves, then she went through the garden again to her study and sat down in the armchair.

After a while she laid her arm across her forehead and half closed her eyes. The arm slid lower till it quite covered them; her breathing became as soft and even as a little child's sleep. But she was not asleep.

She fancied one day she went into the garden and the man said quite frankly, "I have come to see you." And she went up to him just as one little child goes up to another who has come to play with it. She said, "Come and I'll show you all my things!" And she took him into her study. She led him to the corner where her statue stood on the little bracket. She told him what she felt about it; and he told her about where he got it, and what exactly it was. Then she took him to the glass cupboard and showed him the fossils. They took out each one and she told him where she had found them and how. She told him especially all about the large dicynodont's head she had dug out in the krans [1] in the river bed, how she had

¹ Cliff.

felt when, bathed in perspiration in the streaming sunshine one day, the last stone broke away and she held in her hand the old head that so many million years had lain under the sand, come out to see the sunshine it once loved, the same old sun shining, the same old life beating in her hand that had once beat in the old sightless head; she showed him the beautiful winged reptile fossil, that had played so large a part in her system of thought for so many years, being the first thing that had forced on her the knowledge how much of beauty and good has been killed out for ever on earth by the brute struggle of animal power to kill; she explained to him all she felt about that, and he argued it with her; and then they went to her bookshelf and he held in his hand the little handbook of physiology which she had bought with her hoarded pence when a little child, and he understood how she had loved it; and she showed him his own old copy of *Plants and Animals* and his own notes in it, and hers written against them; and they argued over many things she'd wanted to argue with him for years; and she showed him great piles of notes and writing on Woman; and they sat discussing—when the girl from the kitchen came to the study to say the water was boiling and it was time to make the pudding.

Rebekah dropped her arm from her eyes and started up. The drawers of the desk were all shut, and no manuscripts were about and no voices sounded. She rose and followed the maid to make the pudding.

The next day and the next she heard no more of him. On the morning of the third day, just after the children had started for school, Hughie rushed back into the kitchen.

"Mofther, mofther," he cried, "he sayth he wanth to thee you. I've tooked him to your sthudy!" And without waiting to explain he rushed off to join the other boys, who were already going down the avenue.

In her study Rebekah found him standing before her glass case of fossils. He turned quickly.

"I hope the little son has made no mistake in showing me in here!" He glanced round the room at the desk and single chair, showing it was not meant for reception. "He led me in here when I asked for you and planted me before the case, I suppose because I told him I should like to see your stones. They told me you had some."

"Oh, it's quite right," Rebekah said quickly.

"I came," he said, "to ask a favor—whether you would allow your colored boy to come over for a few minutes and help me to cord some of the heavier boxes I am packing to send to Europe."

"I will send him at once," Rebekah said, and made a movement as though she would have moved to the door.

But he had turned to the case. "You seem to have some very interesting things here," he said. "That's a fine head. I got three of the same kind when I was in Africa before, but yours is larger and more perfect."

She took the key down from the corner of the hanging bookshelf and unlocked the glass case quickly. He took down the head and asked where it was found. She said on a farm in the Midlands.

"Mine came from that part. May I look at the rest?"

She opened the other door wide and he took them out one after the other: bits of great leg bone and huge claws and prints of footmarks. Then he took up the small square slate with her winged reptile upon it. "This is very curious, very valuable," he said. He turned, walked a step nearer the door to get more light on it. "Where was it found?"

"About two hundred feet from the head in the same bed of a mountain stream."

He looked at it closely.

"What is it?" she said.

"I don't know. I have never seen anything quite like it. Did you find it yourself?"

"Yes," she said.

He walked another step towards the door to look at it, then turned to return it to the case.

"Won't you take it?" she said. "I don't need it."

"Oh, I could not. It's the crown of your collection," he said quickly.

"I'd like you to," she said.

He hesitated: "I don't collect for myself, you know. I send all my collections to a friend of mine at Vienna, and he puts them in his private museum or distributes them in public collections where others can make use of them. They are a kind of blood money with me, you see. One must, I suppose, contribute something to the world's scot and lot. So I do this and then I feel I'm free to do what I like with the rest of my life with a clear conscience." He laughed, still holding the stone in his hand.

"It's better so," she said. "Some one might make use of it. I never will."

He looked down at it, hesitating for a moment; then, "Thank you, I will take it," he said. "Have you noticed how beautifully clear the veinings in the wings are?" He was moving towards the door. "I will not interrupt you any more: I am sure you are busy. Any time to-day will do for the boy to come over."

At the door he turned and wished her good morning and went down the steps with the stone in his hand. She stood before the case. She closed it and began to pace up and down. He had been there; she had shown him nothing. All the things she had to tell him she had not said! She walked to the corner and looked at the statue he had bought, and to the shelf, and looked at his Darwin with the notes in it.

That night at eight, when the smaller children had been put to bed and the two elder boys were amusing themselves in the large room, she sat on the veranda of the house. A tin lamp with a reflector was fastened on the wall behind her and threw its light down over her as she sat in the rocking-chair under it, darning the week's stockings. A cloud of little night flies and moths fluttered round the lamp, so thick they seemed to make a halo about it.

Suddenly the front gate opened and Mrs. Drummond's husband came up the path. He did not go to the steps, but stood below her at the side of the veranda.

"Good evening!" he said. "I have not come on any business; I have merely come to see you. May I sit down?"

She half rose to draw a chair forward for him.

"No, I would rather sit here," he said, seating himself on the side of the stoep, which rose about two feet from the ground. "One likes all the air one can get to-night."

She pushed a little mat towards him, saying that the stones were cool.

"Oh, I shall take no harm: I am an old traveler," he said, but he drew it to him and reseated himself. He sat about five feet from her with his back against the veranda post. He looked out across the garden, the darkness of which was partly lit by the light from the lamp's reflector.

"Would you mind my smoking?" he said. "I don't think the smoke would reach you from here." When she assented he took out his pipe and slowly filled and lit it.

"You should learn to smoke," he said after a pause, turning to her again; "persons who lead a very intense life too quickly, at too great a tension, should smoke to slow down; lymphatic people never should." He put the pipe back to his lips and drew a few long whiffs; then he took it out.

.   .   .   .

"Of course you will say, trivial and insignificant as it is, the man had no right to have even that little picture to himself. Instead of jumping up and lurching out of the wagon and making his coffee and going off to seek for fossils, he should at once have seized writing pad and scribbled it down on it, and spent a day in writing it out in proper form and he should have sent it home to a publisher and said, 'How much will you pay me, one pound or two pounds or three pounds a page, what is it worth to you?'—bargain and chaffer over it, and in the end he loses and the publisher makes everything. A man might as well take a child and put her up to auction— Yes, she is very pretty but her nose is a little too long, her hair doesn't curl quite enough; her arms are nice and firm —he ought to have cut her hair shorter in front." He drew some more short draughts at his pipe. "Pugh! Their blame and their praise are alike an insult. Who thinks a man begets children for them? Of course, if he's starving, he may have to put her up, but it's rather like eating your own flesh!"

By this time he had discovered his pipe was dead, and knocked it out vigorously against the brickwork of the stoep and began refilling it.

"I did publish a thing once," he said; "it was many years ago when I was a student. That friend I told you of needed money; the doctor thought they could perform an operation and cure him of his deformity, and he hadn't funds. I gave him a thing I'd written, a little thing, but I cared for it; and I said he could publish it without my name and use what he got for it. I hadn't means at that time. He arranged with a publisher, but he didn't have the papers properly signed; they promised him so much a copy; in the end he got £50, and the publisher made hundreds. The publisher said he could give him one-third of what he had arranged for. A lawyer friend said we had better go to law. That would have been the ultimate prostitution: you have got my daughter, you have used her, and now you don't pay me properly. I got hundreds of letters from people all over the world"; he laughed a little inward laugh. "They thought it must have been written to do them good or give them pleasure! I wonder how often, when a man begets a boy, he is thinking of the various instruction of the race it may undertake. One woman wrote me a love letter and said she didn't know my name, but she was sure we were made for each other, and she had four thousand a year. One man, an American, sent me a printed copy which he had had gloriously printed on thick paper in vellum binding, and told me I was please to write my name and an inscription in it, and he could assure me it would be placed in his library in company with the best writers of the day, Tom and Jack and Harry! I threw it into the fire." He put his pipe back in his mouth and pulled. "They think you write it for them! I suppose they think Newton struck on his great thoughts to please humanity, and Milton wrote *Paradise Lost* for the sake of the ten pounds he got: and so, of course, the small ephemera must do the same! They can't understand that their praise is as insolent as their blame, that there's no virtue or vice about the whole thing! It is because it had to be!" He puffed away for a good time in silence, and Rebekah's face was still bent over her work.

Then suddenly he bent nearer her, taking his pipe from his lips.

"There is something I want to ask you," he said. "I wasn't quite sincere in saying I only wanted to come and see you. I've a little thing I wrote ten years ago; would you read it if I sent it over with my Chinaman to-morrow? It took me two days copying it out; I've done it in my best round schoolboy hand twice, so it won't be difficult to read. I've had it ready for some days, but I haven't ventured to send it. You needn't say anything about it. I just want you to read it."

"I shall," she said. "Is it a story?"

"Well yes—and yet—no. Hardly quite that. There are characters, men and women, in it, but you'll see it's Africa." He smoked a little. "Ten years or so ago I traveled there for a year and a half all over the country in my wagon. I went on towards the Kalahari and away to Lake Ngami. I had gone through a time of some stress before, and somehow the country appealed to me greatly. It's strange that ever since, though I've lived longer in so many countries, yet when anything comes to me, it's nearly always Africa,—Africa that sets it. I've a curious feeling for the country as if it had a personal connection with myself; perhaps because I traveled through it when I was particularly open to the influences of nature, as one is when one's mind has been perturbed. I've always thought I should rather like to be buried there at last. I never wrote about it while I was there; one doesn't about things that are present, you know. It was when I'd gone home to England for four months. I was in a little sea-side lodging, busy arranging my specimens and catalogu-ing them to send to my friend before I started on my journey through Russia to the East. It was a drizzly rainy day and I was sitting at my desk writing out a description of Bushmen, and their habits as I'd seen them, to go with some curios; I was just setting down the exact measure-ment of some skulls I'd taken and was feeling rather de-pressed and heavy, when suddenly, in a moment, the whole of this little thing flashed on me. You know those folded-up views of seaside places and cities that you buy in a sort of little book, and as you pull them open they flash out one after the other in a moment. Well, it was so; in an instant, all the pictures in the thing ran out before me with a flash one after the other. I threw down my pen. It was exactly as though some one quite external to myself had shown them me suddenly. I wrote them all out that night, and the next day, when I came to read them, I saw it was Africa, the scenery—but you'll see, I put it away in a box with the other scribbles, and I haven't looked at it since; but I've always liked it best of all. It took me only one night to write the rough, but it's taken me three days and the best part of the night to revise and write fair. I hope you'll like it!" He leaned forward a little and glanced up gently at her, almost like a little child seeking sympathy. Then he drew himself up and relit his pipe and leaned back against the veranda post.

"I sometimes think," she said, "that that curious sense of weight and depression, often appearing quite causeless, which one feels before some sudden flash of perception, is because some part of one's brain we are not conscious of has been working intensely, so that the part we are conscious of is ill supplied with blood; then something bursts and it comes into consciousness. So it is with intuition; I think it's what Socrates felt when he talked of his Demon. We feel so entirely as if it were a flash from something beyond ourselves. I noticed it when I was a little child."

"But is it the brain at all?" he said, leaning back against the post. "I have a conviction, possibly quite wrong but from which I cannot shake myself, that it isn't the brain at all, or not nearly so much as people suppose, with which any kind of imaginary work is done or any unwilled mental process takes place, that it's far more spinal and visceral than people think and that results are simply flashed up to the brain—anyhow, if it is the brain, it's the back part above the spine and the whole body, especially the trunk, that is concerned; why else, if you've been making stories for six hours, should it never be the front of the brain that was weary, as if you'd been calculating miserable figures or learning lists of words, but always the small of one's back and one's body that is tired? I suppose science will work the matter out some day. Why, at first waking, do pictures and things, entirely uncalled for by the will, rush full-fledged into the brain, which they tell us is so ill-fed with blood during sleep? Why, when one lies half dozing on one's back, does one start up with such a rush of ideas that by no power of will could one have evoked?"

He smoked on for a while in silence.

"I suppose," he said at last, "it's the spontaneous nature of imaginative work that makes one so impervious to criticism? If a man tells you you pronounce a word wrong, or don't hold your fork right, you feel pained and try to reform yourself—as to the other things, they are as they are and be damned to him!"

"And yet one can, to a certain extent, determine their coming," she said. "One can put oneself into the condition in which they may come. When, as a little girl, I wanted to be happy, I used to go and lie under a pear tree in the garden or walk up and down, and they nearly always came."

"Yes, that's just it," he said. "You may put yourself into the condition in which they *may* come, but you cannot determine they shall come, or what they shall be within certain limits! Suppose, in some city of Greece, say, a crown of wild olives or a prize of many talents had been offered for a Winged Victory and there were three artists of power. The first might keep his mind and body, especially the body, so absorbed in gymnastics or business or politics, that no picture comes to him, and he has either not to compete or to make up something he never saw, copied from others, and a complete failure. The second turns all his mind towards it and meditates over an ideal of victory, but there come to him only lovely Venuses and ripe cupids that he can wing and call Victories, though they are not so, because in his soft nature lies nothing Victory can shape itself from. But the third, deep in whose nature is something of hope, virility, strength—to him, when he turns his dreams towards it, a hundred Winged Victories leap out; he could not say just how they come, but he would recognize one as the best, and he would seize it, he would embody it in marble; and then, through the ages, without a head, without an arm, smitten and ill-treated, it would still stand the embodiment of Victory, calling men and women to struggle and conquer, though only through its broken fragment; it would do it because it was in the man, because nothing can come out of the man that was not first in him; he must have felt all the Victory speaks before he could make it; it is his soul." He sat looking out at the garden with the pipe in his hand. "All that a man has seen and known and felt, all that lies within him, is, so to speak, the substance out of which his imagination has to work, the bricks laid before it from which it can select for its work. The small man may be an artist; only the great man can be a great artist. A boy might write a song of yearning unrequited love, because youth knows vague yearnings of love at sixteen, but no boy of sixteen could have written *Paradise Lost* or the *Iliad*; the dream-power might be there, but the matter for it to work on could not be there. And yet, you know," he said, "that is not all! Why is art prophetic? Why does a man dream and hear and see things and faces which, as far as he can judge, are suggested to him by nothing he has seen or known?—and yet, long years afterwards, the faces and the people and the incidents, the very characters and actions, which seemed almost impossible and unlikely to him when he first saw them, come out and look at him from real life? Why is it that he can paint the actions and emotions of characters in complex conditions in which he never was and of which he knew nothing—and yet life as it passes verifies his work? I believe that a European man with imagination, lost among savages from his birth, would be haunted by an ideal of a living European face which he had never seen and perhaps never would see!"

"Is it not," she said, "because no individual is an isolated nomad? He may be one minute growth of the life of his race, of humanity, of living things on earth. Is an artist not simply a man in whom some of the accumulated life of his race, of the millions of human creatures who have been his ancestors in the ages past, is stored? Is not much of his work, if it be true artistic work, like the work of the bee who makes her perfect polygonal cell in the first year of her life. Is not the curious confidence of the artist that he is right due to the fact that he is working by a curious inborn necessity? You argue with the bee in vain, a four-sided cell is better; she builds it six; and, if you ask her why, she says she must—it is so, that's all! Her whole cell is meaningless unless you realize the storing of the honey and the bees that have yet to be born whom she has never seen and who will feed on the honey —but she builds."

"Yes," he said, "but it's more than mere hereditary racial instinct; an artist sees that which his race has never seen. Take the matter of wings. Age after age the artists of every race have seen them on their gods and great spiritual beings—on their Winged Victory, on their angels and devils, on their very bull gods: 'And with twain they covered their face and with twain did fly.' It is useless for the superficial onlooker to say those wings wouldn't carry them, that their pectoral muscles are not strong enough to carry them. The artist says, 'I see them.' In after ages, men will have wings; how they will get the force to move them, or so to fasten them on that they will move freely, we cannot say. One day the man of science will realize the poet's dream, that dream—'So it is!'—which he would not and could not be shaken out of. The creative artist does not so much recall the life of the race; he paints its future, just as he often does his own. It can't be explained!"

"Yes," she said, after a pause, "but, isn't the answer something the same? The life and movement in a single finger is quite incomprehensible unless you know that it belongs to a hand and acts as part of it, and a whole hand with all its functions and movements is quite incomprehensible unless you know it as part of a complex body with a life bound to it. We know the man, and we know a little the race and the life on earth which that expresses; but the life of which it is only part,—of that we know nothing; and that is the moving power."

"Oh yes," he said, "the life of which we know nothing —that is it!"

"I wish they gave it a larger name," she said

"Yes," he said, "the name circumscribes it."

She had left off working and was leaning forward with her elbows on her knees. The little moths, who hovered in a cloud about the tin lamp above her, made a little halo round her head, and sometimes settled on her brown hair with its smooth parting.

"I often think," she said after a few seconds, "that why men so misunderstand the nature of art is because there are three distinct processes to be gone through before it is given to the world; and men confuse them, though they are really wholly distinct. The first, the all-important element, without which there can be no art and no creation, is the sudden flash, or the slowly growing and intensified perception, over which, as you say, the man has and can have no control; it shapes itself in him; it is here as clearly and as actually as the outer world, though he knows it to have no connection with it. It can, as you say, be large only in an individual who is large; but it may be as complete, though smaller, in a smaller individuality. It is perfectly spontaneous, made of the man's substance, himself-of-himself; yet he feels in a way that it is something not himself but shown to him, while yet he feels also it belongs to him more than anything else in the world ever can. That is the first stage. When once he has perceived it clearly, it exists absolutely, perfectly and entirely—but within himself. He has no power to unmake it or to make it other than it is. It is this first stage, the really creative stage of the things, which I think people misunderstand so, because they confuse it with the second stage.

"In the second stage, of course, the artist's will does come into play, though only within certain limits. He must will, consciously or unconsciously, to create it as an external image, or it would remain for ever only in his mind. He must seek for the knowledge and the materials and the leisure or other conditions without which it cannot be incarnated. If he is a sculptor, for instance, he must find the marble, the tools, the spot to work in, and the leisure to work. So far his will is acting, but, even in this stage, only within limits. He can determine whether he will work at all, or with what tool or what shade of marble; and he can determine the amount of sacrifice of other labors and interests and passions which he shall give up to his work; but what the work shall be, beyond a certain limit, he cannot determine without artistic adultery, which means the giving of a spurious art to the work. Always, as he works, he must be looking at the copy within, which is his only guarantee of truth and right. He must not reason and question; he must look. He may change, alter, break and try again, but always in the manner of following his copy. Afterwards, when the work is done or when any part is done, he may question it as to meaning and turn a fierce, unblind criticism on it, sterner than that he would throw on the work of any other man; but, while he works actually, there must be only one thought—the vision and the attempts to incarnate it. If the vision fails, the work should cease. Not only is his will bound in this way, but, I think, even in the undertaking, if there is generally (and the truer the artist the more certainly) a sort of restless pressure which *forces* him, or appears to him to force him, to his work. Of course literally he could resist it: the desire for sensual or other pleasures, the desire for wealth and the attempt to gain it, a sense of duty to others whose immediate service he believes must come first—all these may make a man resist it; but I believe with all true artists the desire to incarnate is instinctive; it may defy their reason; it is almost like the necessity of a woman to give birth to her child when the full time has come; she might kill it, as she might herself; but it is rather nature who compels her to give birth.

"Then comes the third stage. Now the work is completed as far as ever it can be. Seldom, probably never, has a great artist looked at any work that has proceeded from him with the infinite satisfaction and certitude of the dream-god of the Semitics, when he looked at his work and saw that it was good and rested. Perhaps that which he alone knows of remains always to him of a completeness and beauty which nothing he can create in the poor medium of words or paint or marble can show; perhaps that is why, to the true artist, no criticism of outsiders makes any difference in *his* estimate of the work; if they blame it, he knows that they have not seen the original which came to him and was not willfully made by him; if they praise it, he knows how much better the original was. But the time comes when, as far as he can or will, the work is done. It is now severed from him; the cord is cut; it has now its organic existence quite apart from himself. As time passes he can turn upon it exactly the same objective criticism which he would on another man's creation. The child is weaned. Then comes the question, what shall he do with it? Here, in this last stage, his will is supreme; the question is one entirely of motive. He can burn or destroy it, he can sell it or keep it, publish or exhibit it, save it to be given to the world after his death, show it to one human being or to the world, as he wishes. I think it is because it is this phase of the giving of art to the world, which alone the ignorant person sees clearly, that makes him think so strangely of it. He supposes that, because a man can decide whether he will publish the book or exhibit the picture, his will was equally independent in determining what it should be; even with the highest work of art, ignorant people are probably of opinion it came into existence only for them to see. That is perhaps why they are so generous with their advice—'You ought to have done so!' 'Why didn't you make it so?'—not simply 'I like it' or 'I don't like it,'—which is quite justified, if their opinion is asked."

He was still leaning back with his arms folded against the veranda post; he glanced round at her and laughed: "And the author says, 'Damn you, take it or leave it, as you like!'"

"Yes,"she laughed, "or something stronger if he knows it!" Then she leaned further forward: "I think all kinds of motives may make him give his work to the world —the feeling that makes a little child, when it finds a pretty flower, always run to its nurse or its mother that they may see it too—perhaps in some cases the idea of helping or comforting others—perhaps in some cases the mere love of fame and notoriety, though I think the art given out for such a cause would have something fraudulent in its very nature and not be true art—very often there is absolute necessity, such that, if a man is to go on producing art, he must live by it, and cannot so live unless he gives it out."

"Often not then! It's the middleman gets it, whether it's a picture or a cradle!" he interjected softly between his teeth, still looking out at the flower beds, which near the veranda were made visible amid the surrounding darkness by the light from the tin reflector of the lamp.

She paused to listen to him, and then said, "I think, with the true artist, whatever other motive there may be, there must always be this, consciously or unconsciously —not to let the thing die! As he has striven and labored to give it a perfect concrete form, that it may exist outside of his own mind, so there is in him a longing that it should live on—completely reflected in another mind as once it lived in his: 'Shall I call to the birth and not cause to bring forth? saith the Lord'—I think it's something like that!"

"Yes," he said, still leaning back and staring away at the flower beds.

"I have never seen any great sculptor's art," she said; "but in my study is a little statue nine inches high; it's a Hercules or a Bacchus (it doesn't matter what it's called) with some vine leaves about its forehead; the man's nude body, with all its gigantic power of muscle, holds in its arms an infant, and the bearded face smiles down at it. I think it was once yours; I bought it for a silk dress. Perhaps you, who have seen so much great art, might think nothing of it; it may be only a copy of some great work. But to me the glory is that—after all these hundreds, perhaps almost thousands, of years it has lain buried, while the man, whose being it first lived in, has for ages been Italian dust or rooted trees and plants on a Greek island—it has sprung out into life again—here, on the opposite side of the earth, after all those ages; with the joy, the comprehension of it, that throbbed in his brain when he saw it, beating here again in mine—the same, alive; it is *not* dead. When I finger it and feel its beauty, the throb in him lives, across all the centuries, as an actual throb in me. It's something like the feeling when you break off the last flake of stone and out comes the head of the creature that was an actual living being, having his day, as you are having yours, and as real; and it comes out into the sunshine, the very sunshine it loved and lived in millions of years ago. You feel and touch it—your fellow life—from across all the countless ages; and all life seems to be knit together even across boundless time." She was speaking quickly, but stopped suddenly.

Then as though her thoughts had been wandering, she said after a few moments, "I can fancy that, if a man were shut for years in some lonely castle by a lake, with no human companion and no hope of escape, he yet might find life tolerable if he found in his prison an old block and carved it year after year; and that, when the time came for him to be led out to execution, rather than that his captor should see it, rather than that they should possess it who could not understand it, he might take out his knife and utterly destroy it; but I have fancied also how he would have clambered up and dropped it out of the small window into the lake below, in the hope, as they led him to death, that some day it might be found and might fall into the hands of one who would understand it, and that all the agony and all the hope and despair graven into the block in those long years would find an answer in another heart. They would never know who had carved it, but the thing would live in another soul; and so I have fancied death would be easier to him. I think no artist need fear to give his work to the world because there are none who can understand. No human soul is so lonely as it feels itself, because no man is merely an individual but is a part of the great body of life; the thoughts he thinks are part of humanity's thoughts, the visions he sees are part of humanity's visions; the artist is only an eye in the great human body, seeing for those who share his life: somewhere, some time, his own exist."

She was softly rumpling a tiny rumple in her little black

silk apron between her thumb and forefinger. "I have sometimes thought," she said, "that ages ago in Ancient Chaldea there might have been some thinker whose thought seemed to have no relation to the men about him, whose vision seemed for himself alone; yet, recorded on a mud tablet and preserved through the years and coming to the light to-day, it might be found most closely connected with our needs and new life, might find its own here to-day and live again, though the man who made it might be forgotten. I cannot feel there is anything ignoble in the wish that, when we pass, the thing we love should live on its own life. Even a woman feels that when she gives birth to a child; though, if she has not loved the man she lived with, she has not conceived it for the good it might do or the beauty it might show,— yet, even then, when she is in the agony of childbirth, the thought will flash in her with sudden joy, 'Perhaps it will live on when I am gone and be the beautiful and the good to others'; and the thought gives her joy, though those who win good and beauty from the child may never know it had a mother or who she was. I think there is nothing ignoble in this wish—that the thing we have loved, that has been so beautiful to us, should live on a little in the love of other souls, though we gain nothing by it and our names are not even known."

"Yes," he said, "that is true." She had gathered up her darning again and was beginning to work. He laughed a little soft internal laugh, such as people do who live much alone, conversing only with themselves.

Then turning to her and looking up at her, he said, "You know, turning from the world-wide discussion of art and creation to a very trivial and insignificant thing, if you will allow me—what you say is true. Even with my own insignificant little scribblings, which might never be of the slightest value to anyone but myself, I always have deep down a curious feeling that I don't want *them* to die. Somewhere deep down in my mind I've always had a feeling that, when I grow old and have lived enough and seen enough and am wearying, then will be the time to settle down peacefully somewhere and throw them into such form that they could live for others. Ever since I was a boy," he said, bending towards her and leaning the palm of one hand on the floor of the veranda, "I've had an old deal box with a slipping lid that came to me from Germany full of wooden bricks, and ever since all or nearly all I've written has gone in there. I believe why I haven't written so much lately is because it's nearly full," he laughed; "but some day, I'm always conscious deep down in my heart I'm going to make it fair and square. They can publish them after I die; it won't hurt me."

She had dropped her work again. "But life is so short," she said.

He moved quickly. "Yes!" Then he laughed again and sat upright. "I am forty; I have another forty years to live. I've had only one serious illness in my life, and then I was too small to remember it. I'm good for eighty! May I smoke again?" He took out his pipe.

She was passing the needle evenly in and out in her darning. "I have sometimes thought," she said, "it would be a terrible thing if, when death came to a man or woman, there stood about his bed, reproaching him, not for his sins, not for his crimes of commission and omission toward his fellow-men, but for the thoughts and the visions that had come to him, and which he, not for the sake of sensuous pleasure or gain, had thrust always into the background, saying, 'Because of my art, my love and my relations to my fellow-men shall never suffer; there shall be no loaf of bread less baked, no sick left untended, no present human creature's need of me left unsatisfied because of it.' And then, when he is dying, they gather round him, the things he might have incarnated and given life to—and would not. All that might have lived, and now must never live for ever, look at him with their large reproachful eyes—his own dead visions reproaching him; as the children a woman has aborted and refused to give life to might gather about her at last, saying, 'We came to you; you, only you, could have given us life. Now we are dead forever. Was it worth it? All the sense of duty you satisfied, the sense of necessity you labored under: should you not have violated it and given us birth?' It has come upon me so vividly sometimes," she said, "that I have almost leaped out of bed to gain air —that suffocating sense that all his life long a man or a woman might live striving to do his duty and then at the end find it all wrong." She had stopped in her work again and was breathing quickly.

"Yes," he said slowly, as he smoked with his face turned to the garden and almost his back towards her, "but remember this—that no art, no creative thought can be greater all round than the creature from whom it takes its birth. If the man or the woman dwarf himself for the sake of art, in devotion to thought, the art and the thought are both shorn. Is a lovely life also nothing? Is it not the highest ideal to realize it? Many a man has shorn his life of all devotion to any aims except his art and thought, and in the end they have died starved out and weaklings."

She had taken up her work again.

"I see that," she said; "but life is so terribly difficult. Men say it is so hard to do the right. I have never found that. The moment one knows what is right, I do it; it is easy to do it; the difficulty is to find what *is* right! There are such absolutely conflicting ideals; the ideal of absolute submission and endurance of wrong towards one-self—the ideal of noble resistance to all injustice and wrong, even when done to oneself—the ideal of the abso-lute devotion to the smaller, always present, call of life— and the ideal of a devotion to the larger aims sweeping all before it—all are beautiful. The agony of life is not the choice between good and evil, but between two evils or two goods !"

"Why don't you follow your demon? I do," he said.

"I used to," she replied. "Long ago I always knew with absolute certainty, not what was the right course for

another man, but for me—and I took it. But life grows
so terribly complex as you grow older; there comes always
the thought, 'if I should be choosing the wrong.' "

"Life doesn't become more complex to me," he said;
"it lies right ahead. I know which path you would always
choose," he added.

"Which?" she asked.

"Whichever gave you most pain or least pleasure. You
would always think that was the right one."

At that moment the great clock in the hall struck half-
past nine and the two elder boys, whose bedtime it was,
came rushing out from the new room to their bedroom in
the large house. As they saw Drummond they raised the
war shout, which was their appointed mode of greeting
him. They begged to be allowed to sit up just ten minutes
more to sit and talk to him, and sat down beside him on
the edge of the stoep, Charles on his right hand and Frank,
who was generally demonstrative, on his left with his
arm across his shoulder.

"Put your watch on your knee, so we can see exactly
how the time's going."

"I have been trying to paint reindeer like the one you
told us the story of, standing by her young when it was
wounded. I can manage the reindeer and the blue, but I
can't make the snow glitter; does it ——"

"Oh, don't talk about your old picture; let him tell
us an adventure instead; the time's half gone already."

They talked till the ten minutes were over and then
trooped away to bed, and Rebekah rose to go to the rooms
to see if the three young ones were all right.

He rose. "I also must go," he said.

"It's very early," she said. "I shall be back again in
an instant."

"Then if you will allow me I will smoke this pipe out."
He relit it and sat down again.

When she returned he was still sitting absorbed in
smoking and she took up her work, but neither spoke till
the pipe was empty. Then as he took it from his lips and

knocked it out carefully against the side of the veranda, he said, "It was a nice old custom of the Indians for a man to hand his pipe to another in token of amity and union. We lose much in modern life by doing away with these old symbols of deeper things." He put the pipe away in his breast pocket as he stood up. He stood below the veranda, looking at her as she darned. "Should I be trespassing too much if I asked you to allow me to see your fossils again? I did not half examine them, and some, I think, will be quite new to me."

"You can come and see them at any time you like," Rebekah said; "the door of the room is hardly ever shut; if it is, you will find the key on the ledge above the door; and the little key of the cabinet is in the top left-hand drawer of the desk. Please come at any time you like."

"Thank you. Good night."

Without offering his hand he turned down the path towards the front gate; when he had almost reached it he turned back and stood just within the circle of light the lamp shed.

"Wouldn't you care to come and see my fossils? I have not finished packing them yet. I could easily show them you."

She hesitated a moment. "No, thank you," she said.

"They are in an outer room on the other side of the house; I have two rooms there; you would interfere with no one."

"No, thank you," she said.

"All right. Good night!" He turned and walked quickly down to the gate.

Olive Schreiner told me briefly how this novel was to end.

Drummond, persisting in his search for Bertie, found her in a house of ill fame at Simon's Town, stricken down by a loathsome and terrible disease. Rebekah took this dearly loved sister to her own house at Rondelbosch, where everything that love and medical science could do was lavished upon her. But, alas, the rescue came too late; the ravages wrought in this tender but helpless woman were too far advanced; and her death approaches. Possibly it was after depicting this deeply-wronged woman's death that Olive did the "outburst" on Veronica and Mrs. Drummond that "relieved her so." (*Life*, p. 180.) Something of the intensity of the scene and of the "outburst" may perhaps be inferred from the extract from Olive's letter to Ellis of the 5th April, 1889. (*Letters*, p. 160.) With regard to the death scene, Olive told me what were the last words, or among the last words, of Bertie. Some people were gathered round the dying woman's bed; I do not know all who were present, nor how it came that Mrs. Drummond was among them; but that evil woman was there. Baby-Bertie's simple nature had presumably never been troubled by the doubts, still less had it reached the conclusions, inevitable in the case of a cultured modern mind of the caliber of Rebekah's; Bertie had no doubt retained the primitive beliefs implanted early in her mind by her childlike "little mother." However that may be, as the end drew near, Rebekah leaned over her dying sister and asked her whether she would like them to pray. It is no great mental effort to remember the very words of the reply, because they seemed to me so terrific and because Olive chuckled over them. She used to style such a cut "the stroke oblique," and was always pleased, as in this instance, when she got it in at the right moment. "Let Mrs. Drummond pray," said Baby-Bertie; "she is a Christian." And so one of the two women Olive loved so passionately passed into the Silence.

Rebekah lived on. The sense of full comprehension and close fellowship between her and Drummond increased until they realized mutually the depth and the fitness of the undying love between them. But, as they were situated, a more intimate relationship was unwarrantable to such a woman as Rebekah; for her it was impossible to do anything which could degrade such a love; it therefore became inevitable that she must give up and leave the one man who she felt could be her life's close companion; and so they parted forever. Leaving Frank, she went to Matjesfontein with her children and the little colored girl Sartje. There she lived, educating the children and rearing Sartje as though a child of her own.

There is a little koppie in the flat at Matjesfontein, some distance west of the lonely Station, towards the bare and rocky mountains Olive so loved. This koppie she often referred to in her letters as "my koppie." From the Station, away across the vast and barren flat to the koppie, was a favorite walk of hers. There we see the last of Rebekah. As the sun sets, flooding the Karoo flats with radiance and glowing the brilliant mountains as it disappears behind them, Rebekah stands on the summit of the lonely koppie in the soft effulgence of the evening light, in something of that unutterable beauty of wild nature that suffused the veld and comforted the mind of Waldo of the *African Farm* when he went out "to sit in the sunshine."

Of the subsidiary characters I know no more. Possibly, however, this is of little moment. What happens to them does not seem to me to be of much interest after they cease to impinge upon Rebekah and Bertie; and those two women are now, we know, beyond them.

                                        S. C. C. S.